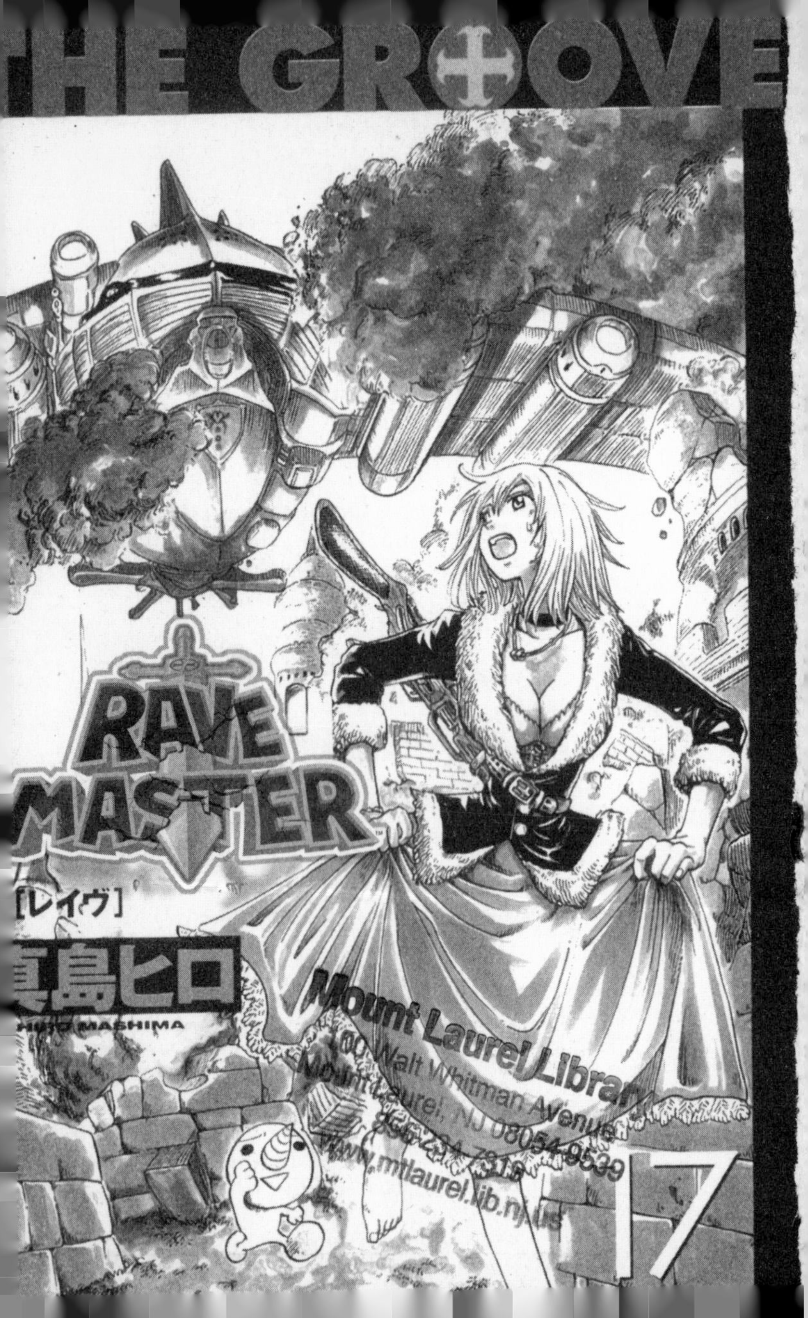
THE GROOVE
RAVE MASTER
【レイヴ】
島ヒロ
MASHIMA
17

Rave Master Vol. 17
Created by Hiro Mashima

Translation - Jeremiah Bourque
English Adaptation - Jake Forbes
Associate Editor - Suzanne Waldman
Retouch and Lettering - Rafael Nadjarian
Production Artist - James Dashiell
Cover Design - Al-Insan Lashley

Editor - Troy Lewter
Digital Imaging Manager - Chris Buford
Production Managers - Jennifer Miller and Mutsumi Miyazaki
Managing Editor - Lindsey Johnston
VP of Production - Ron Klamert
Publisher and E.I.C. - Mike Kiley
President and C.O.O. - John Parker
C.E.O. - Stuart Levy

A 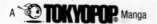 Manga

TOKYOPOP Inc.
5900 Wilshire Blvd. Suite 2000
Los Angeles, CA 90036

E-mail: info@TOKYOPOP.com
Come visit us online at www.TOKYOPOP.com

ISBN: 1-59532-022-9

First TOKYOPOP printing: October 2005
10 9 8 7 6 5 4 3 2 1
Printed in the USA

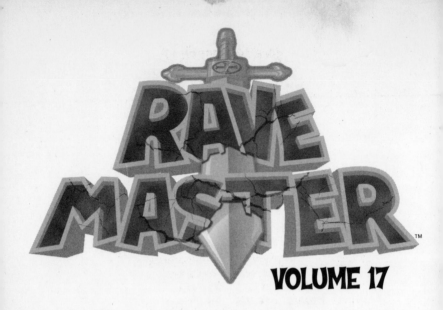

VOLUME 17

Story and Art by

HIRO MASHIMA

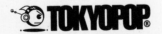

HAMBURG // LONDON // LOS ANGELES // TOKYO

THE STORY SO FAR...

The road to the fourth **Rave Stone** continues to be a perilous one as Haru, gravely injured after his battle with **Doryu**, was rescued by none other than **Ruby** and his **Magic Blade Holy Bell.** Ruby used it to whisk them both to safety, where a walrus-like creature named **Dalmatian** tended to Haru's wounds. Elsewhere, **Demon Card** confronted **Ogre** aboard the ship **River Saly**, which is actually the **Sliver Ray. Reina** and **Musica's** combined **Silver Bonds** power destroyed Ogre. However, Reina pushed Musica out of the ship at the last minute, sacrificing her life to blow it up. Meanwhile, Haru hobbles off for a rematch against Doryu—but not before telling Ruby the name of the **third Rave Master...**

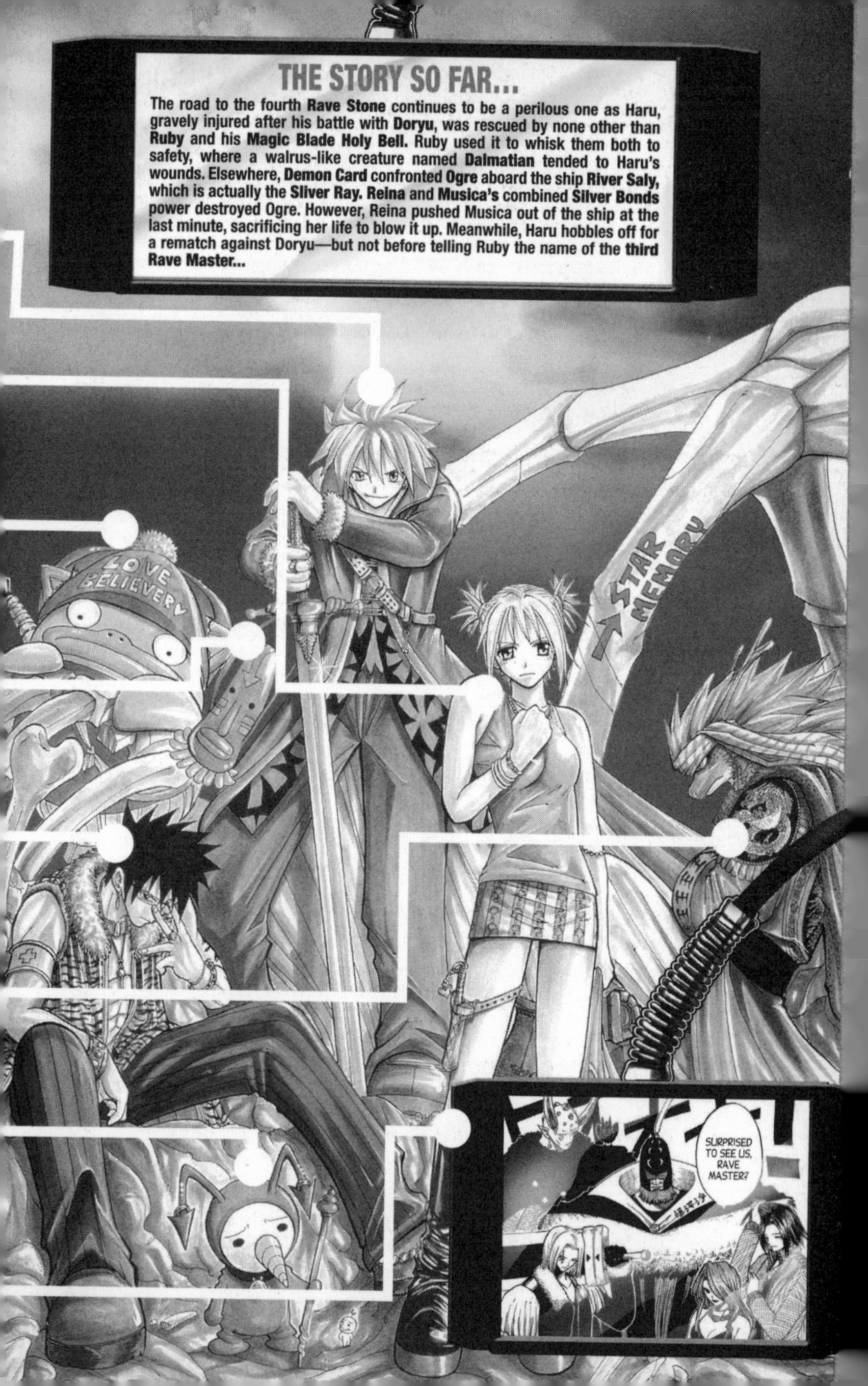
LOVE BELIEVER
STAR MEMORY
SURPRISED TO SEE US, RAVE MASTER?

THE RAVE MASTER CREW

HARU GLORY

A small-town boy turned savior of the world. As the **Rave Master** (the only one capable of using the holy weapon RAVE), Haru set forth to find the missing Rave Stones and defeat **Demon Card**. He fights with the **Ten Powers Sword,** a weapon that takes on different forms at his command. With Demon Card seemingly out of the way, Haru now seeks the remaining two Rave Stones in order to open the way to Star Memory.

ELIE

The girl without memories. Elie joined Haru on his quest when he promised to help her find out about her past. She's cute, spunky and loves gambling and shopping in equal measure. Locked inside of her is the power of **Etherion.**

RUBY

A "penguin-type" sentenoid, Ruby loves rare and unusual items. After Haru saved him from Pumpkin Doryu's gang, Ruby agreed to sponsor Haru's team in their search for the ultimate rare treasures: the Rave Stones!

GRIFFON KATO (GRIFF)

Griff is a loyal friend, even if he is a bit of a coward. His rubbery body can stretch and change shape as needed. Griff's two greatest pleasures in life are mapmaking and peeping on Elie.

MUSICA

A **"Silverclaimer"** (an alchemist who can shape silver at will) and a former street punk who made good. He joined Haru for the adventure, but now that Demon Card is defeated, does he have any reason to stick around?

LET

A member of the **Dragon Race,** he was formerly a member of the Demon Card's Five Palace Guardians. He was so impressed by Haru's fighting skills and pureness of heart that he made a truce with the Rave Master. After passing his Dragon Trial, he gained a human body, but his blood is still Dragon Race.

PLUE

The **Rave Bearer,** Plue is the faithful companion to the Rave Master. In addition to being Haru's guide, Plue also has powers of his own. When he's not getting Haru into or out of trouble, Plue can be found enjoying a sucker, his favorite treat.

THE ORACION SIX

Demon Card's six generals. Haru defeated **Shuda** after finding the Rave of Wisdom. The other five generals were presumed dead after King destroyed Demon Card Headquarters.

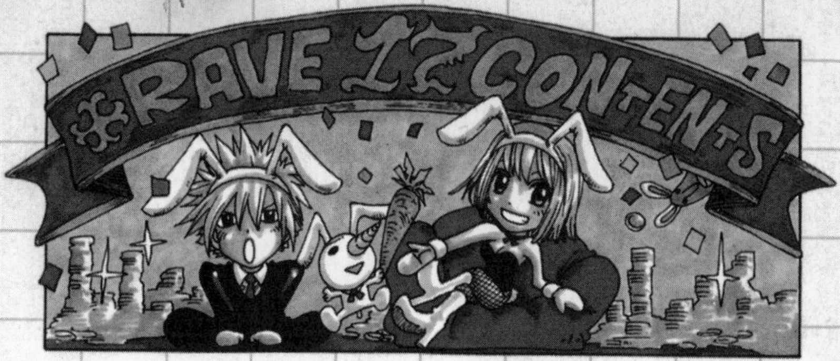
RAVE 17 CONTENTS

THE GROOVE ADVENTURE

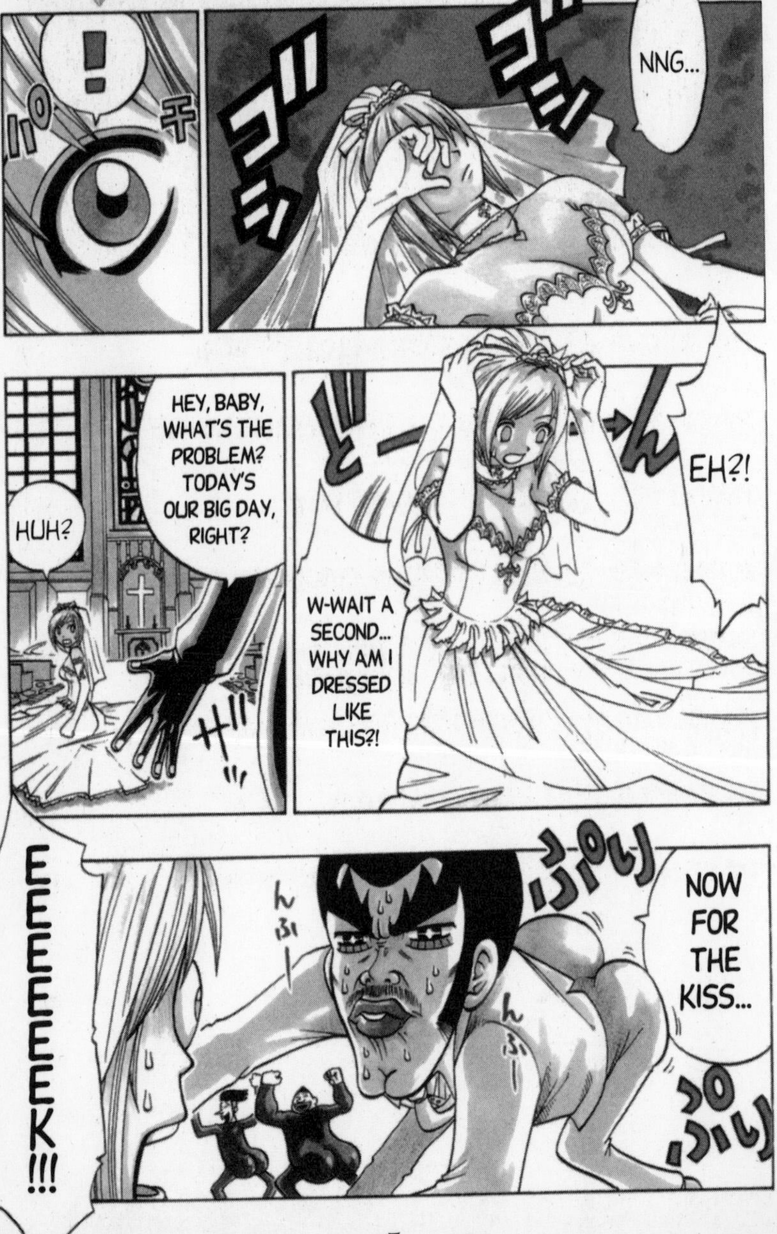
NNG...
!
EH?!
W-WAIT A SECOND... WHY AM I DRESSED LIKE THIS?!
HEY, BABY, WHAT'S THE PROBLEM? TODAY'S OUR BIG DAY, RIGHT?
HUH?
NOW FOR THE KISS...
EEEEEEEEK!!!

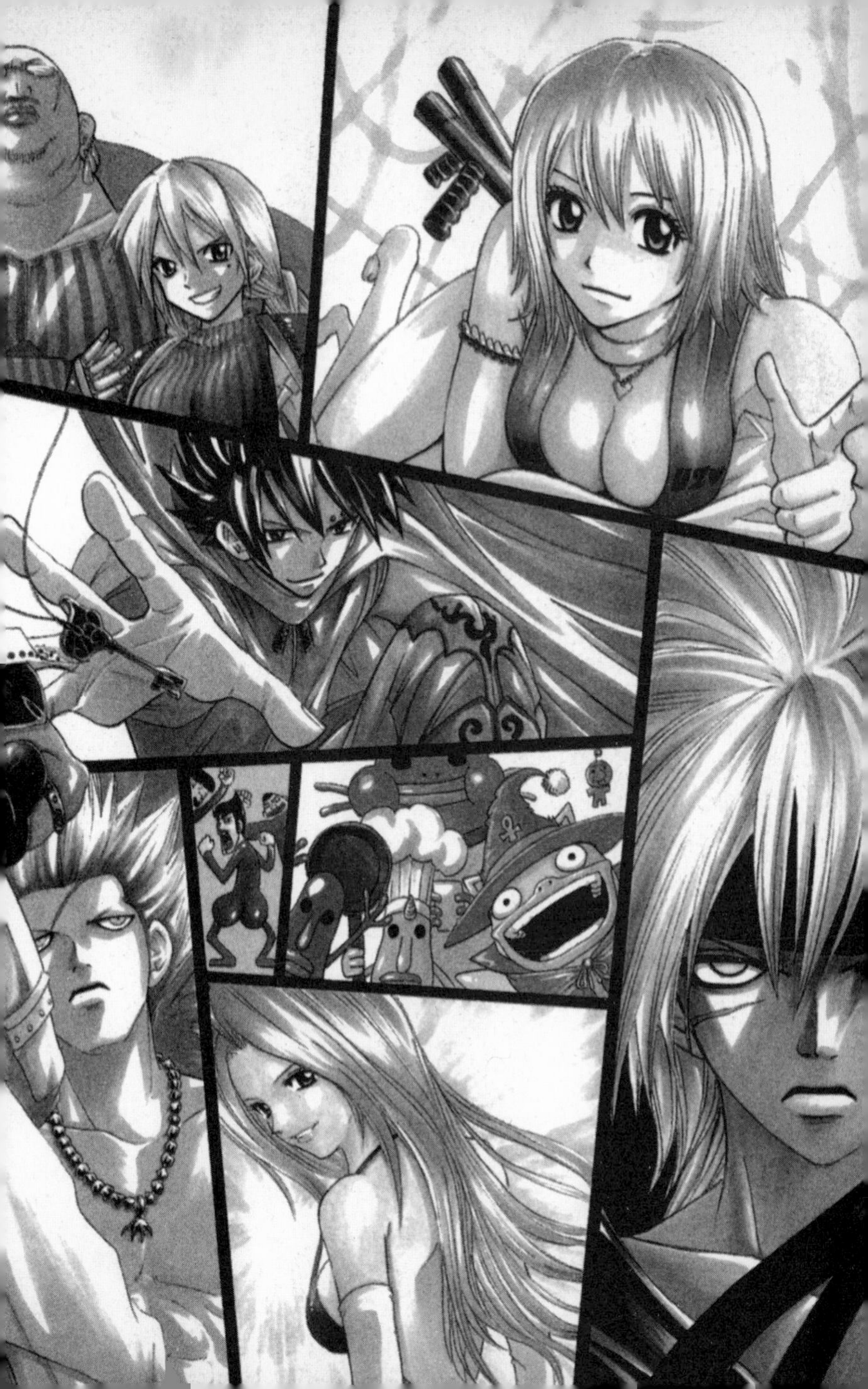

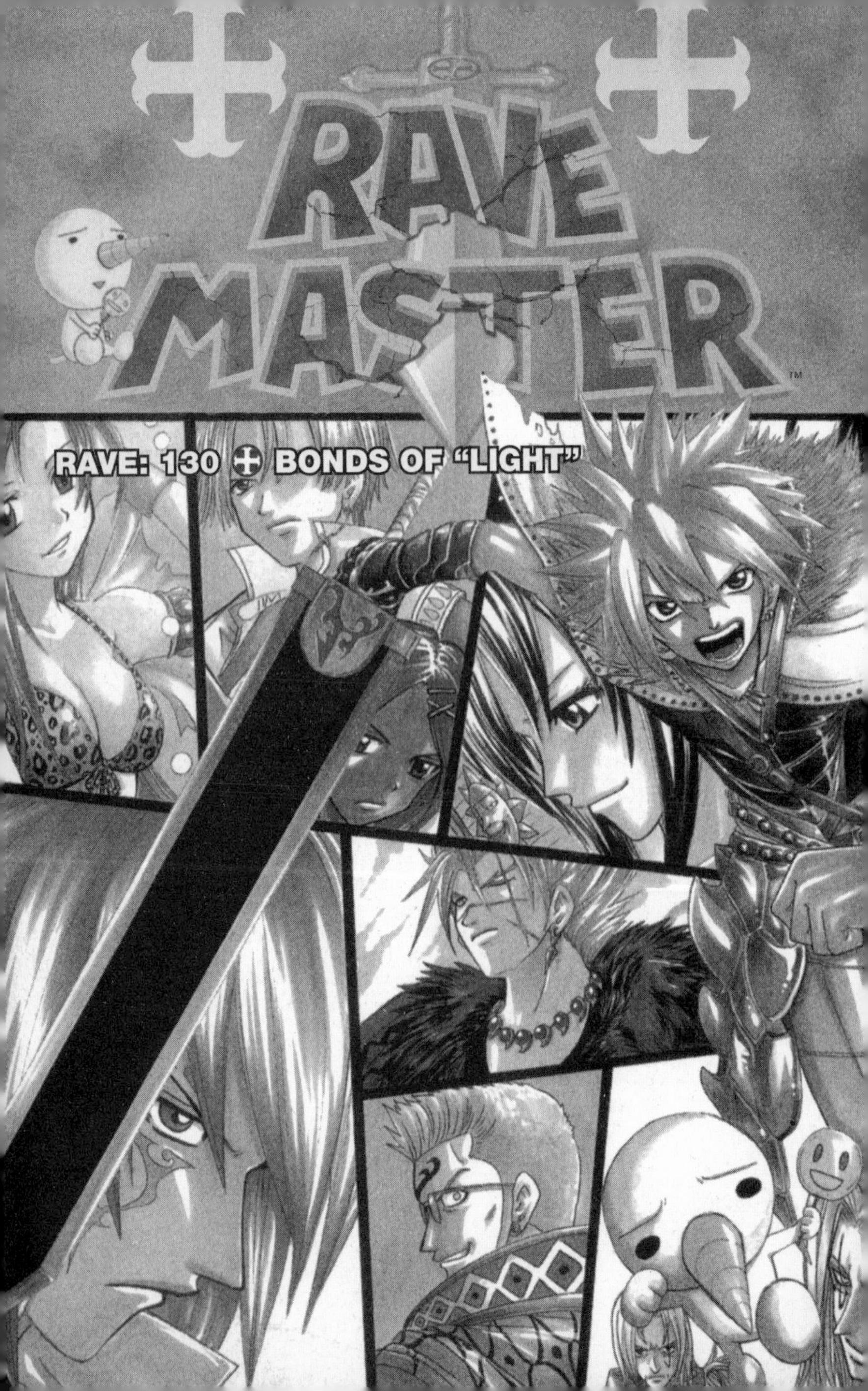
RAVE MASTER™
RAVE: 130 BONDS OF "LIGHT"

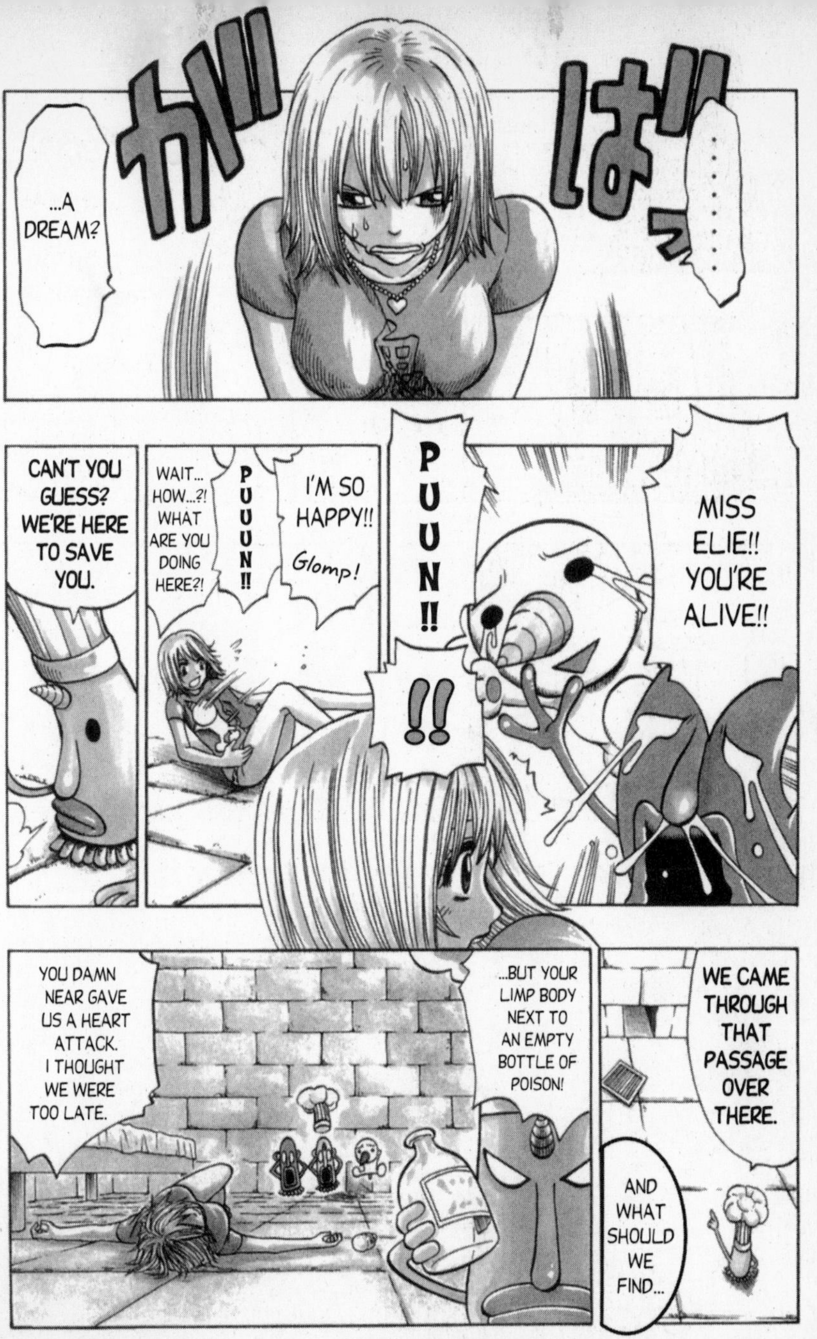
がばっ
......
...A DREAM?
MISS ELIE!! YOU'RE ALIVE!!
PUUN!!
!!
I'M SO HAPPY!!
Glomp!
PUUUN!!
WAIT... HOW...?! WHAT ARE YOU DOING HERE?!
CAN'T YOU GUESS? WE'RE HERE TO SAVE YOU.
WE CAME THROUGH THAT PASSAGE OVER THERE.
AND WHAT SHOULD WE FIND...
...BUT YOUR LIMP BODY NEXT TO AN EMPTY BOTTLE OF POISON!
YOU DAMN NEAR GAVE US A HEART ATTACK. I THOUGHT WE WERE TOO LATE.

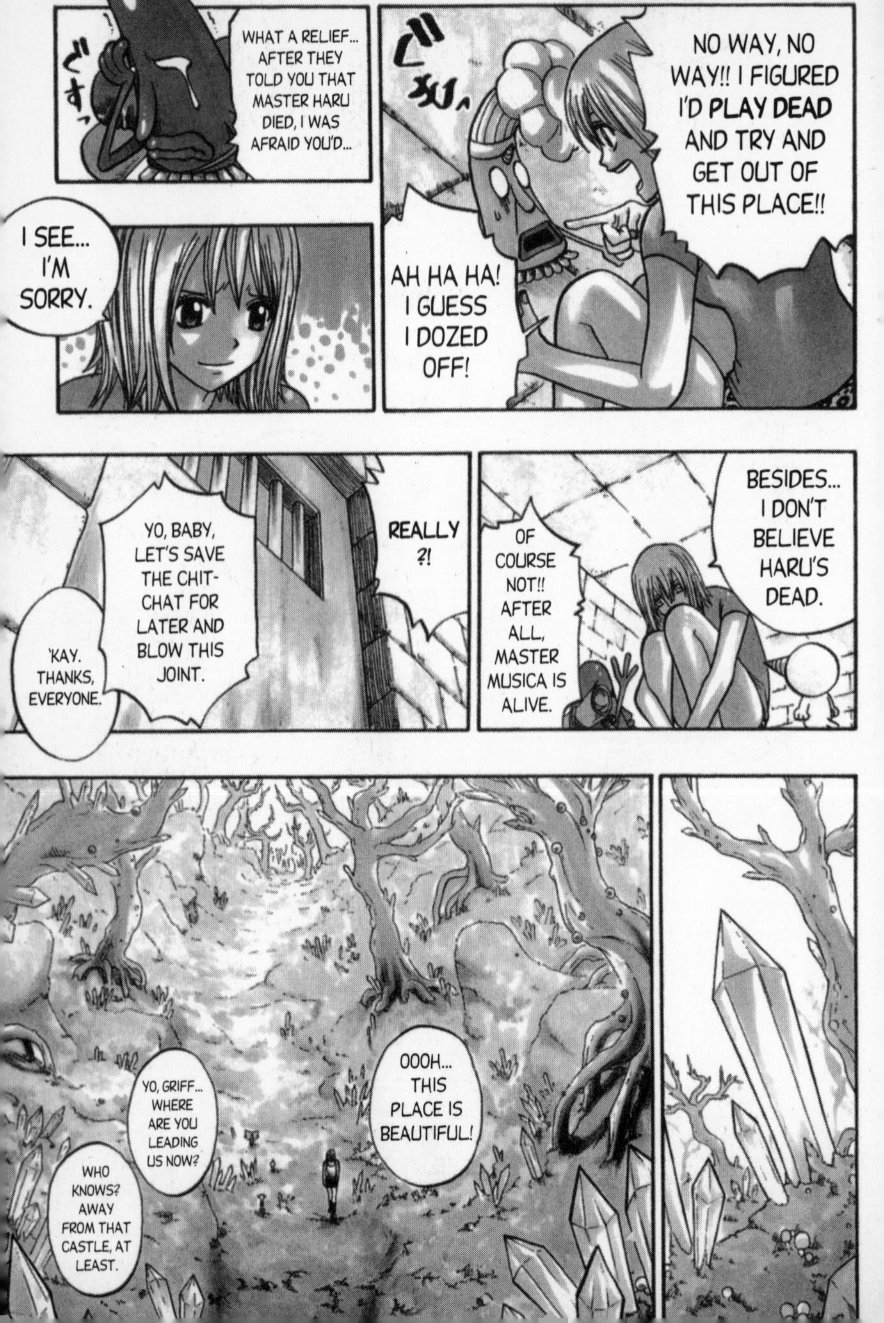
NO WAY, NO WAY!! I FIGURED I'D **PLAY DEAD** AND TRY AND GET OUT OF THIS PLACE!!
AH HA HA! I GUESS I DOZED OFF!
WHAT A RELIEF... AFTER THEY TOLD YOU THAT MASTER HARU DIED, I WAS AFRAID YOU'D...
I SEE... I'M SORRY.
BESIDES... I DON'T BELIEVE HARU'S DEAD.
OF COURSE NOT!! AFTER ALL, MASTER MUSICA IS ALIVE.
REALLY?!
YO, BABY, LET'S SAVE THE CHIT-CHAT FOR LATER AND BLOW THIS JOINT.
'KAY. THANKS, EVERYONE.
OOOH... THIS PLACE IS BEAUTIFUL!
YO, GRIFF... WHERE ARE YOU LEADING US NOW?
WHO KNOWS? AWAY FROM THAT CASTLE, AT LEAST.

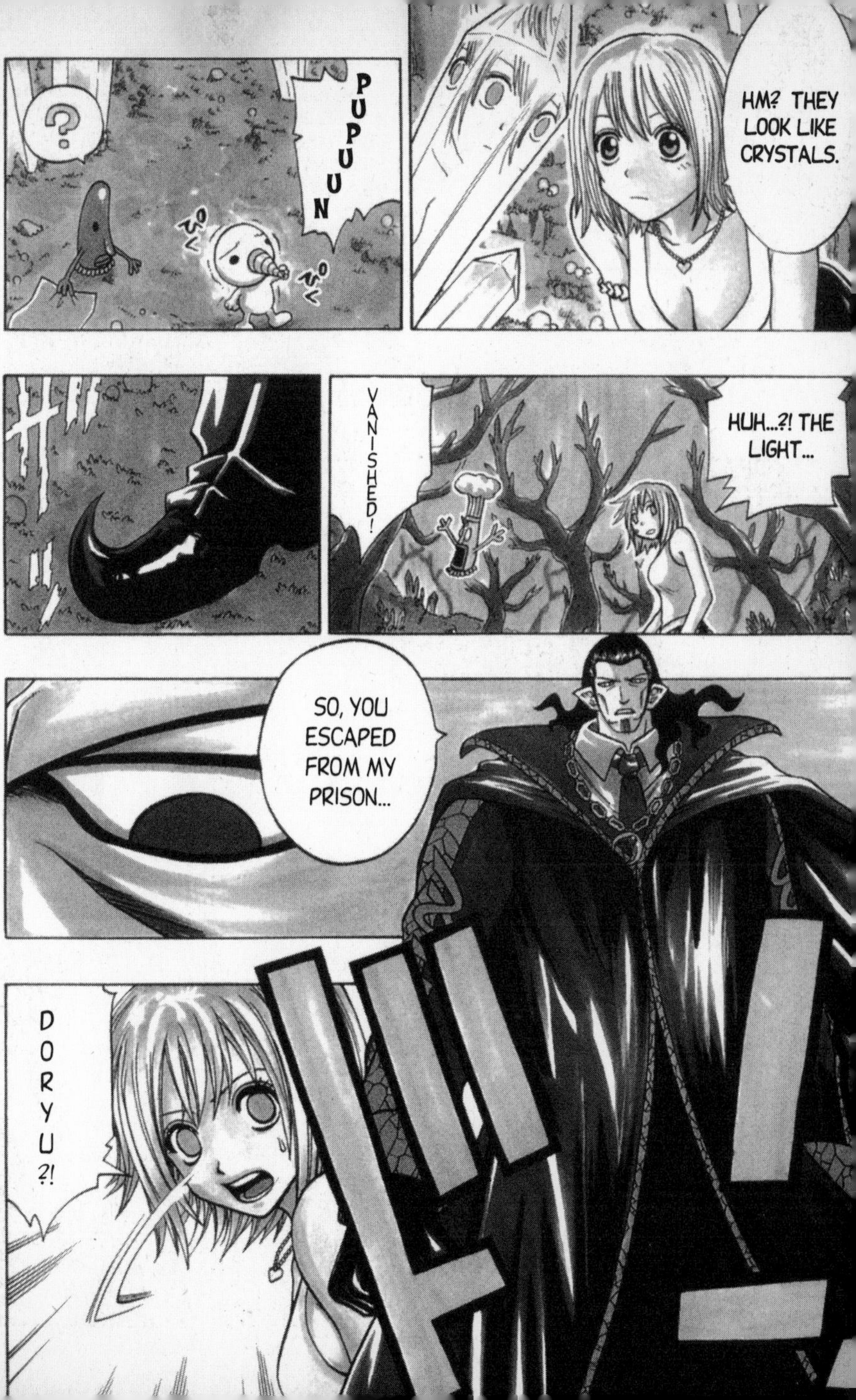
HM? THEY LOOK LIKE CRYSTALS.
?
PUPUUN
HUH...?! THE LIGHT...
VANISHED!
SO, YOU ESCAPED FROM MY PRISON...
DORYU?!

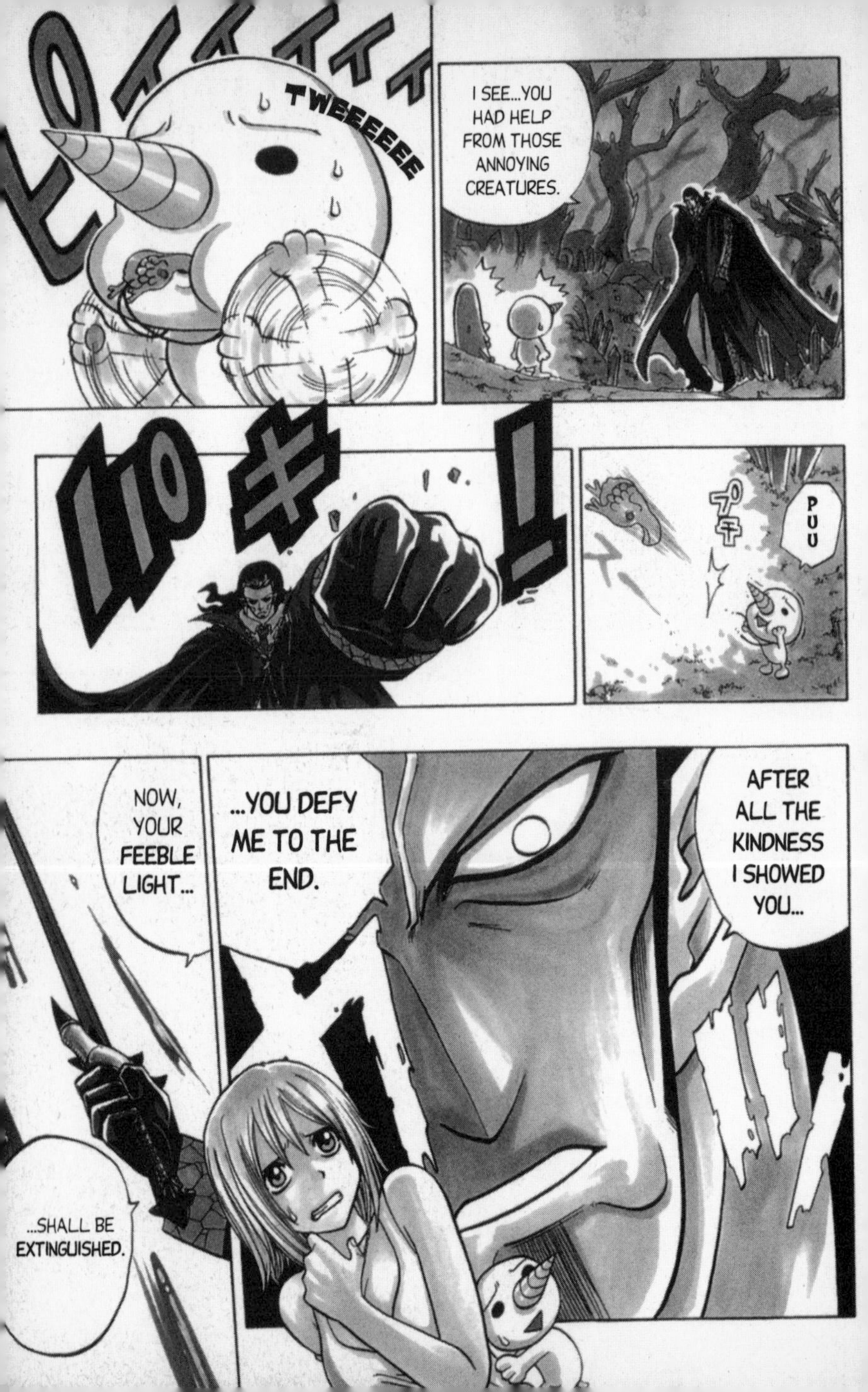
I SEE...YOU HAD HELP FROM THOSE ANNOYING CREATURES.
TWEEEEEEE
PUU
AFTER ALL THE KINDNESS I SHOWED YOU...
...YOU DEFY ME TO THE END.
NOW, YOUR FEEBLE LIGHT...
...SHALL BE EXTINGUISHED.

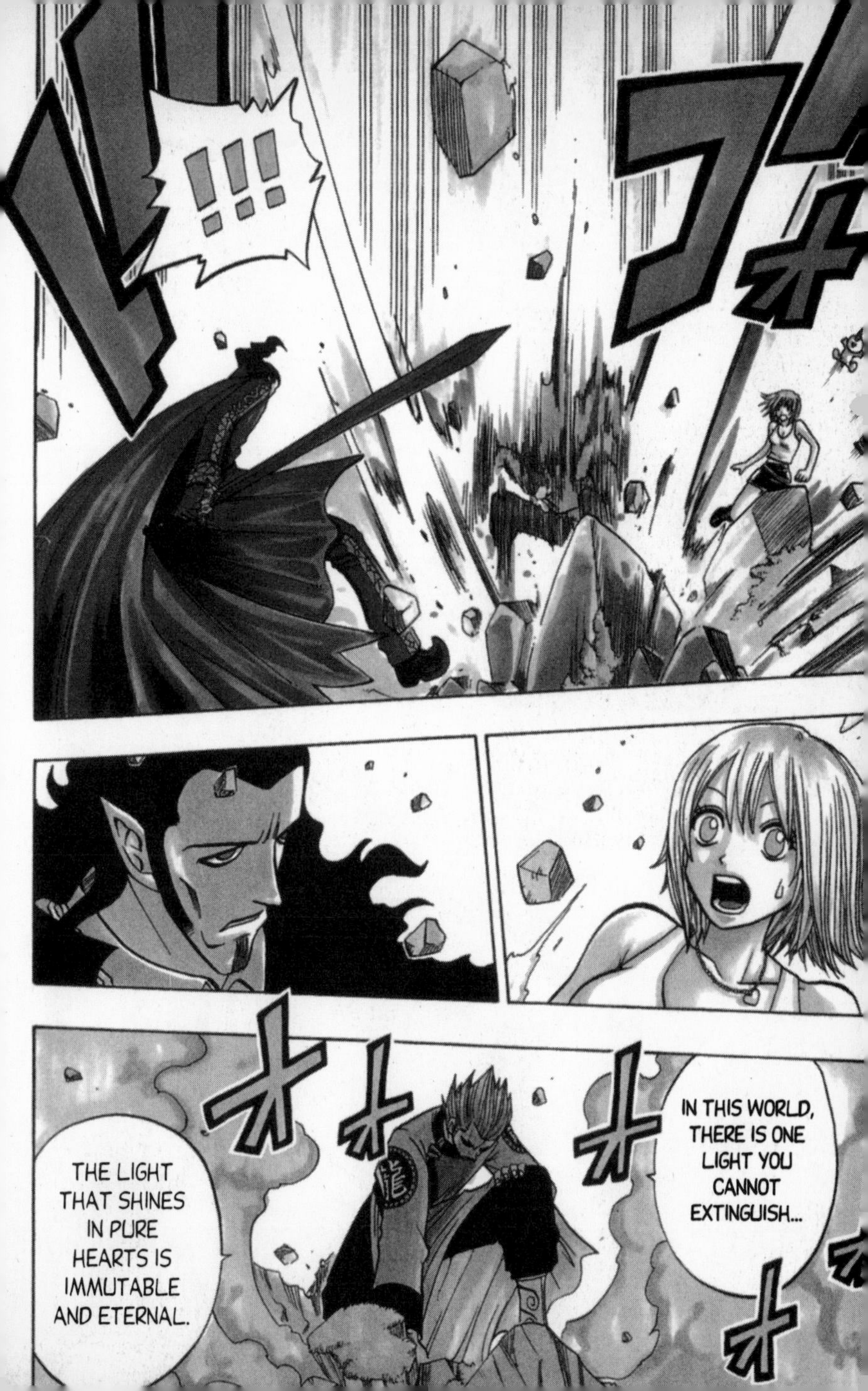
!!!
IN THIS WORLD, THERE IS ONE LIGHT YOU CANNOT EXTINGUISH...
THE LIGHT THAT SHINES IN PURE HEARTS IS IMMUTABLE AND ETERNAL.

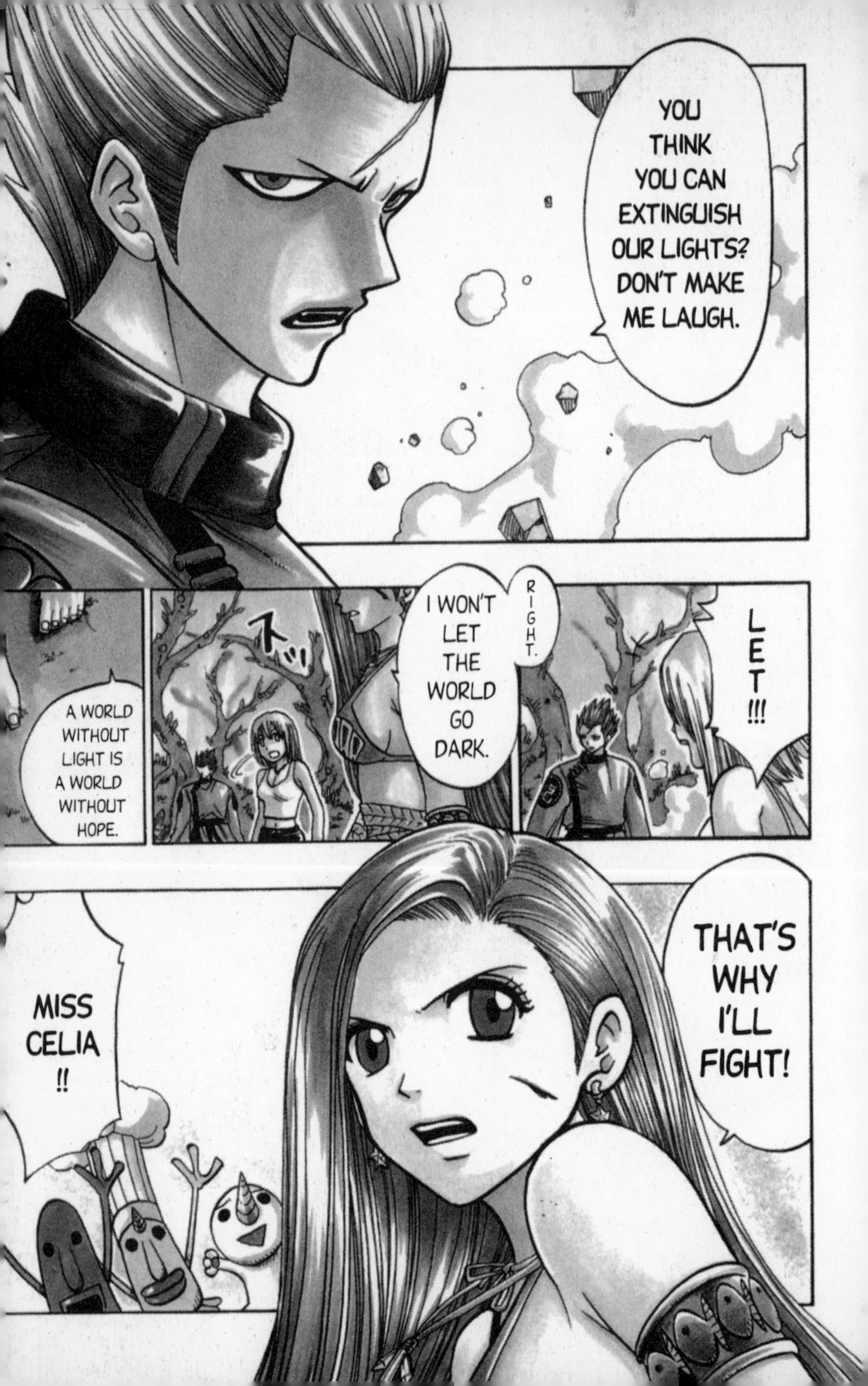
YOU THINK YOU CAN EXTINGUISH OUR LIGHTS? DON'T MAKE ME LAUGH.
LET!!!
RIGHT.
I WON'T LET THE WORLD GO DARK.
A WORLD WITHOUT LIGHT IS A WORLD WITHOUT HOPE.
THAT'S WHY I'LL FIGHT!
MISS CELIA !!

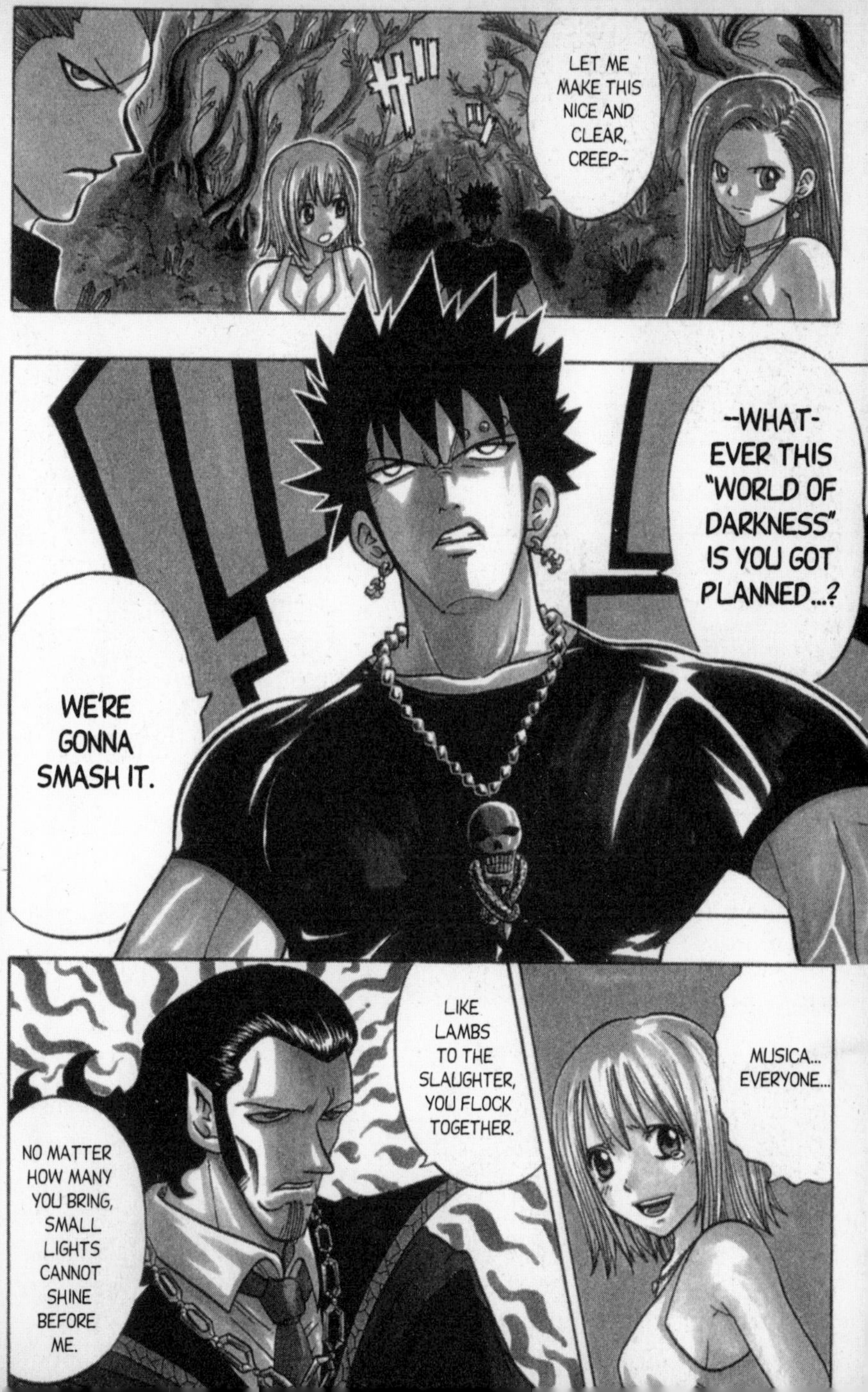
LET ME MAKE THIS NICE AND CLEAR, CREEP--
--WHAT-EVER THIS "WORLD OF DARKNESS" IS YOU GOT PLANNED...?
WE'RE GONNA SMASH IT.
MUSICA... EVERYONE...
LIKE LAMBS TO THE SLAUGHTER, YOU FLOCK TOGETHER.
NO MATTER HOW MANY YOU BRING, SMALL LIGHTS CANNOT SHINE BEFORE ME.

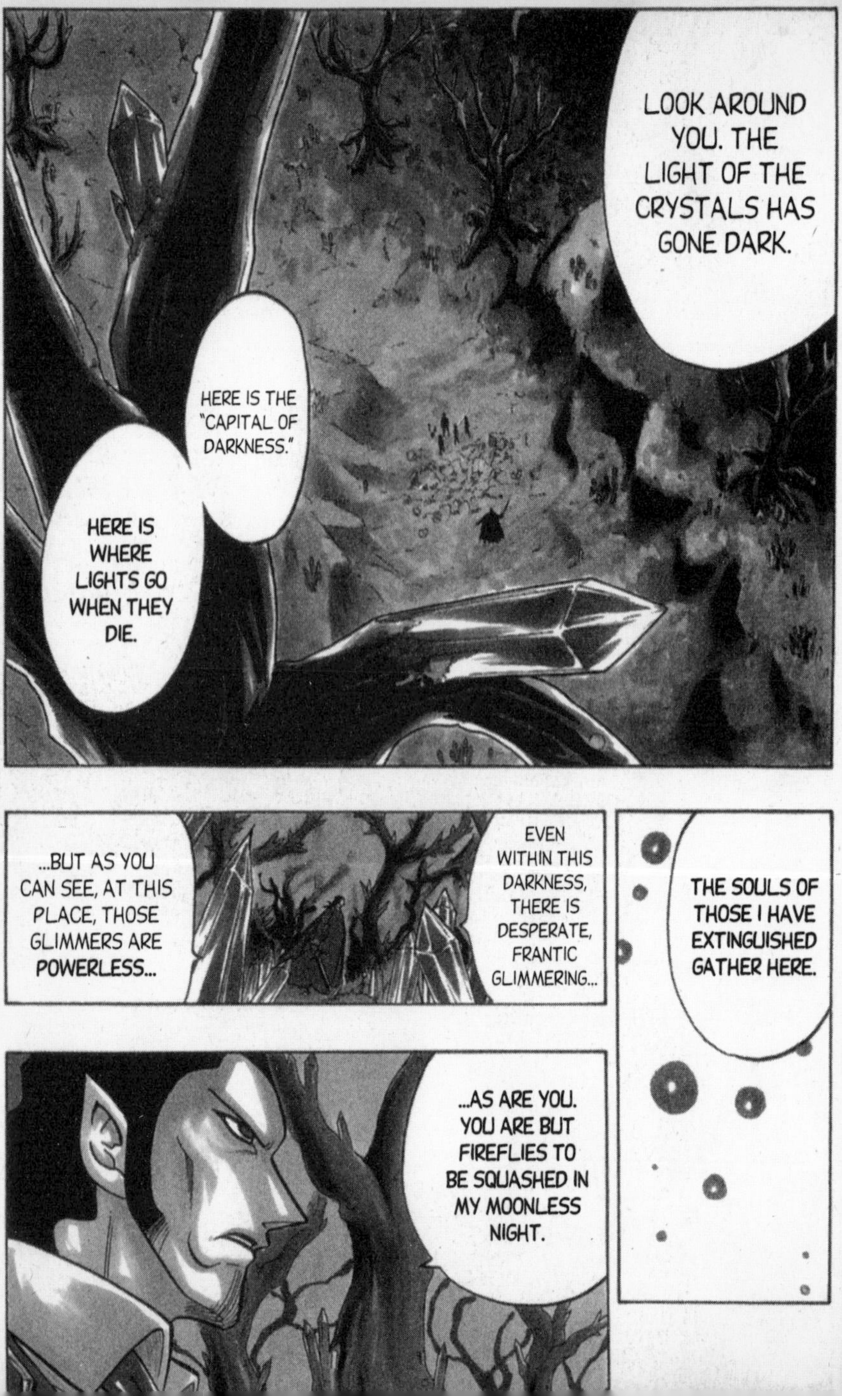
LOOK AROUND YOU. THE LIGHT OF THE CRYSTALS HAS GONE DARK.
HERE IS THE "CAPITAL OF DARKNESS."
HERE IS WHERE LIGHTS GO WHEN THEY DIE.
THE SOULS OF THOSE I HAVE EXTINGUISHED GATHER HERE.
EVEN WITHIN THIS DARKNESS, THERE IS DESPERATE, FRANTIC GLIMMERING...
...BUT AS YOU CAN SEE, AT THIS PLACE, THOSE GLIMMERS ARE POWERLESS...
...AS ARE YOU. YOU ARE BUT FIREFLIES TO BE SQUASHED IN MY MOONLESS NIGHT.

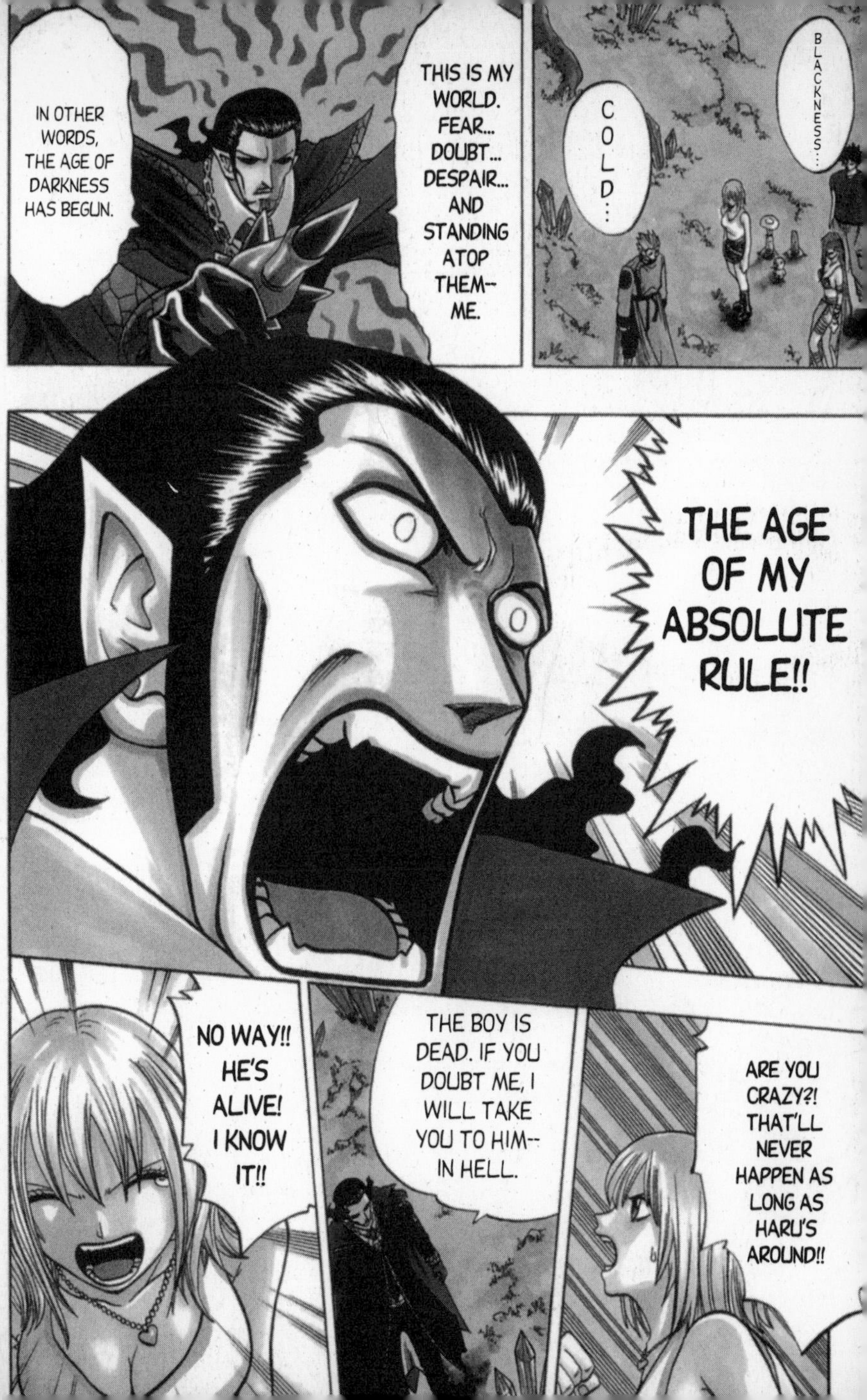
BLACKNESS...
COLD...
THIS IS MY WORLD. FEAR... DOUBT... DESPAIR... AND STANDING ATOP THEM-- ME.
IN OTHER WORDS, THE AGE OF DARKNESS HAS BEGUN.
THE AGE OF MY ABSOLUTE RULE!!
ARE YOU CRAZY?! THAT'LL NEVER HAPPEN AS LONG AS HARU'S AROUND!!
THE BOY IS DEAD. IF YOU DOUBT ME, I WILL TAKE YOU TO HIM-- IN HELL.
NO WAY!! HE'S ALIVE! I KNOW IT!!

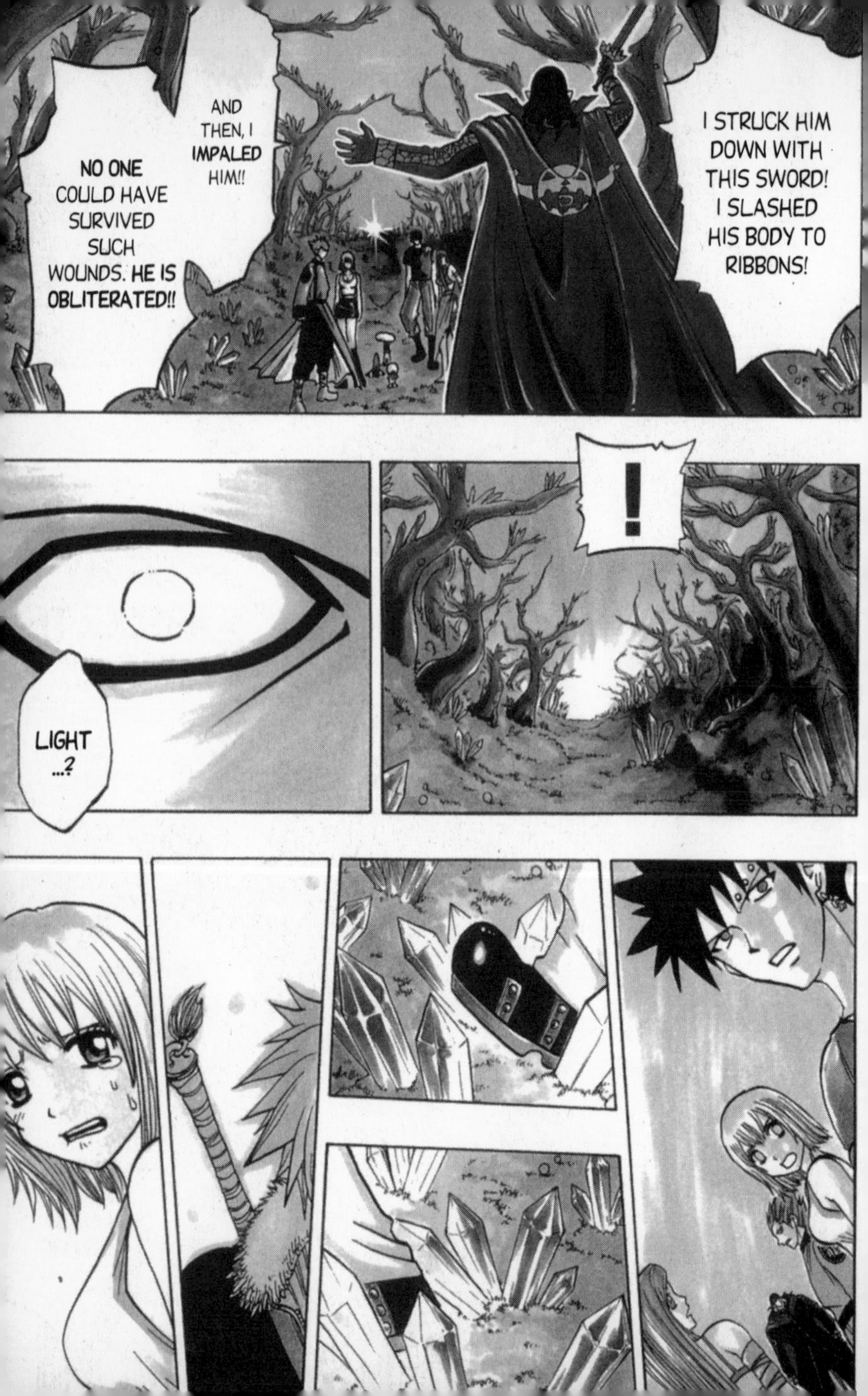
I STRUCK HIM DOWN WITH THIS SWORD! I SLASHED HIS BODY TO RIBBONS!
AND THEN, I IMPALED HIM!!
NO ONE COULD HAVE SURVIVED SUCH WOUNDS. HE IS OBLITERATED!!
!
LIGHT ...?

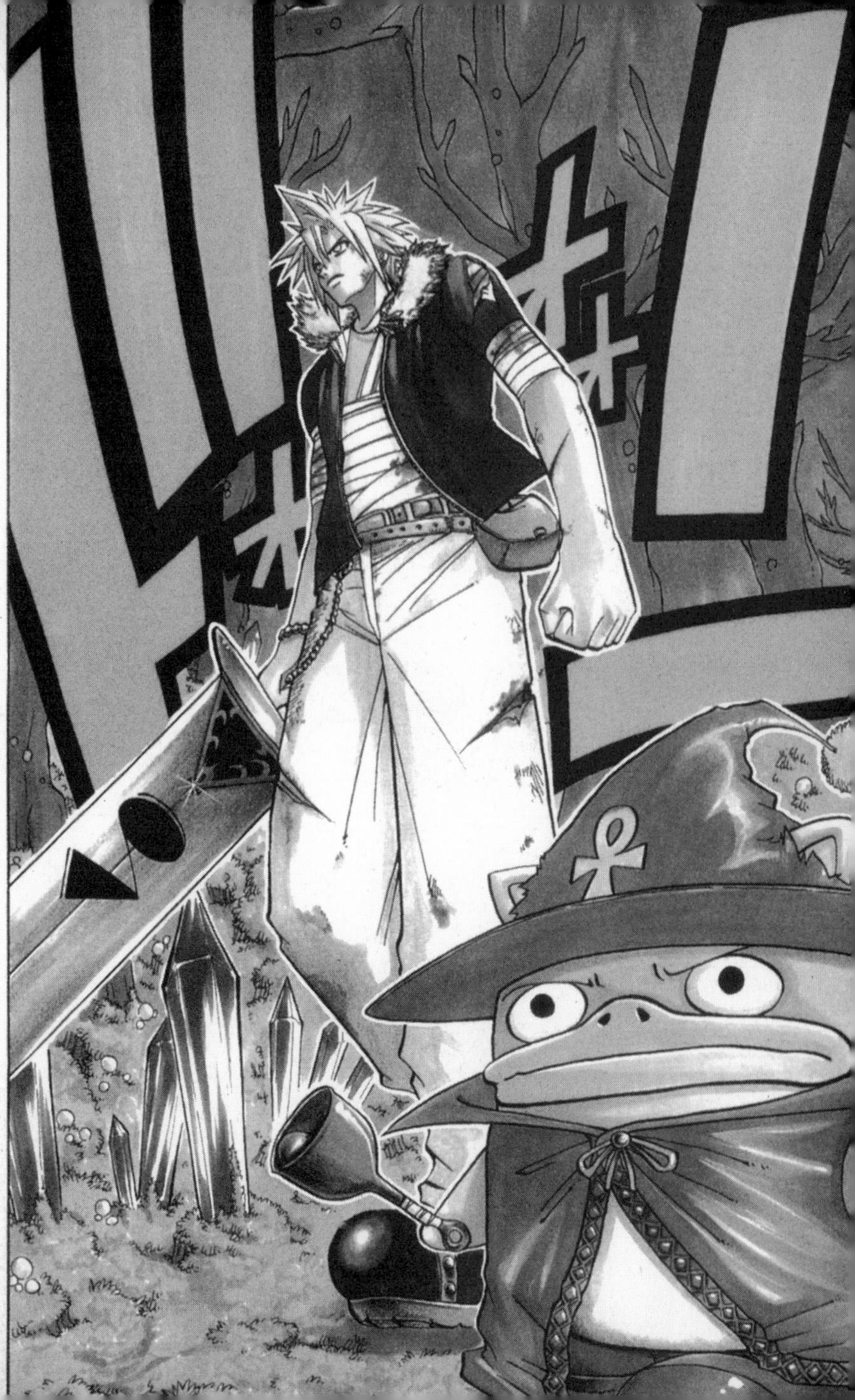

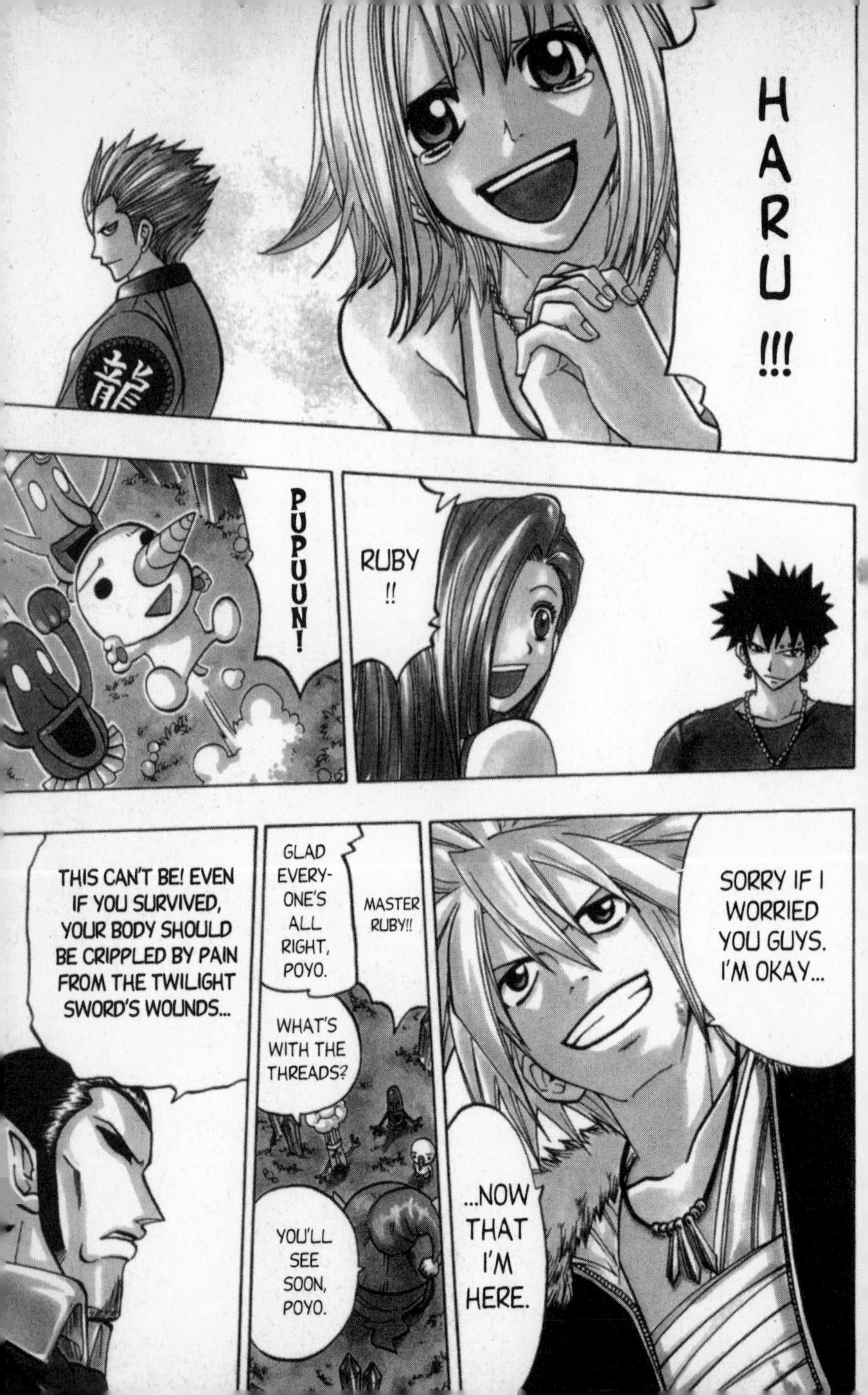
HARU!!!
RUBY !!
PUPUUUN!
SORRY IF I WORRIED YOU GUYS. I'M OKAY...
...NOW THAT I'M HERE.
MASTER RUBY!!
GLAD EVERYONE'S ALL RIGHT, POYO.
WHAT'S WITH THE THREADS?
YOU'LL SEE SOON, POYO.
THIS CAN'T BE! EVEN IF YOU SURVIVED, YOUR BODY SHOULD BE CRIPPLED BY PAIN FROM THE TWILIGHT SWORD'S WOUNDS...

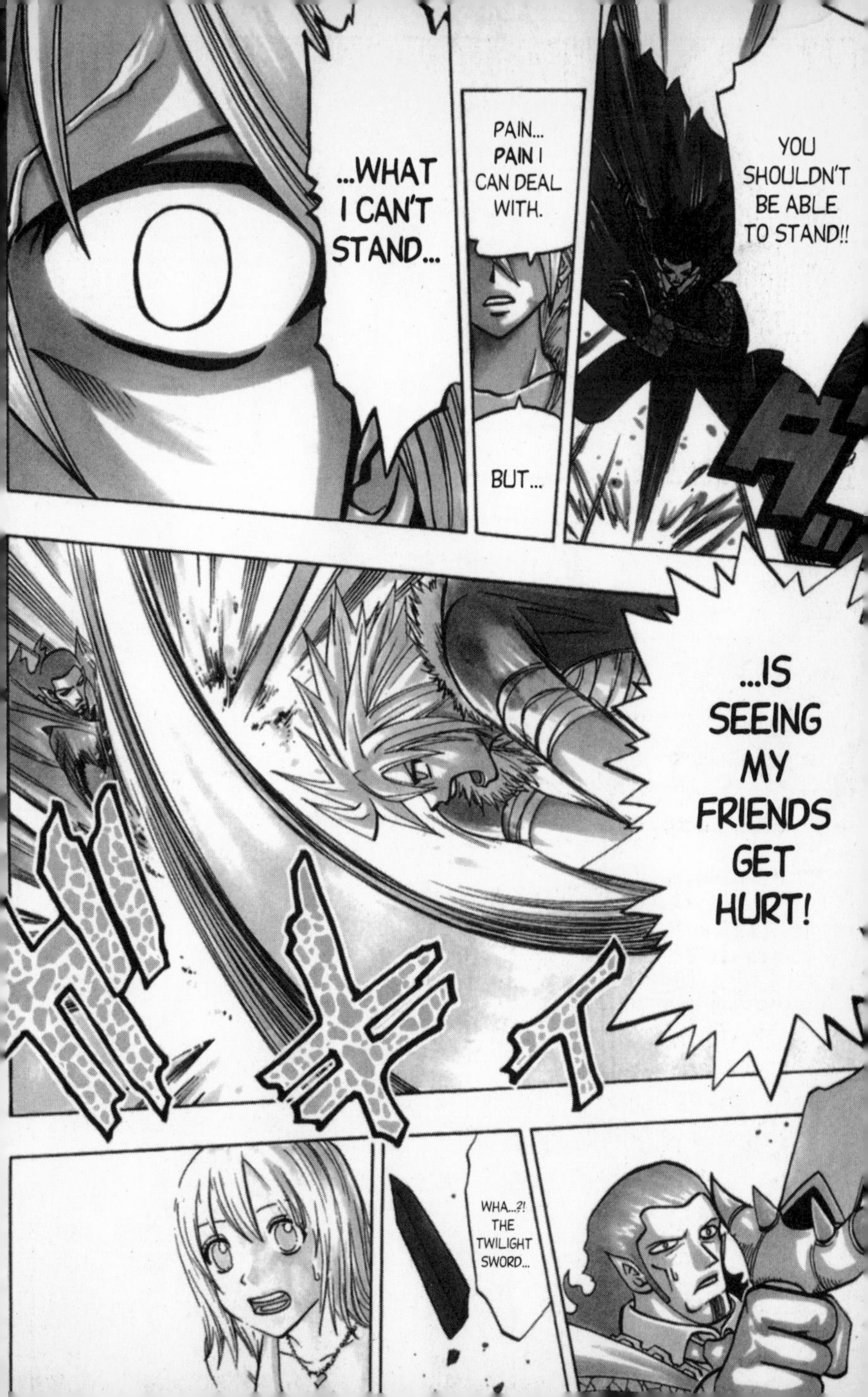
YOU SHOULDN'T BE ABLE TO STAND!!
PAIN... PAIN I CAN DEAL WITH.
BUT...
...WHAT I CAN'T STAND...
...IS SEEING MY FRIENDS GET HURT!
WHA...?! THE TWILIGHT SWORD...

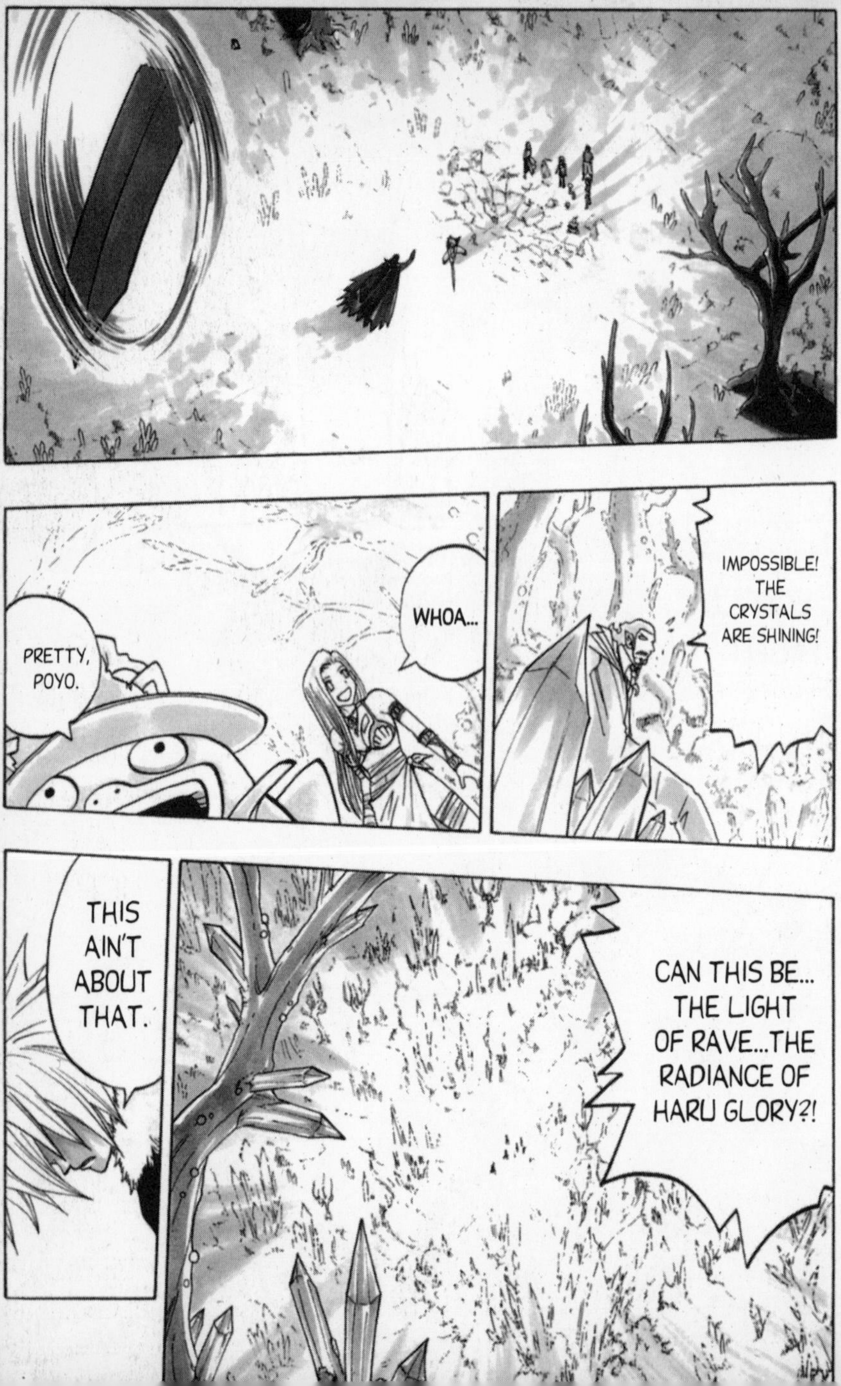
IMPOSSIBLE! THE CRYSTALS ARE SHINING!
WHOA...
PRETTY, POYO.
CAN THIS BE... THE LIGHT OF RAVE...THE RADIANCE OF HARU GLORY?!
THIS AIN'T ABOUT THAT.

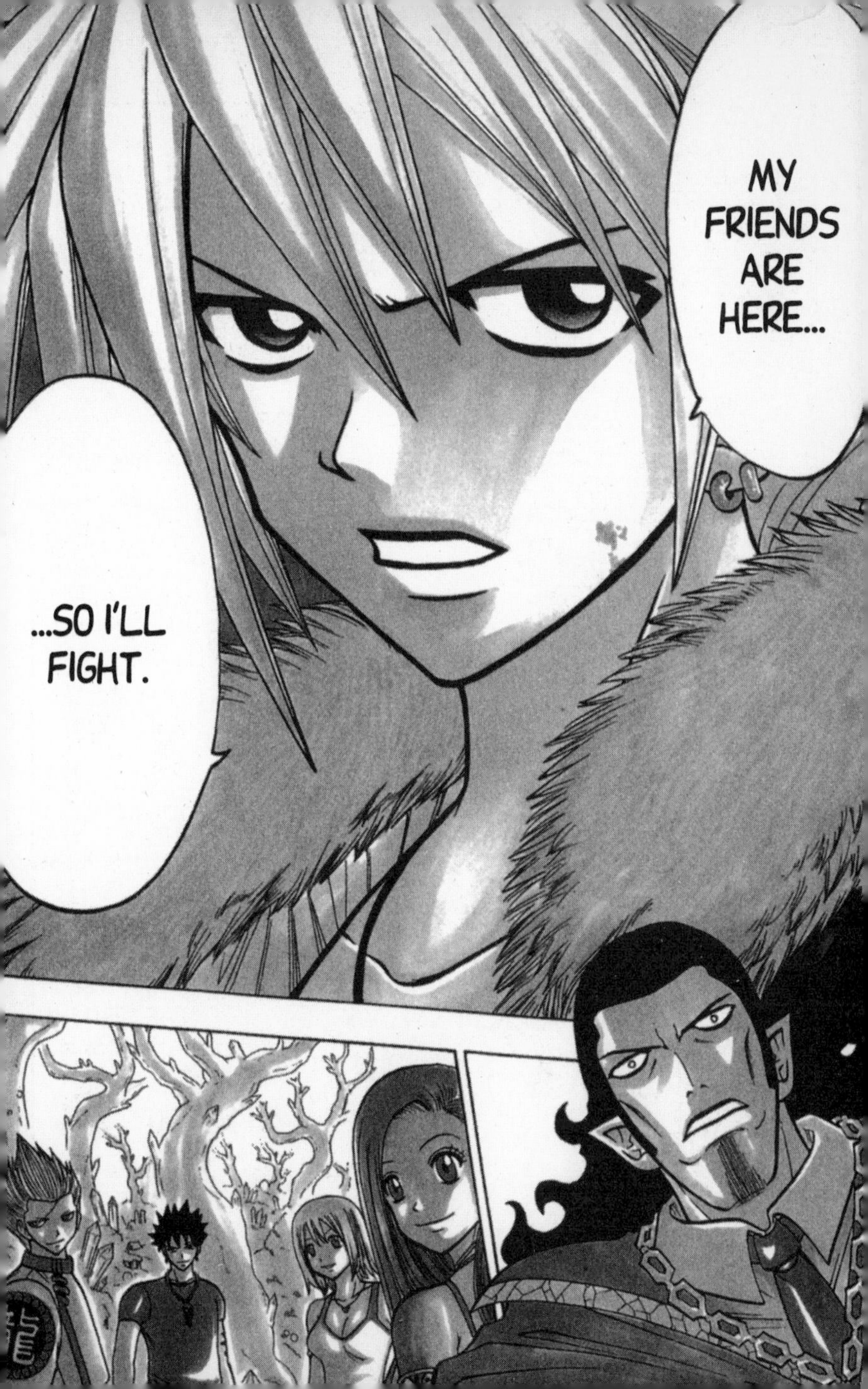
MY FRIENDS ARE HERE...
...SO I'LL FIGHT.

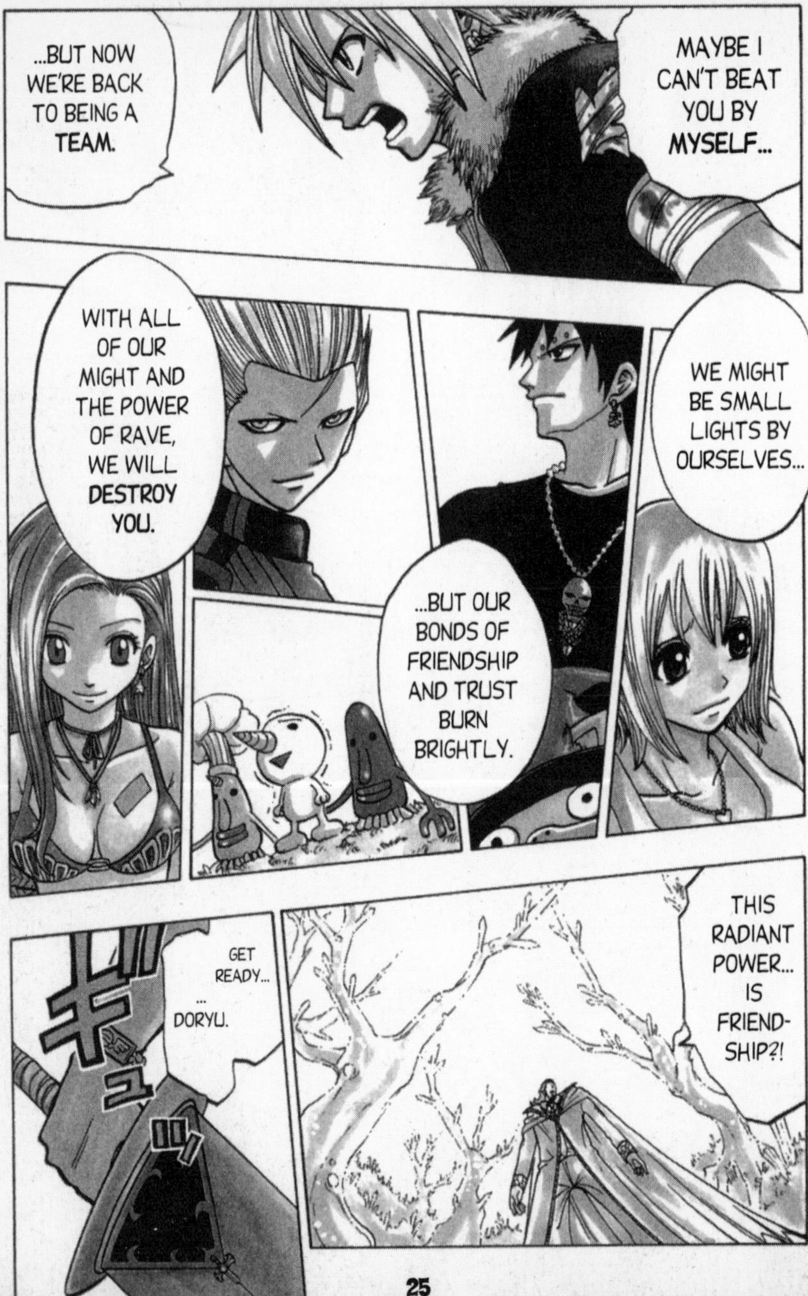
MAYBE I CAN'T BEAT YOU BY MYSELF...
...BUT NOW WE'RE BACK TO BEING A TEAM.
WE MIGHT BE SMALL LIGHTS BY OURSELVES...
...BUT OUR BONDS OF FRIENDSHIP AND TRUST BURN BRIGHTLY.
WITH ALL OF OUR MIGHT AND THE POWER OF RAVE, WE WILL DESTROY YOU.
THIS RADIANT POWER... IS FRIEND-SHIP?!
GET READY...
... DORYU.

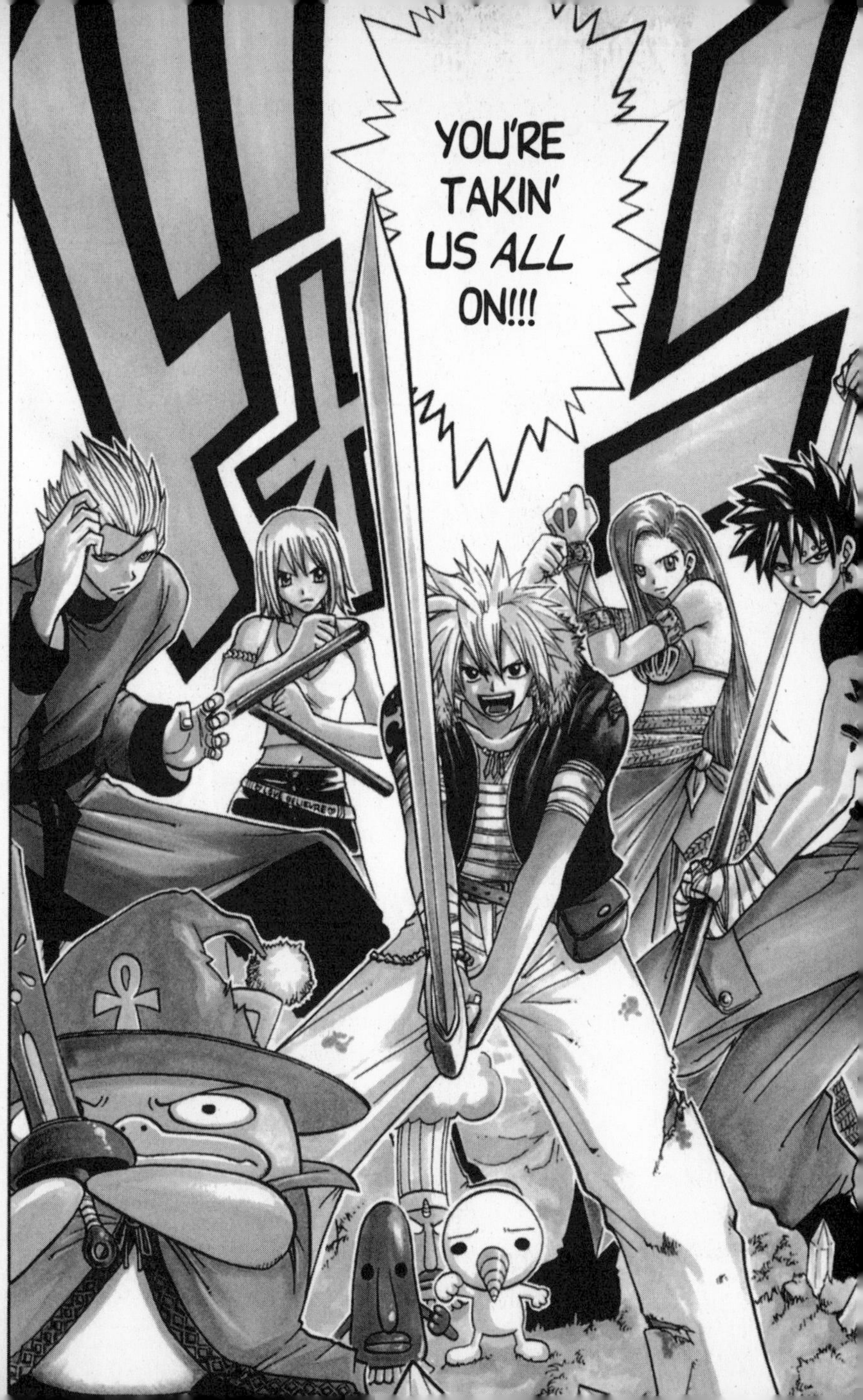
YOU'RE TAKIN' US *ALL* ON!!!

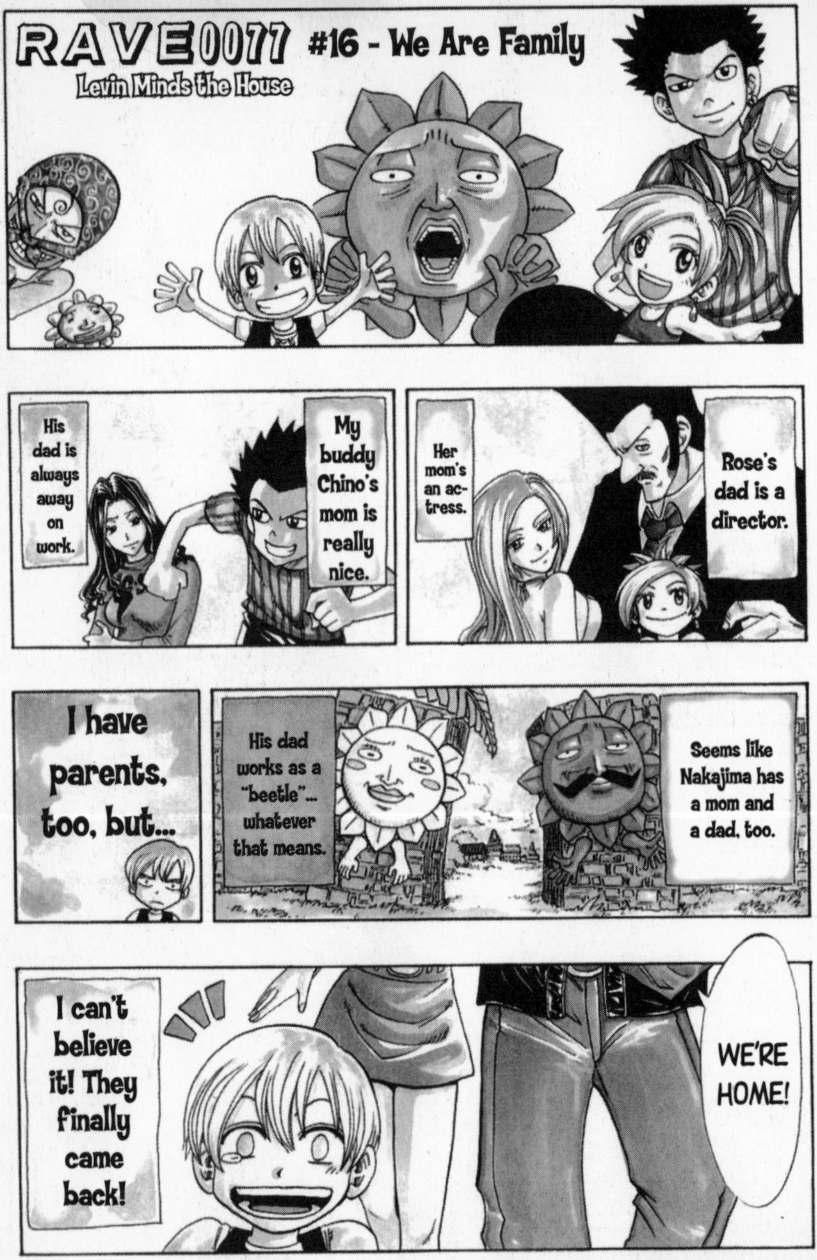
RAVE0077
#16 - We Are Family
Levin Minds the House
Rose's dad is a director.
Her mom's an ac-tress.
My buddy Chino's mom is really nice.
His dad is always away on work.
Seems like Nakajima has a mom and a dad, too.
His dad works as a "beetle"... whatever that means.
I have parents, too, but...
WE'RE HOME!
I can't believe it! They finally came back!

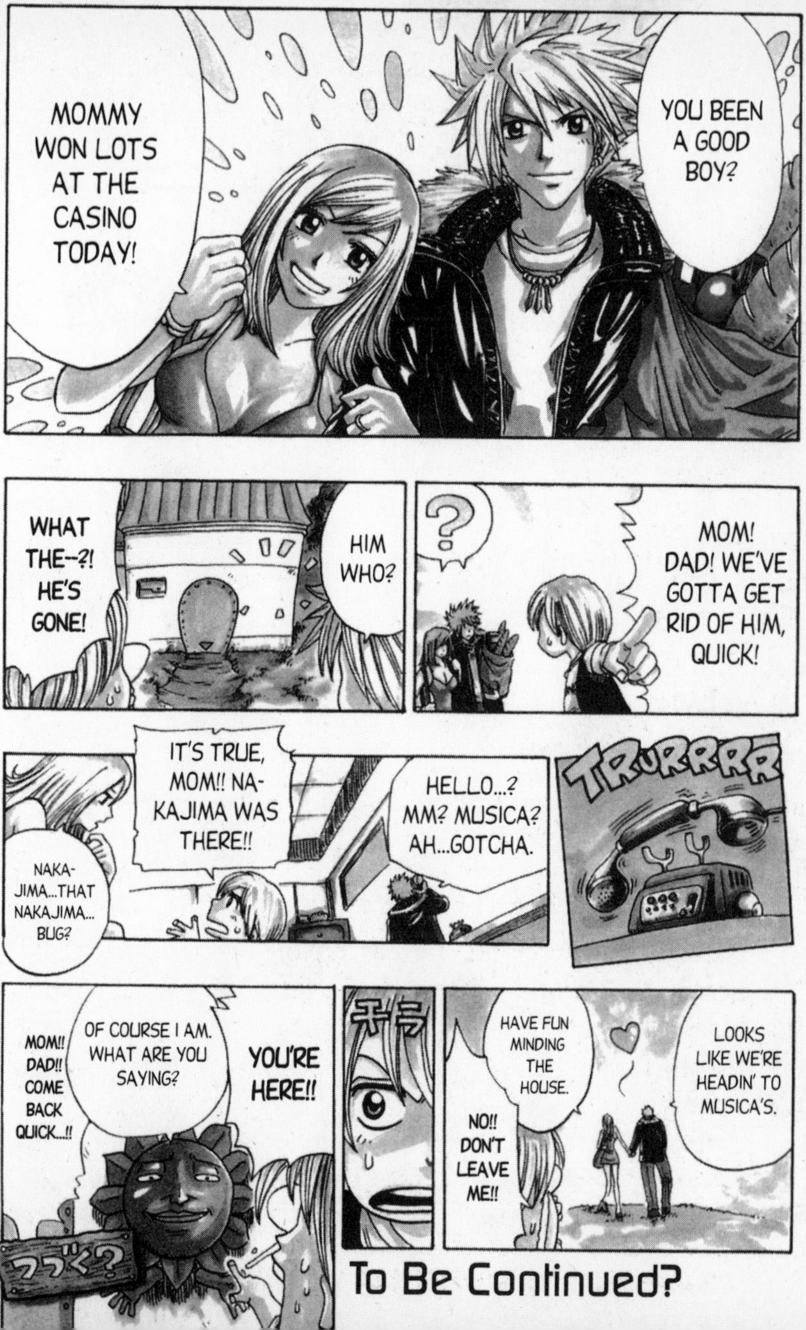
YOU BEEN A GOOD BOY?
MOMMY WON LOTS AT THE CASINO TODAY!
?
MOM! DAD! WE'VE GOTTA GET RID OF HIM, QUICK!
HIM WHO?
WHAT THE--?! HE'S GONE!
TRURRRR
HELLO...? MM? MUSICA? AH...GOTCHA.
IT'S TRUE, MOM!! NA-KAJIMA WAS THERE!!
NAKA-JIMA...THAT NAKAJIMA... BUG?
LOOKS LIKE WE'RE HEADIN' TO MUSICA'S.
HAVE FUN MINDING THE HOUSE.
NO!! DON'T LEAVE ME!!
YOU'RE HERE!!
OF COURSE I AM. WHAT ARE YOU SAYING?
MOM!! DAD!! COME BACK QUICK...!!
つづく?

To Be Continued?

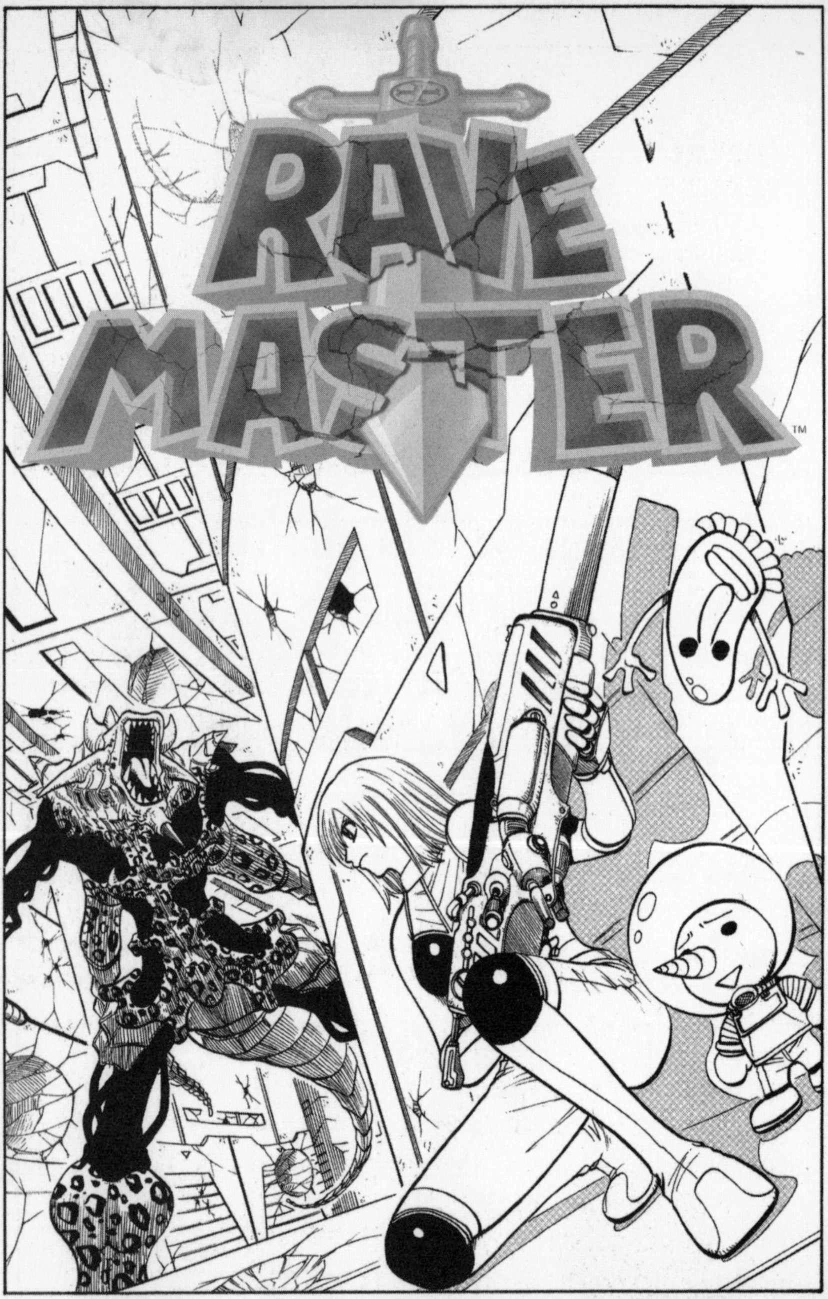
RAVE MASTER™

RAVE:131 ✥ DOOR TO THE NIGHTMARE

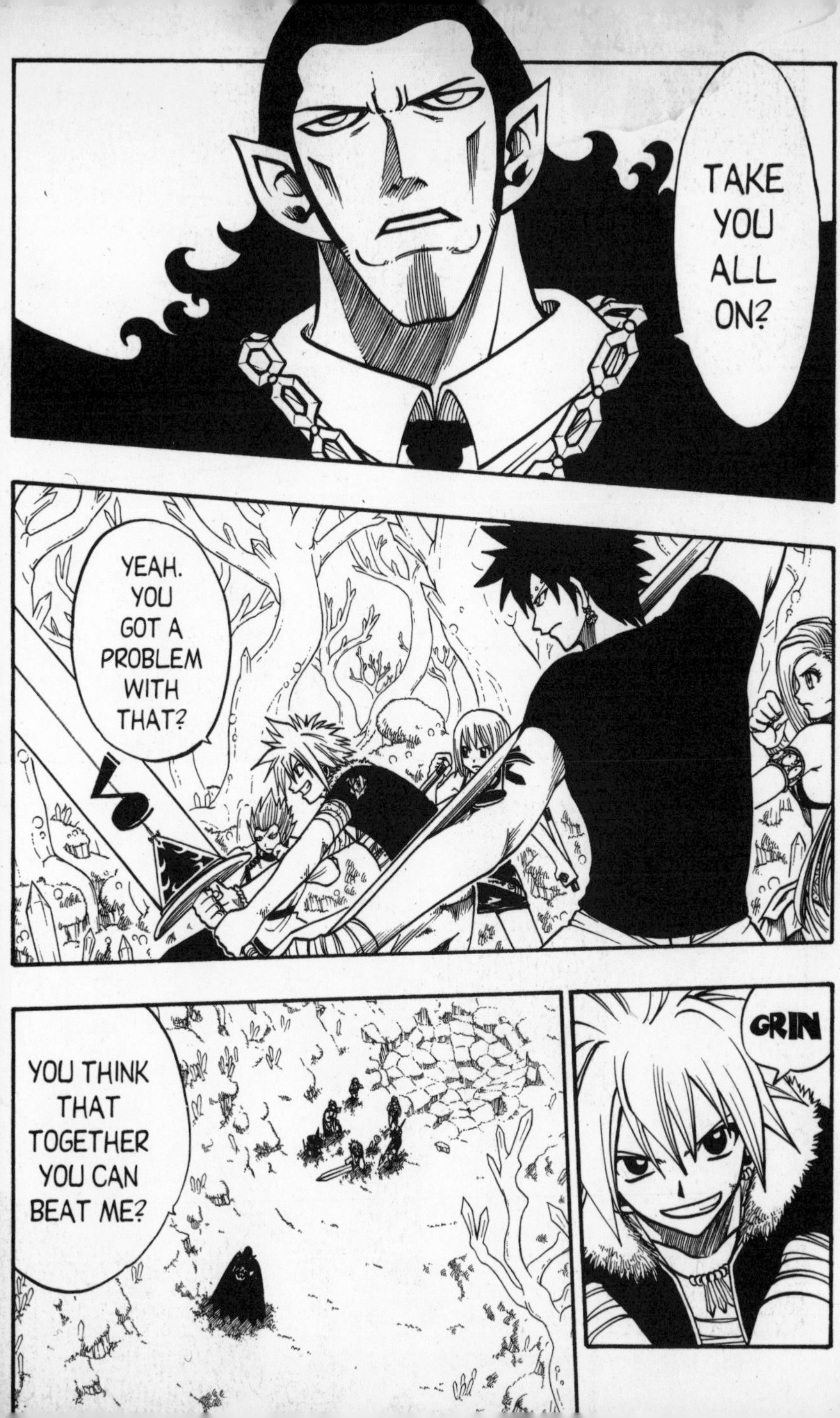
TAKE YOU ALL ON?
YEAH. YOU GOT A PROBLEM WITH THAT?
GRIN
YOU THINK THAT TOGETHER YOU CAN BEAT ME?

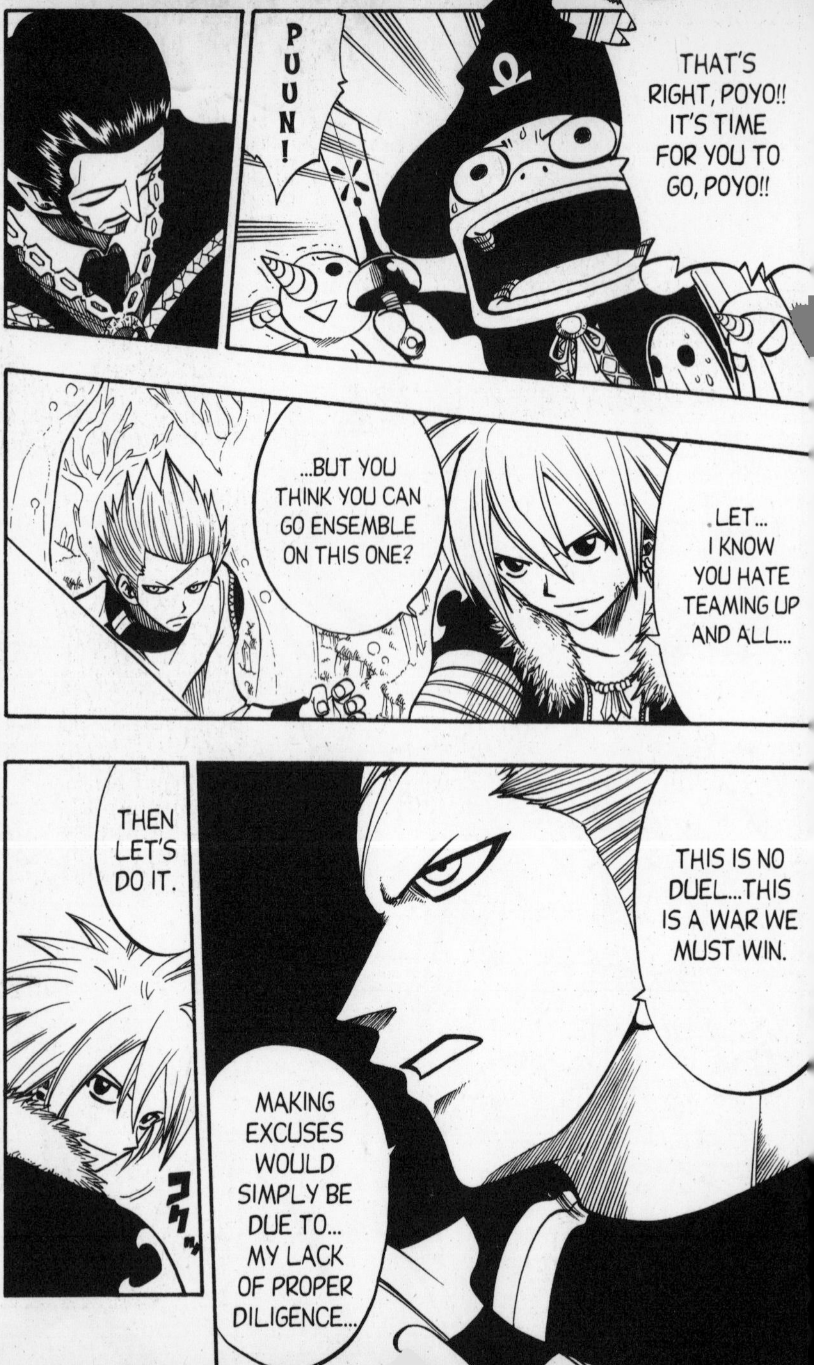
THAT'S RIGHT, POYO!! IT'S TIME FOR YOU TO GO, POYO!!
PUUN!
LET... I KNOW YOU HATE TEAMING UP AND ALL...
...BUT YOU THINK YOU CAN GO ENSEMBLE ON THIS ONE?
THIS IS NO DUEL...THIS IS A WAR WE MUST WIN.
MAKING EXCUSES WOULD SIMPLY BE DUE TO... MY LACK OF PROPER DILIGENCE...
THEN LET'S DO IT.

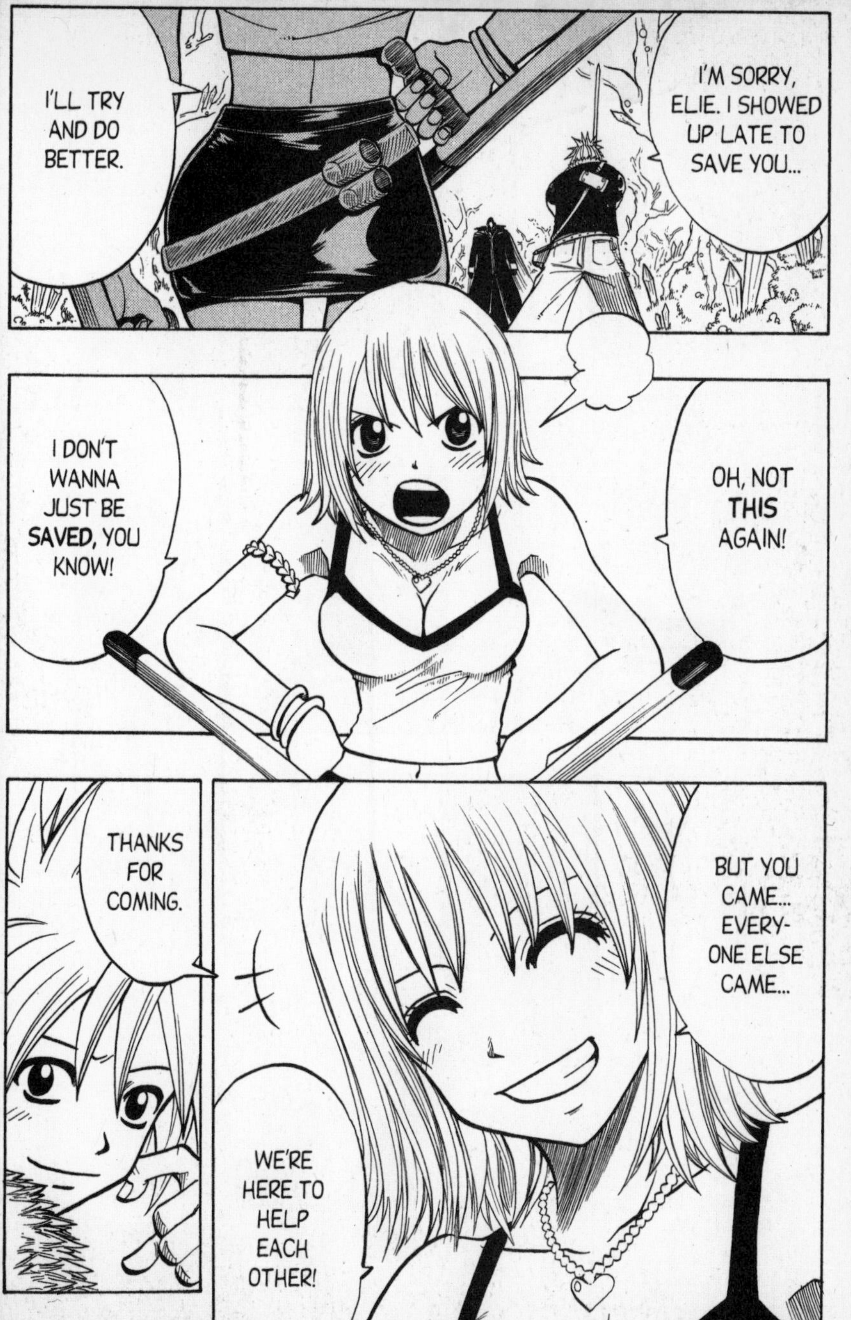
I'M SORRY, ELIE. I SHOWED UP LATE TO SAVE YOU...
I'LL TRY AND DO BETTER.
OH, NOT THIS AGAIN!
I DON'T WANNA JUST BE SAVED, YOU KNOW!
BUT YOU CAME... EVERY-ONE ELSE CAME...
WE'RE HERE TO HELP EACH OTHER!
THANKS FOR COMING.

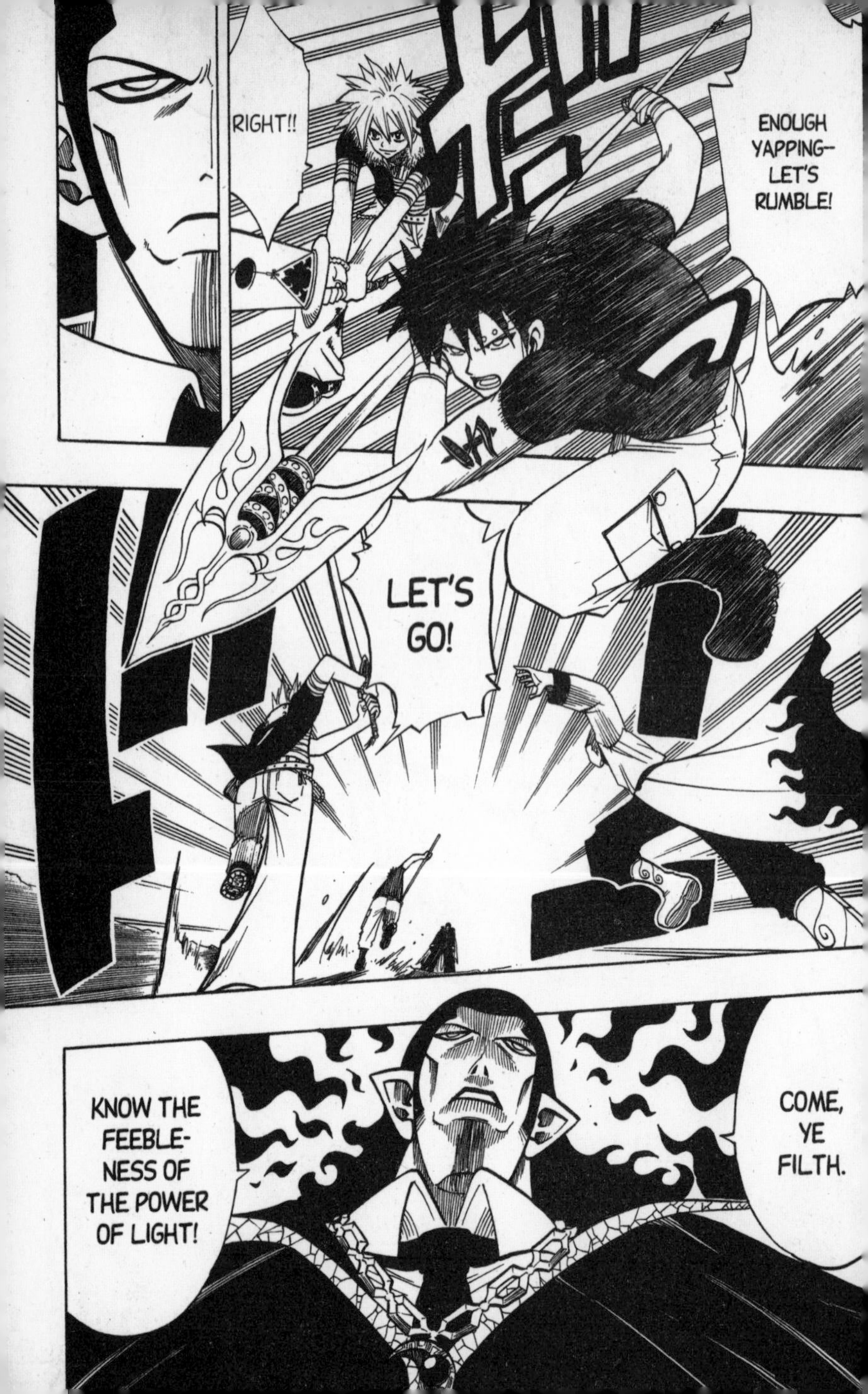
ENOUGH YAPPING— LET'S RUMBLE!
RIGHT!!
LET'S GO!
COME, YE FILTH.
KNOW THE FEEBLE- NESS OF THE POWER OF LIGHT!

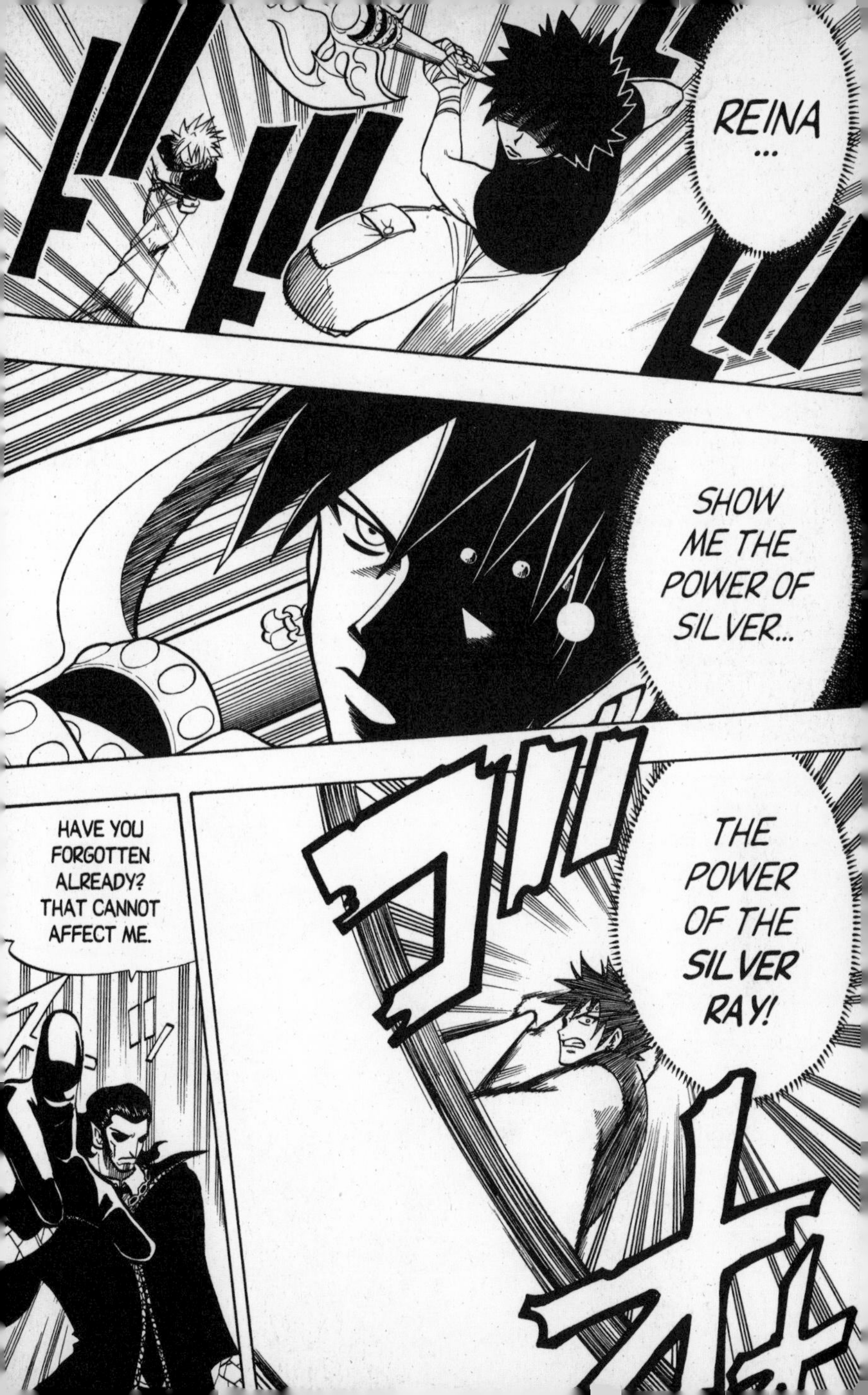
REINA ...
SHOW ME THE POWER OF SILVER...
THE POWER OF THE SILVER RAY!
HAVE YOU FORGOTTEN ALREADY? THAT CANNOT AFFECT ME.

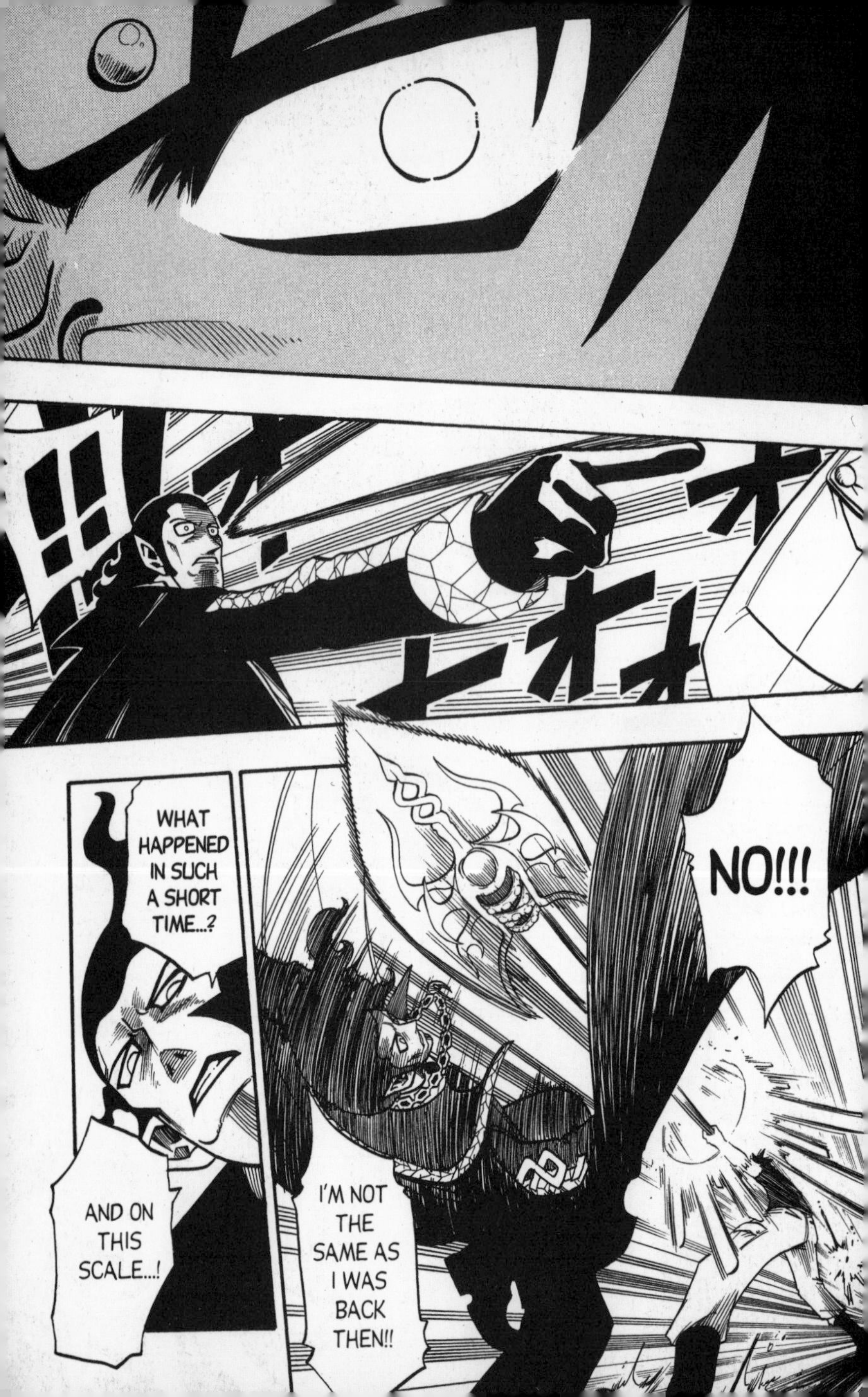
NO!!!
I'M NOT THE SAME AS I WAS BACK THEN!!
WHAT HAPPENED IN SUCH A SHORT TIME...?
AND ON THIS SCALE...!

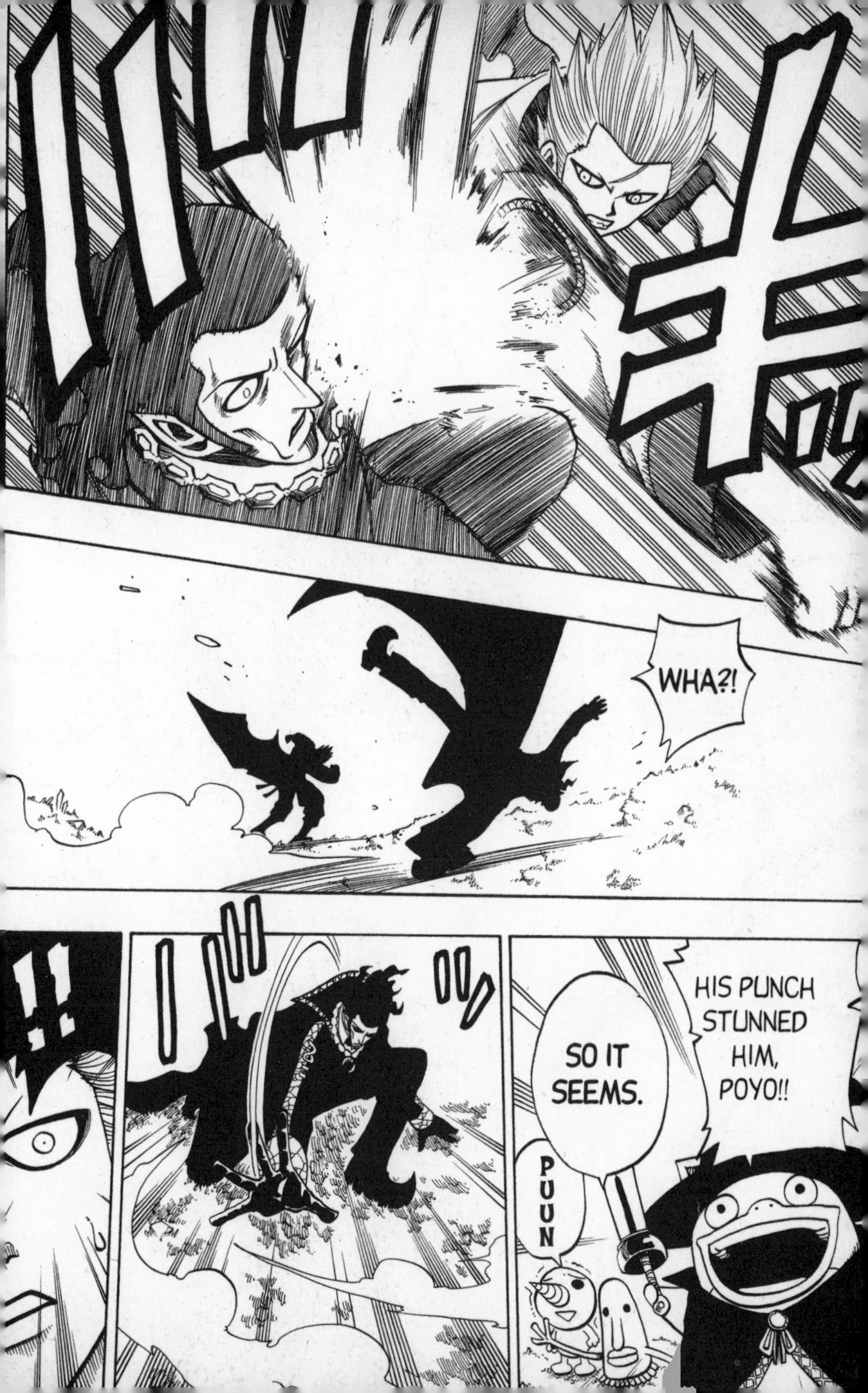
WHA?!
HIS PUNCH STUNNED HIM, POYO!!
SO IT SEEMS.
PUUN
!!

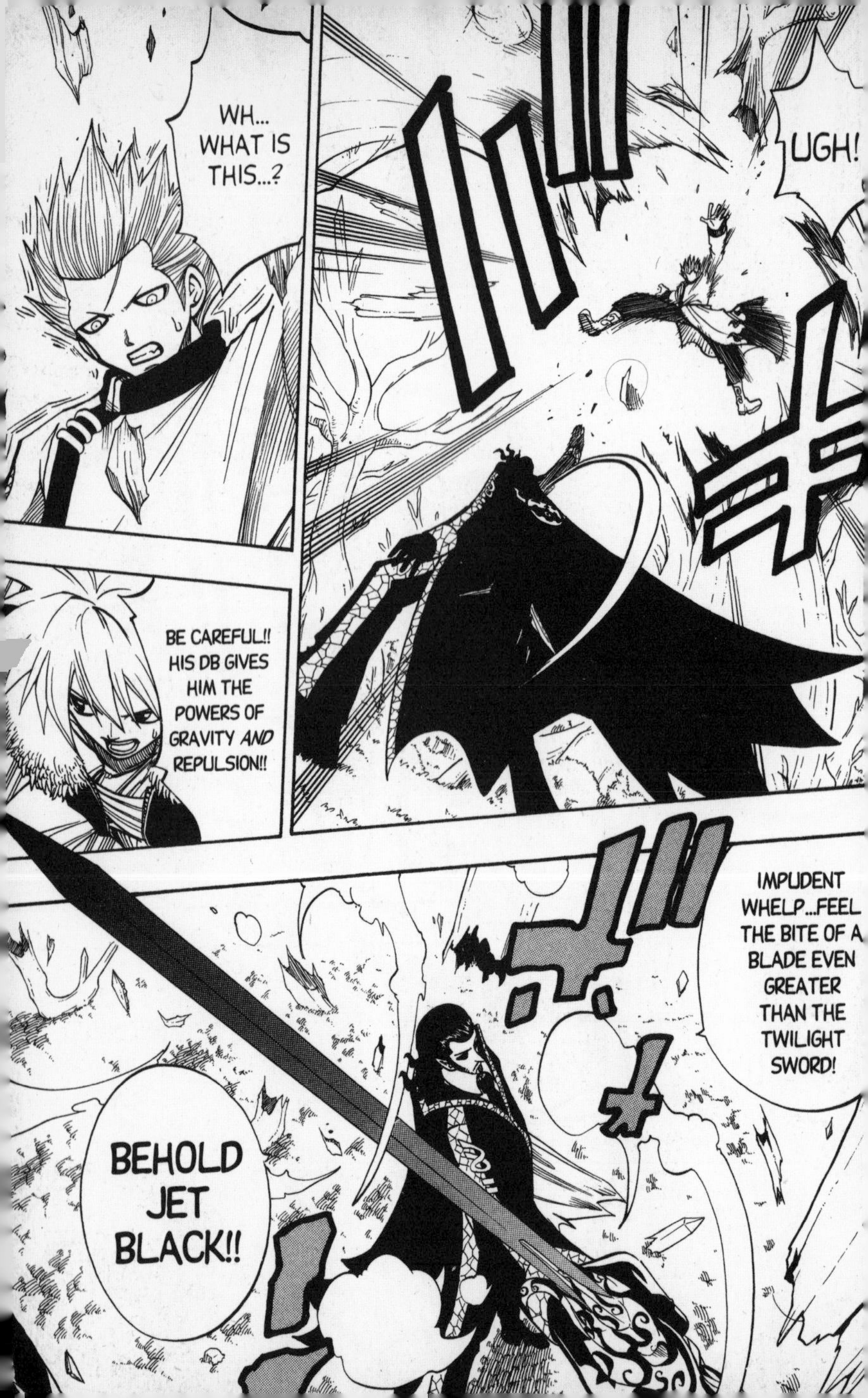
UGH!
WH... WHAT IS THIS...?
BE CAREFUL!! HIS DB GIVES HIM THE POWERS OF GRAVITY *AND* REPULSION!!
IMPUDENT WHELP...FEEL THE BITE OF A BLADE EVEN GREATER THAN THE TWILIGHT SWORD!
BEHOLD JET BLACK!!

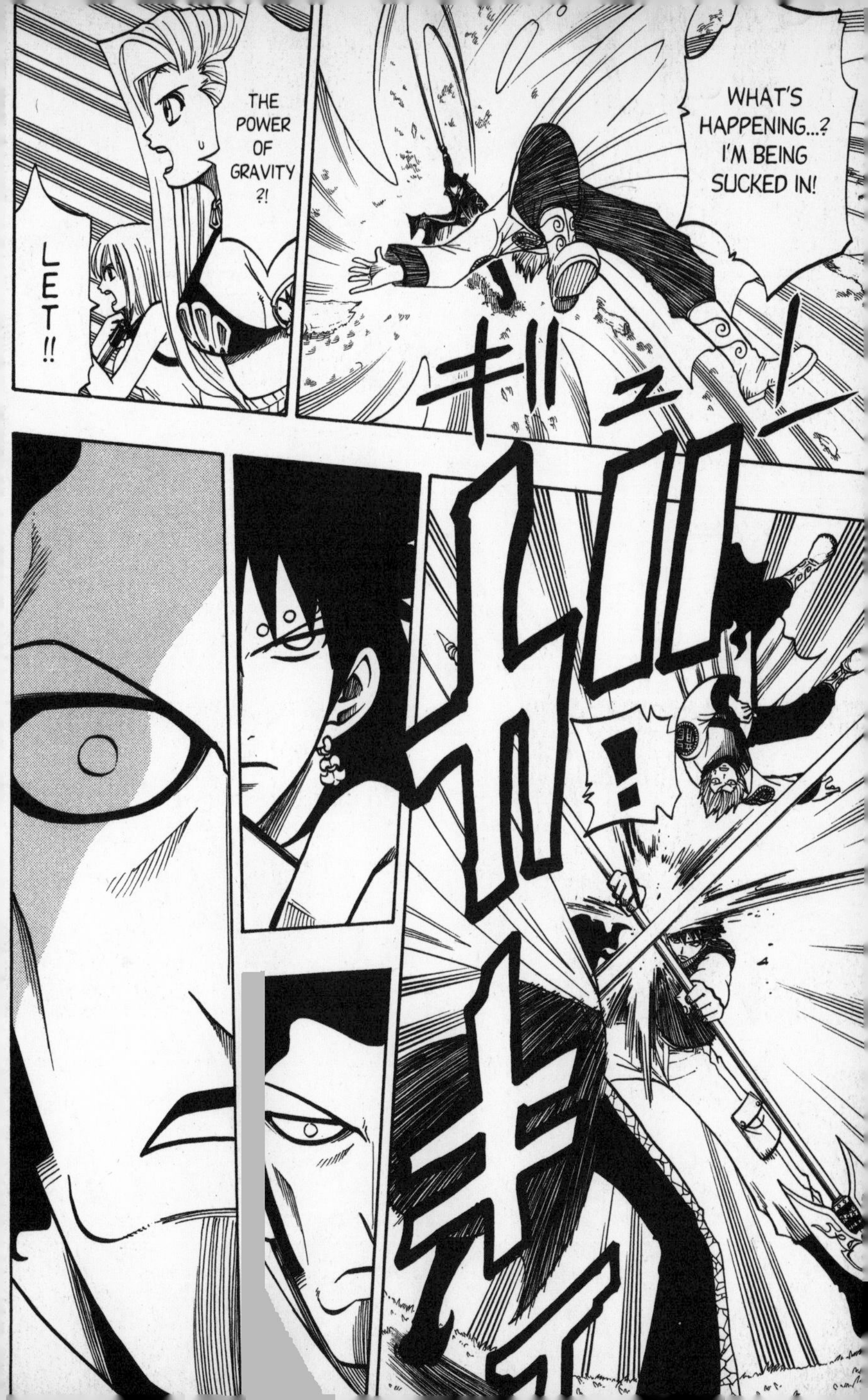
WHAT'S HAPPENING...? I'M BEING SUCKED IN!
THE POWER OF GRAVITY ?!
LET!!
!

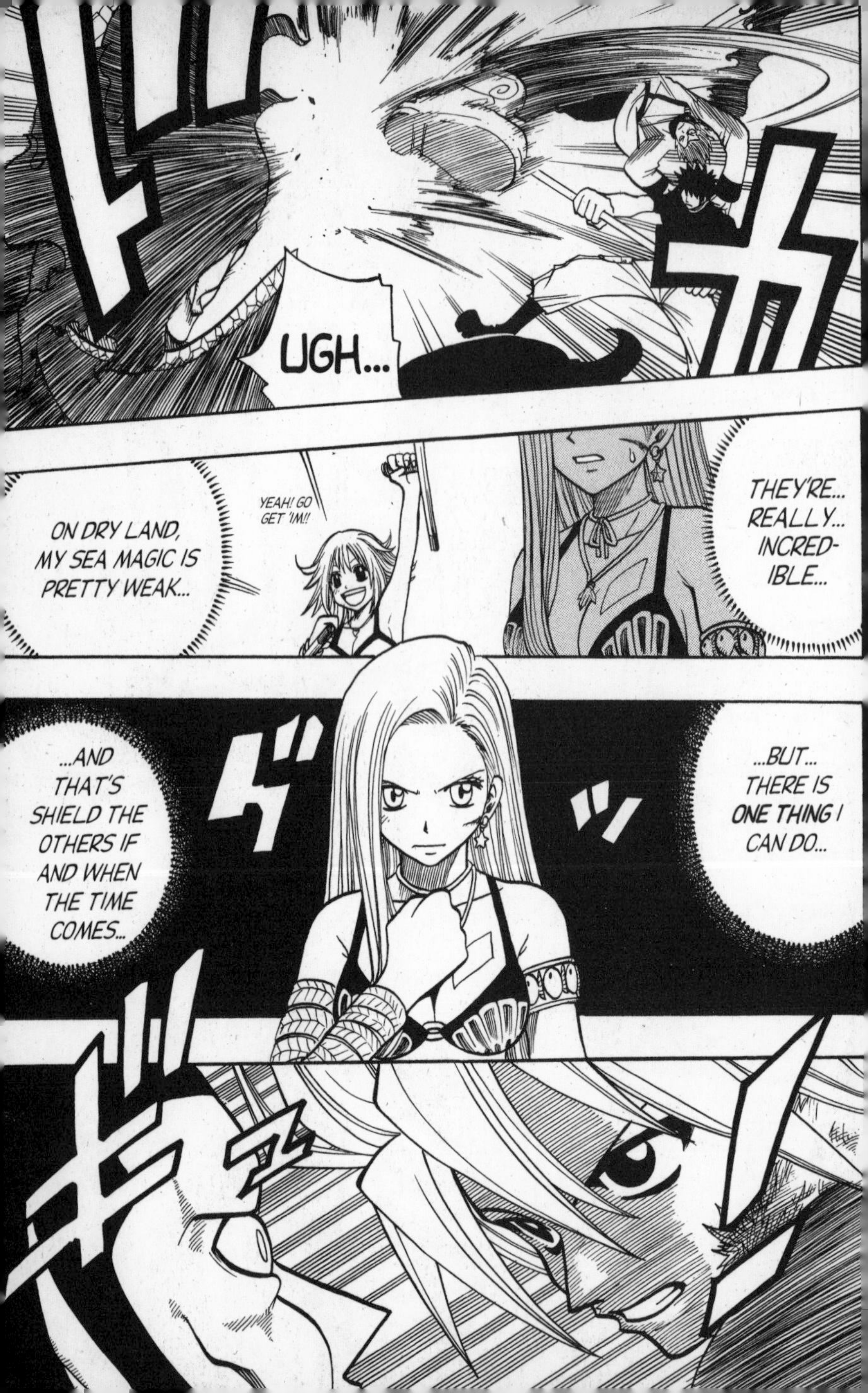
UGH...
THEY'RE... REALLY... INCRED-IBLE...
YEAH! GO GET 'IM!!
ON DRY LAND, MY SEA MAGIC IS PRETTY WEAK...
...BUT... THERE IS ONE THING I CAN DO...
...AND THAT'S SHIELD THE OTHERS IF AND WHEN THE TIME COMES...

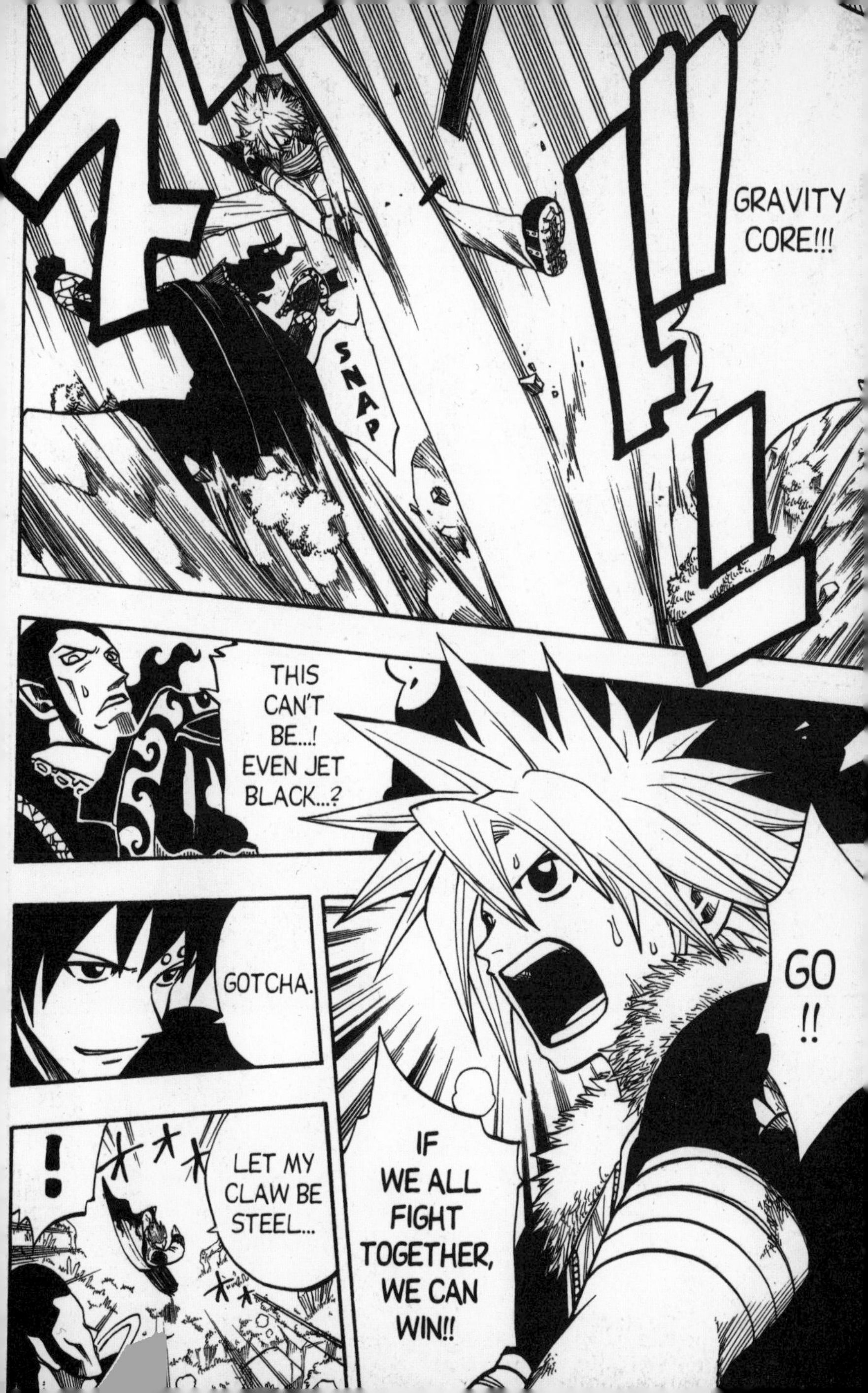
GRAVITY CORE!!!
SNAP
GO !!
IF WE ALL FIGHT TOGETHER, WE CAN WIN!!
THIS CAN'T BE...! EVEN JET BLACK...?
GOTCHA.
LET MY CLAW BE STEEL...

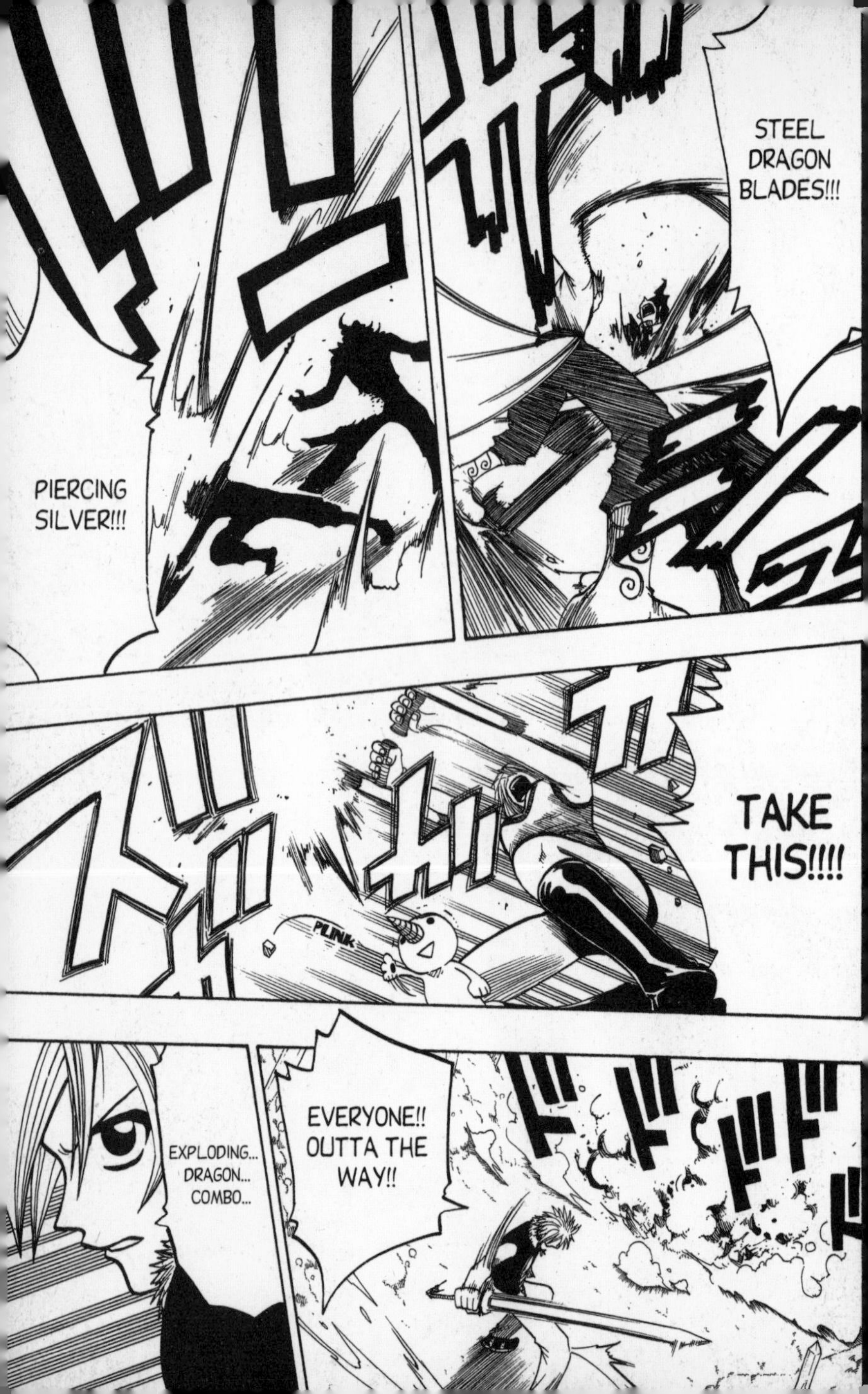
STEEL DRAGON BLADES!!!
PIERCING SILVER!!!
TAKE THIS!!!!
PLINK
EVERYONE!! OUTTA THE WAY!!
EXPLODING... DRAGON... COMBO...

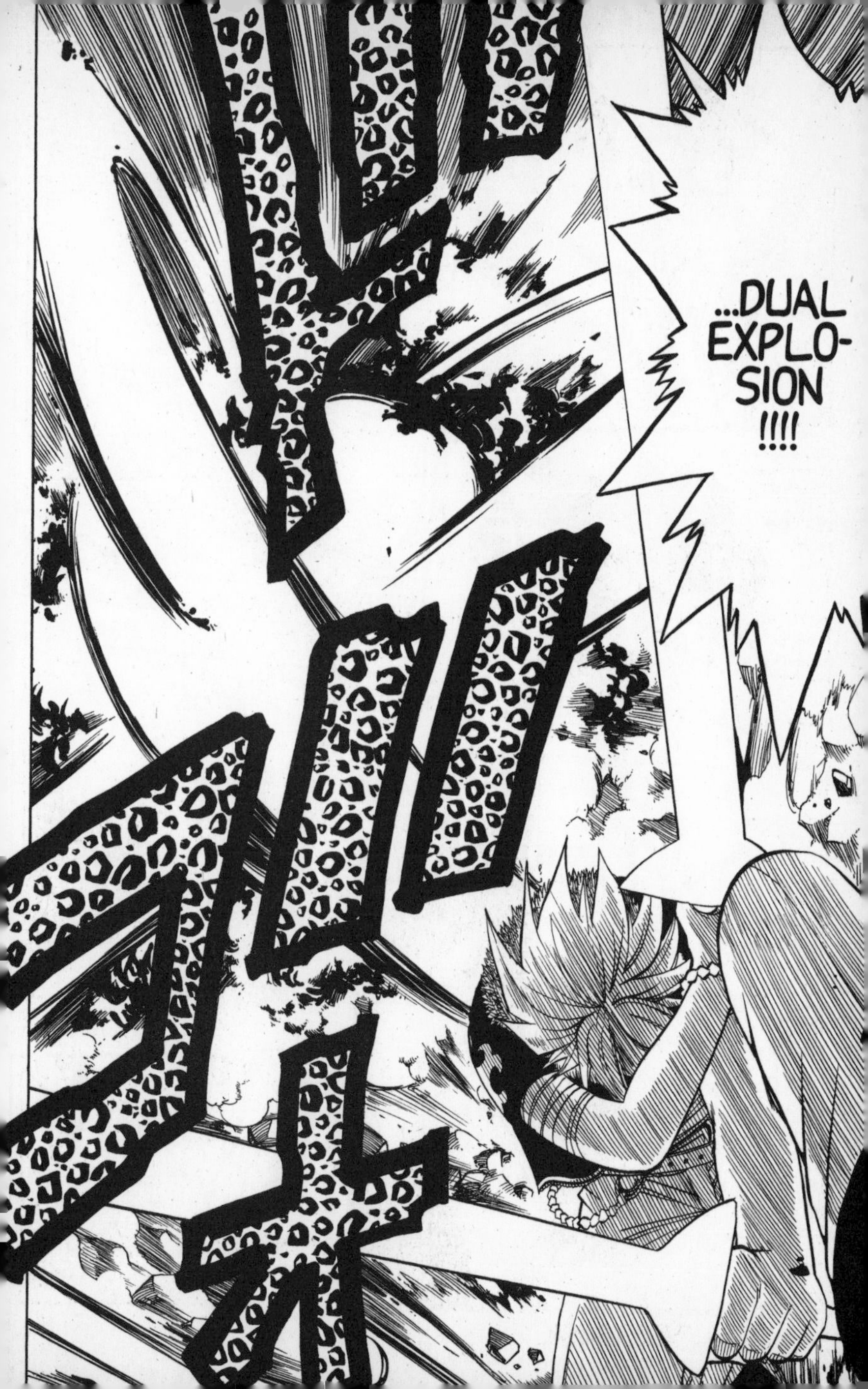
...DUAL EXPLO- SION !!!!

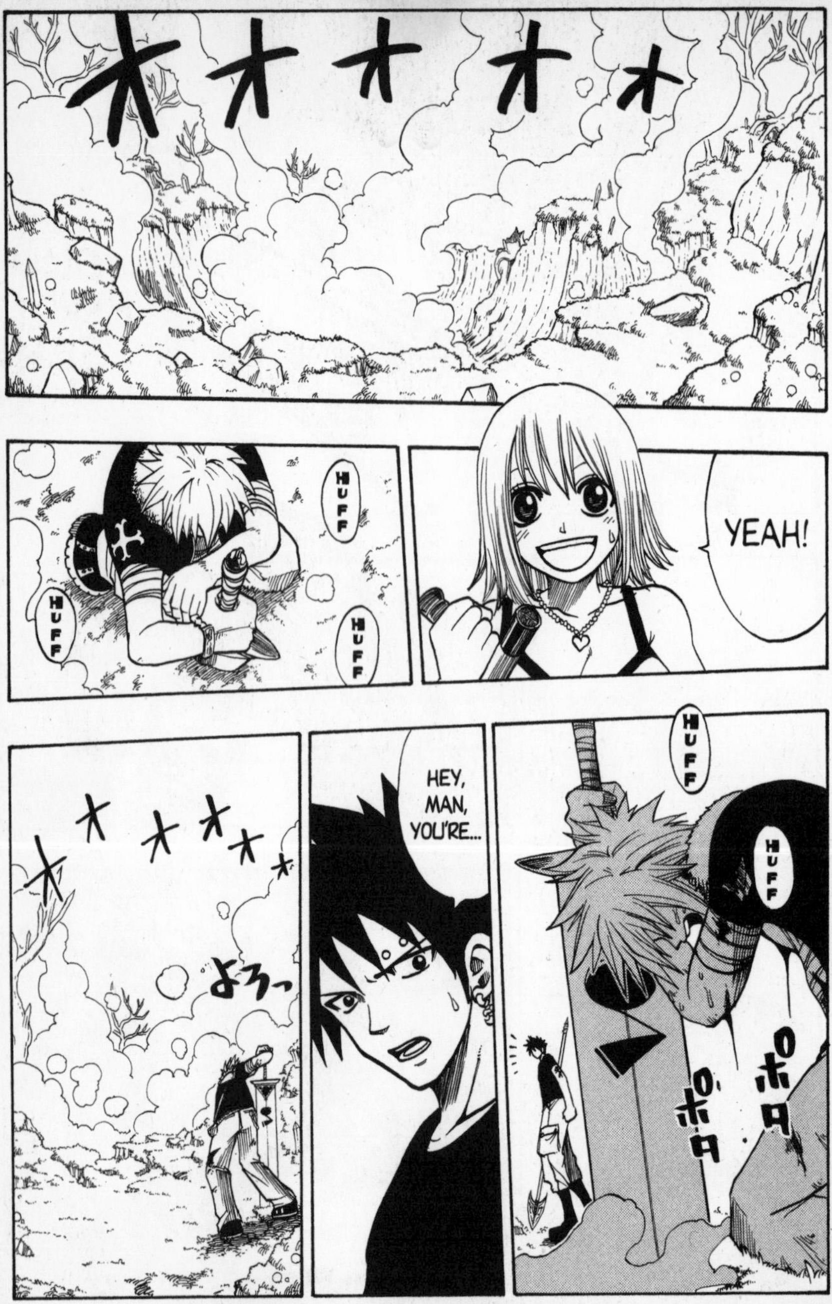
オオオオオ
YEAH!
HUFF
HUFF
HUFF
HUFF
HUFF
ポタ
ポタ
HEY, MAN, YOU'RE...
オオオオオ
よろっ

STAGGER...

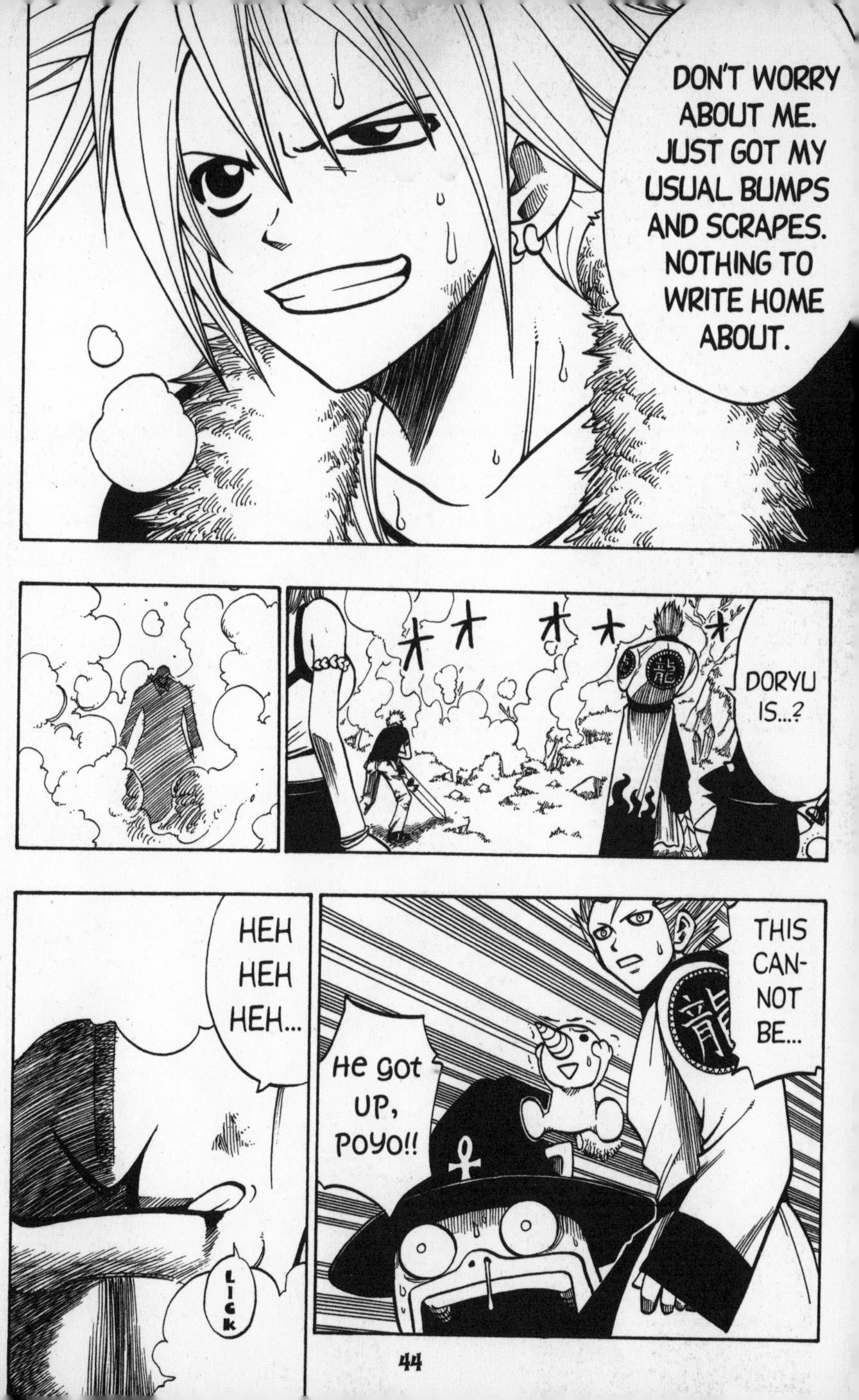
DON'T WORRY ABOUT ME. JUST GOT MY USUAL BUMPS AND SCRAPES. NOTHING TO WRITE HOME ABOUT.
DORYU IS...?
THIS CAN-NOT BE...
He got UP, POYO!!
HEH HEH HEH...
LICK

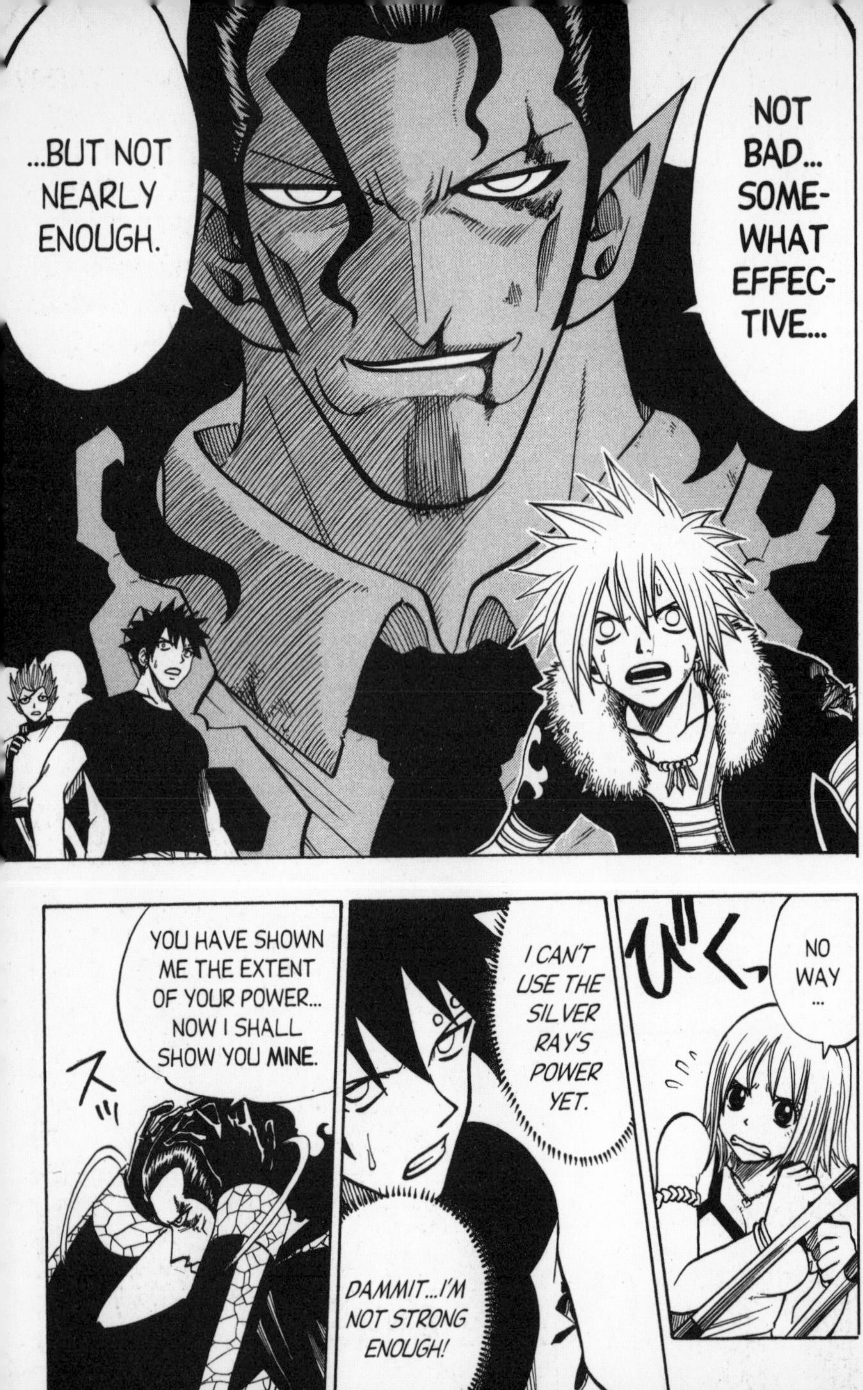
NOT BAD... SOME-WHAT EFFEC-TIVE...
...BUT NOT NEARLY ENOUGH.
びくっ
NO WAY ...
I CAN'T USE THE SILVER RAY'S POWER YET.
DAMMIT...I'M NOT STRONG ENOUGH!
YOU HAVE SHOWN ME THE EXTENT OF YOUR POWER... NOW I SHALL SHOW YOU MINE.
スッ

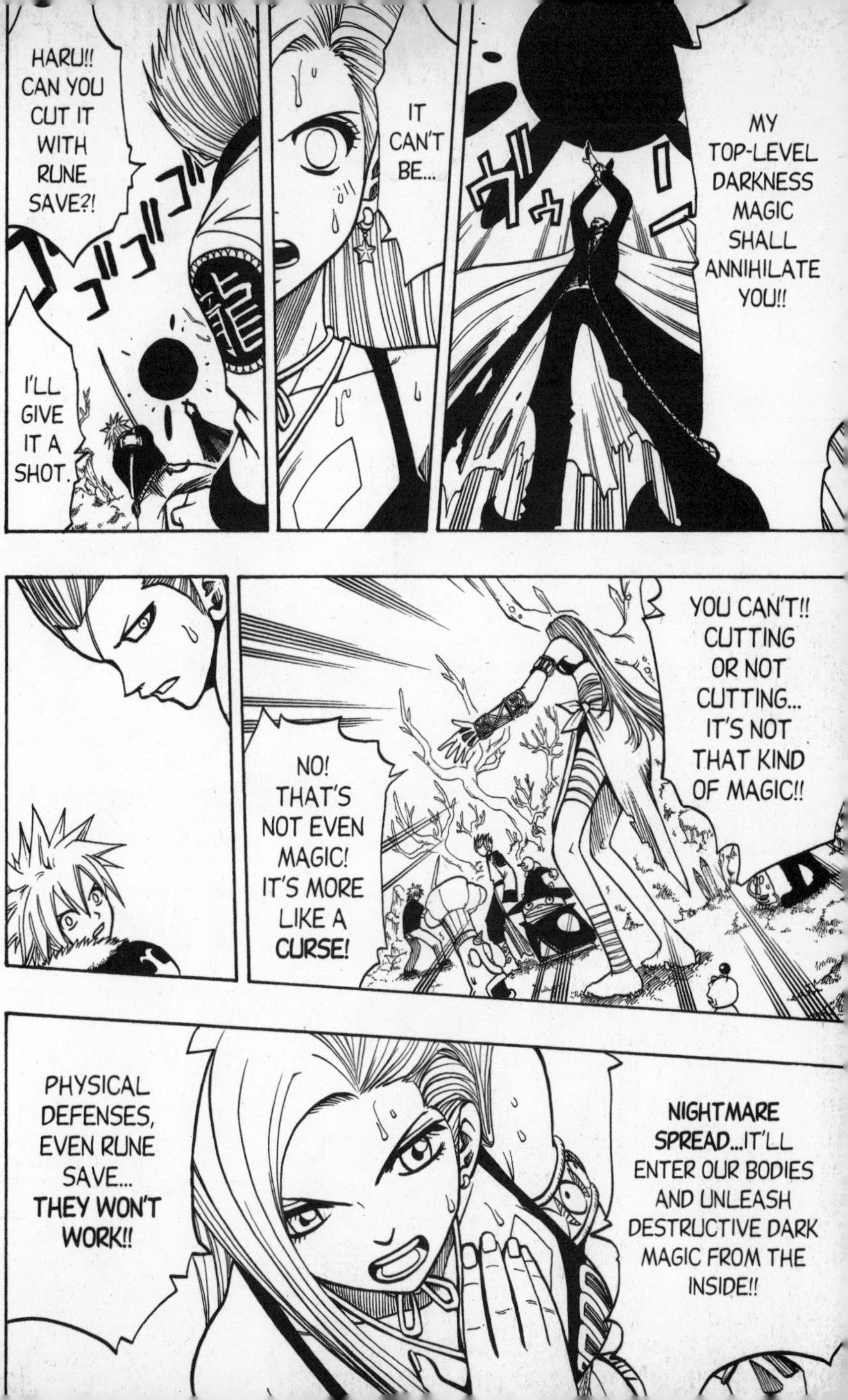
MY TOP-LEVEL DARKNESS MAGIC SHALL ANNIHILATE YOU!!
IT CAN'T BE...
HARU!! CAN YOU CUT IT WITH RUNE SAVE?!
I'LL GIVE IT A SHOT.
YOU CAN'T!! CUTTING OR NOT CUTTING... IT'S NOT THAT KIND OF MAGIC!!
NO! THAT'S NOT EVEN MAGIC! IT'S MORE LIKE A **CURSE!**
NIGHTMARE SPREAD...IT'LL ENTER OUR BODIES AND UNLEASH DESTRUCTIVE DARK MAGIC FROM THE INSIDE!!
PHYSICAL DEFENSES, EVEN RUNE SAVE... **THEY WON'T WORK!!**

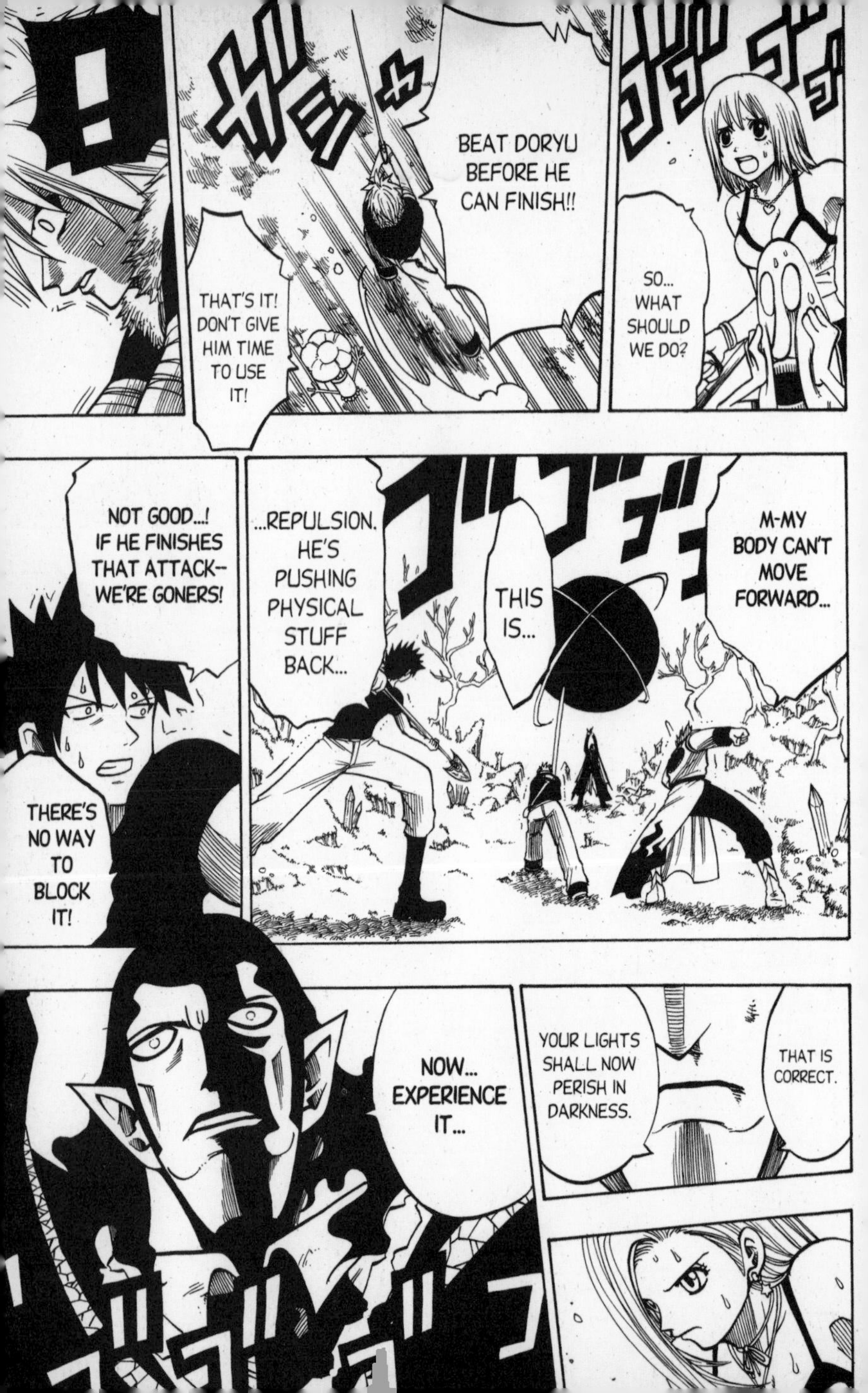
SO... WHAT SHOULD WE DO?
BEAT DORYU BEFORE HE CAN FINISH!!
THAT'S IT! DON'T GIVE HIM TIME TO USE IT!
!
M-MY BODY CAN'T MOVE FORWARD...
THIS IS...
...REPULSION. HE'S PUSHING PHYSICAL STUFF BACK...
NOT GOOD...! IF HE FINISHES THAT ATTACK-- WE'RE GONERS!
THERE'S NO WAY TO BLOCK IT!
THAT IS CORRECT.
YOUR LIGHTS SHALL NOW PERISH IN DARKNESS.
NOW... EXPERIENCE IT...

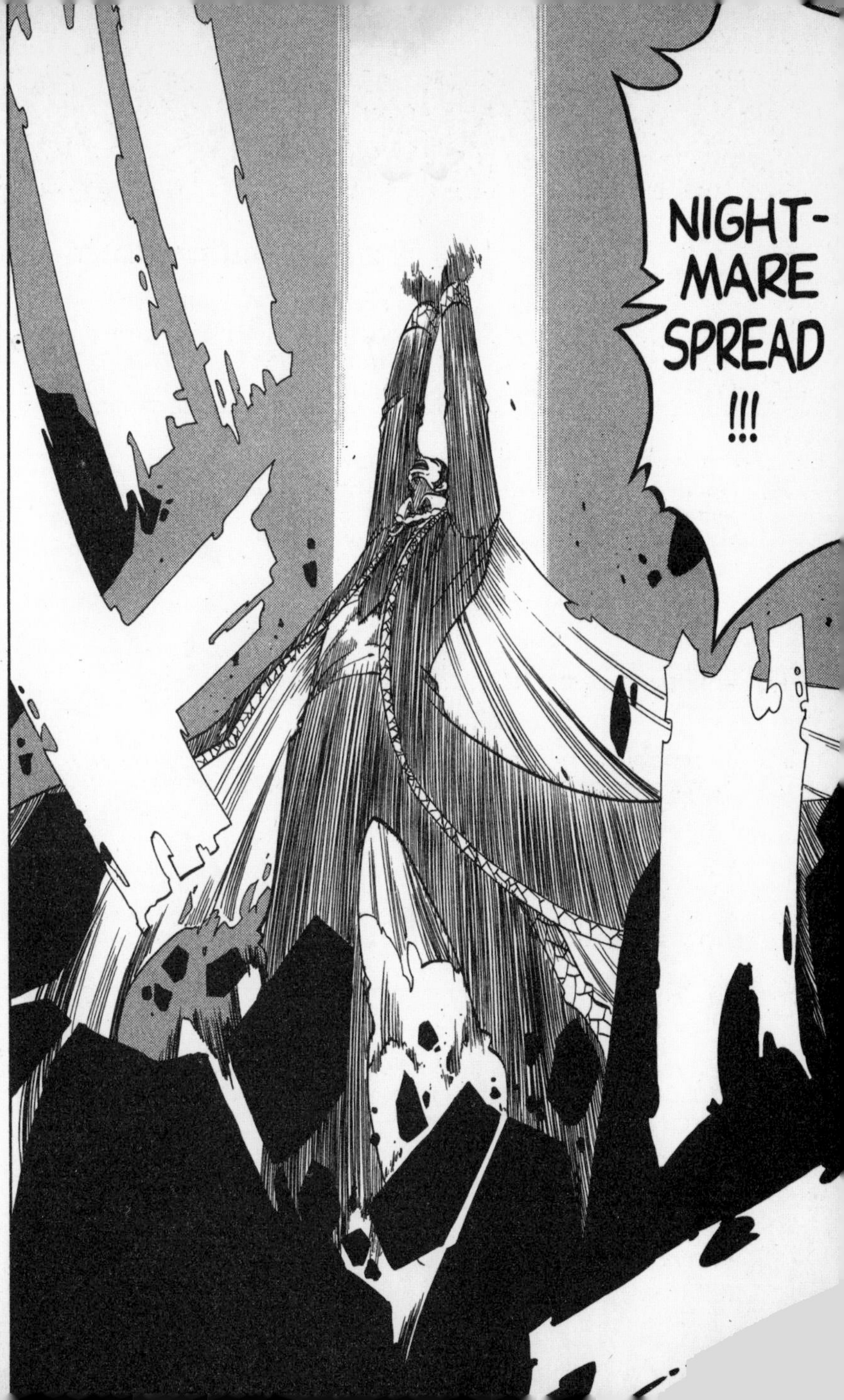
NIGHT-
MARE
SPREAD
!!!

RAVEOOQA

It's the Question Corner!

Q. MUSICA & REINA ANNIHILATED OGRE WITH BONDS OF SILVER IN VOL. 16, BUT WAS THE "LAST PHYSICS" DB AROUND OGRE'S NECK DESTROYED? DID REINA'S "WHITE KISS" GET DESTROYED?

(SHIGA-KEN - LITTLE DARK)

A. LAST PHYSICS WASN'T ANNIHILATED. IT TAKES MORE THAN THAT TO DESTROY A MOTHER DB. IT MUST'VE FALLEN INTO THE SEA. REINA'S WHITE KISS WASN'T ANNIHILATED EITHER-- RATHER, IT'S NOW A PART OF MUSICA'S SILVER RAY.

Q. WHICH IS MORE DESTRUCTIVE--THE SILVER RAY ACTIVATING OR OVERDRIVE?

(MIE-KEN - SETSU)

A. OVERDRIVE, DEFINITELY. WE DON'T KNOW JUST HOW POWERFUL THE SILVER RAY IS BE-CAUSE IT DIDN'T GO OFF. THIS MANGA REALLY IS FULL OF DESTRUCTIVE THINGS, ISN'T IT?

Q. IN VOL. 15, WHEN DR. MUMMY TURNS INTO THE BONE KNIGHT, THE SOUND EFFECT IN JAPANESE SAYS "BONE." IS THIS A GAG? (TOKYO - TOSHIO OKAWA)

A. IT'S A GAG. SORRY.

Q. I NOTICED WHILE READING *RAVE MASTER* THAT THE EXPLOSION/SPEED COMBO IN VOL. 6 IS EXPLODING DRAGON WINGS, BUT IN VOL. 14, IT'S WRITTEN AS SILVER DRIVE. WHICH IS WHICH?

(AICHI-KEN - KOBAKATSU)

A. HE WASN'T USING EXPLODING DRAGON WINGS FOR TWO REASONS. ONE, SIEG DEFLECTED IT WITH EASE. TWO, HARU FIGURED HE SHOULD REFRAIN USING THE WORD "DRAGON" IN ATTACK NAMES UNTIL HE COMBINES EXPLOSION WITH THE TWIN DRAGON BLADES (PROBABLY)!!

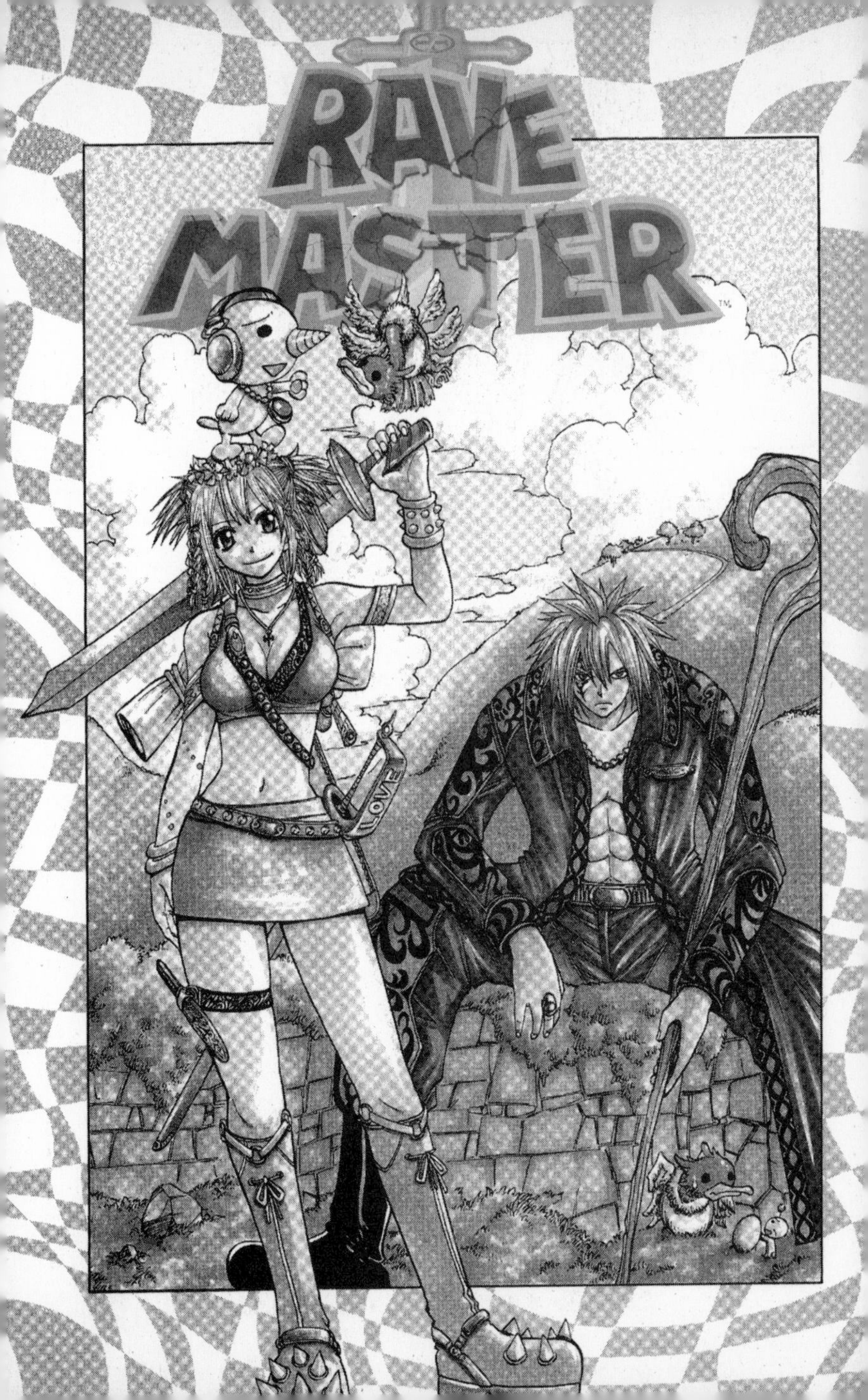
RAVE MASTER™
LOVE

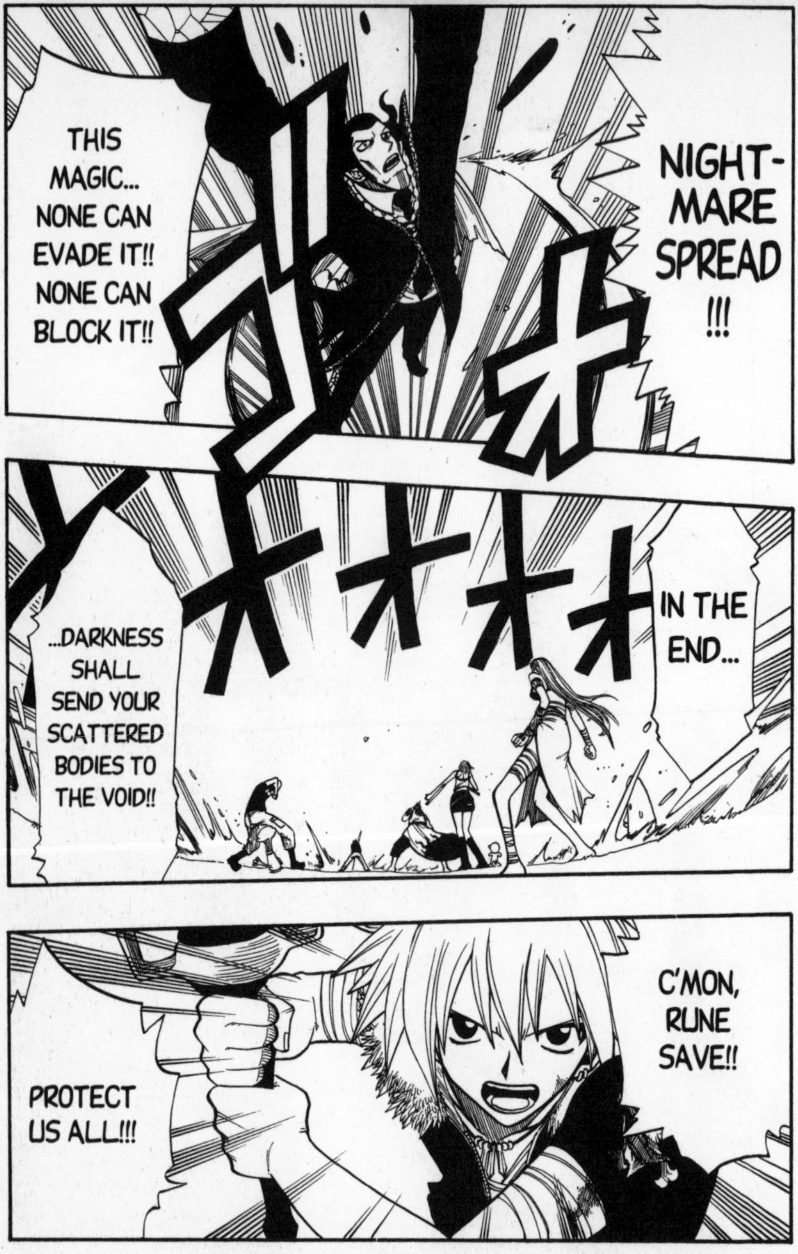
NIGHT-MARE SPREAD!!!
THIS MAGIC... NONE CAN EVADE IT!! NONE CAN BLOCK IT!!
ゴオオオオオ
IN THE END...
...DARKNESS SHALL SEND YOUR SCATTERED BODIES TO THE VOID!!
C'MON, RUNE SAVE!!
PROTECT US ALL!!!

RAVE: 132 ✠ BLACK SOUL

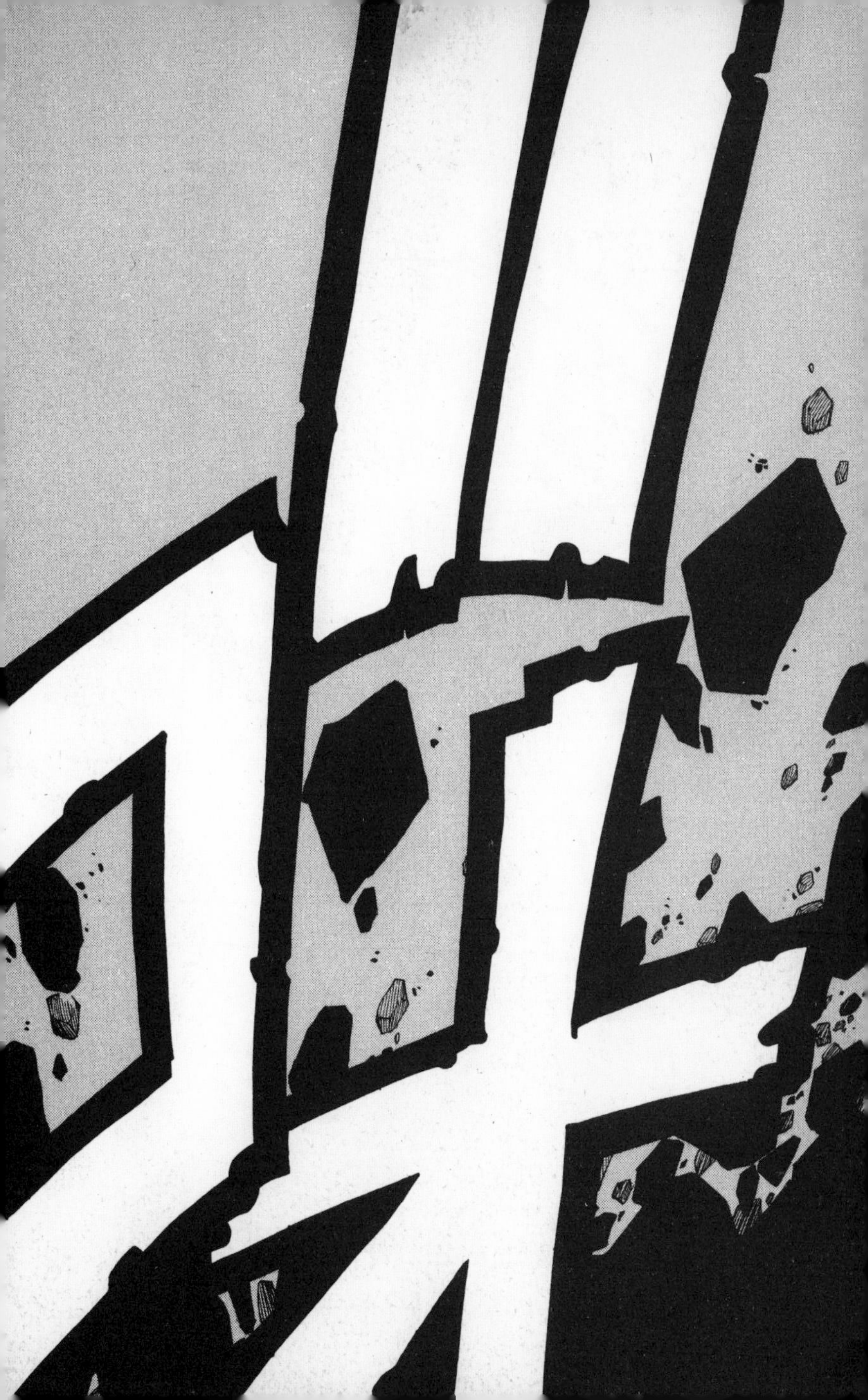

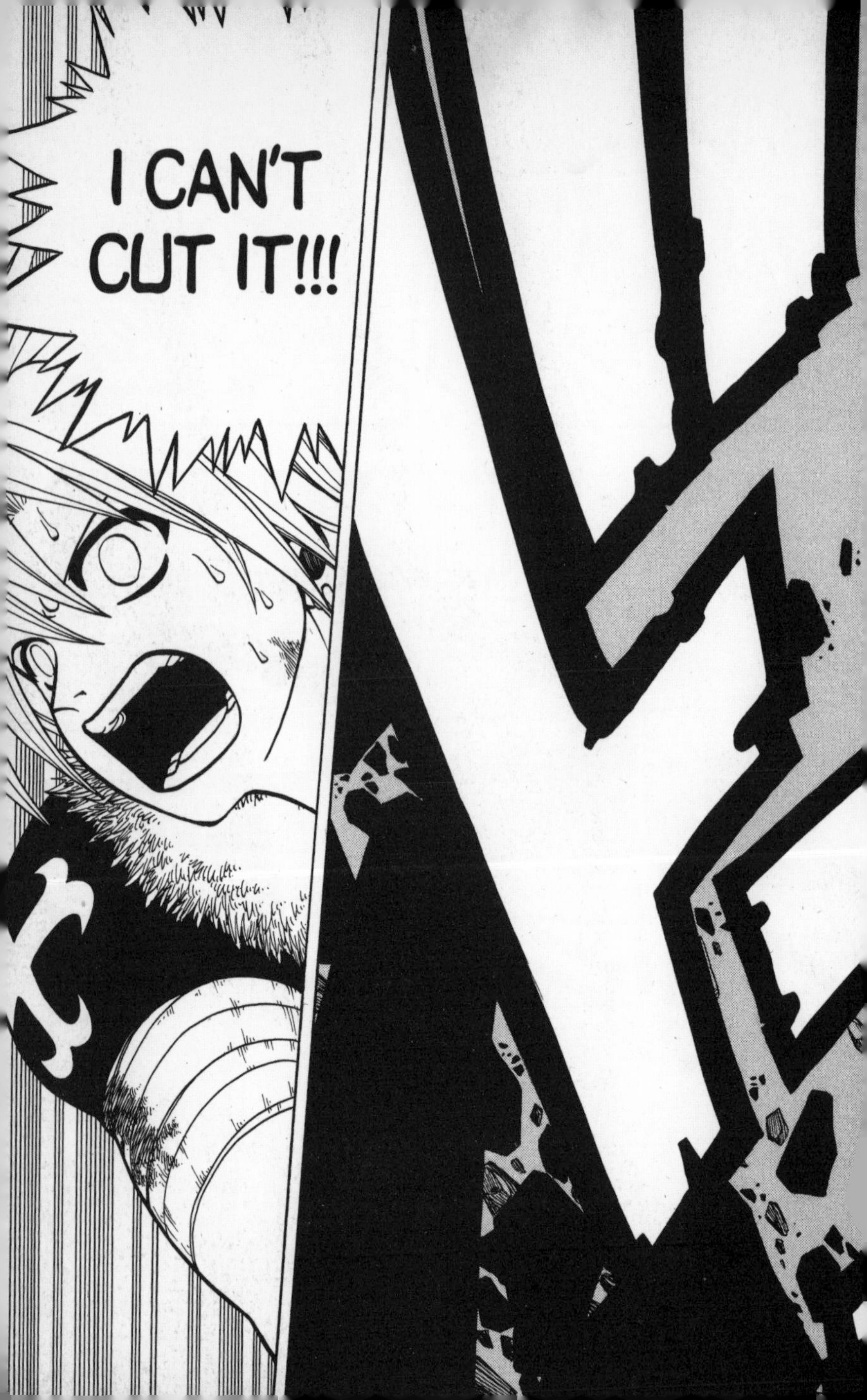
I CAN'T CUT IT!!!

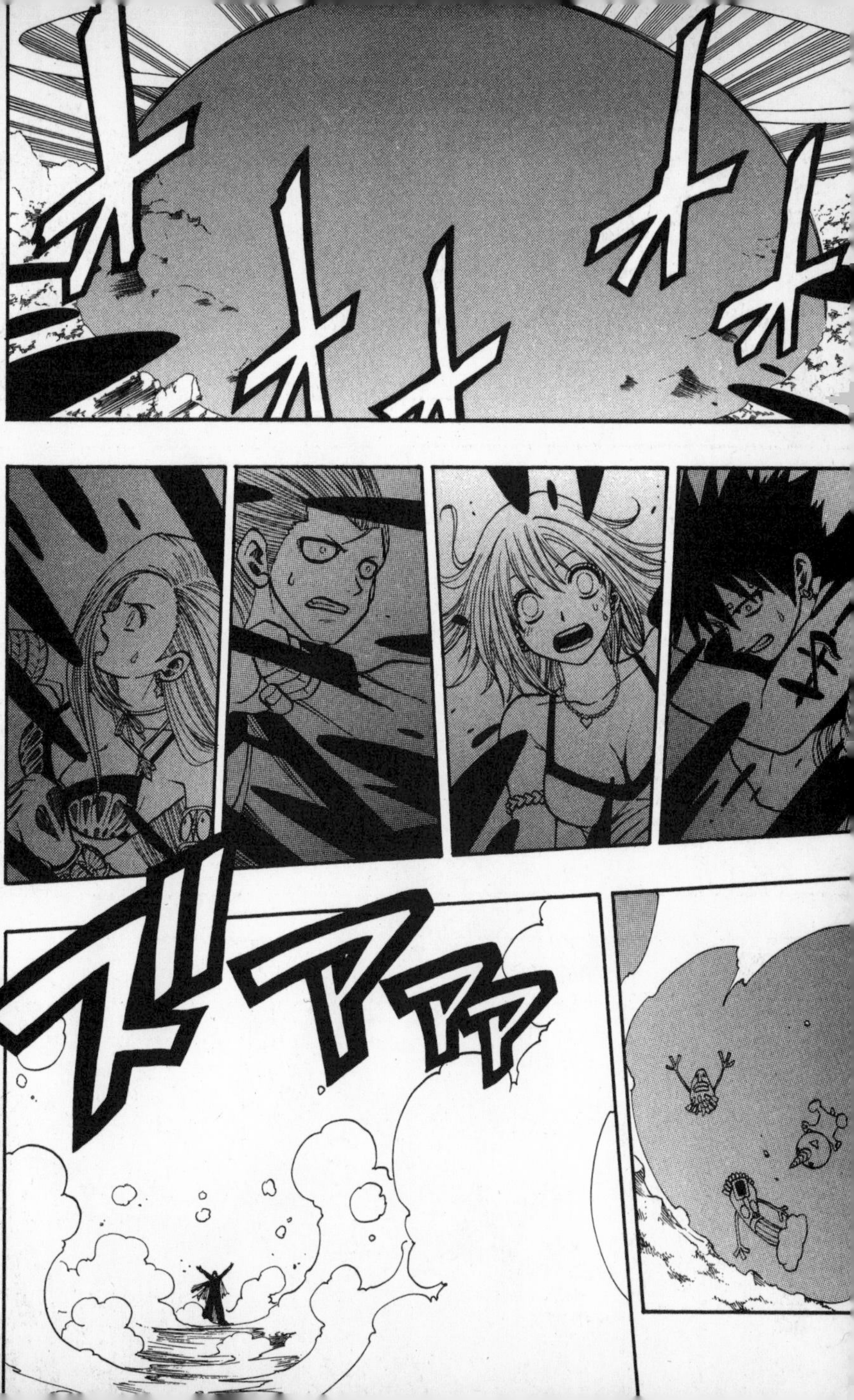
オオオオオ
ズアァァ

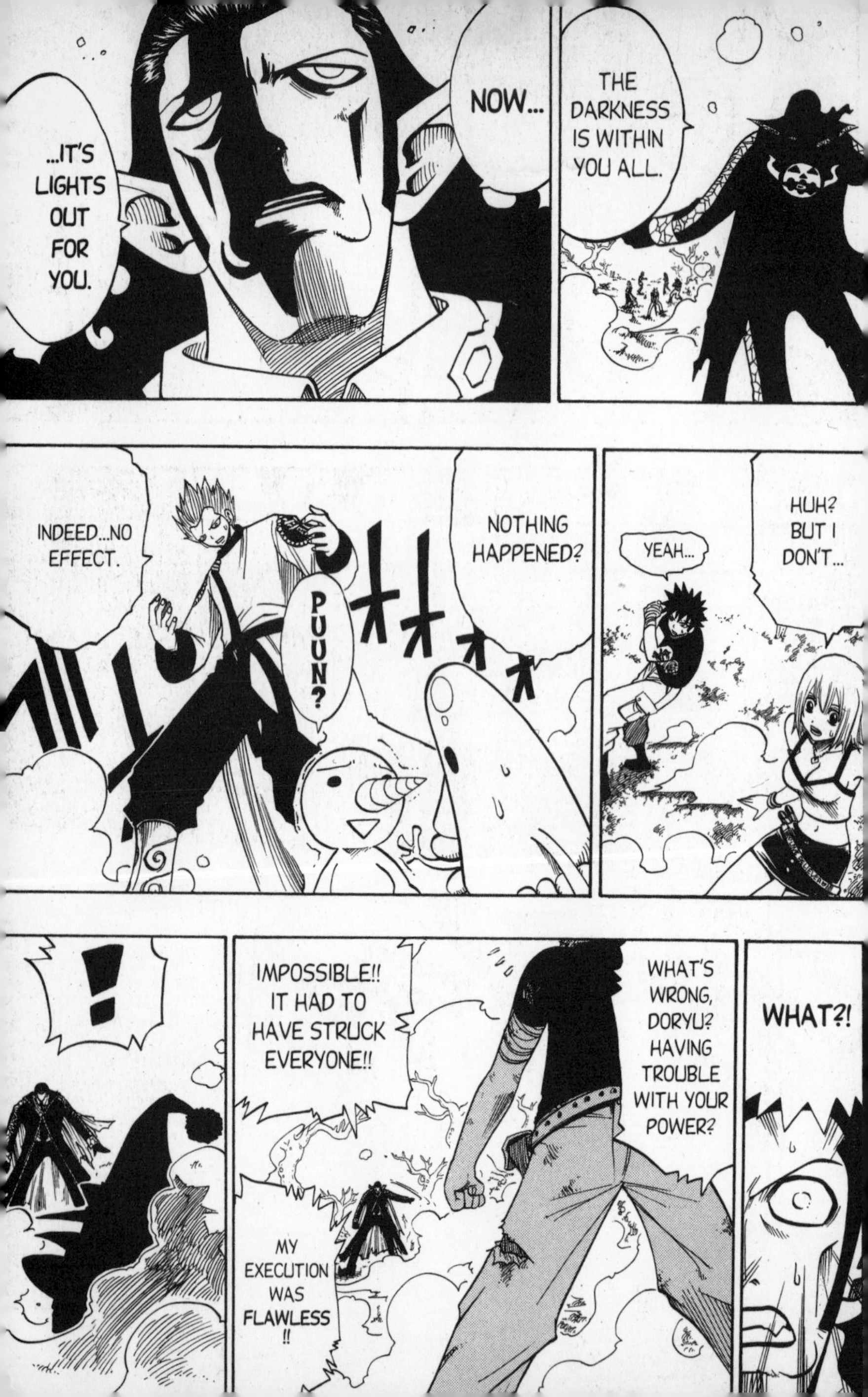
THE DARKNESS IS WITHIN YOU ALL.
NOW...
...IT'S LIGHTS OUT FOR YOU.
HUH? BUT I DON'T...
YEAH...
NOTHING HAPPENED?
PUUN?
INDEED...NO EFFECT.
WHAT?!
WHAT'S WRONG, DORYU? HAVING TROUBLE WITH YOUR POWER?
IMPOSSIBLE!! IT HAD TO HAVE STRUCK EVERYONE!!
MY EXECUTION WAS FLAWLESS!!
!

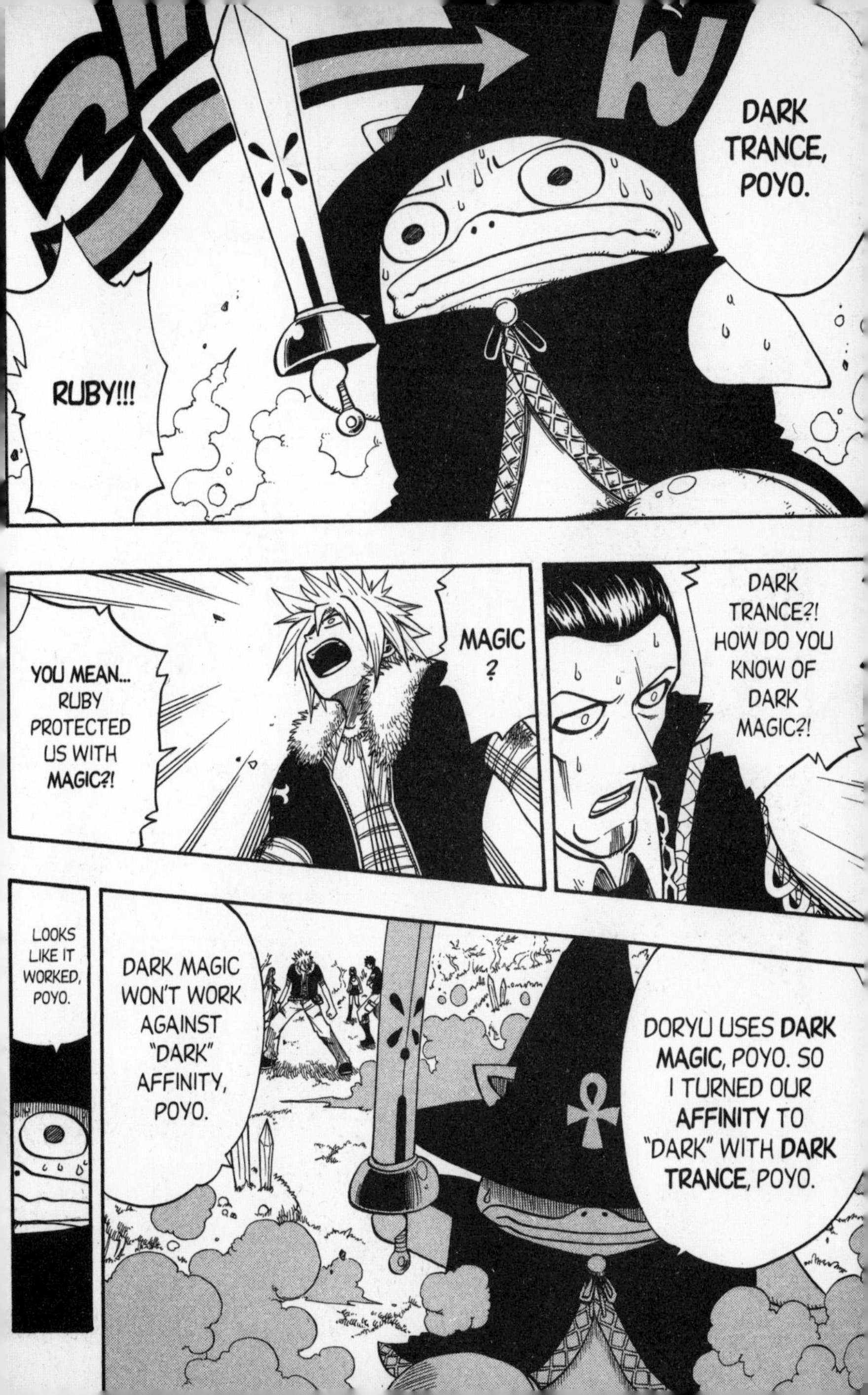
DARK TRANCE, POYO.
RUBY!!!
DARK TRANCE?! HOW DO YOU KNOW OF DARK MAGIC?!
MAGIC?
YOU MEAN... RUBY PROTECTED US WITH MAGIC?!
DORYU USES DARK MAGIC, POYO. SO I TURNED OUR AFFINITY TO "DARK" WITH DARK TRANCE, POYO.
DARK MAGIC WON'T WORK AGAINST "DARK" AFFINITY, POYO.
LOOKS LIKE IT WORKED, POYO.

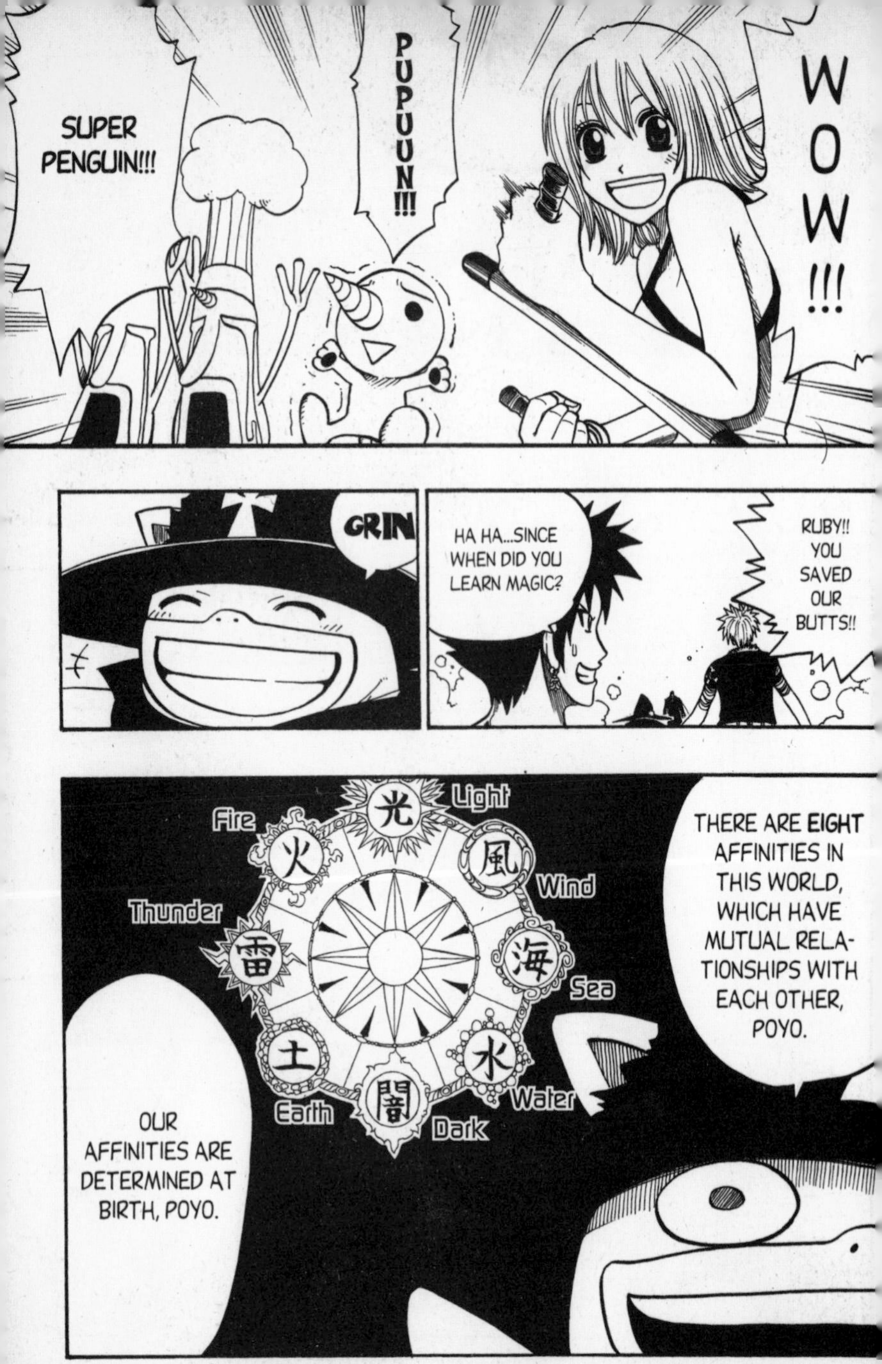
WOW!!!
PUPUUN!!!
SUPER PENGUIN!!!
RUBY!! YOU SAVED OUR BUTTS!!
HA HA...SINCE WHEN DID YOU LEARN MAGIC?
GRIN
THERE ARE EIGHT AFFINITIES IN THIS WORLD, WHICH HAVE MUTUAL RELATIONSHIPS WITH EACH OTHER, POYO.
光 Light
風 Wind
海 Sea
水 Water
闇 Dark
土 Earth
雷 Thunder
火 Fire
OUR AFFINITIES ARE DETERMINED AT BIRTH, POYO.

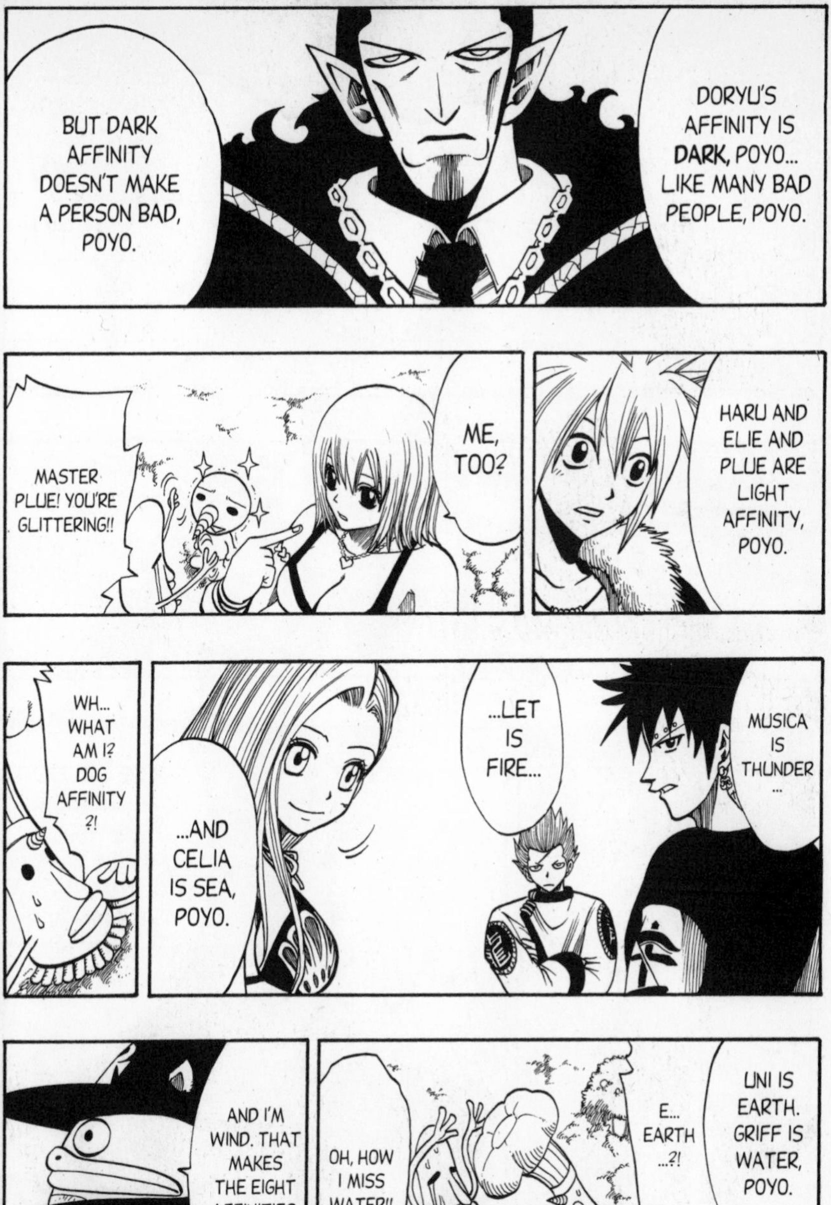
DORYU'S AFFINITY IS DARK, POYO... LIKE MANY BAD PEOPLE, POYO.
BUT DARK AFFINITY DOESN'T MAKE A PERSON BAD, POYO.
HARU AND ELIE AND PLUE ARE LIGHT AFFINITY, POYO.
ME, TOO?
MASTER PLUE! YOU'RE GLITTERING!!
MUSICA IS THUNDER ...
...LET IS FIRE...
...AND CELIA IS SEA, POYO.
WH... WHAT AM I? DOG AFFINITY ?!
UNI IS EARTH. GRIFF IS WATER, POYO.
E... EARTH ...?!
OH, HOW I MISS WATER!!
AND I'M WIND. THAT MAKES THE EIGHT AFFINITIES, POYO.

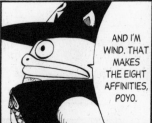

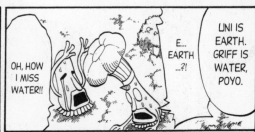

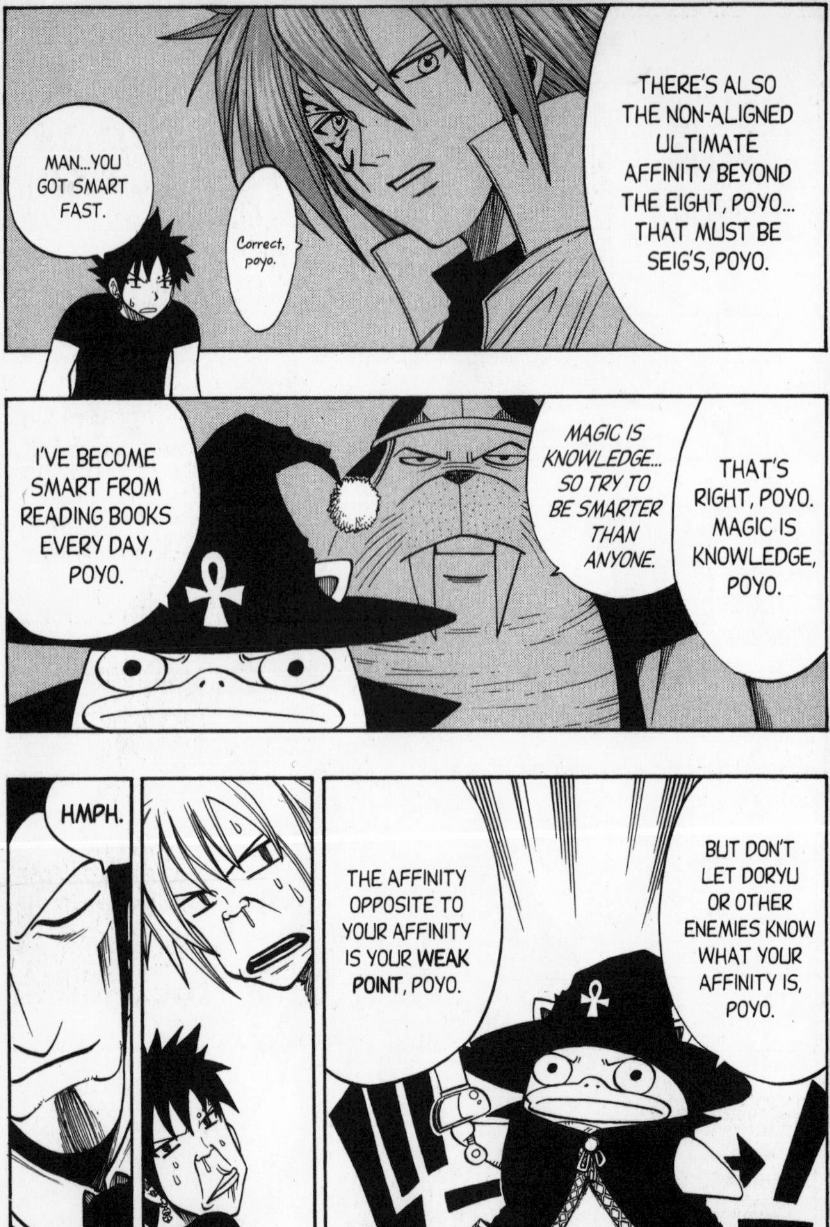
THERE'S ALSO THE NON-ALIGNED ULTIMATE AFFINITY BEYOND THE EIGHT, POYO... THAT MUST BE SEIG'S, POYO.
Correct, poyo.
MAN...YOU GOT SMART FAST.
THAT'S RIGHT, POYO. MAGIC IS KNOWLEDGE, POYO.
MAGIC IS KNOWLEDGE... SO TRY TO BE SMARTER THAN ANYONE.
I'VE BECOME SMART FROM READING BOOKS EVERY DAY, POYO.
BUT DON'T LET DORYU OR OTHER ENEMIES KNOW WHAT YOUR AFFINITY IS, POYO.
THE AFFINITY OPPOSITE TO YOUR AFFINITY IS YOUR WEAK POINT, POYO.
HMPH.

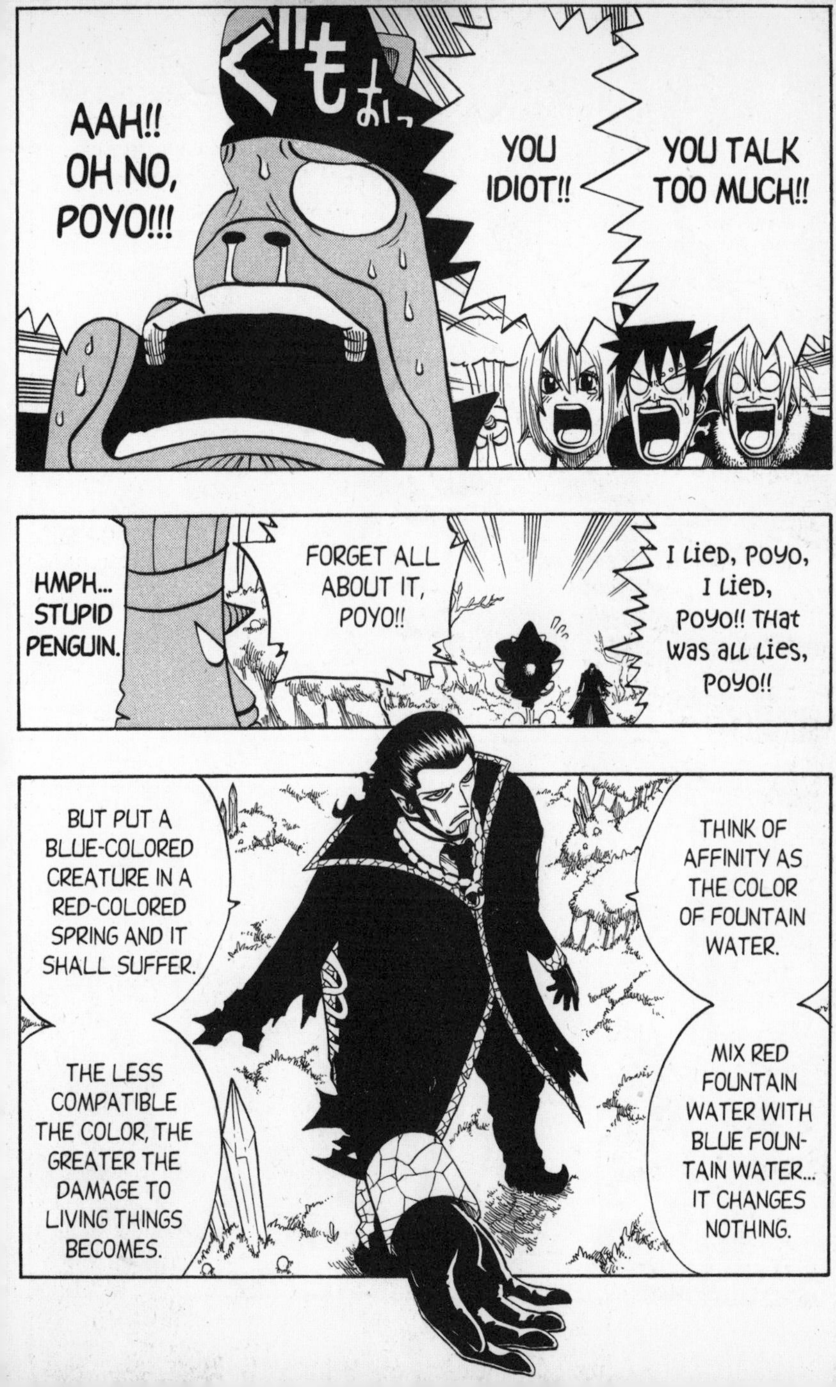
YOU TALK TOO MUCH!!
YOU IDIOT!!
AAH!! OH NO, POYO!!!
I LIED, POYO, I LIED, POYO!! THAT WAS ALL LIES, POYO!!
FORGET ALL ABOUT IT, POYO!!
HMPH... STUPID PENGUIN.
THINK OF AFFINITY AS THE COLOR OF FOUNTAIN WATER.
BUT PUT A BLUE-COLORED CREATURE IN A RED-COLORED SPRING AND IT SHALL SUFFER.
MIX RED FOUNTAIN WATER WITH BLUE FOUN-TAIN WATER... IT CHANGES NOTHING.
THE LESS COMPATIBLE THE COLOR, THE GREATER THE DAMAGE TO LIVING THINGS BECOMES.

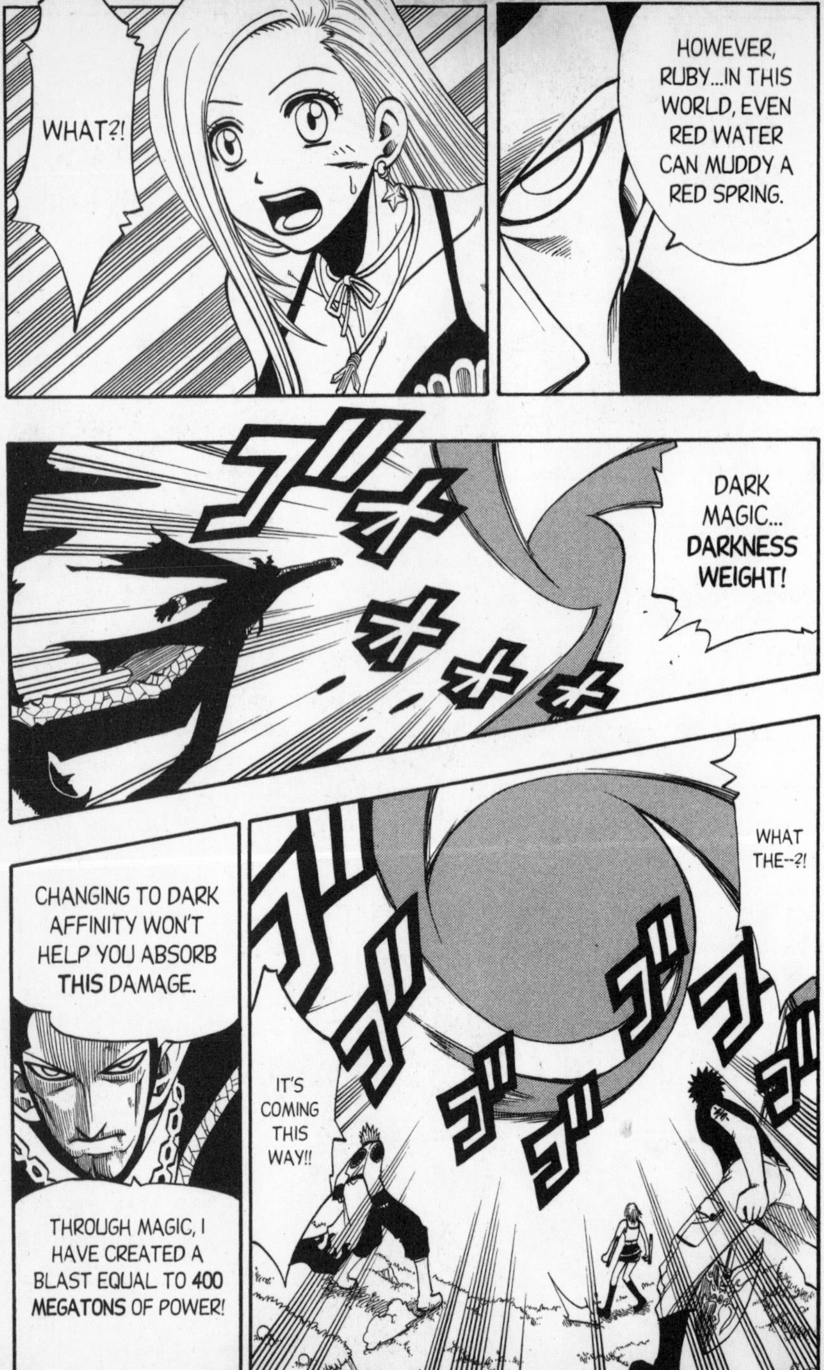
HOWEVER, RUBY...IN THIS WORLD, EVEN RED WATER CAN MUDDY A RED SPRING.
WHAT?!
DARK MAGIC... DARKNESS WEIGHT!
WHAT THE--?!
IT'S COMING THIS WAY!!
CHANGING TO DARK AFFINITY WON'T HELP YOU ABSORB THIS DAMAGE.
THROUGH MAGIC, I HAVE CREATED A BLAST EQUAL TO 400 MEGATONS OF POWER!

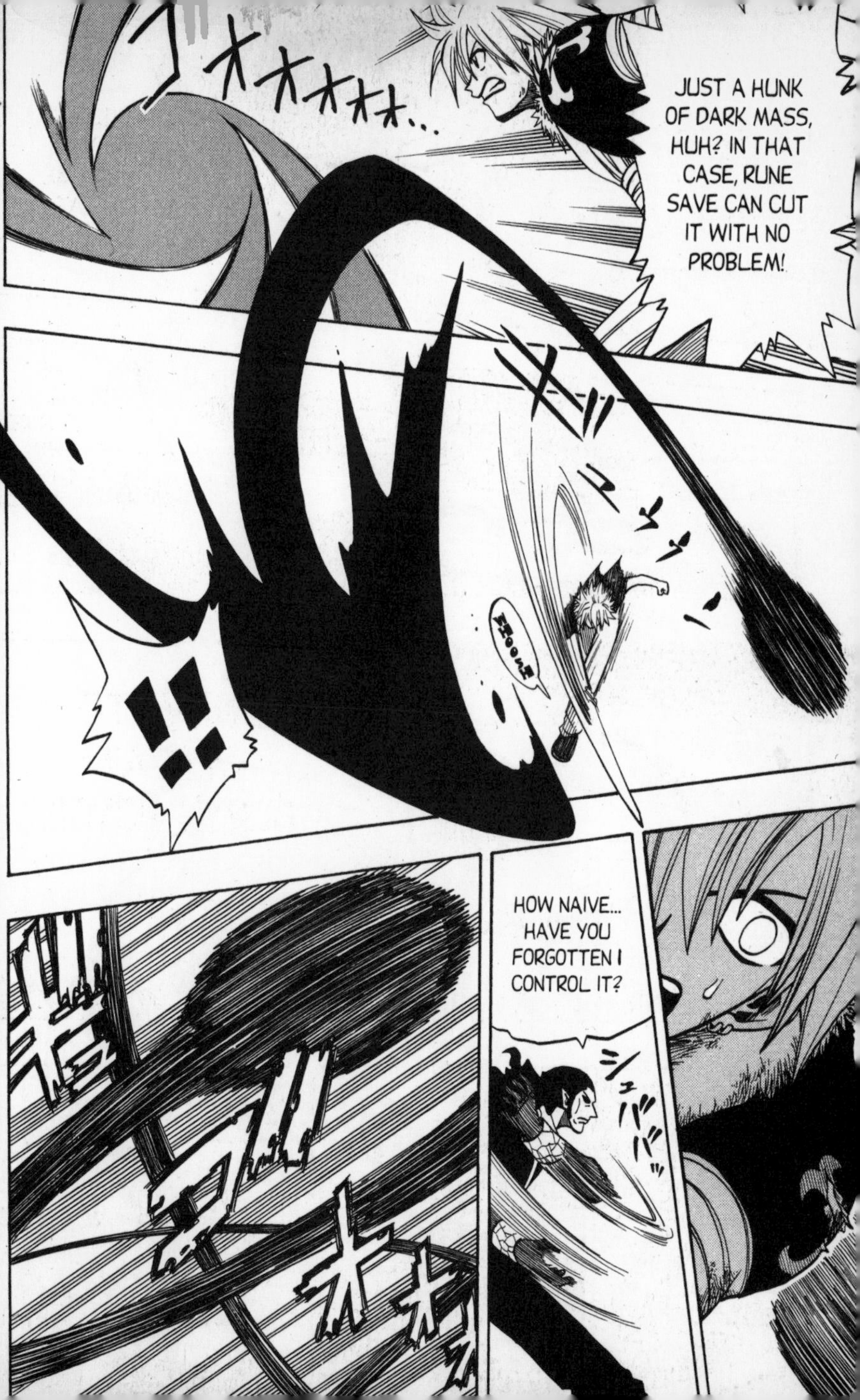

JUST A HUNK OF DARK MASS, HUH? IN THAT CASE, RUNE SAVE CAN CUT IT WITH NO PROBLEM!
WHOOSH
HOW NAIVE... HAVE YOU FORGOTTEN I CONTROL IT?

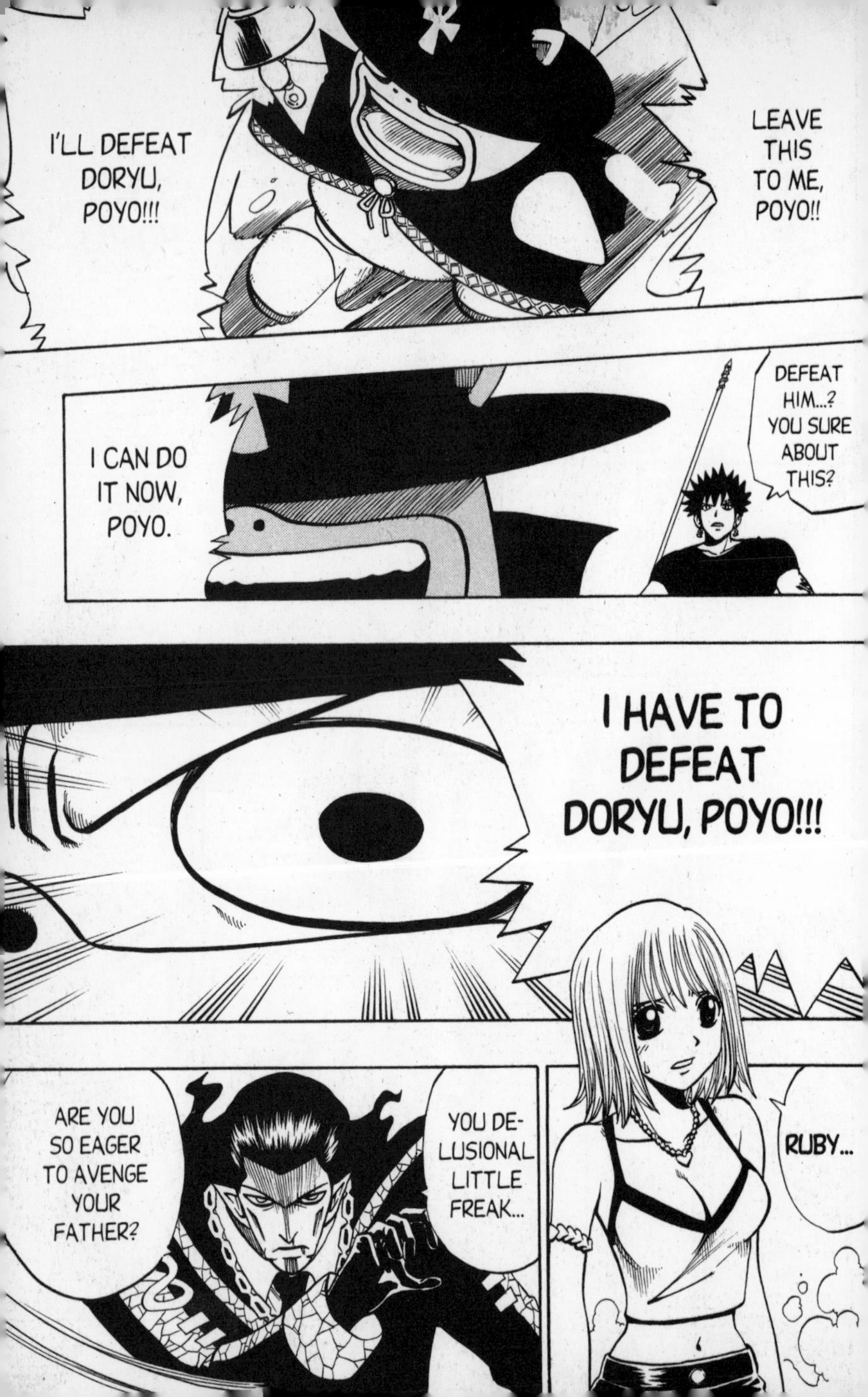
LEAVE THIS TO ME, POYO!!
I'LL DEFEAT DORYU, POYO!!!
DEFEAT HIM...? YOU SURE ABOUT THIS?
I CAN DO IT NOW, POYO.
I HAVE TO DEFEAT DORYU, POYO!!!
RUBY...
YOU DE-LUSIONAL LITTLE FREAK...
ARE YOU SO EAGER TO AVENGE YOUR FATHER?

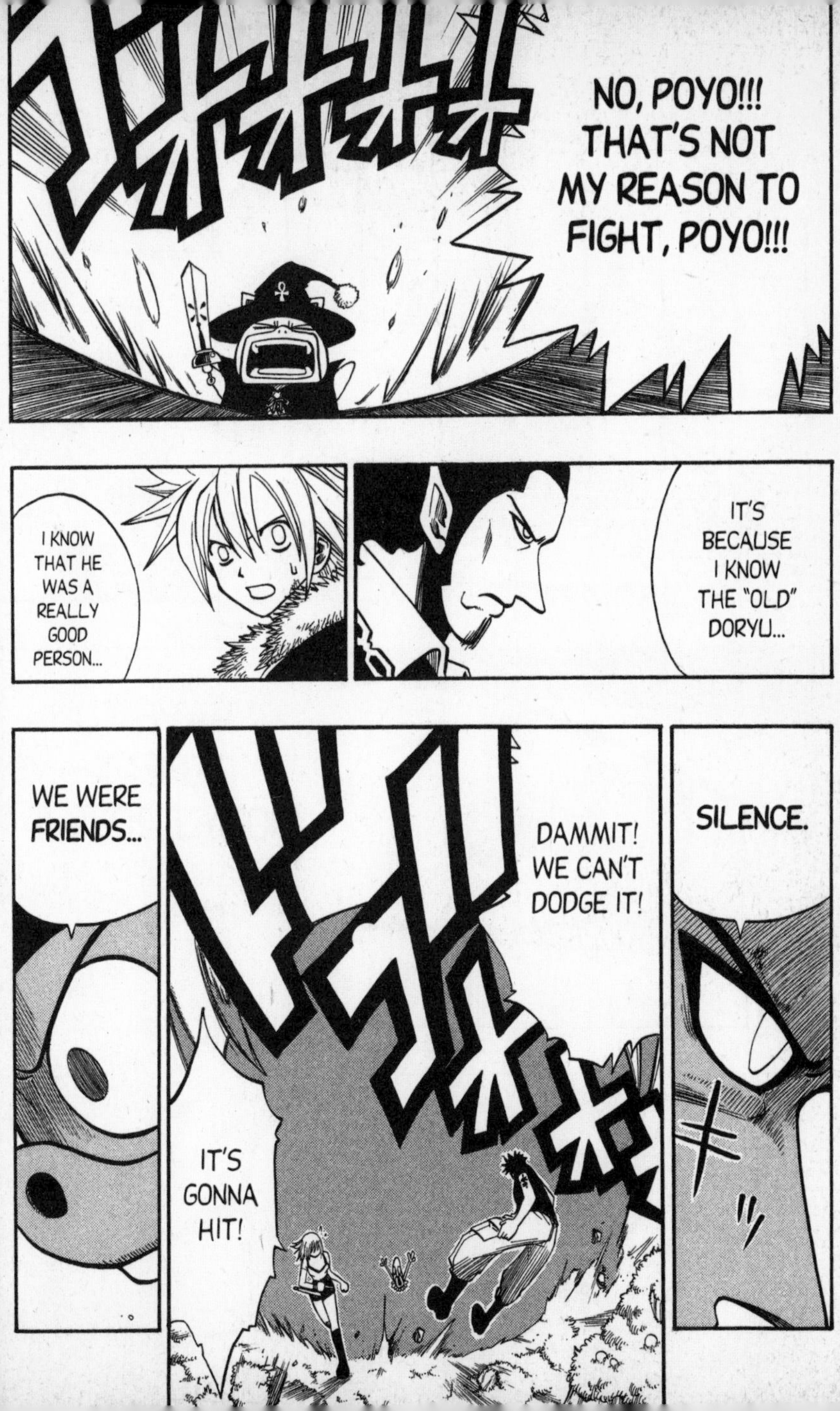
NO, POYO!!! THAT'S NOT MY REASON TO FIGHT, POYO!!!
IT'S BECAUSE I KNOW THE "OLD" DORYU...
I KNOW THAT HE WAS A REALLY GOOD PERSON...
SILENCE.
DAMMIT! WE CAN'T DODGE IT!
IT'S GONNA HIT!
WE WERE FRIENDS...

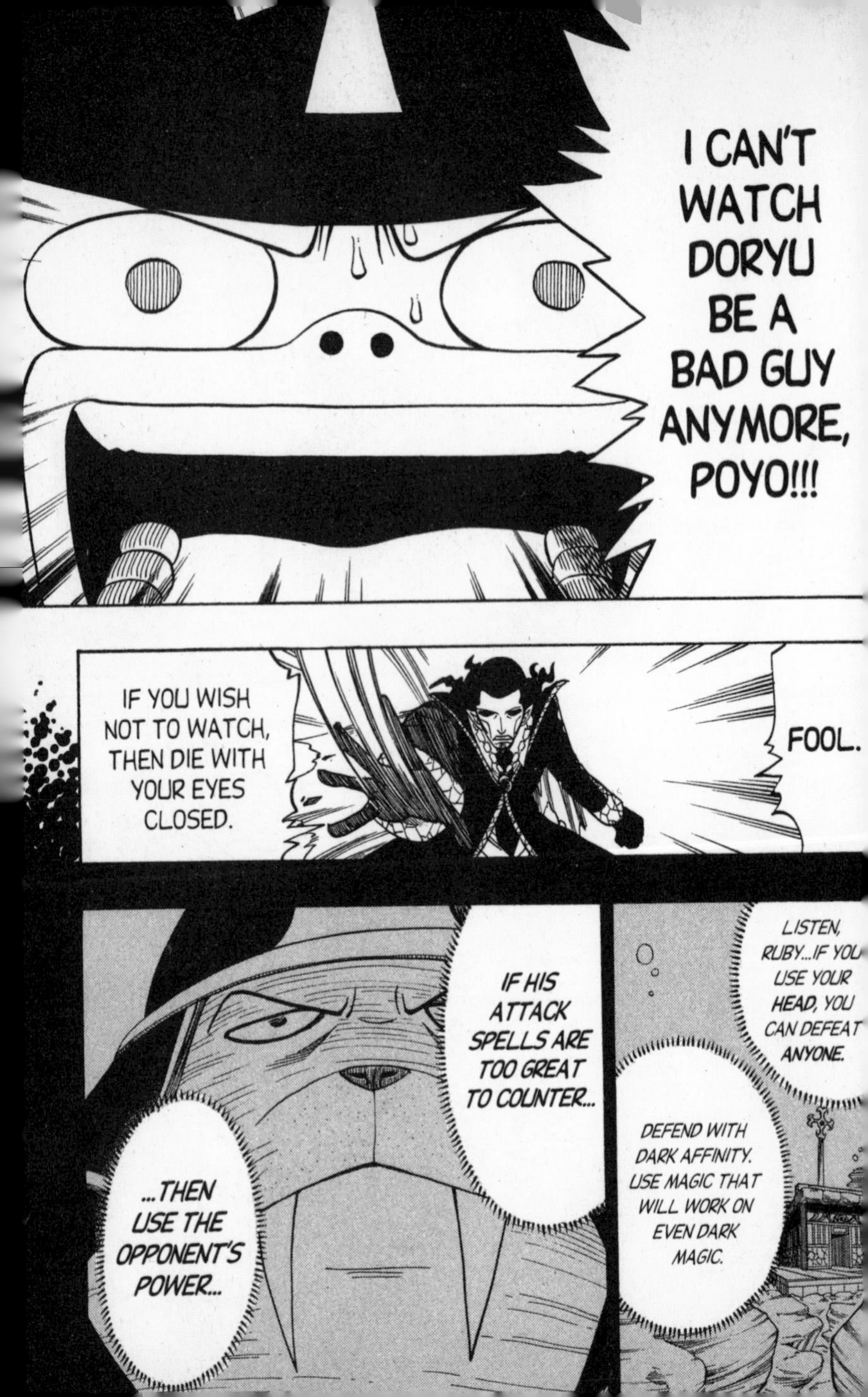
I CAN'T WATCH DORYU BE A BAD GUY ANYMORE, POYO!!!
FOOL.
IF YOU WISH NOT TO WATCH, THEN DIE WITH YOUR EYES CLOSED.
LISTEN, RUBY...IF YOU USE YOUR HEAD, YOU CAN DEFEAT ANYONE.
DEFEND WITH DARK AFFINITY. USE MAGIC THAT WILL WORK ON EVEN DARK MAGIC.
IF HIS ATTACK SPELLS ARE TOO GREAT TO COUNTER...
...THEN USE THE OPPONENT'S POWER...

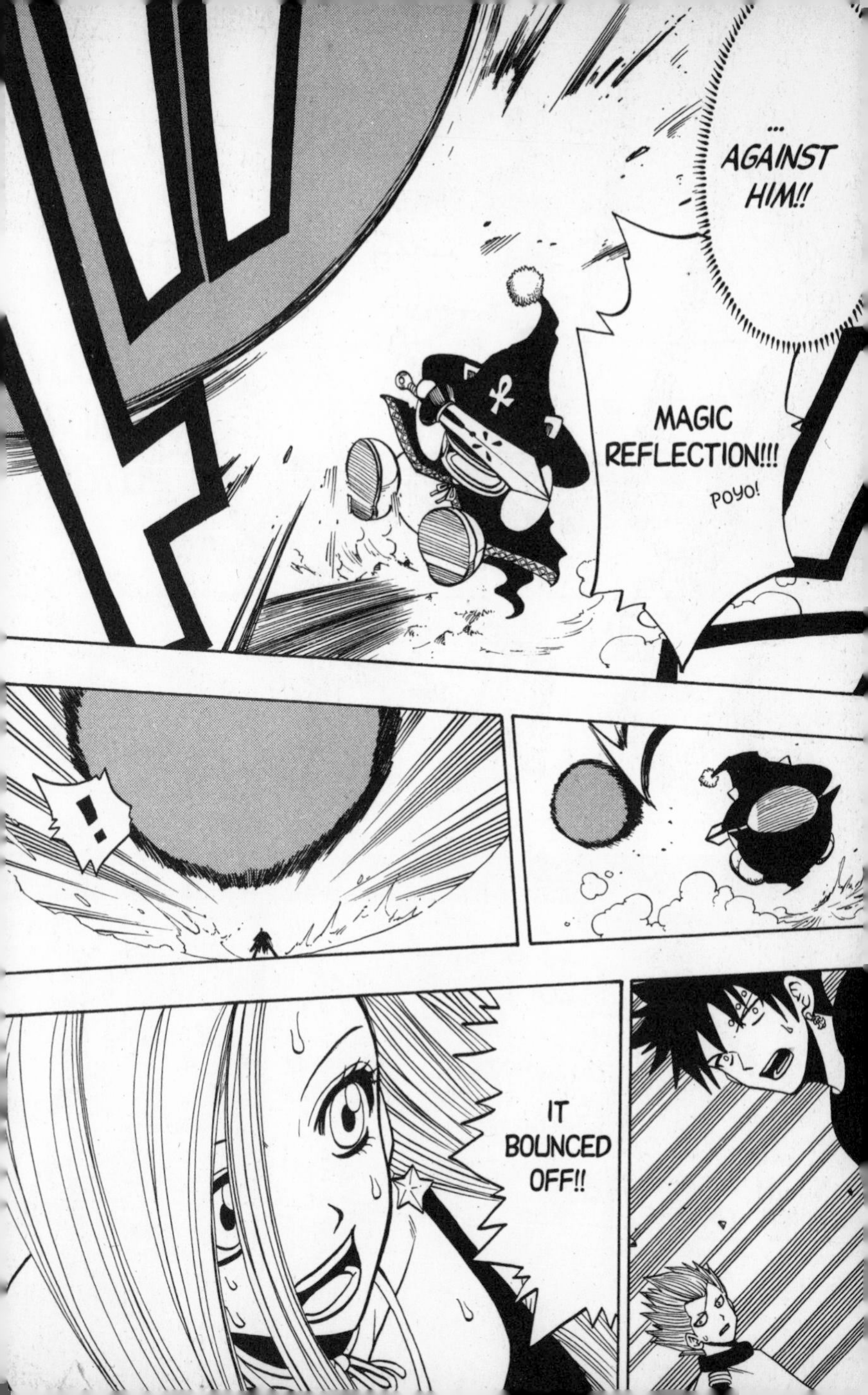
...AGAINST HIM!!
MAGIC REFLECTION!!!
POYO!
!
IT BOUNCED OFF!!

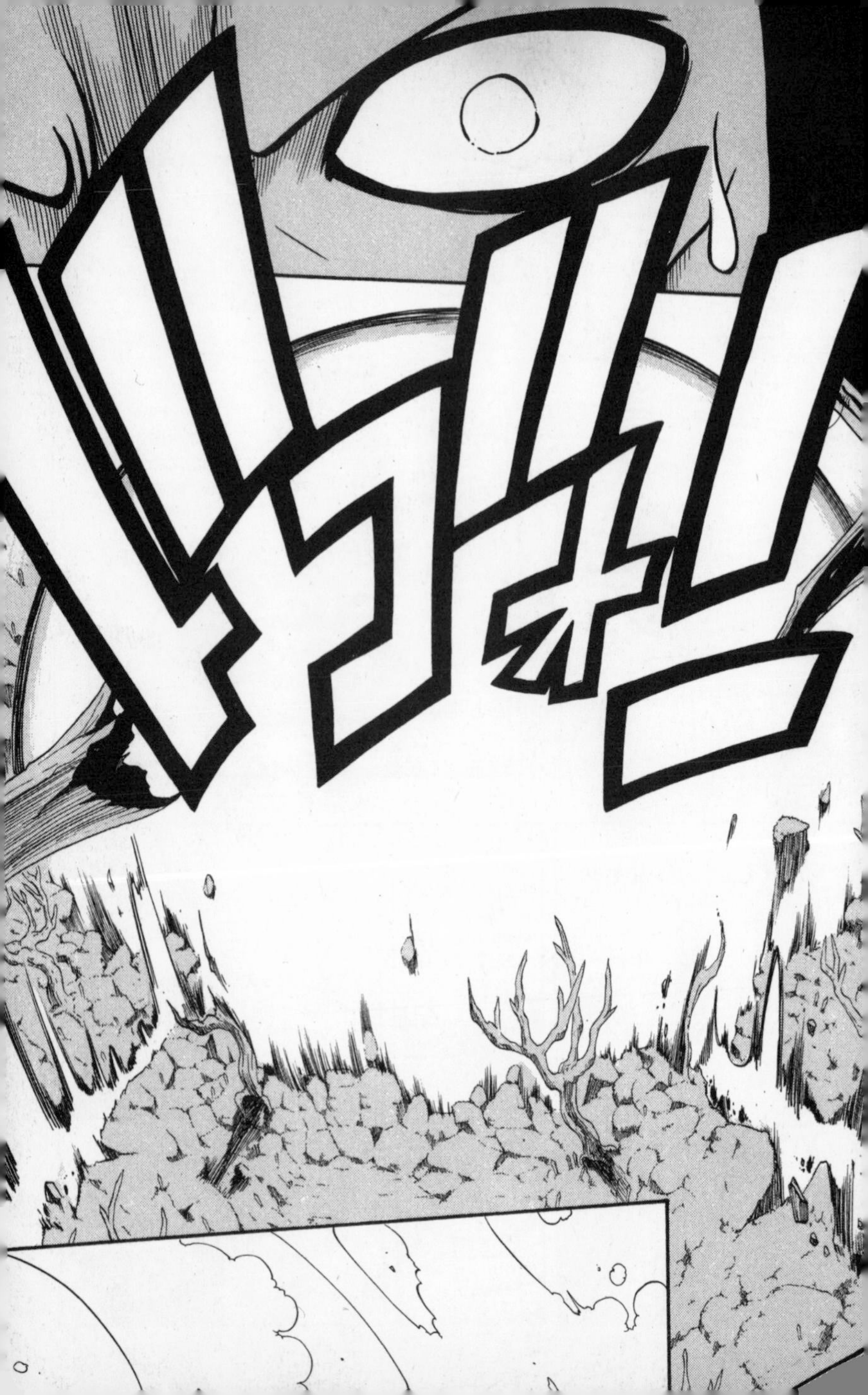

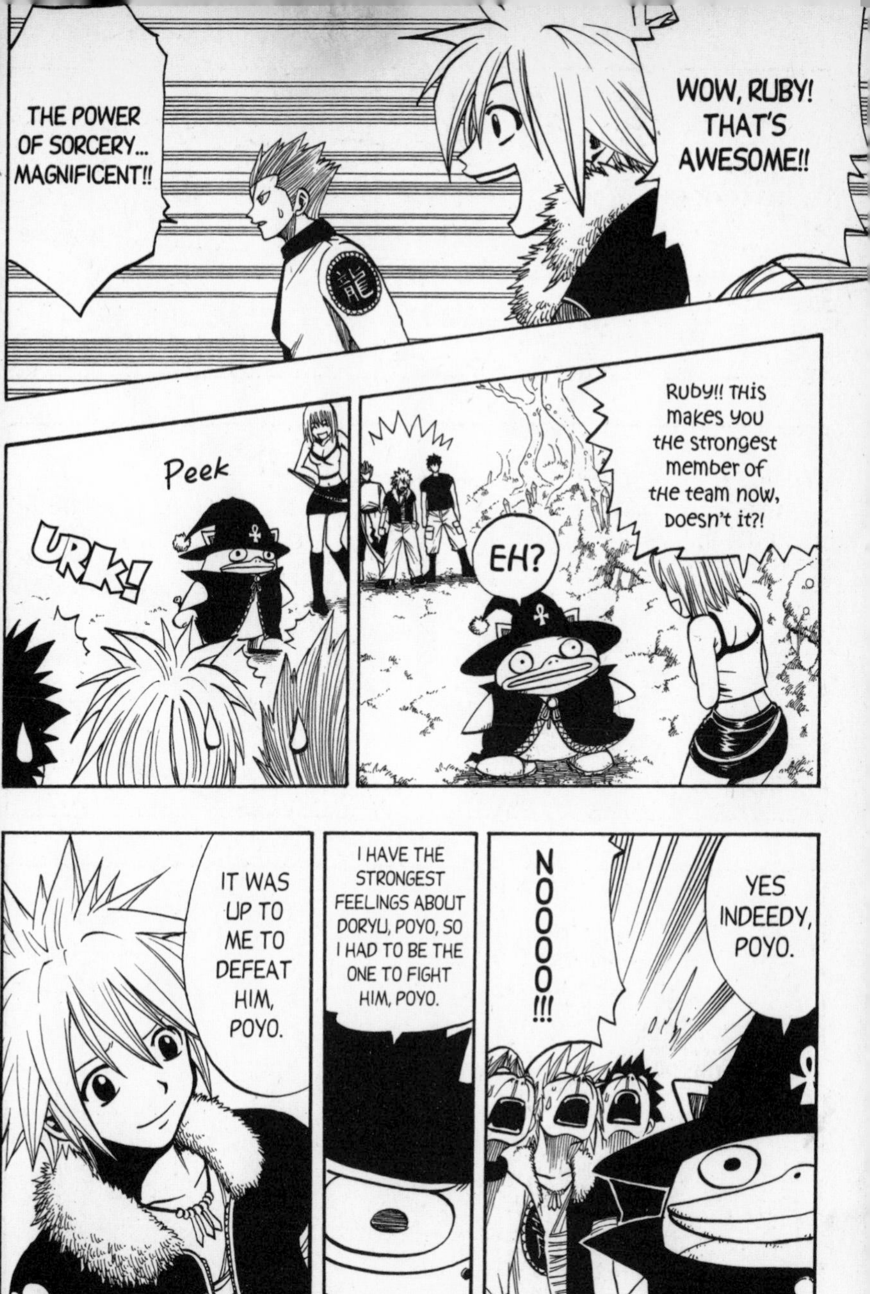
WOW, RUBY! THAT'S AWESOME!!
THE POWER OF SORCERY... MAGNIFICENT!!
RUBY!! THIS makes you the strongest member of the team now, Doesn't it?!
EH?
Peek
URK!
YES INDEEDY, POYO.
NOOOOO!!!
I HAVE THE STRONGEST FEELINGS ABOUT DORYU, POYO, SO I HAD TO BE THE ONE TO FIGHT HIM, POYO.
IT WAS UP TO ME TO DEFEAT HIM, POYO.

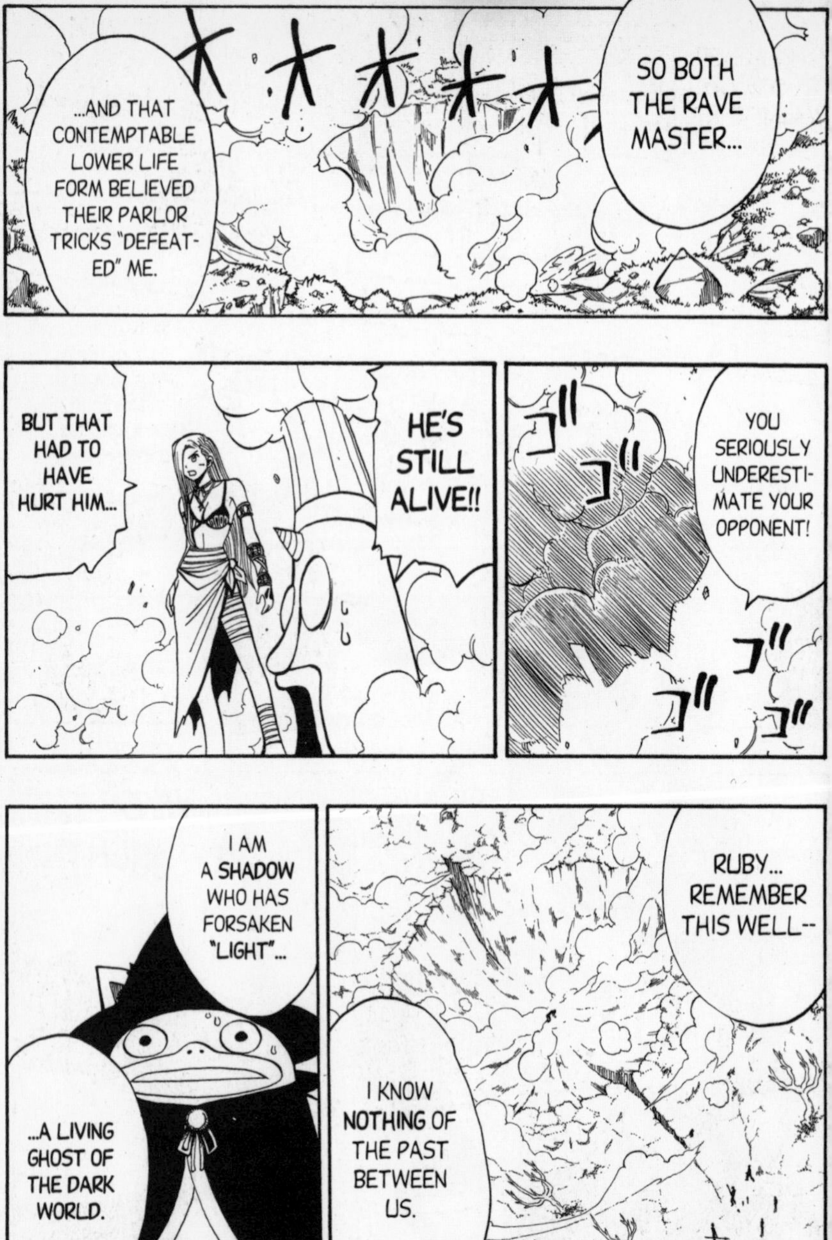
SO BOTH THE RAVE MASTER...
オオオオオオ
...AND THAT CONTEMPTABLE LOWER LIFE FORM BELIEVED THEIR PARLOR TRICKS "DEFEAT-ED" ME.
YOU SERIOUSLY UNDERESTI-MATE YOUR OPPONENT!
ゴゴゴゴゴ
HE'S STILL ALIVE!!
BUT THAT HAD TO HAVE HURT HIM...
RUBY... REMEMBER THIS WELL--
I KNOW NOTHING OF THE PAST BETWEEN US.
I AM A SHADOW WHO HAS FORSAKEN "LIGHT"...
...A LIVING GHOST OF THE DARK WORLD.

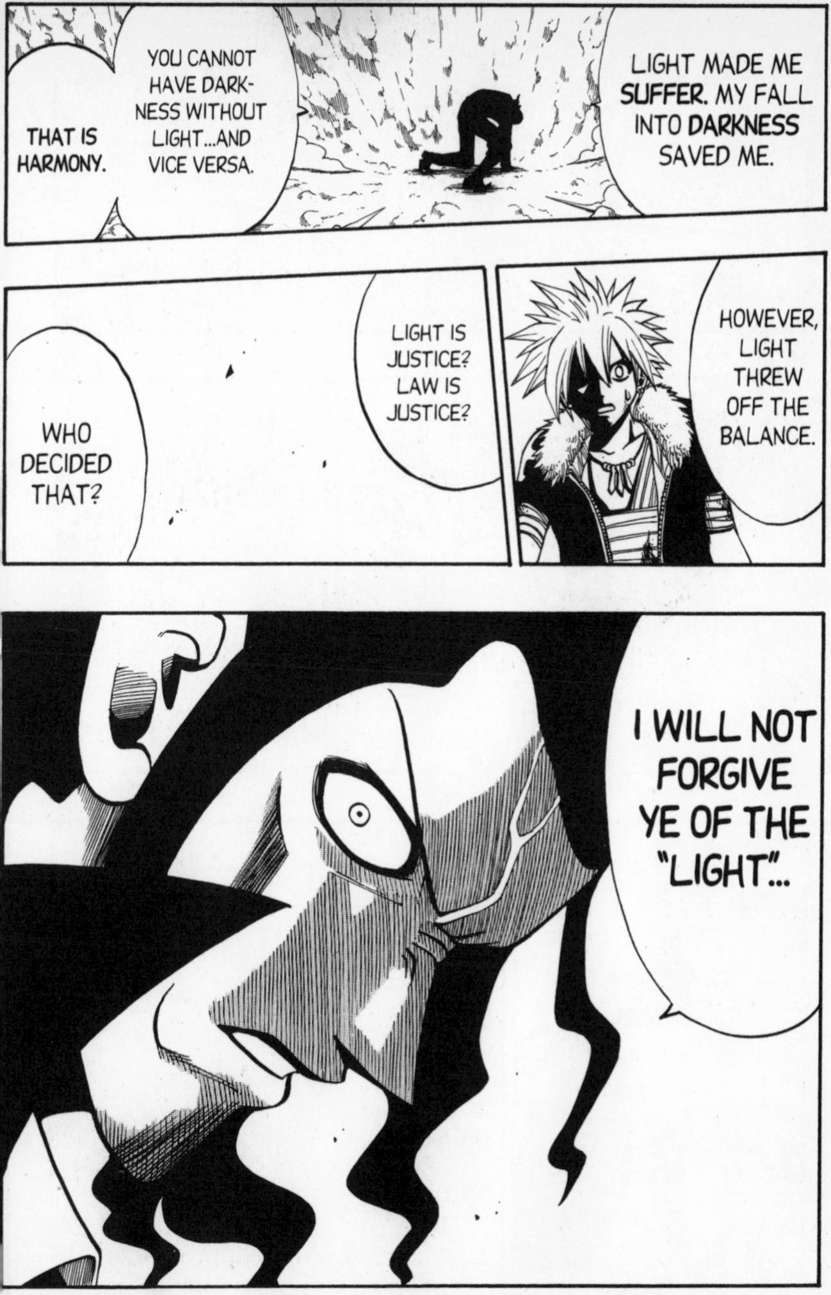
LIGHT MADE ME SUFFER. MY FALL INTO DARKNESS SAVED ME.
YOU CANNOT HAVE DARKNESS WITHOUT LIGHT...AND VICE VERSA.
THAT IS HARMONY.
HOWEVER, LIGHT THREW OFF THE BALANCE.
LIGHT IS JUSTICE? LAW IS JUSTICE?
WHO DECIDED THAT?
I WILL NOT FORGIVE YE OF THE "LIGHT"...

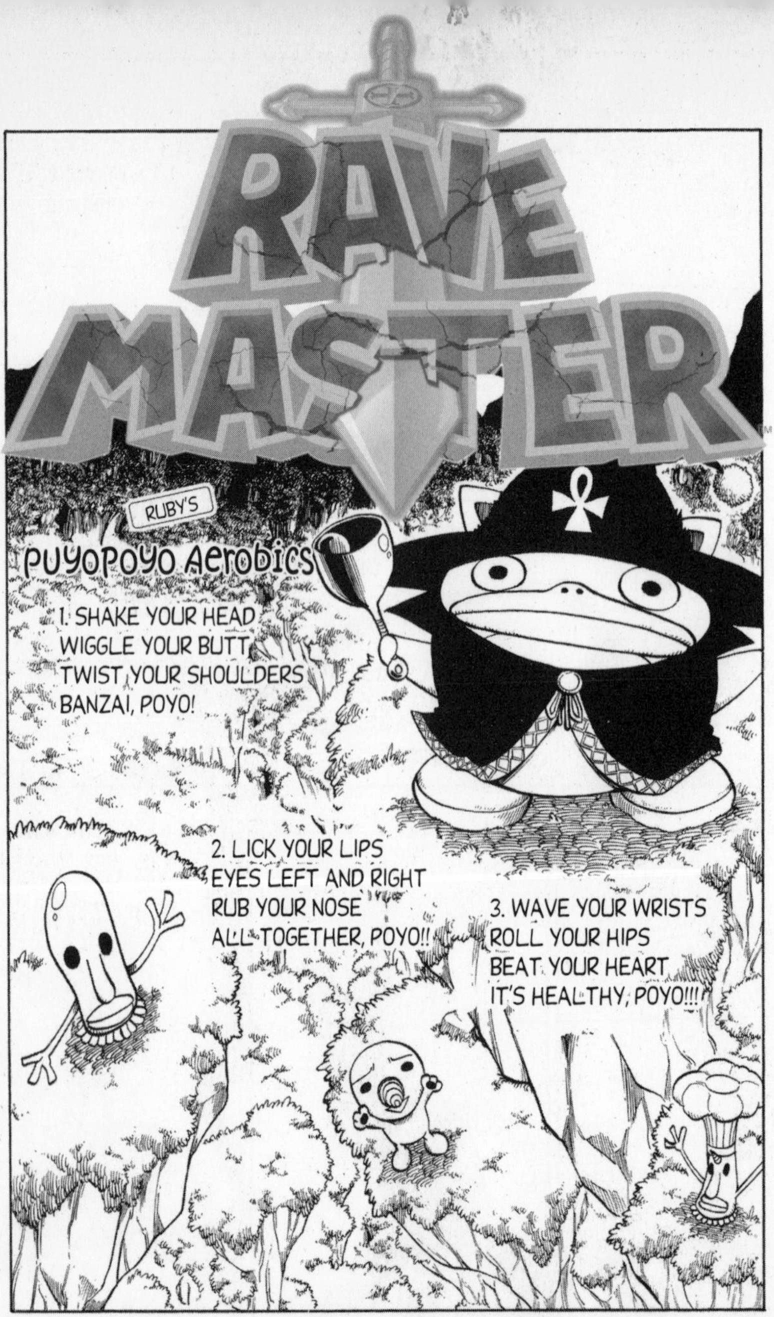
RAVE MASTER
RUBY'S
PUYOPOYO AEROBICS
1. SHAKE YOUR HEAD
WIGGLE YOUR BUTT
TWIST YOUR SHOULDERS
BANZAI, POYO!
2. LICK YOUR LIPS
EYES LEFT AND RIGHT
RUB YOUR NOSE
ALL TOGETHER, POYO!!
3. WAVE YOUR WRISTS
ROLL YOUR HIPS
BEAT YOUR HEART
IT'S HEALTHY, POYO!!!

RAVE: 133 ✠ SHATTERED DREAMS

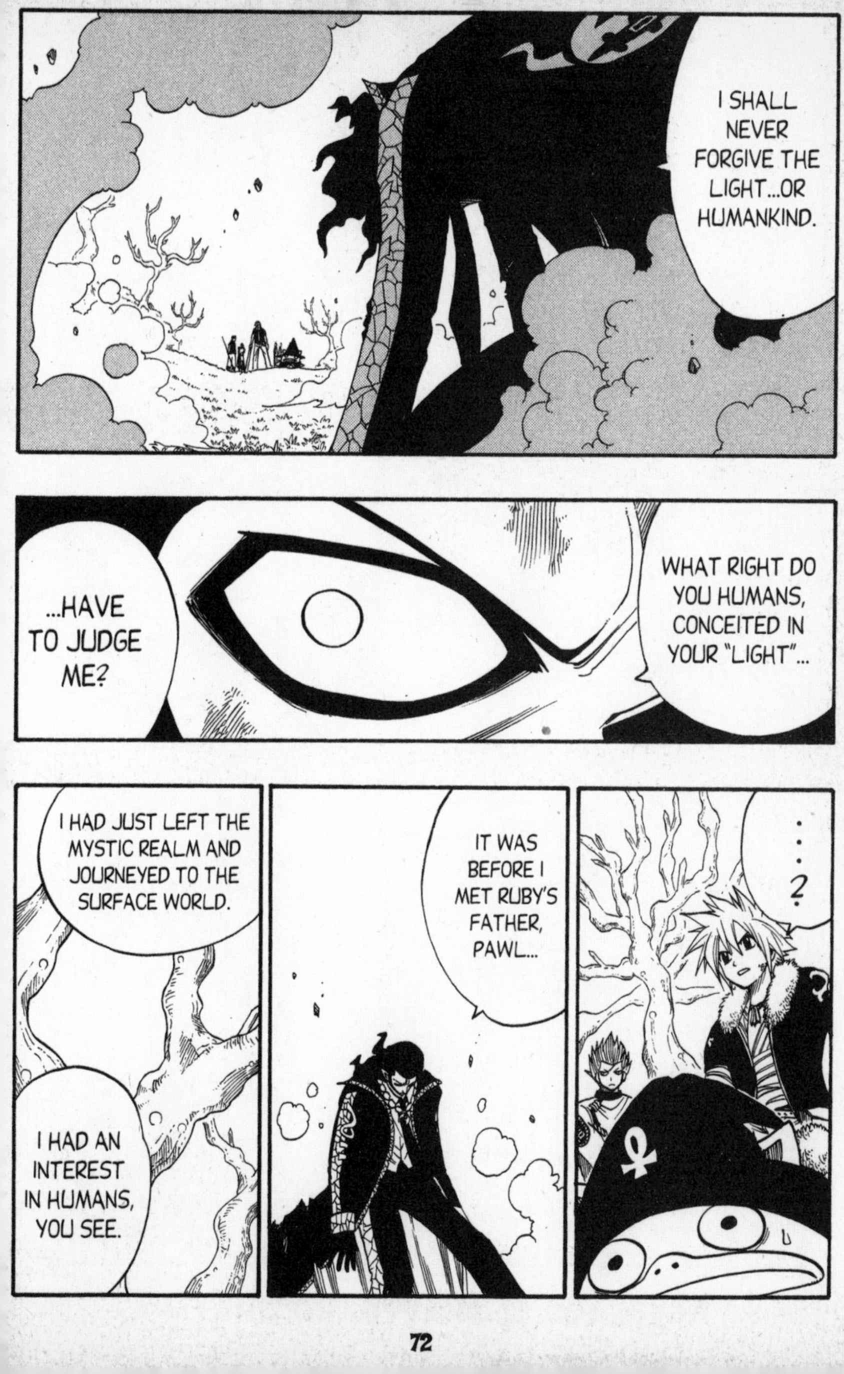
I SHALL NEVER FORGIVE THE LIGHT...OR HUMANKIND.
WHAT RIGHT DO YOU HUMANS, CONCEITED IN YOUR "LIGHT"...
...HAVE TO JUDGE ME?
...?
IT WAS BEFORE I MET RUBY'S FATHER, PAWL...
I HAD JUST LEFT THE MYSTIC REALM AND JOURNEYED TO THE SURFACE WORLD.
I HAD AN INTEREST IN HUMANS, YOU SEE.

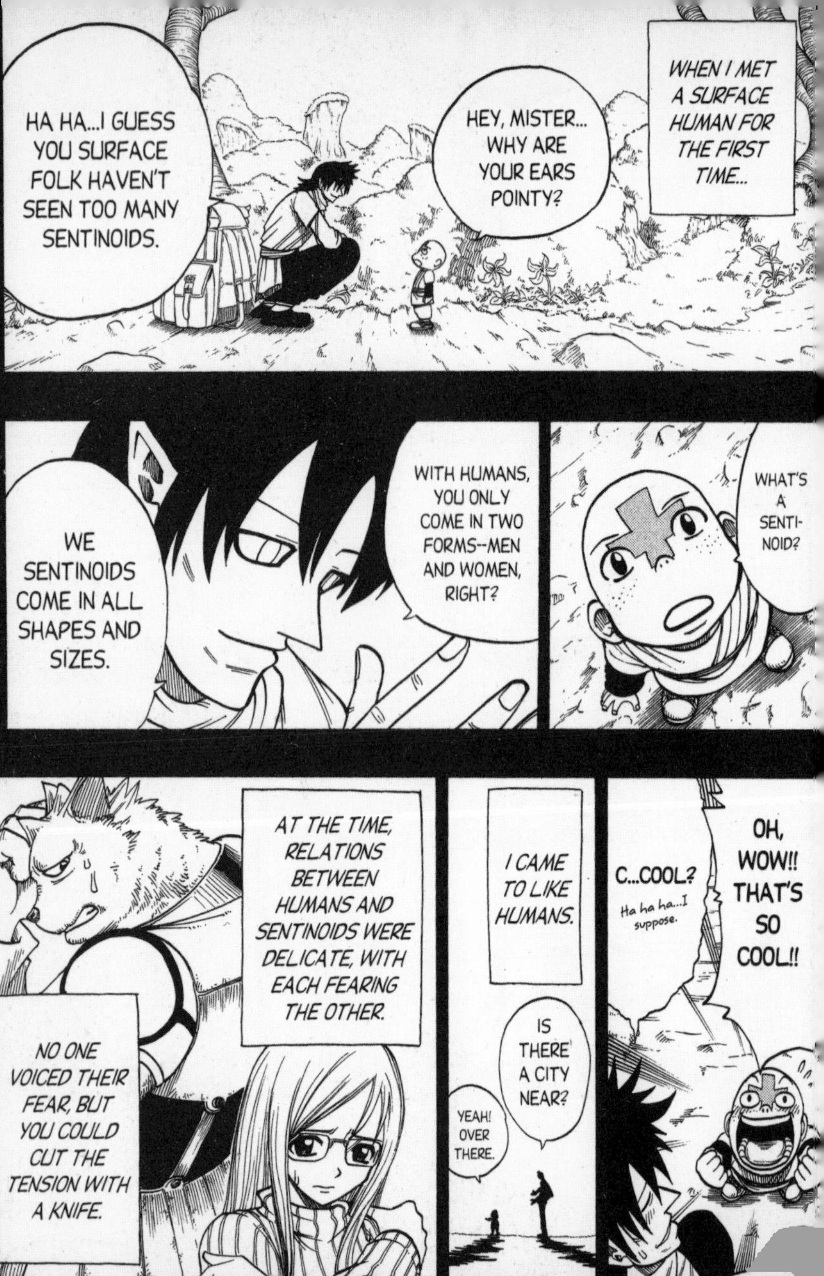
WHEN I MET A SURFACE HUMAN FOR THE FIRST TIME...
HEY, MISTER... WHY ARE YOUR EARS POINTY?
HA HA...I GUESS YOU SURFACE FOLK HAVEN'T SEEN TOO MANY SENTINOIDS.
WHAT'S A SENTI-NOID?
WITH HUMANS, YOU ONLY COME IN TWO FORMS--MEN AND WOMEN, RIGHT?
WE SENTINOIDS COME IN ALL SHAPES AND SIZES.
OH, WOW!! THAT'S SO COOL!!
C...COOL?
Ha ha ha...I suppose.
I CAME TO LIKE HUMANS.
IS THERE A CITY NEAR?
YEAH! OVER THERE.
AT THE TIME, RELATIONS BETWEEN HUMANS AND SENTINOIDS WERE DELICATE, WITH EACH FEARING THE OTHER.
NO ONE VOICED THEIR FEAR, BUT YOU COULD CUT THE TENSION WITH A KNIFE.

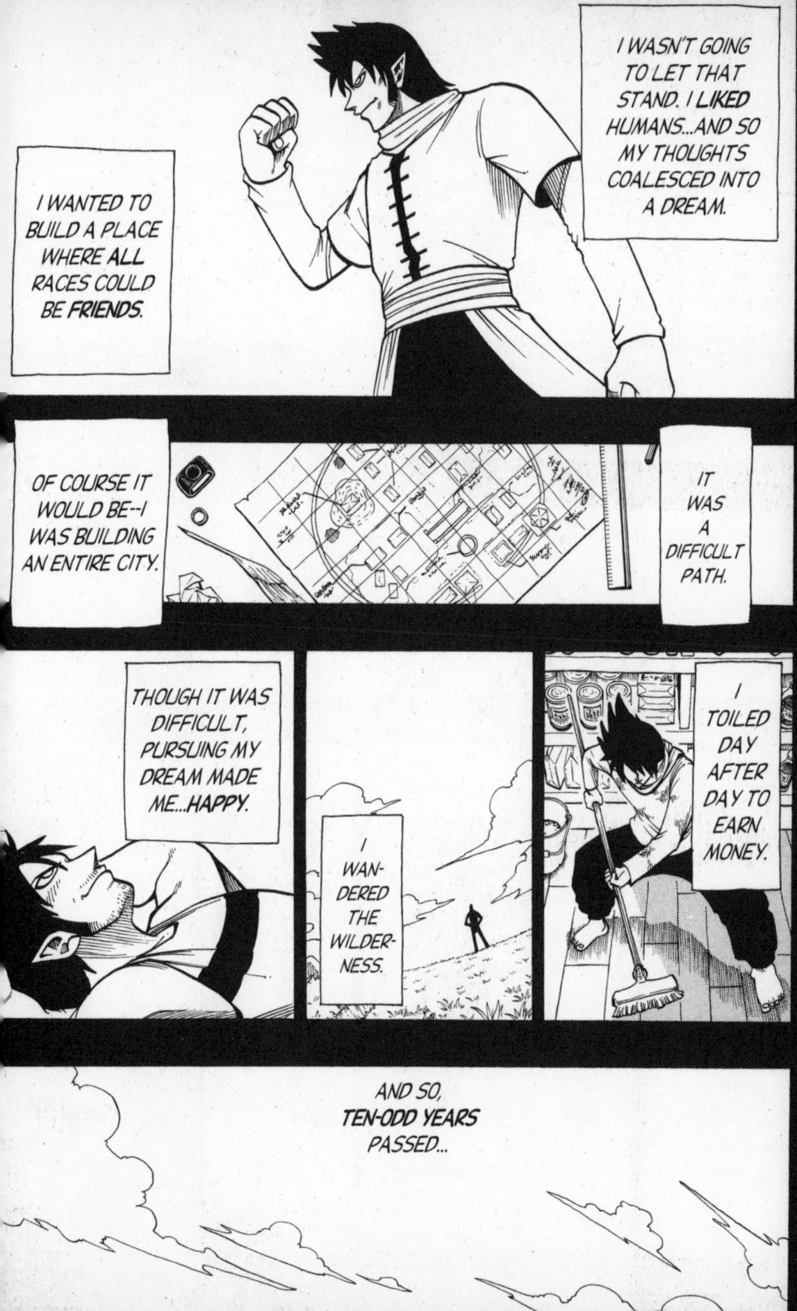
I WASN'T GOING TO LET THAT STAND. I LIKED HUMANS...AND SO MY THOUGHTS COALESCED INTO A DREAM.
I WANTED TO BUILD A PLACE WHERE ALL RACES COULD BE FRIENDS.
IT WAS A DIFFICULT PATH.
OF COURSE IT WOULD BE--I WAS BUILDING AN ENTIRE CITY.
I TOILED DAY AFTER DAY TO EARN MONEY.
I WAN-DERED THE WILDER-NESS.
THOUGH IT WAS DIFFICULT, PURSUING MY DREAM MADE ME...HAPPY.
AND SO, TEN-ODD YEARS PASSED...

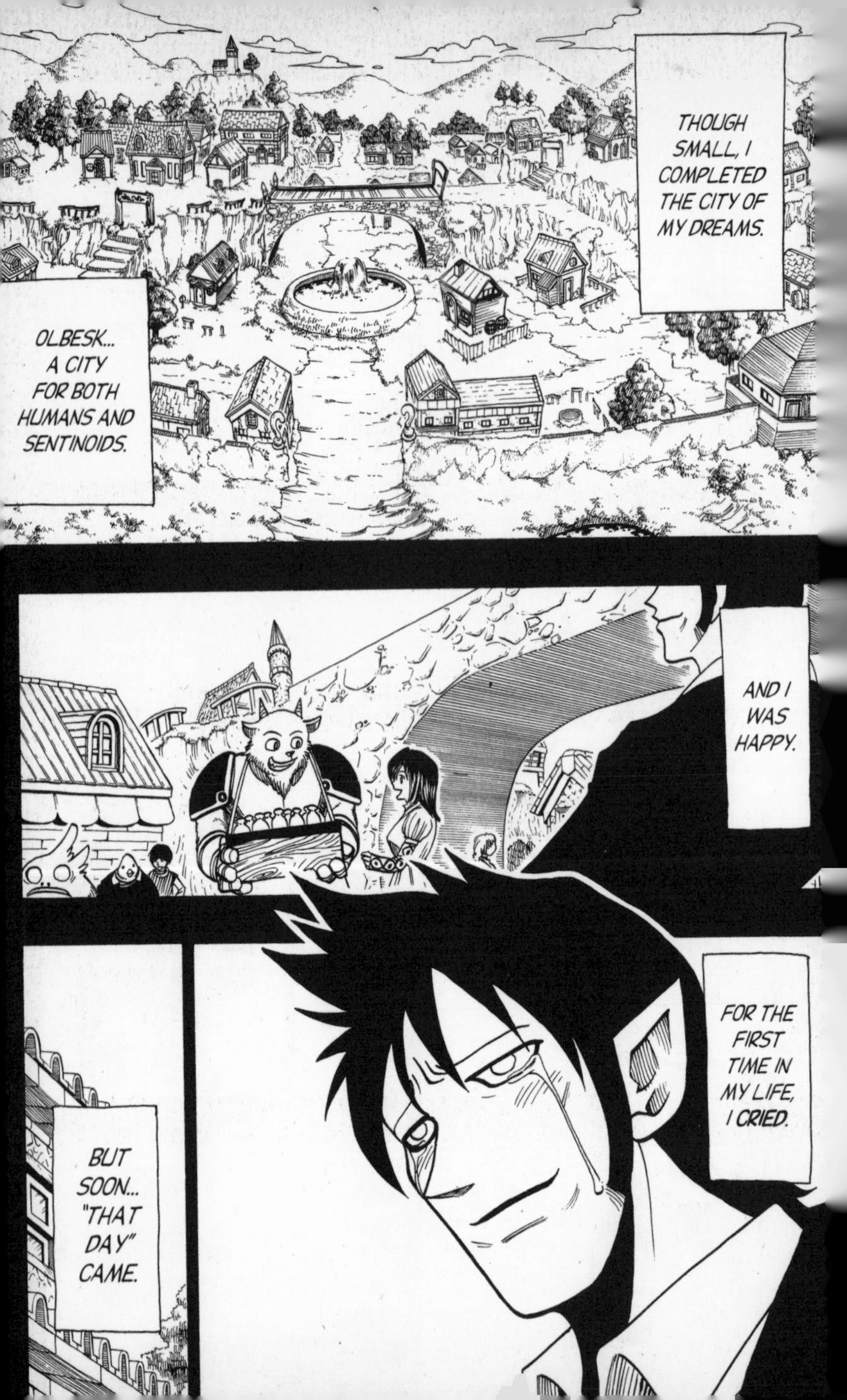
THOUGH SMALL, I COMPLETED THE CITY OF MY DREAMS.
OLBESK... A CITY FOR BOTH HUMANS AND SENTINOIDS.
AND I WAS HAPPY.
FOR THE FIRST TIME IN MY LIFE, I CRIED.
BUT SOON... "THAT DAY" CAME.

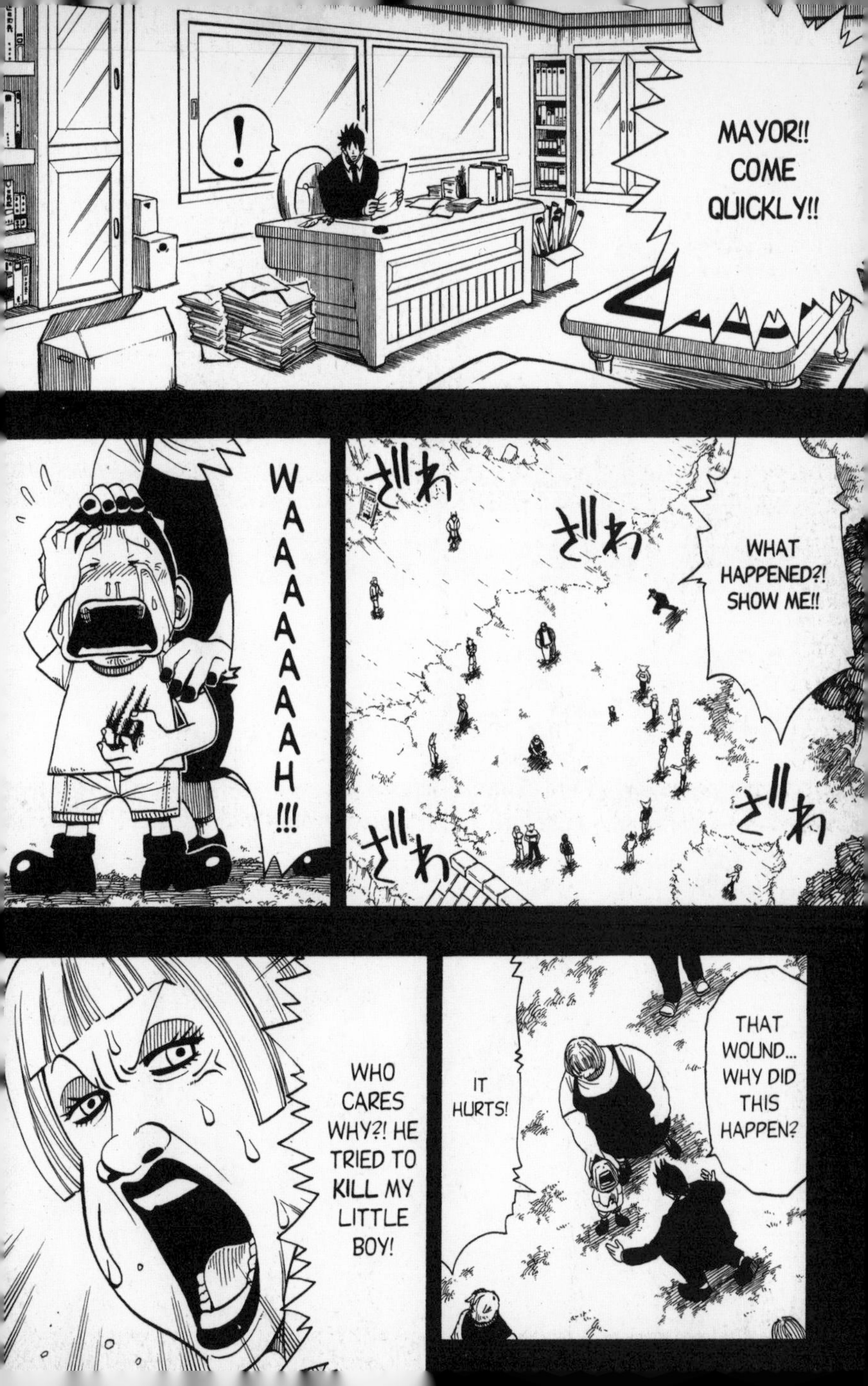
MAYOR!! COME QUICKLY!!
!
WHAT HAPPENED?! SHOW ME!!
ざわ
ざわ
ざわ
ざわ
WAAAAAAAAAH!!!
THAT WOUND... WHY DID THIS HAPPEN?
IT HURTS!
WHO CARES WHY?! HE TRIED TO KILL MY LITTLE BOY!

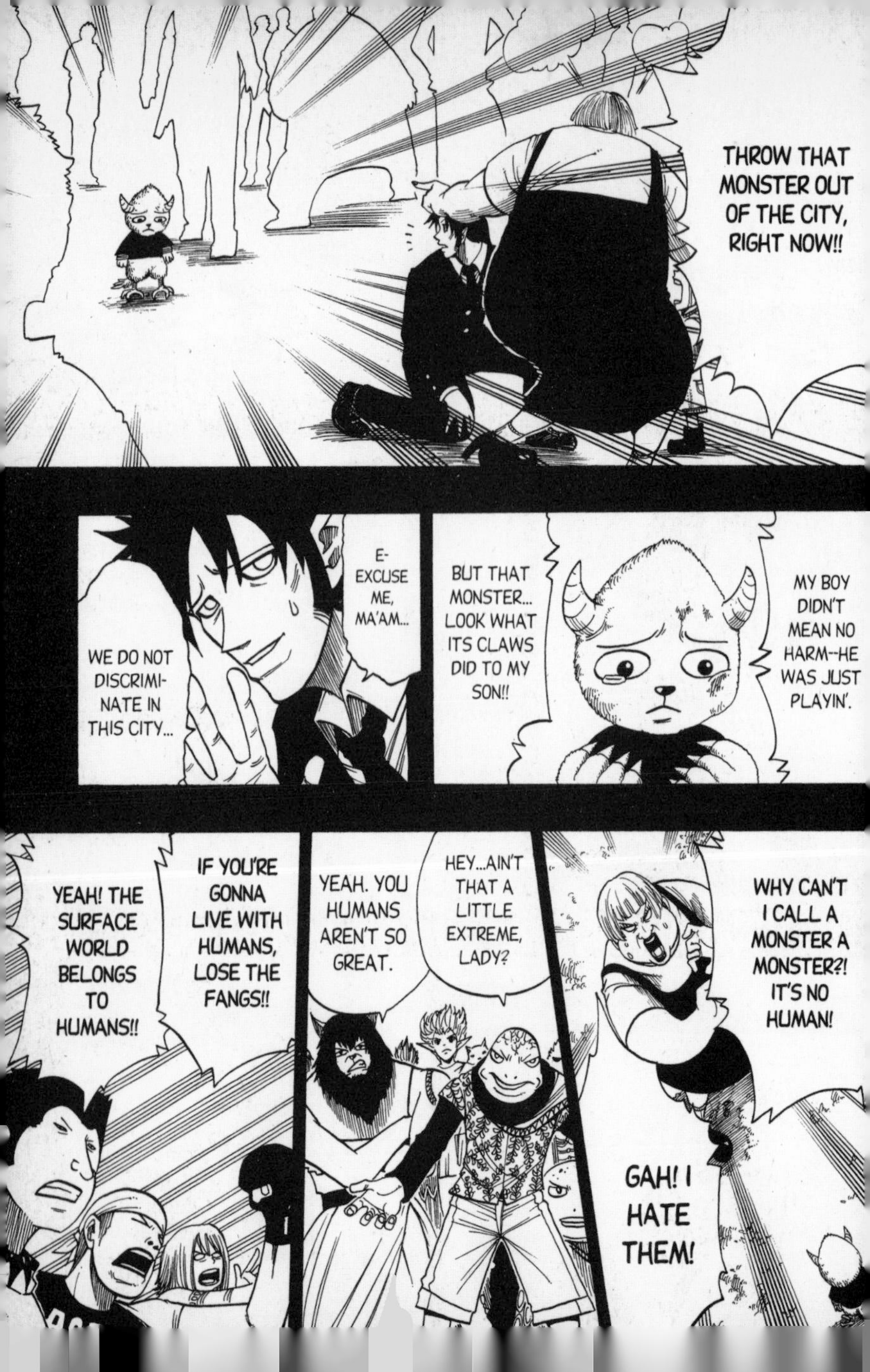
THROW THAT MONSTER OUT OF THE CITY, RIGHT NOW!!
MY BOY DIDN'T MEAN NO HARM--HE WAS JUST PLAYIN'.
BUT THAT MONSTER... LOOK WHAT ITS CLAWS DID TO MY SON!!
E- EXCUSE ME, MA'AM...
WE DO NOT DISCRIMINATE IN THIS CITY...
WHY CAN'T I CALL A MONSTER A MONSTER?! IT'S NO HUMAN!
GAH! I HATE THEM!
HEY...AIN'T THAT A LITTLE EXTREME, LADY?
YEAH. YOU HUMANS AREN'T SO GREAT.
IF YOU'RE GONNA LIVE WITH HUMANS, LOSE THE FANGS!!
YEAH! THE SURFACE WORLD BELONGS TO HUMANS!!

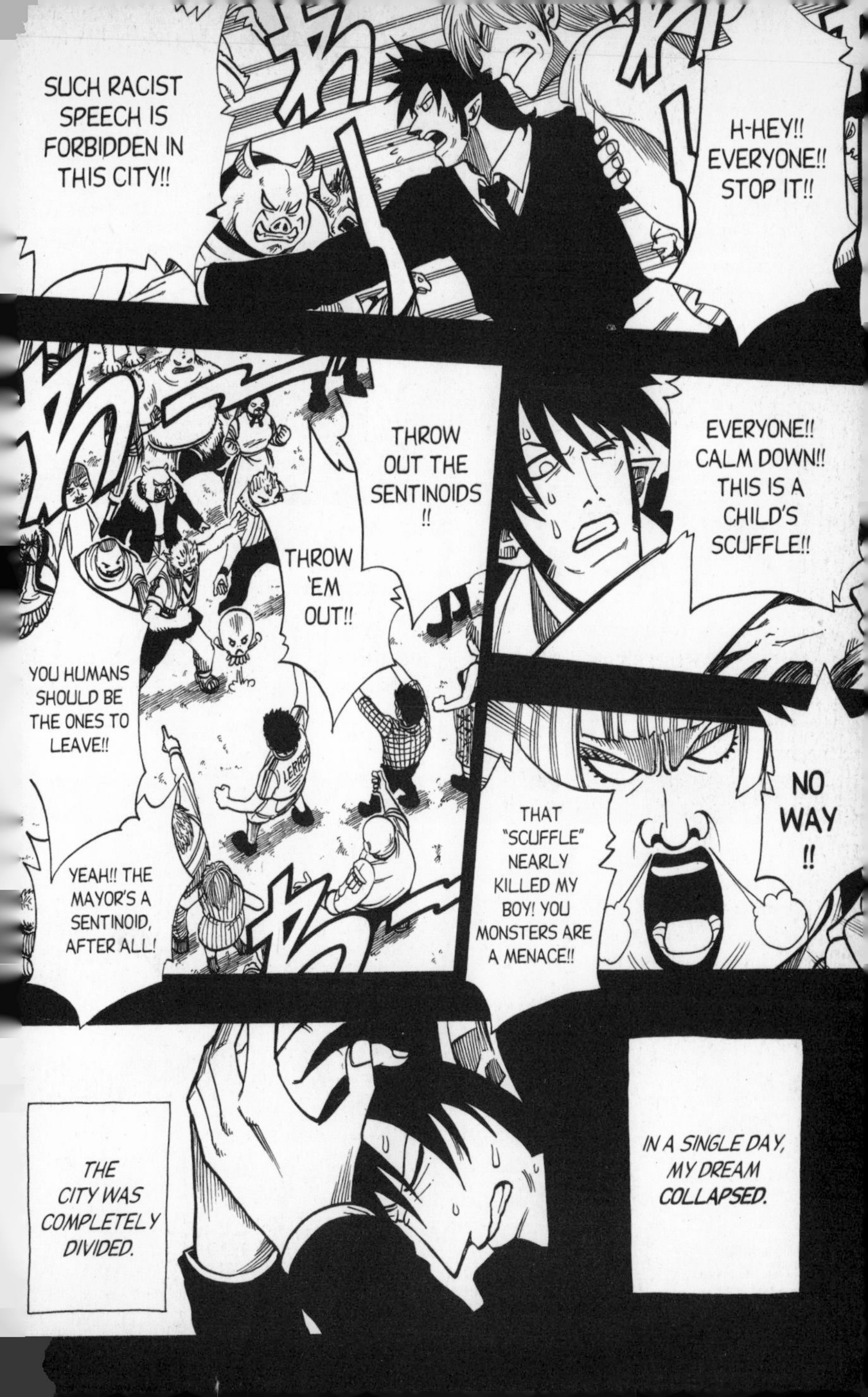
H-HEY!! EVERYONE!! STOP IT!!
SUCH RACIST SPEECH IS FORBIDDEN IN THIS CITY!!
EVERYONE!! CALM DOWN!! THIS IS A CHILD'S SCUFFLE!!
NO WAY!!
THAT "SCUFFLE" NEARLY KILLED MY BOY! YOU MONSTERS ARE A MENACE!!
THROW OUT THE SENTINOIDS!!
THROW 'EM OUT!!
YOU HUMANS SHOULD BE THE ONES TO LEAVE!!
YEAH!! THE MAYOR'S A SENTINOID, AFTER ALL!
IN A SINGLE DAY, MY DREAM COLLAPSED.
THE CITY WAS COMPLETELY DIVIDED.

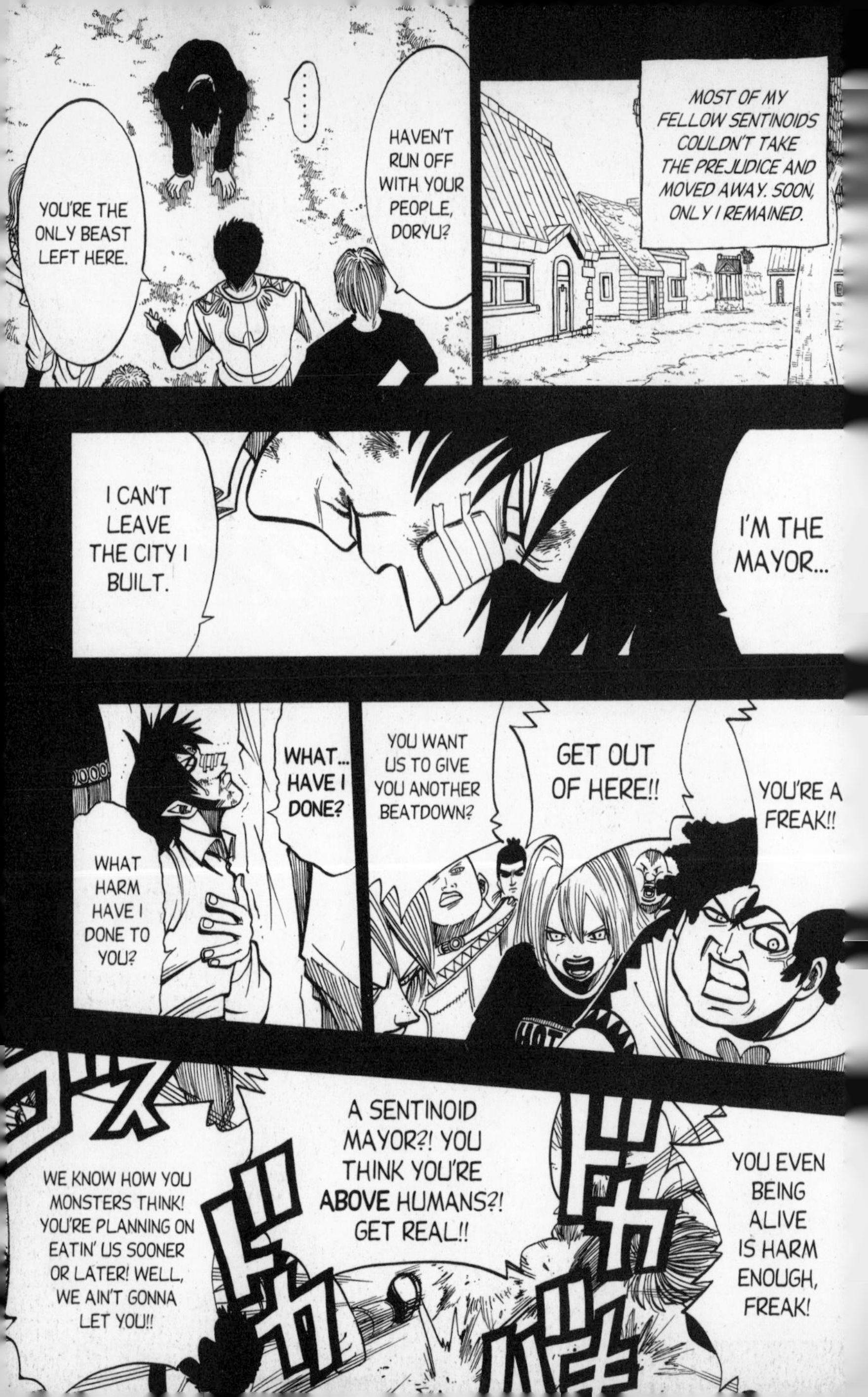
MOST OF MY FELLOW SENTINOIDS COULDN'T TAKE THE PREJUDICE AND MOVED AWAY. SOON, ONLY I REMAINED.
HAVEN'T RUN OFF WITH YOUR PEOPLE, DORYU?
......
YOU'RE THE ONLY BEAST LEFT HERE.
I'M THE MAYOR...
I CAN'T LEAVE THE CITY I BUILT.
YOU'RE A FREAK!!
GET OUT OF HERE!!
YOU WANT US TO GIVE YOU ANOTHER BEATDOWN?
WHAT... HAVE I DONE?
WHAT HARM HAVE I DONE TO YOU?
YOU EVEN BEING ALIVE IS HARM ENOUGH, FREAK!
A SENTINOID MAYOR?! YOU THINK YOU'RE ABOVE HUMANS?! GET REAL!!
WE KNOW HOW YOU MONSTERS THINK! YOU'RE PLANNING ON EATIN' US SOONER OR LATER! WELL, WE AIN'T GONNA LET YOU!!

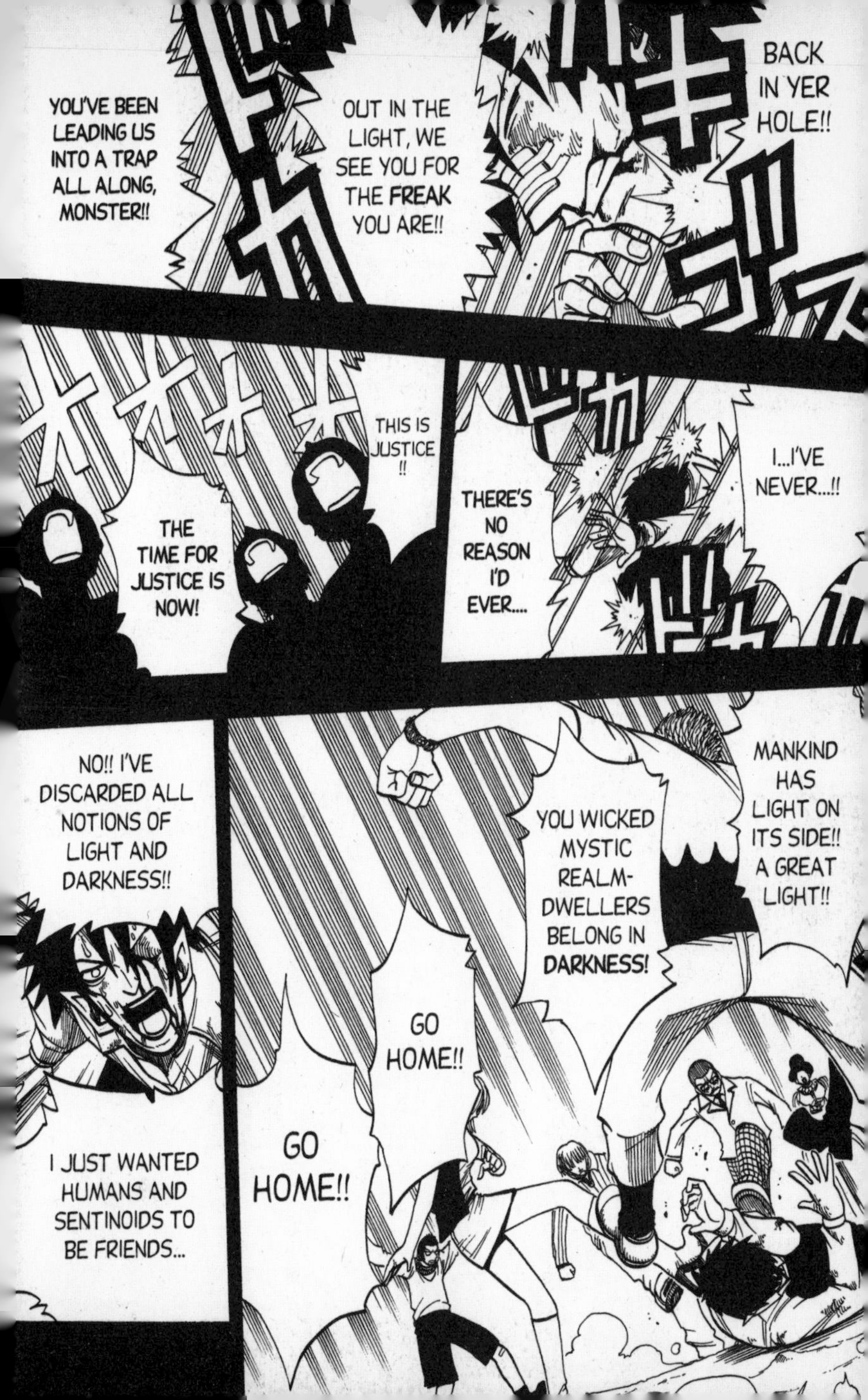
BACK IN YER HOLE!!
OUT IN THE LIGHT, WE SEE YOU FOR THE FREAK YOU ARE!!
YOU'VE BEEN LEADING US INTO A TRAP ALL ALONG, MONSTER!!
I...I'VE NEVER...!!
THERE'S NO REASON I'D EVER....
THIS IS JUSTICE !!
THE TIME FOR JUSTICE IS NOW!
MANKIND HAS LIGHT ON ITS SIDE!! A GREAT LIGHT!!
YOU WICKED MYSTIC REALM-DWELLERS BELONG IN DARKNESS!
GO HOME!!
GO HOME!!
NO!! I'VE DISCARDED ALL NOTIONS OF LIGHT AND DARKNESS!!
I JUST WANTED HUMANS AND SENTINOIDS TO BE FRIENDS...

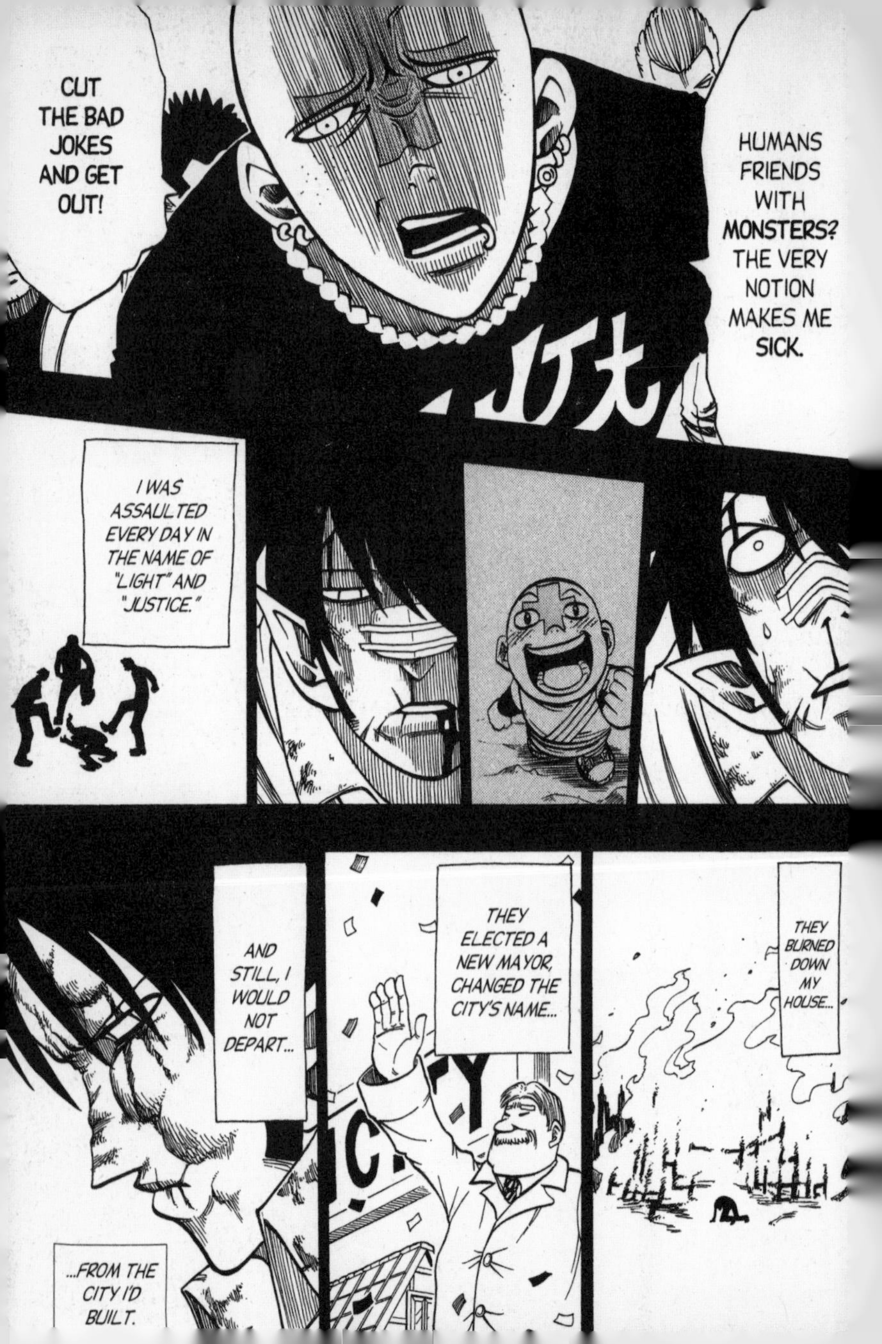
HUMANS FRIENDS WITH MONSTERS? THE VERY NOTION MAKES ME SICK.
CUT THE BAD JOKES AND GET OUT!
I WAS ASSAULTED EVERY DAY IN THE NAME OF "LIGHT" AND "JUSTICE."
THEY BURNED DOWN MY HOUSE...
THEY ELECTED A NEW MAYOR, CHANGED THE CITY'S NAME...
AND STILL, I WOULD NOT DEPART...
...FROM THE CITY I'D BUILT.

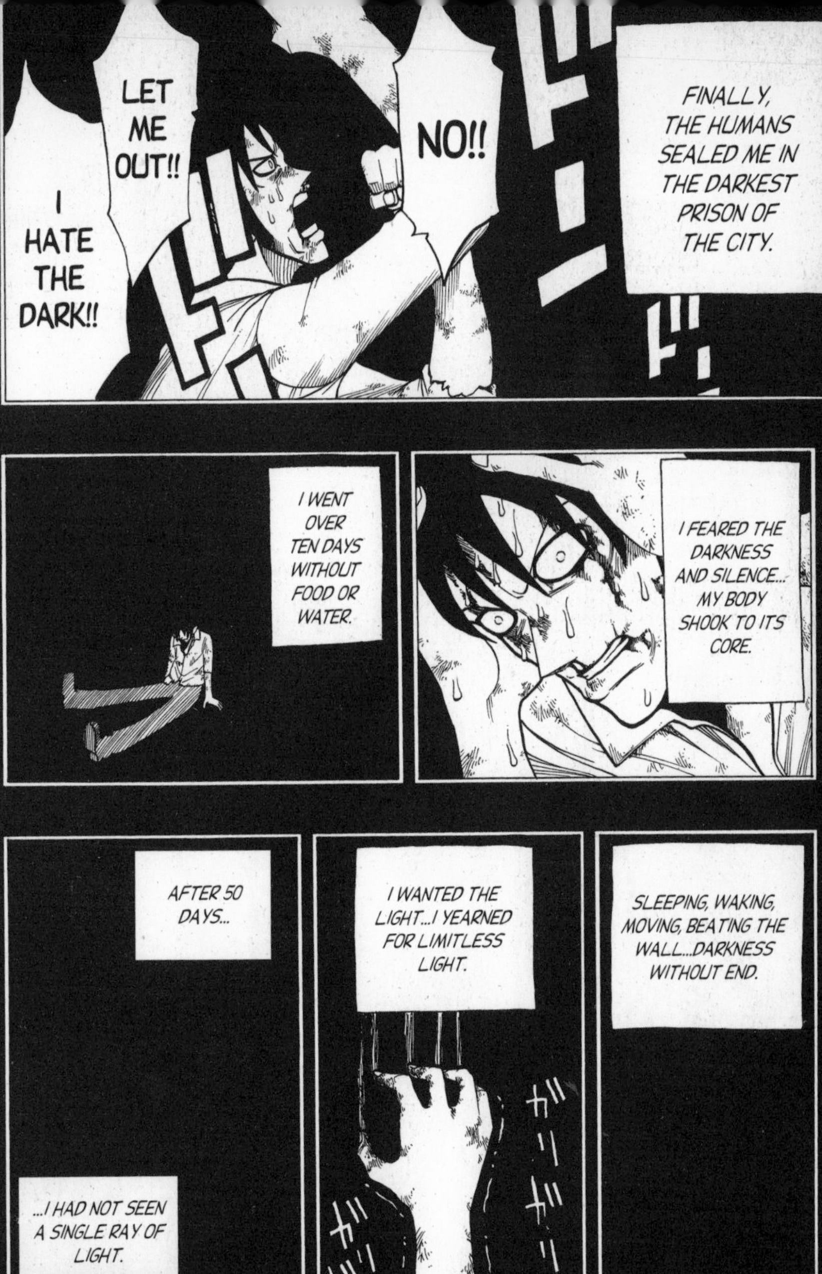
FINALLY, THE HUMANS SEALED ME IN THE DARKEST PRISON OF THE CITY.
NO!!
LET ME OUT!!
I HATE THE DARK!!
I FEARED THE DARKNESS AND SILENCE... MY BODY SHOOK TO ITS CORE.
I WENT OVER TEN DAYS WITHOUT FOOD OR WATER.
SLEEPING, WAKING, MOVING, BEATING THE WALL...DARKNESS WITHOUT END.
I WANTED THE LIGHT...I YEARNED FOR LIMITLESS LIGHT.
AFTER 50 DAYS...
...I HAD NOT SEEN A SINGLE RAY OF LIGHT.

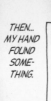

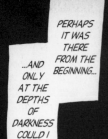

OVER 100 DAYS PASSED.
DARKNESS TRANSFORMED ME INTO A MOCKERY OF LIFE.
THEN... MY HAND FOUND SOMETHING.
GRAB
PERHAPS IT WAS THERE FROM THE BEGINNING...
...AND ONLY AT THE DEPTHS OF DARKNESS COULD I SEE IT.
THE MOTHER DARK BRING-- SINCLAIRE.
A MONUMENT OF DARKNESS, ONLY FIVE IN THE WORLD...AND IT CHOSE ME.
ALL THE MURDEROUS DESIRES THAT I HAD BEEN SUPPRESSING WITHIN ME UNTIL THEN....
...FINALLY SURGED FORTH.
REVENGE AGAINST HUMANS... REVENGE AGAINST LIGHT... WITH THE OVERWHELMING POWER OF DARKNESS...
...BOTH WERE WITHIN MY REACH.

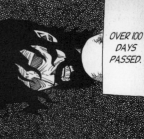

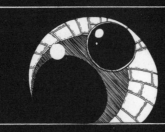

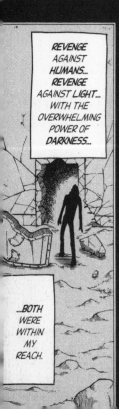

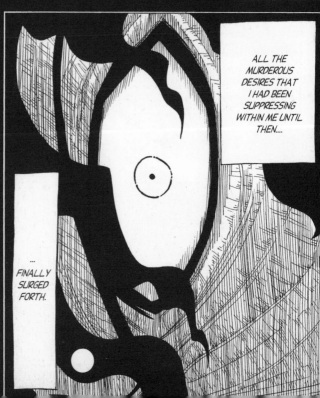

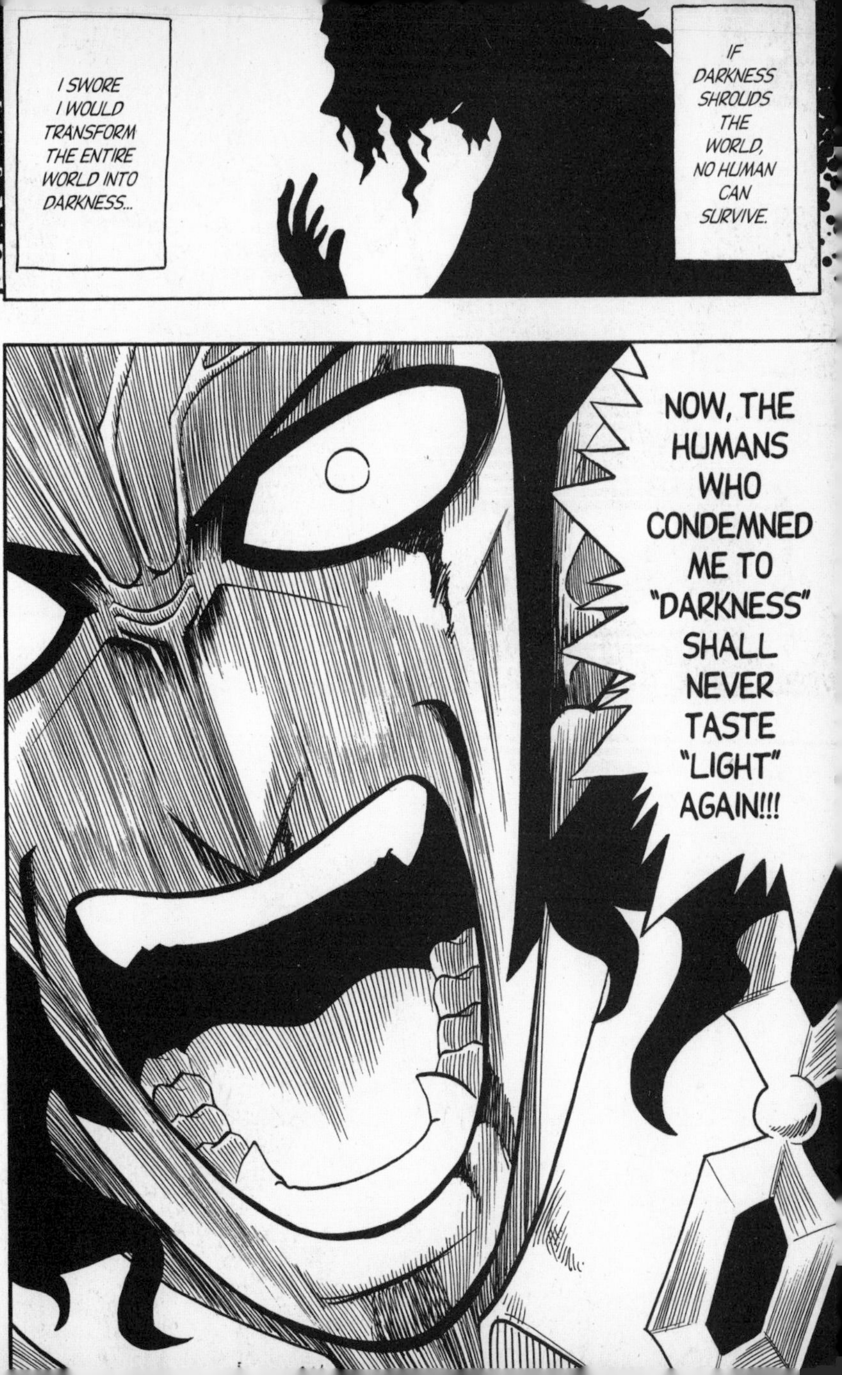
IF DARKNESS SHROUDS THE WORLD, NO HUMAN CAN SURVIVE.
I SWORE I WOULD TRANSFORM THE ENTIRE WORLD INTO DARKNESS...
NOW, THE HUMANS WHO CONDEMNED ME TO "DARKNESS" SHALL NEVER TASTE "LIGHT" AGAIN!!!

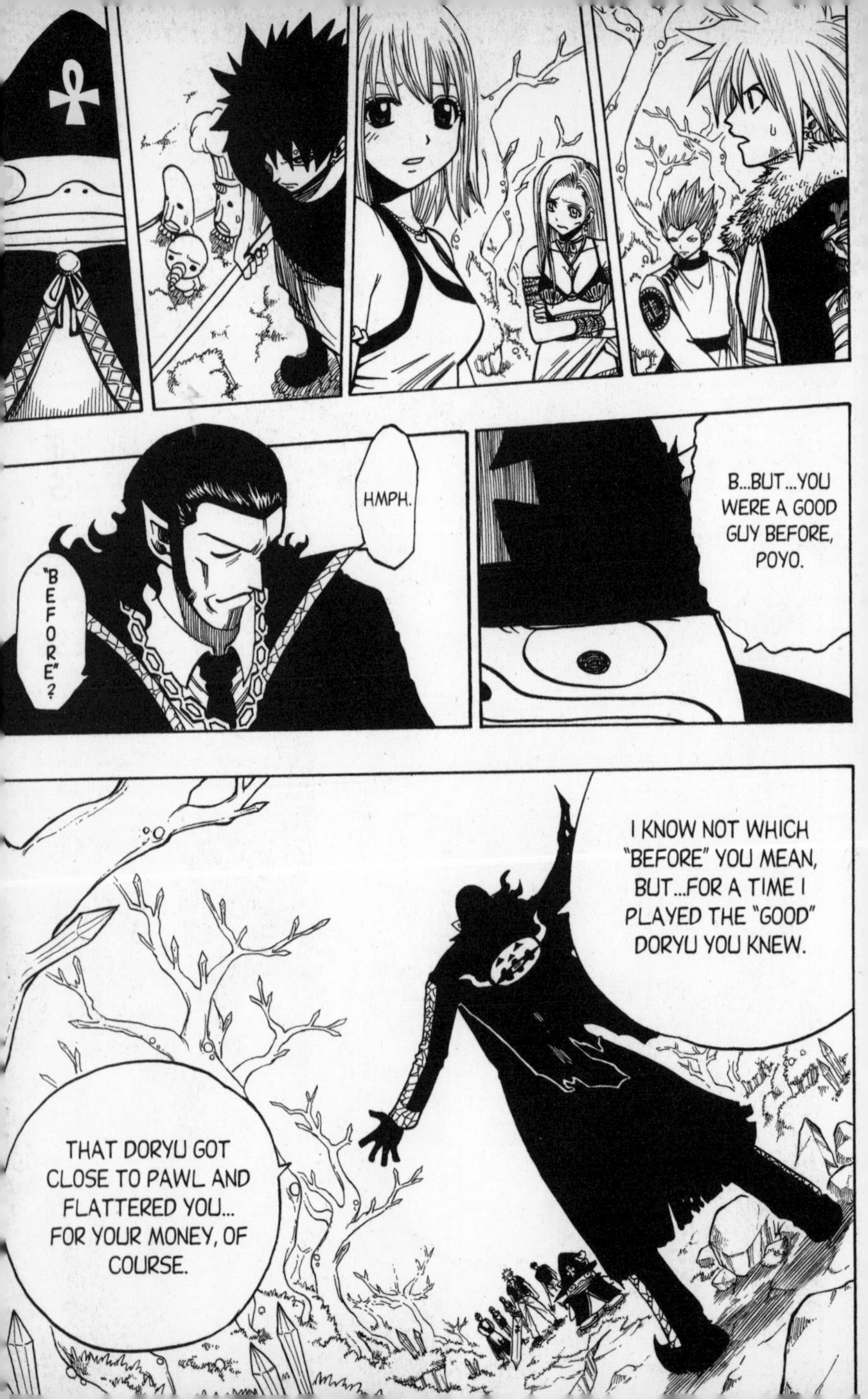
B...BUT...YOU WERE A GOOD GUY BEFORE, POYO.
HMPH.
"BEFORE"?
I KNOW NOT WHICH "BEFORE" YOU MEAN, BUT...FOR A TIME I PLAYED THE "GOOD" DORYU YOU KNEW.
THAT DORYU GOT CLOSE TO PAWL AND FLATTERED YOU... FOR YOUR MONEY, OF COURSE.

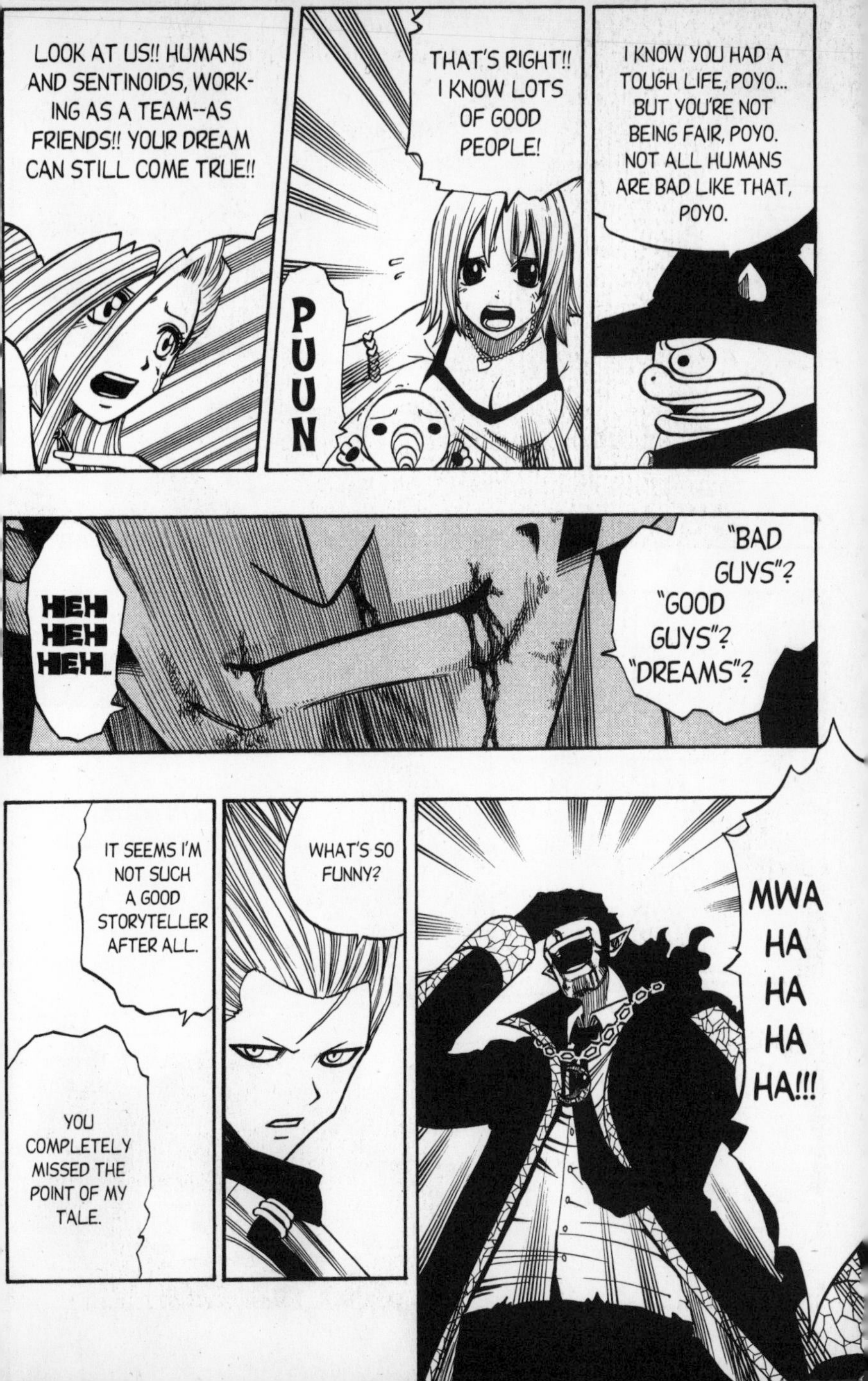
I KNOW YOU HAD A TOUGH LIFE, POYO... BUT YOU'RE NOT BEING FAIR, POYO. NOT ALL HUMANS ARE BAD LIKE THAT, POYO.
THAT'S RIGHT!! I KNOW LOTS OF GOOD PEOPLE!
PUUN
LOOK AT US!! HUMANS AND SENTINOIDS, WORKING AS A TEAM--AS FRIENDS!! YOUR DREAM CAN STILL COME TRUE!!
"BAD GUYS"? "GOOD GUYS"? "DREAMS"?
HEH HEH HEH...
MWA HA HA HA HA!!!
WHAT'S SO FUNNY?
IT SEEMS I'M NOT SUCH A GOOD STORYTELLER AFTER ALL.
YOU COMPLETELY MISSED THE POINT OF MY TALE.

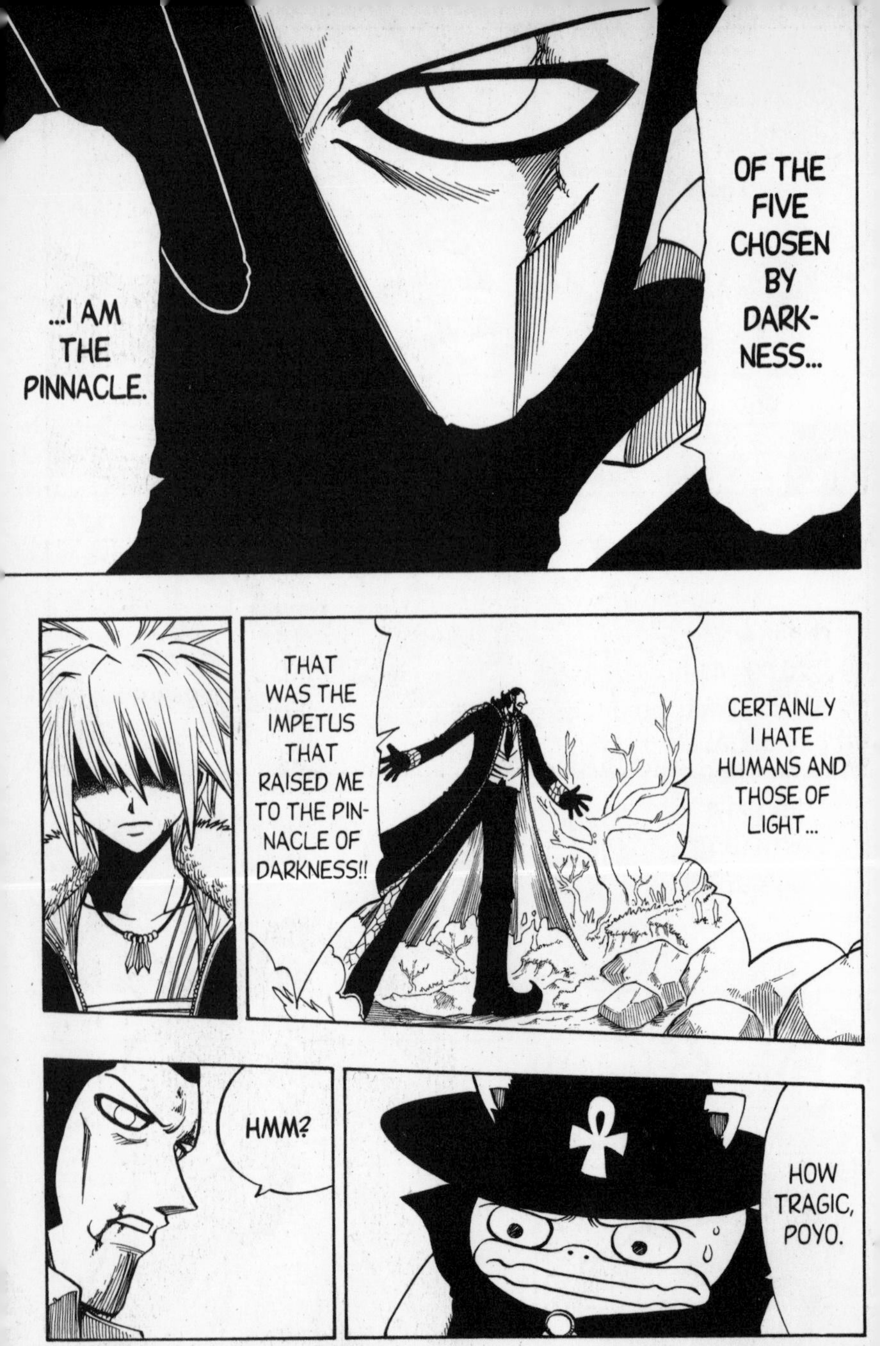
OF THE FIVE CHOSEN BY DARK-NESS...
...I AM THE PINNACLE.
CERTAINLY I HATE HUMANS AND THOSE OF LIGHT...
THAT WAS THE IMPETUS THAT RAISED ME TO THE PIN-NACLE OF DARKNESS!!
HOW TRAGIC, POYO.
HMM?

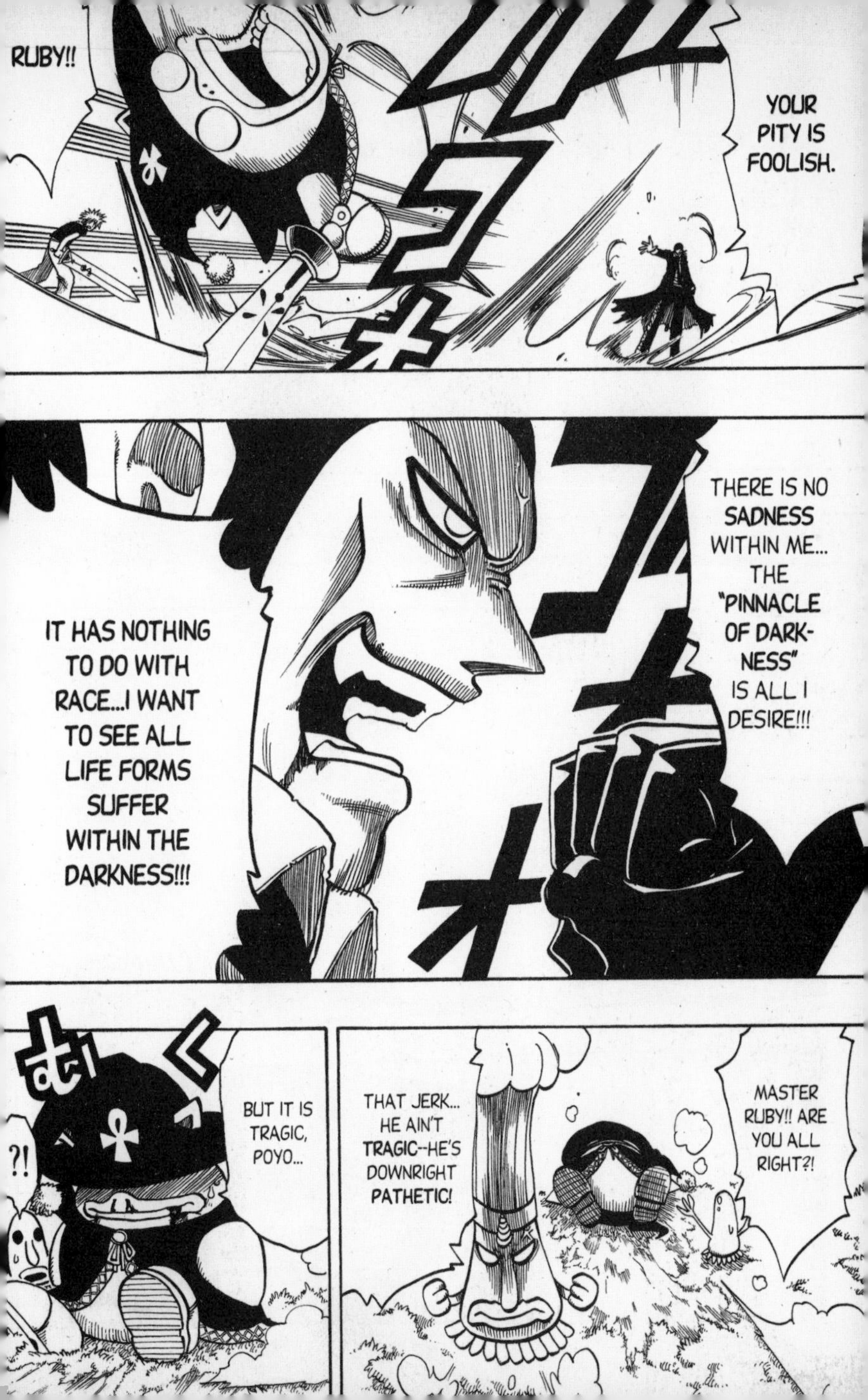
YOUR PITY IS FOOLISH.
RUBY!!
THERE IS NO SADNESS WITHIN ME... THE "PINNACLE OF DARK-NESS" IS ALL I DESIRE!!!
IT HAS NOTHING TO DO WITH RACE...I WANT TO SEE ALL LIFE FORMS SUFFER WITHIN THE DARKNESS!!!
MASTER RUBY!! ARE YOU ALL RIGHT?!
THAT JERK... HE AIN'T TRAGIC--HE'S DOWNRIGHT PATHETIC!
BUT IT IS TRAGIC, POYO...
?!

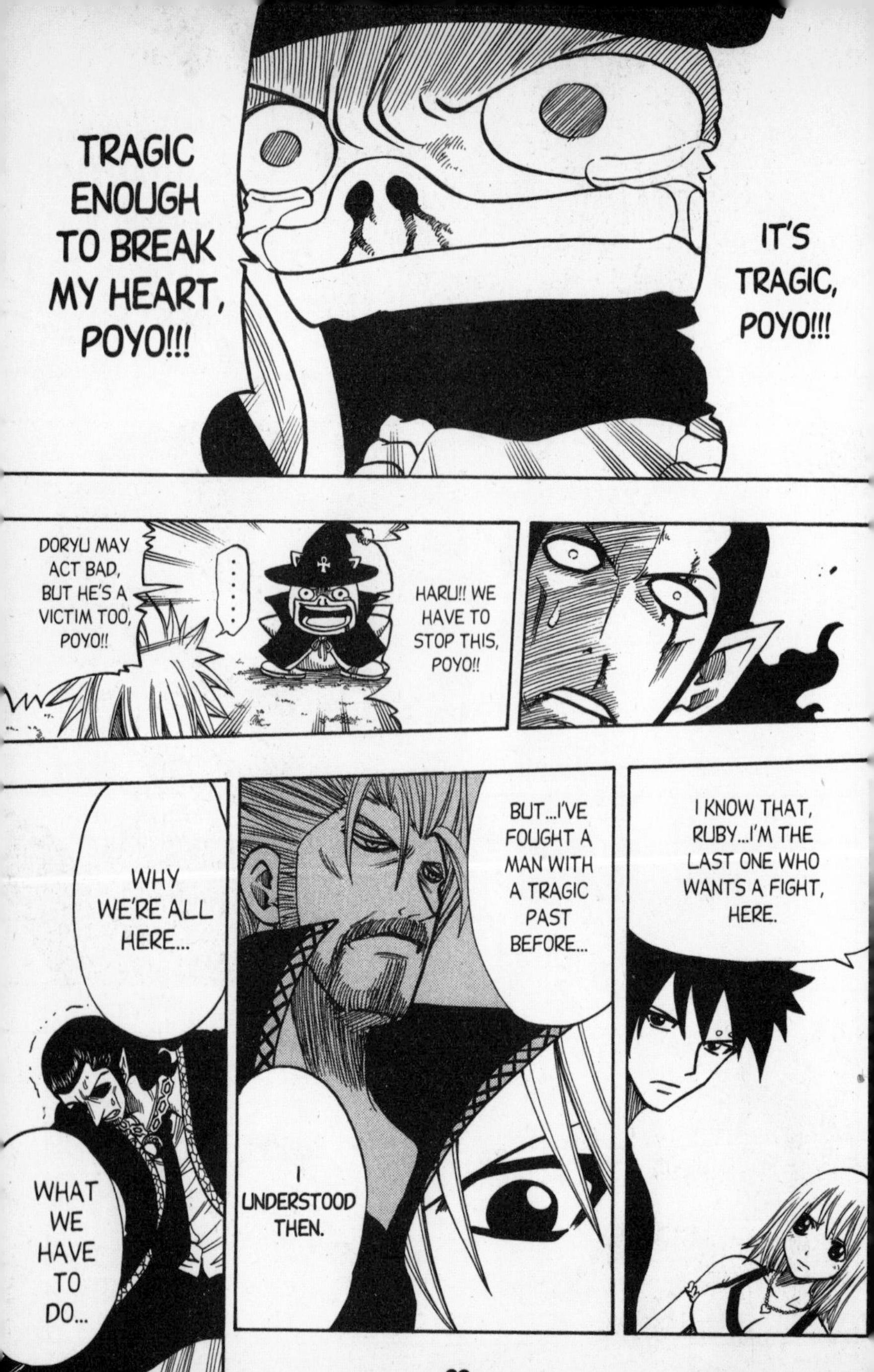
IT'S TRAGIC, POYO!!!
TRAGIC ENOUGH TO BREAK MY HEART, POYO!!!
HARU!! WE HAVE TO STOP THIS, POYO!!
......
DORYU MAY ACT BAD, BUT HE'S A VICTIM TOO, POYO!!
I KNOW THAT, RUBY...I'M THE LAST ONE WHO WANTS A FIGHT, HERE.
BUT...I'VE FOUGHT A MAN WITH A TRAGIC PAST BEFORE...
I UNDERSTOOD THEN.
WHY WE'RE ALL HERE...
WHAT WE HAVE TO DO...

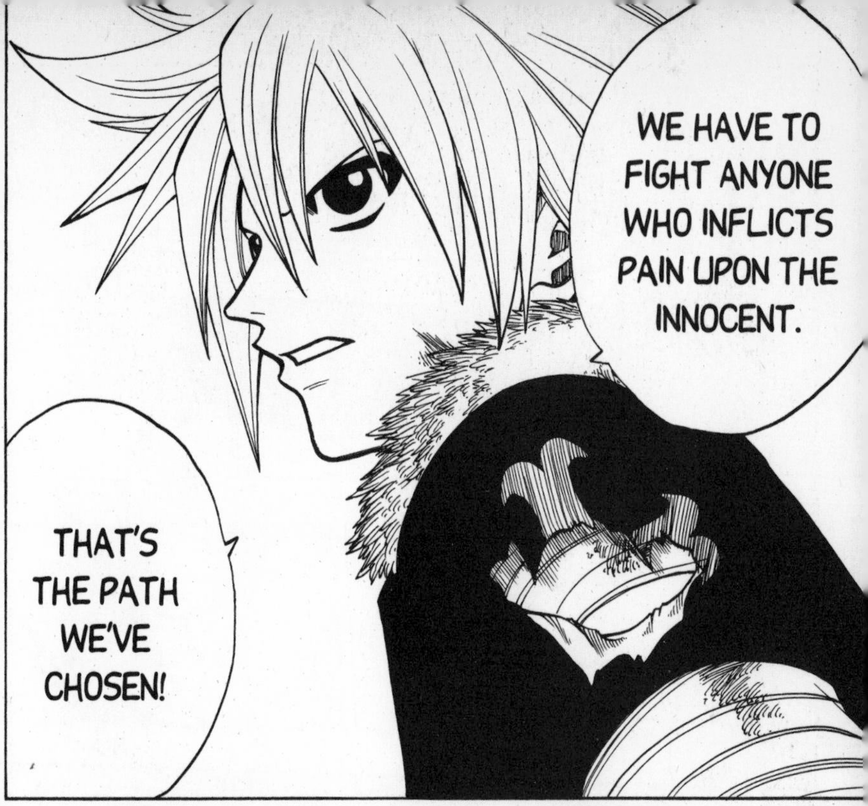
WE HAVE TO FIGHT ANYONE WHO INFLICTS PAIN UPON THE INNOCENT.
THAT'S THE PATH WE'VE CHOSEN!

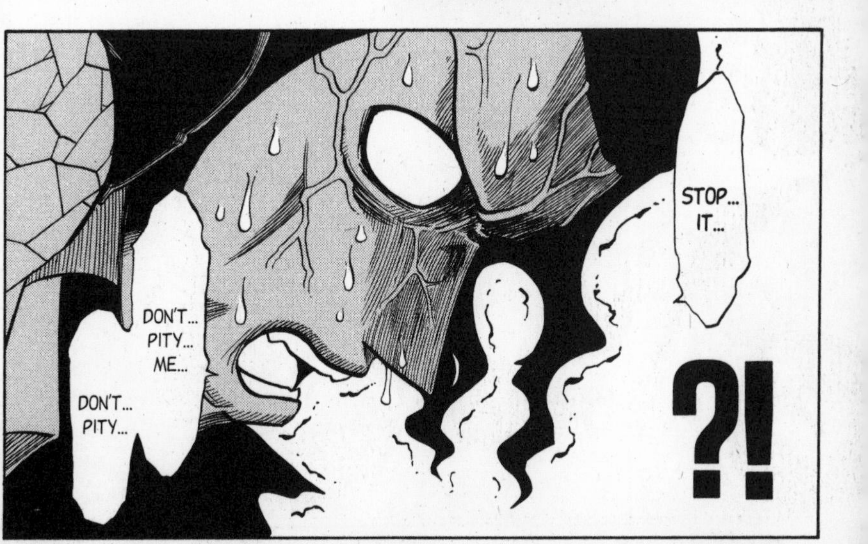
STOP... IT...
?!
DON'T... PITY... ME...
DON'T... PITY...

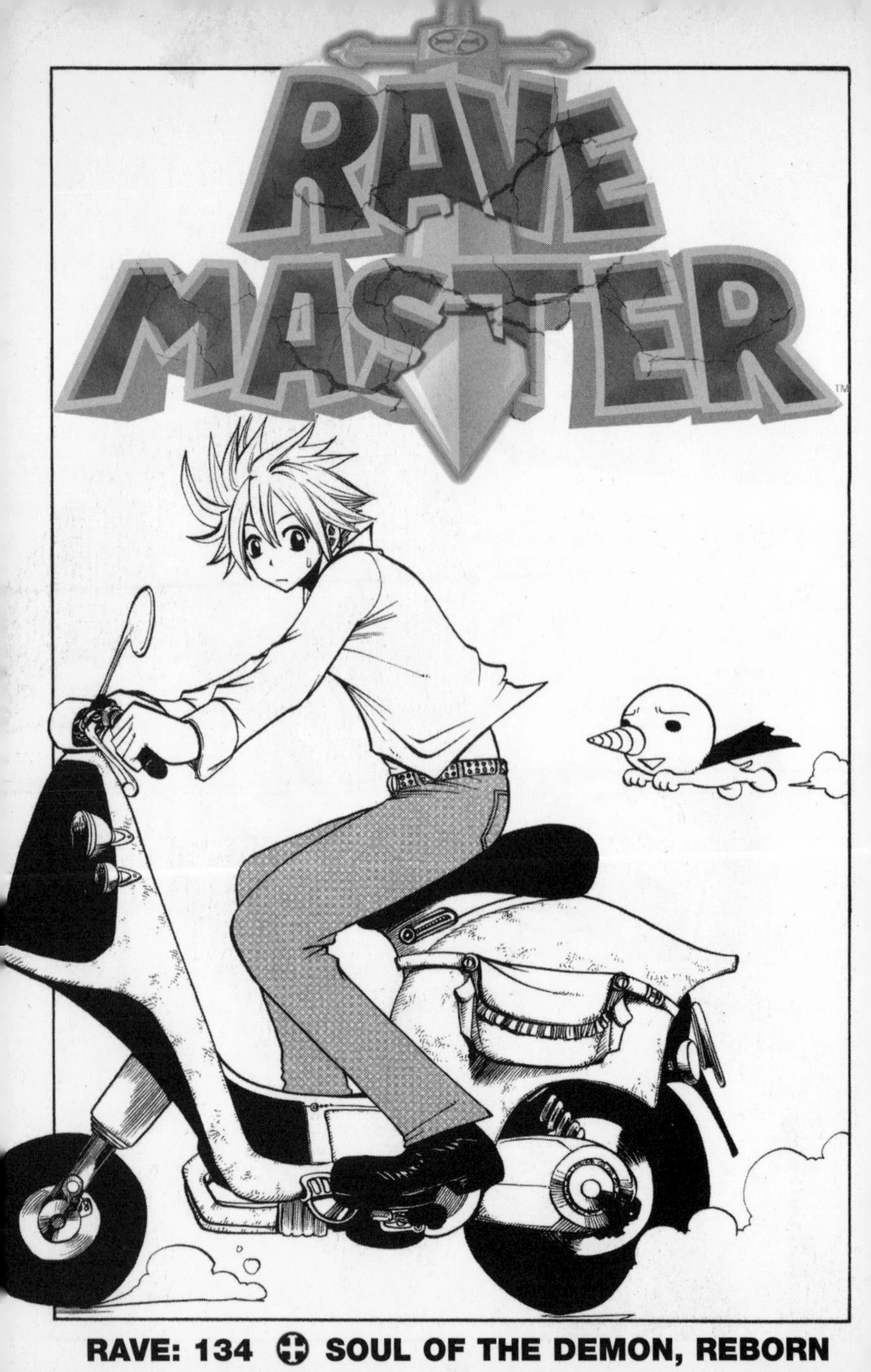
RAVE MASTER

RAVE: 134 ✠ SOUL OF THE DEMON, REBORN

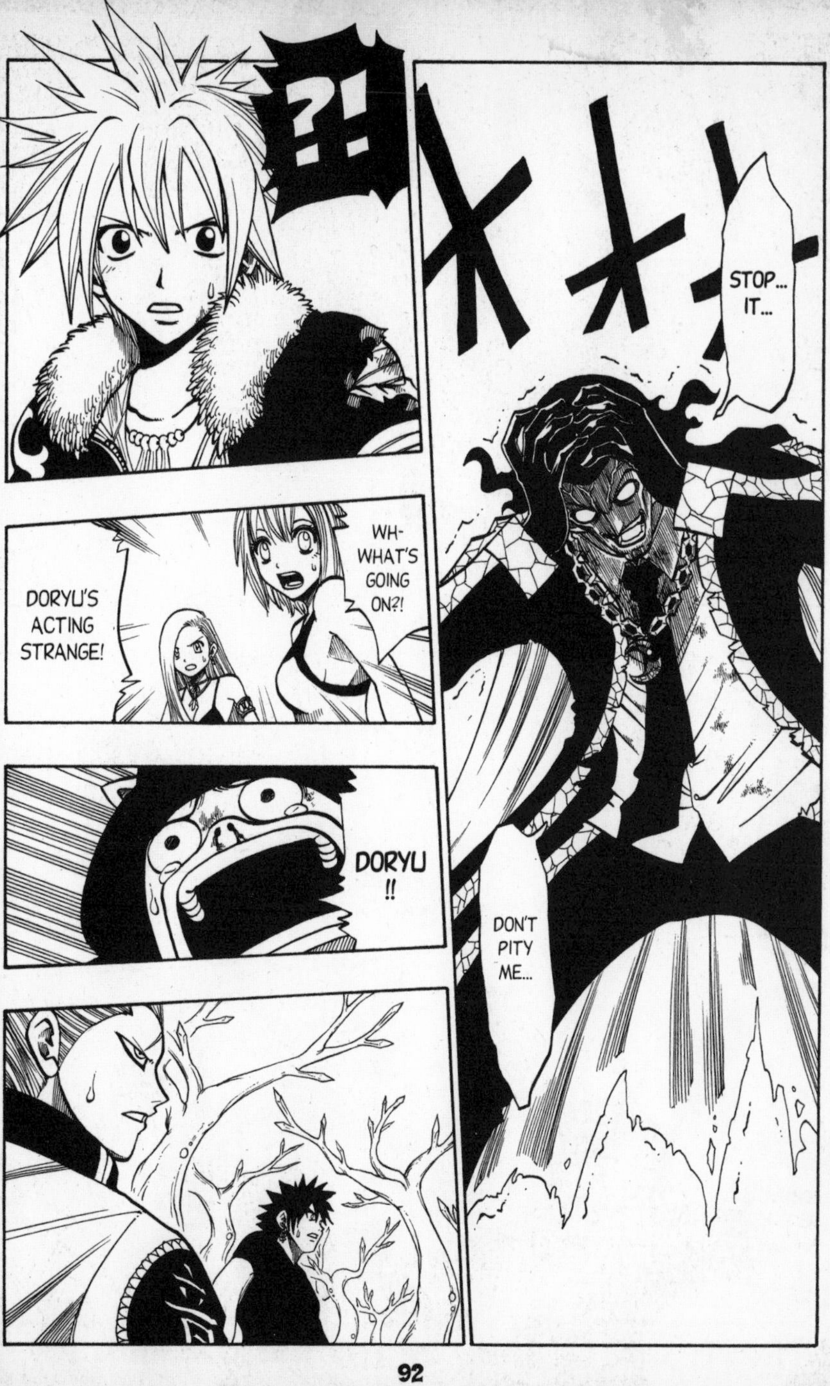
STOP... IT...
DON'T PITY ME...
?!
WH- WHAT'S GOING ON?!
DORYU'S ACTING STRANGE!
DORYU !!

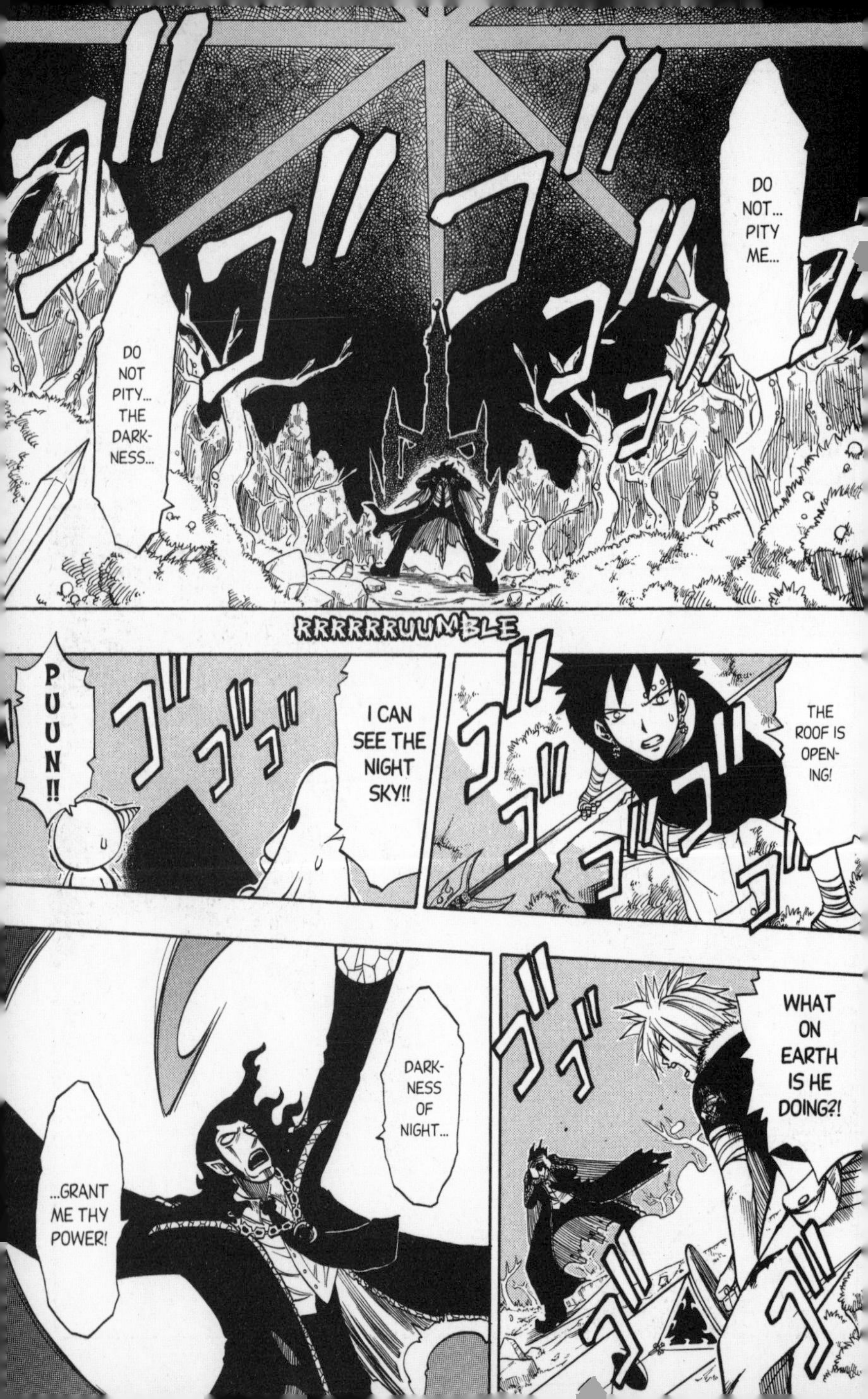
DO NOT... PITY ME...
DO NOT PITY... THE DARKNESS...
RRRRRRUUMBLE
THE ROOF IS OPENING!
I CAN SEE THE NIGHT SKY!!
PUUN!!
WHAT ON EARTH IS HE DOING?!
DARKNESS OF NIGHT...
...GRANT ME THY POWER!

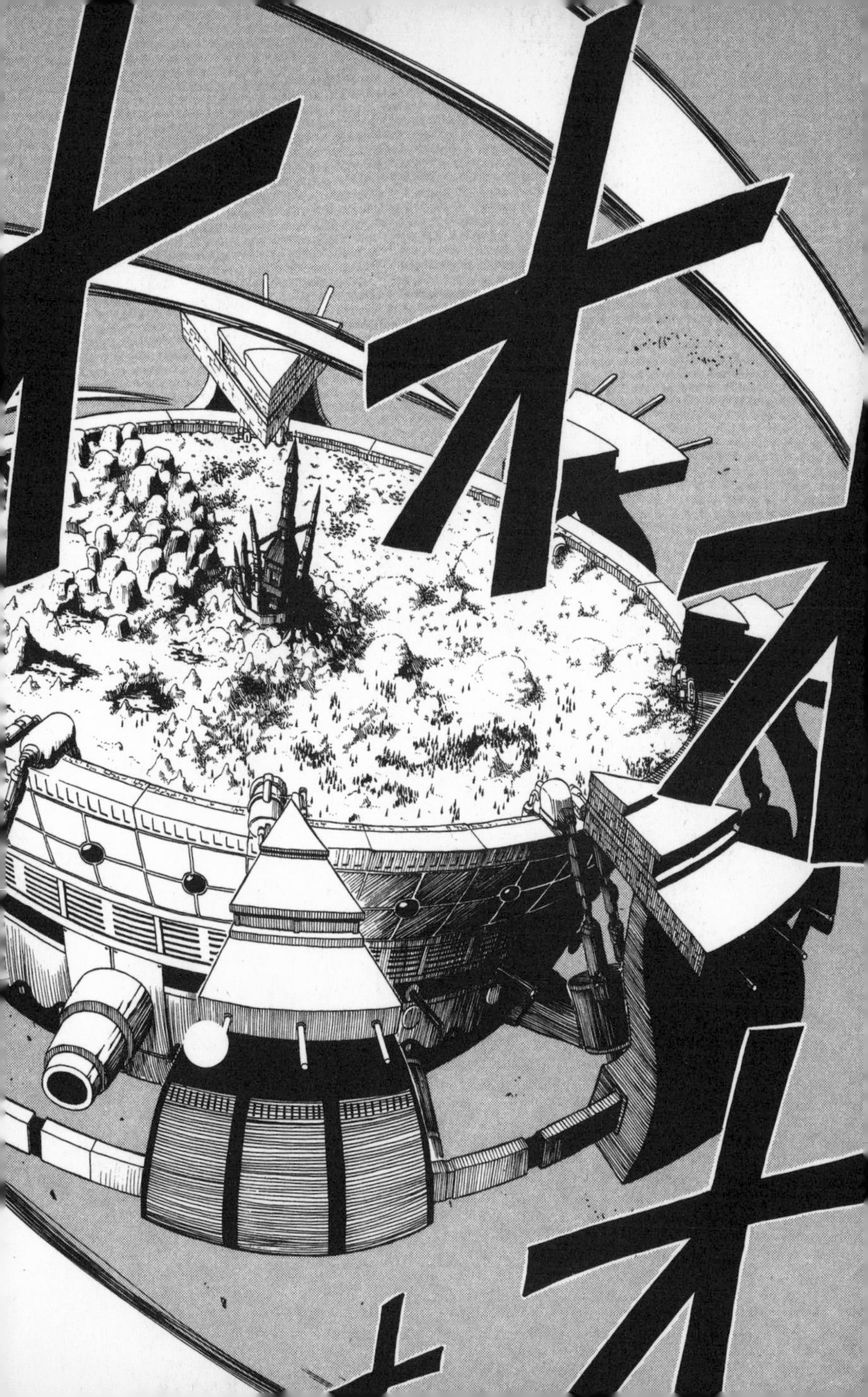

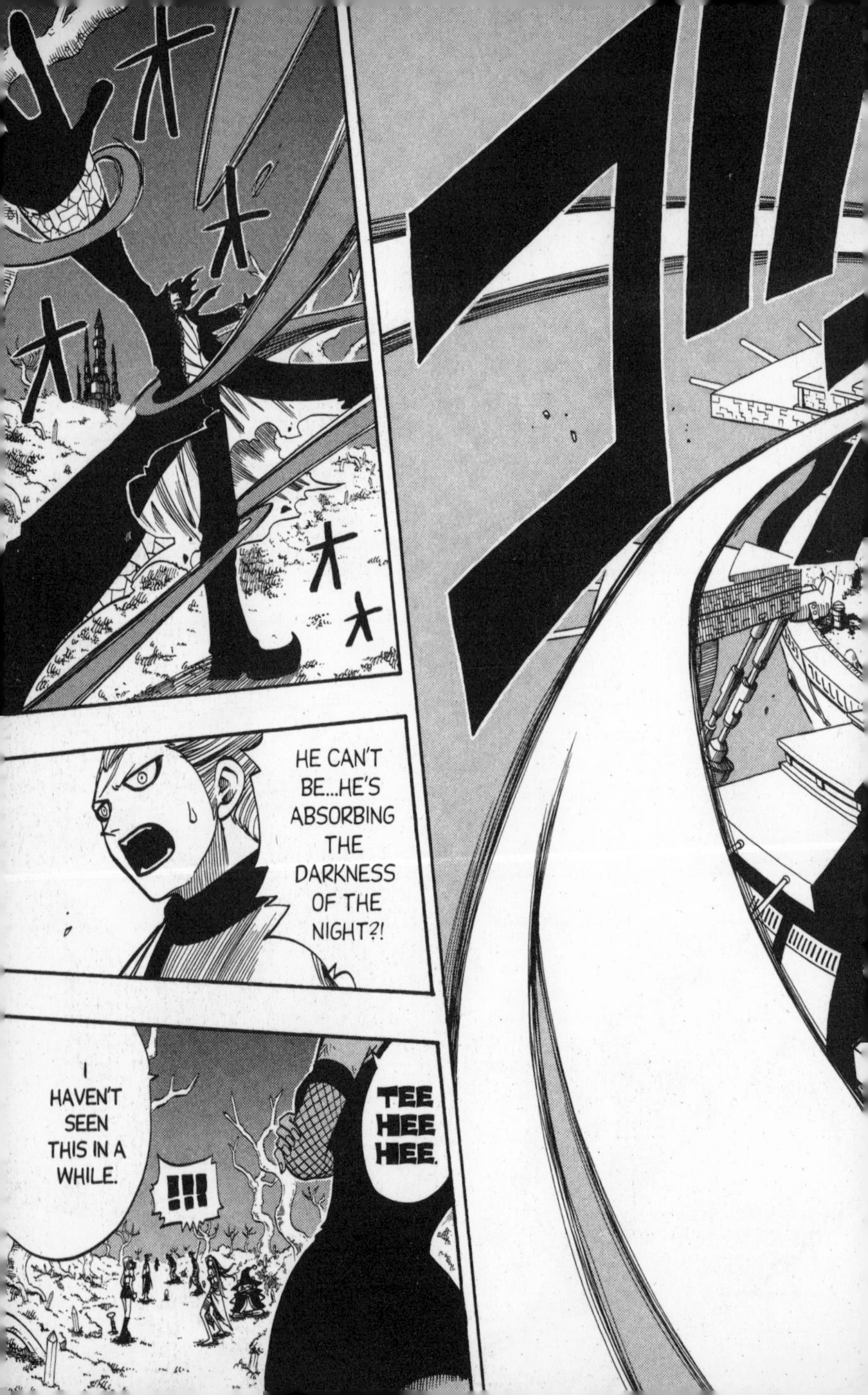
HE CAN'T BE...HE'S ABSORBING THE DARKNESS OF THE NIGHT?!
TEE HEE HEE.
I HAVEN'T SEEN THIS IN A WHILE.
!!!

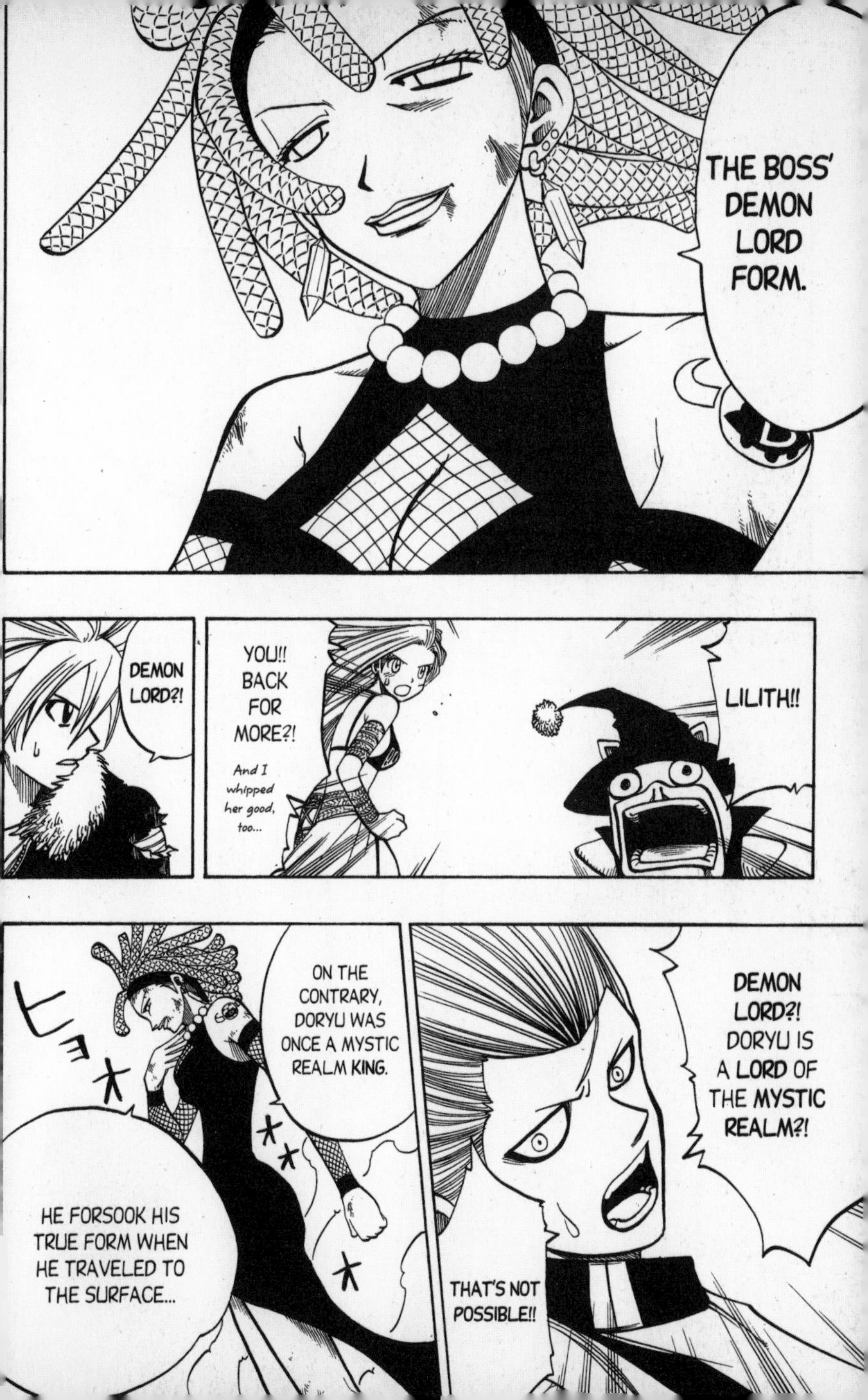
THE BOSS' DEMON LORD FORM.
LILITH!!
YOU!! BACK FOR MORE?!
And I whipped her good, too...
DEMON LORD?!
DEMON LORD?! DORYU IS A LORD OF THE MYSTIC REALM?!
THAT'S NOT POSSIBLE!!
ON THE CONTRARY, DORYU WAS ONCE A MYSTIC REALM KING.
HE FORSOOK HIS TRUE FORM WHEN HE TRAVELED TO THE SURFACE...

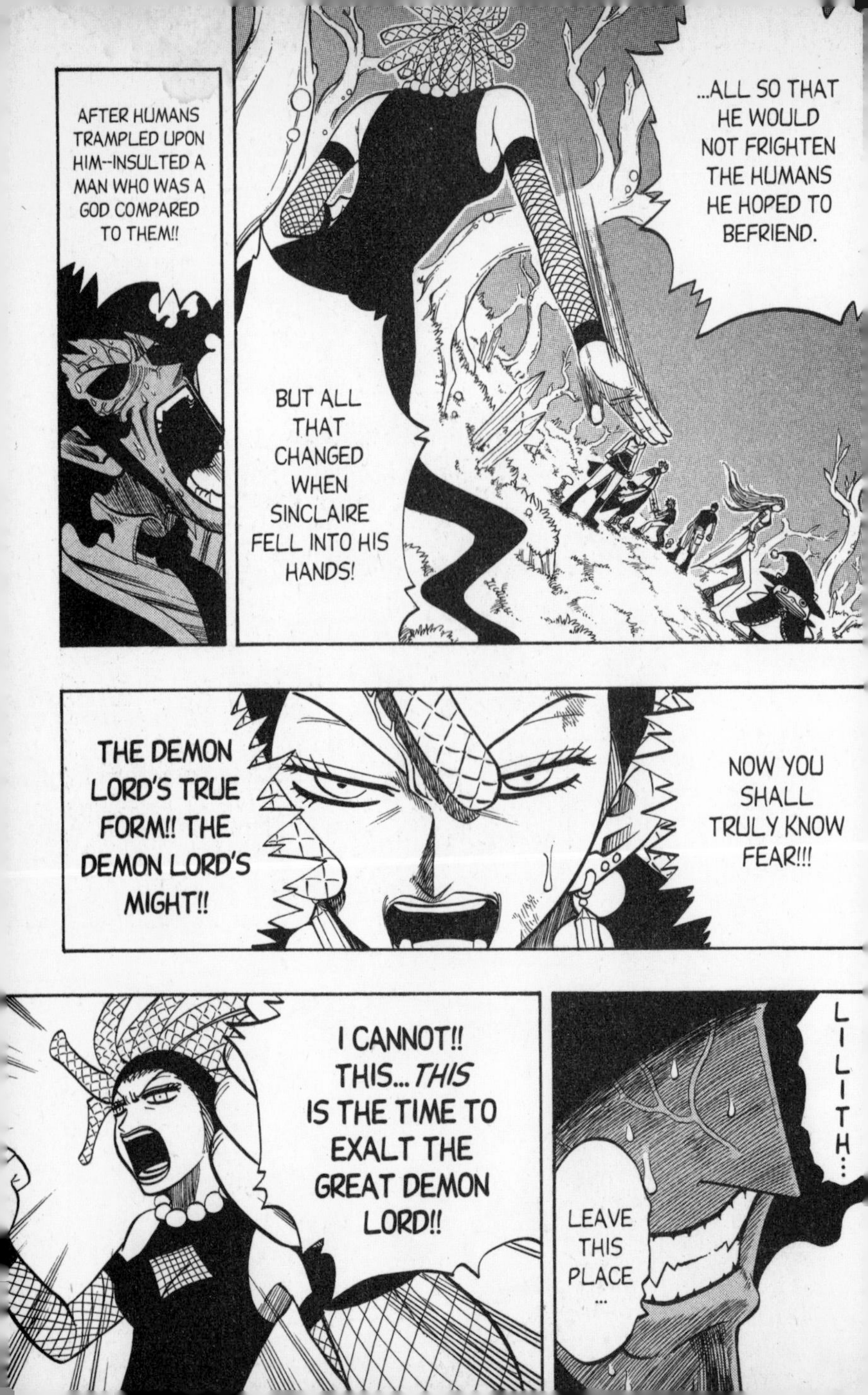
...ALL SO THAT HE WOULD NOT FRIGHTEN THE HUMANS HE HOPED TO BEFRIEND.
BUT ALL THAT CHANGED WHEN SINCLAIRE FELL INTO HIS HANDS!
AFTER HUMANS TRAMPLED UPON HIM--INSULTED A MAN WHO WAS A GOD COMPARED TO THEM!!
NOW YOU SHALL TRULY KNOW FEAR!!!
THE DEMON LORD'S TRUE FORM!! THE DEMON LORD'S MIGHT!!
LILITH...
LEAVE THIS PLACE...
I CANNOT!! THIS...*THIS* IS THE TIME TO EXALT THE GREAT DEMON LORD!!

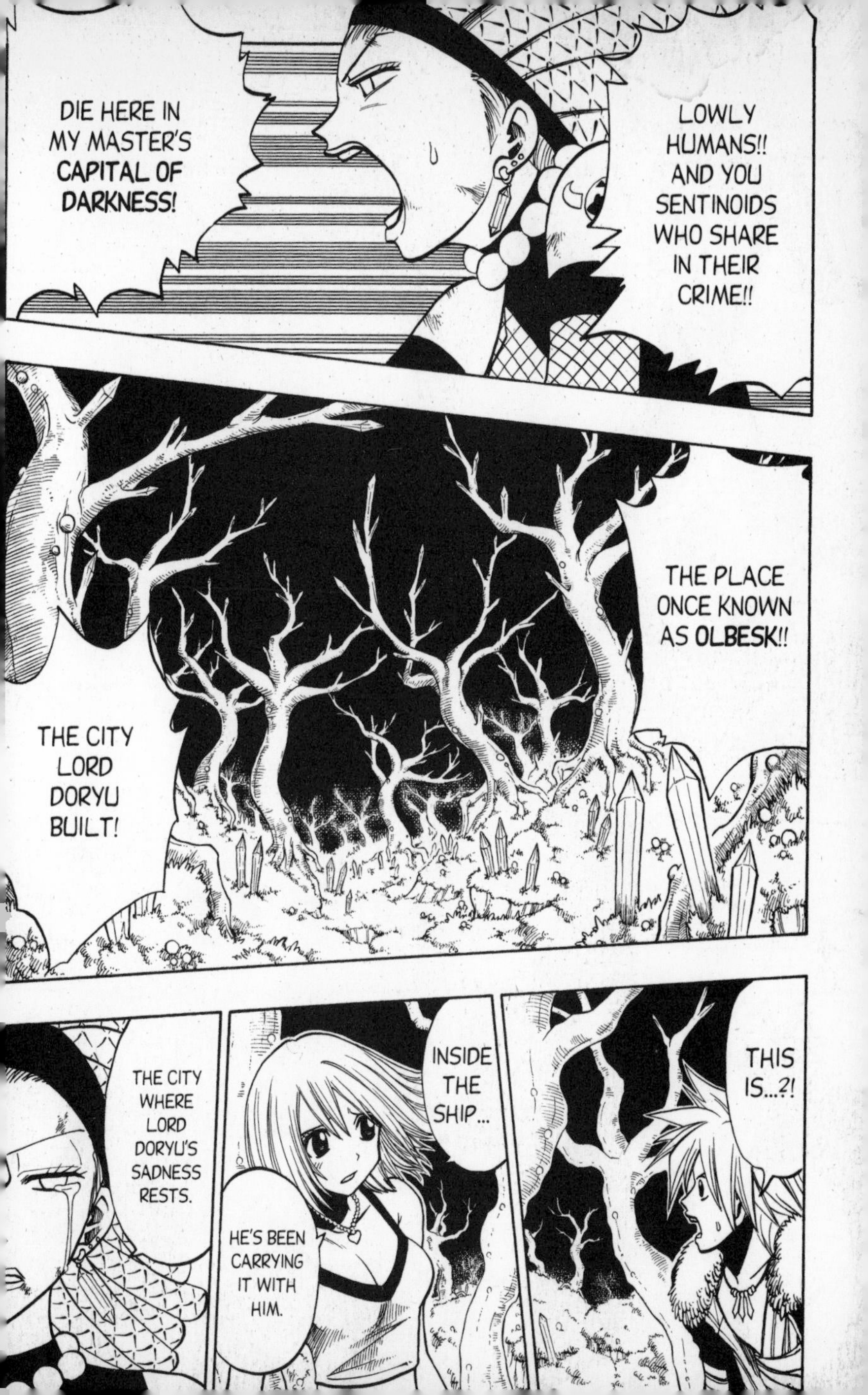
LOWLY HUMANS!! AND YOU SENTINOIDS WHO SHARE IN THEIR CRIME!!
DIE HERE IN MY MASTER'S CAPITAL OF DARKNESS!
THE PLACE ONCE KNOWN AS OLBESK!!
THE CITY LORD DORYU BUILT!
THIS IS...?!
INSIDE THE SHIP...
HE'S BEEN CARRYING IT WITH HIM.
THE CITY WHERE LORD DORYU'S SADNESS RESTS.

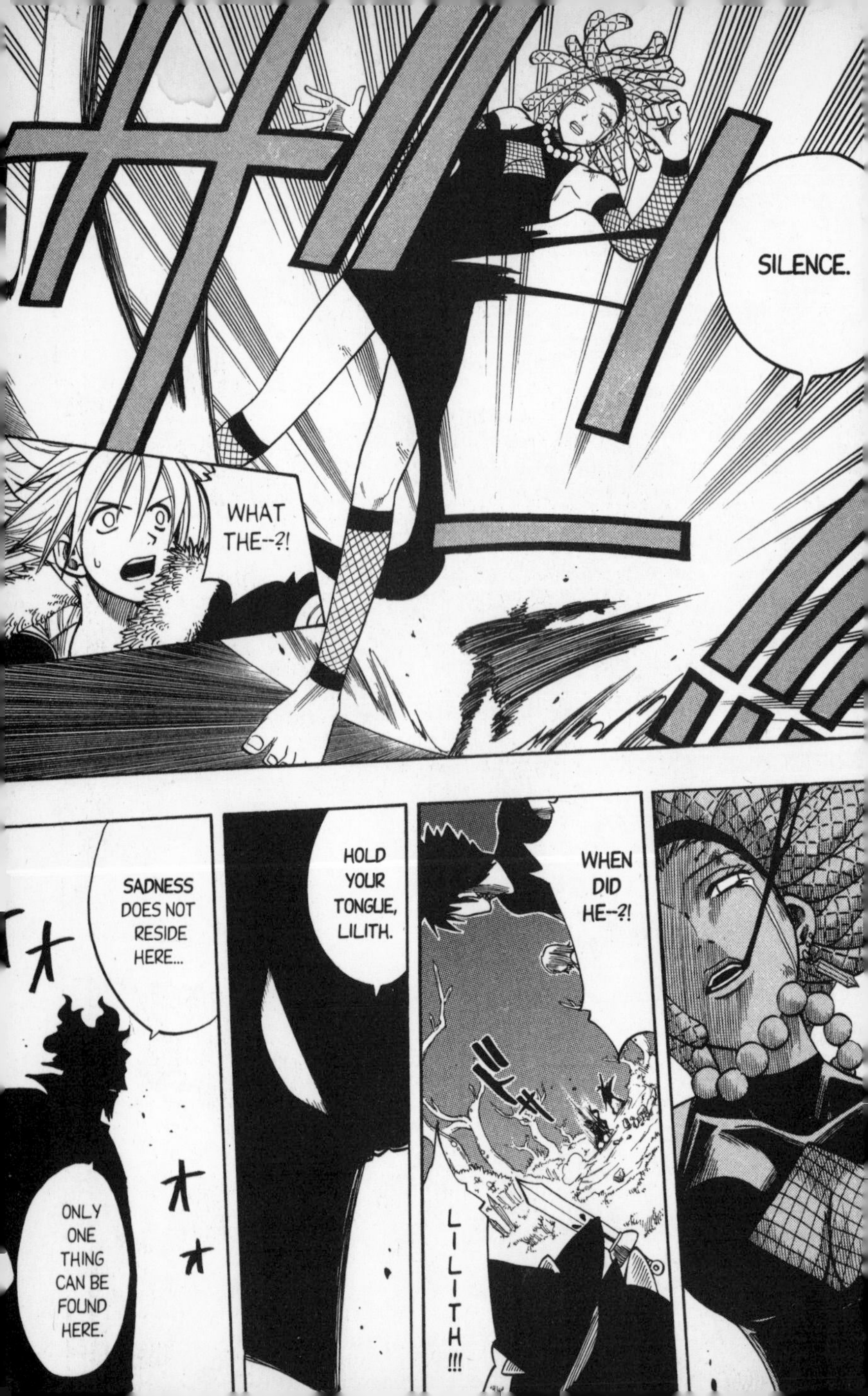
SILENCE.
WHAT THE--?!
WHEN DID HE--?!
LILITH!!!
HOLD YOUR TONGUE, LILITH.
SADNESS DOES NOT RESIDE HERE...
ONLY ONE THING CAN BE FOUND HERE.

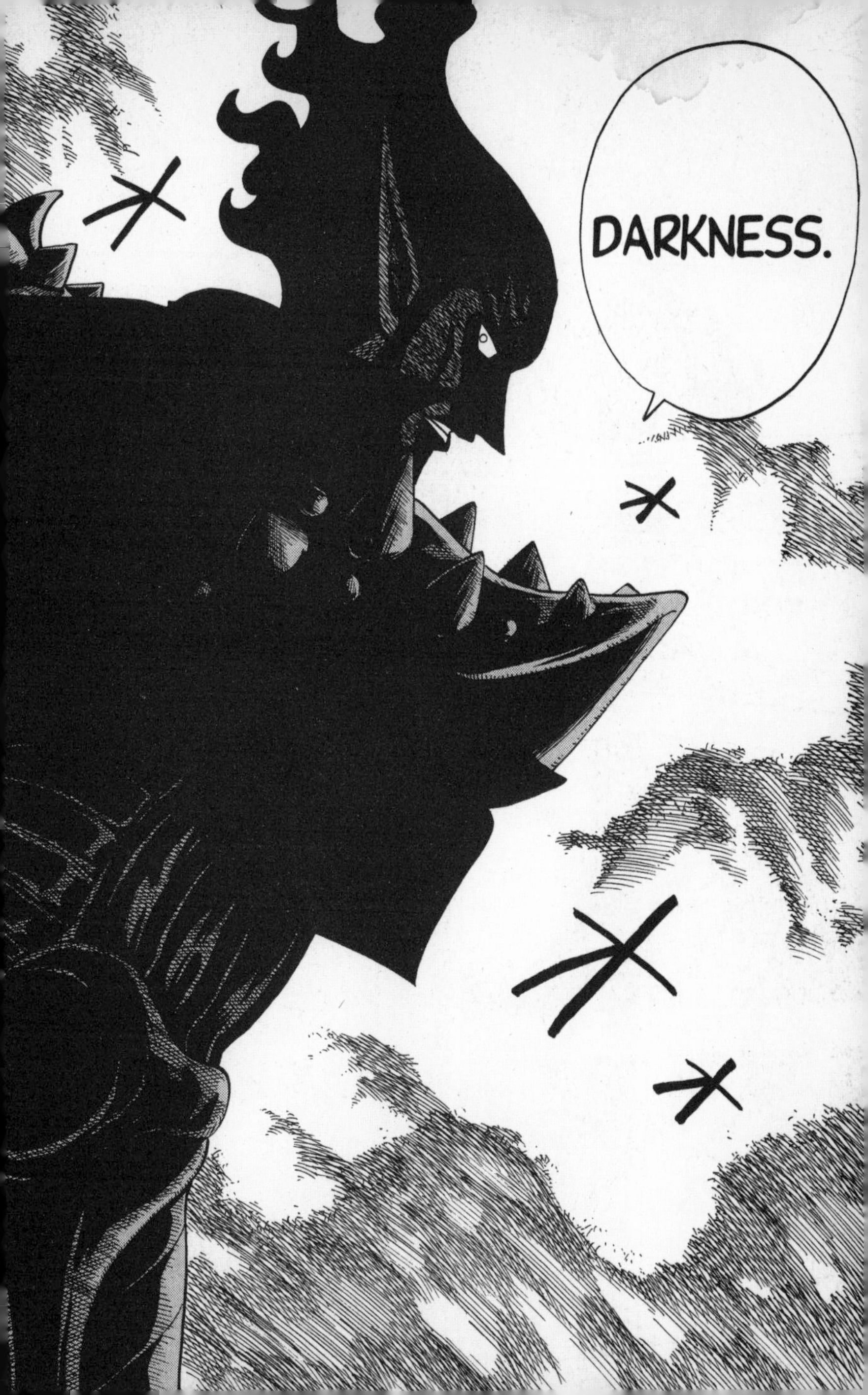
DARKNESS.

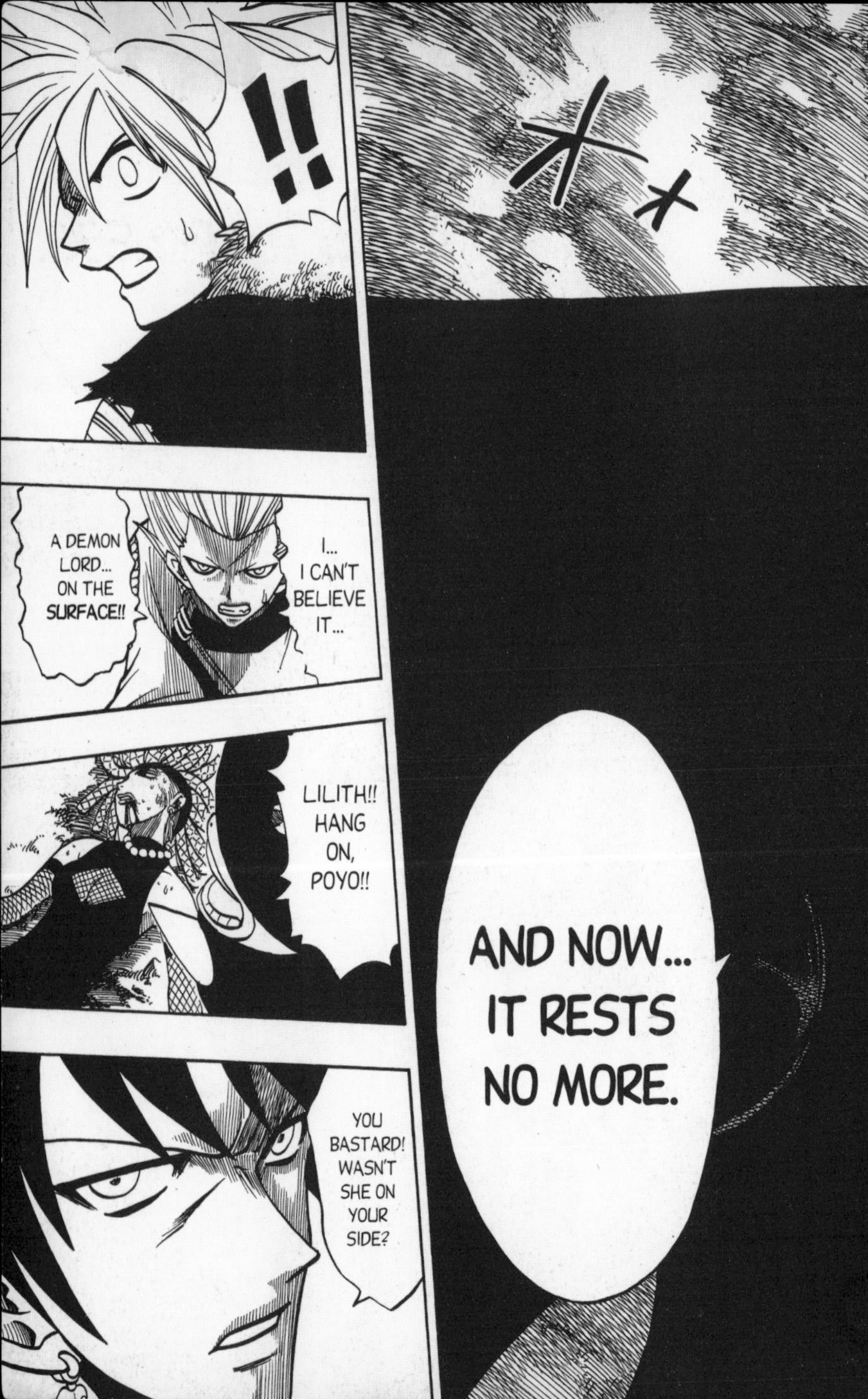
AND NOW... IT RESTS NO MORE.
!!
I... I CAN'T BELIEVE IT...
A DEMON LORD... ON THE SURFACE!!
LILITH!! HANG ON, POYO!!
YOU BASTARD! WASN'T SHE ON YOUR SIDE?

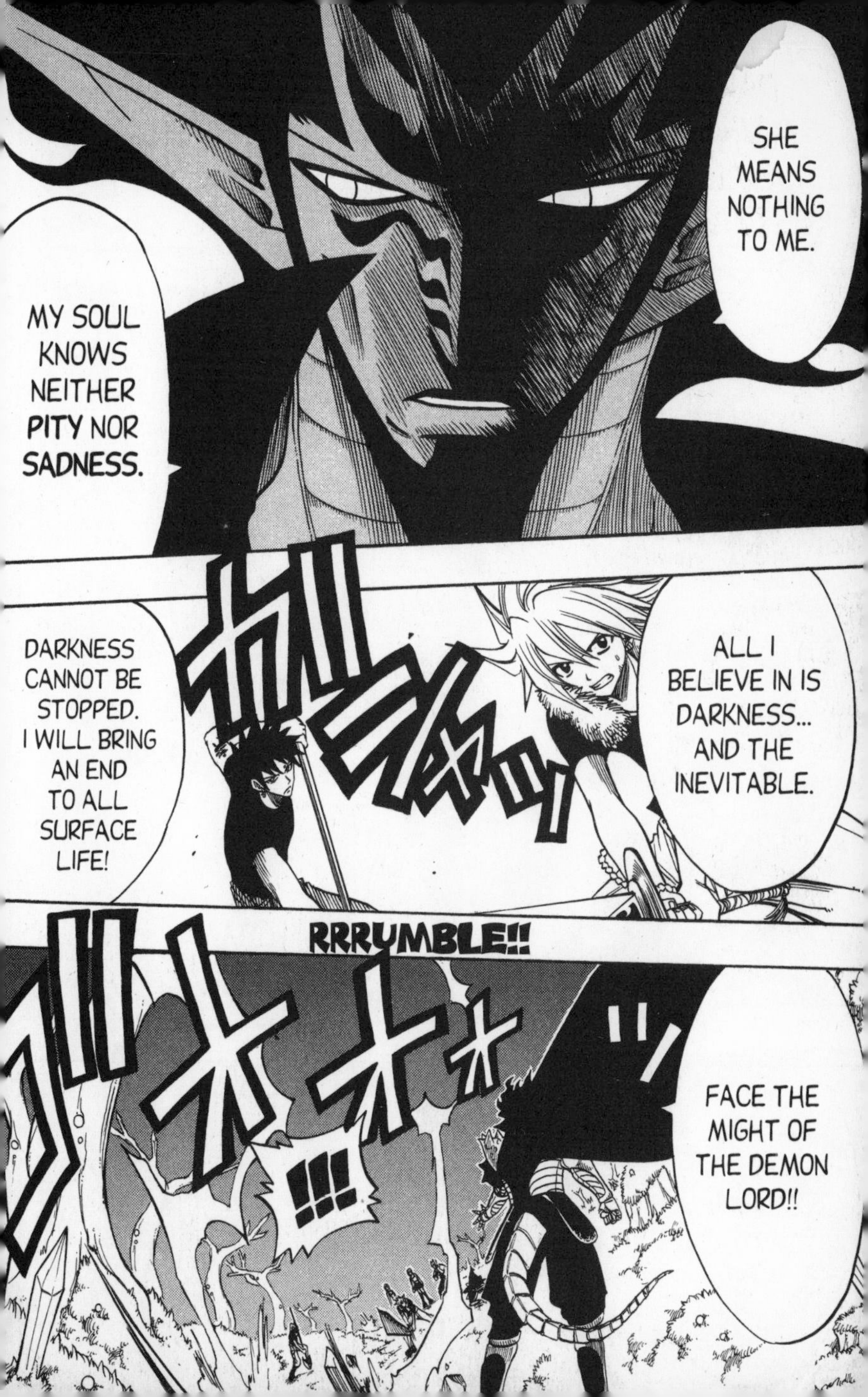
SHE MEANS NOTHING TO ME.
MY SOUL KNOWS NEITHER PITY NOR SADNESS.
ALL I BELIEVE IN IS DARKNESS... AND THE INEVITABLE.
DARKNESS CANNOT BE STOPPED. I WILL BRING AN END TO ALL SURFACE LIFE!
RRRUMBLE!!
FACE THE MIGHT OF THE DEMON LORD!!
!!!

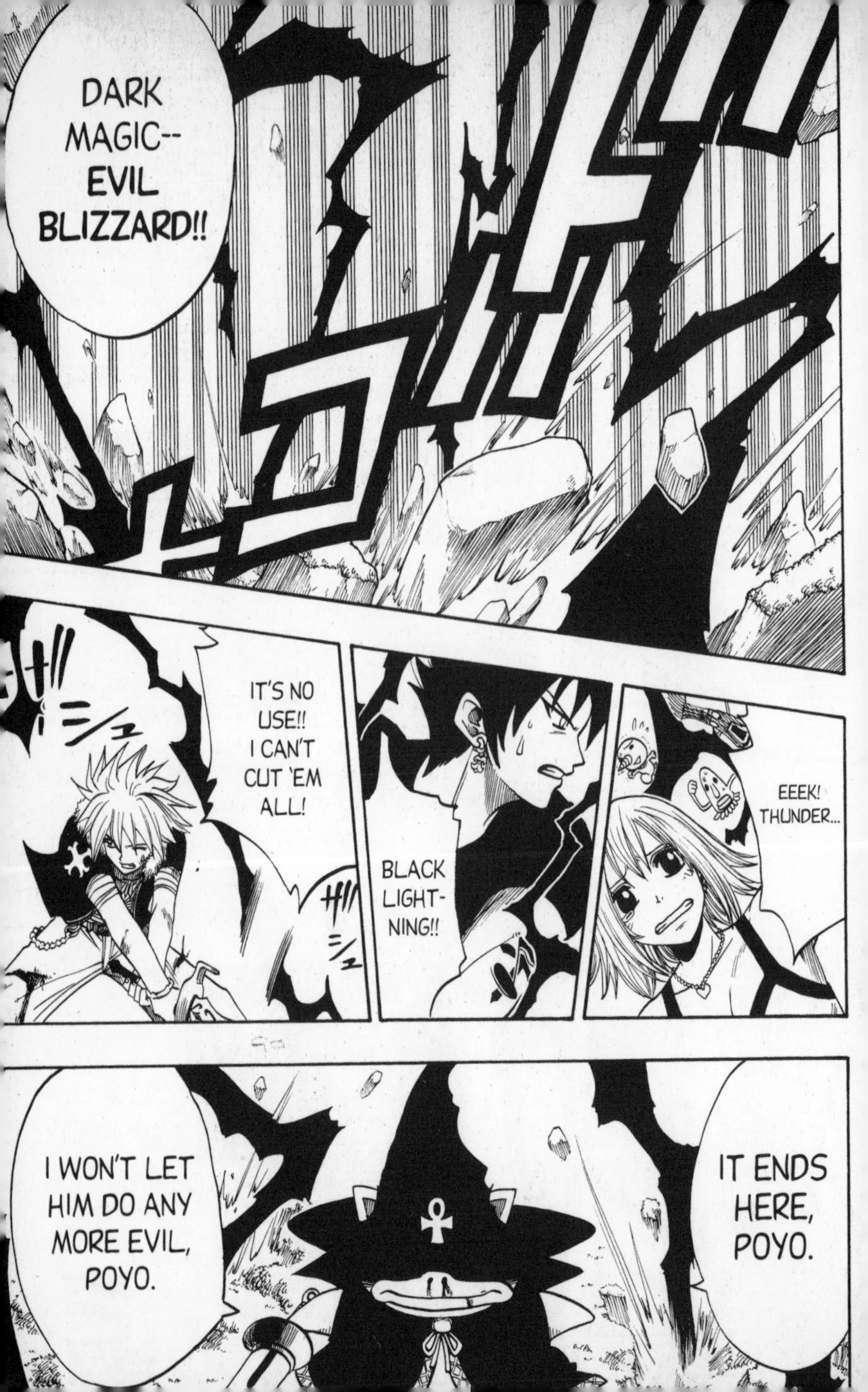
DARK MAGIC-- EVIL BLIZZARD!!
EEEK! THUNDER...
BLACK LIGHT-NING!!
IT'S NO USE!! I CAN'T CUT 'EM ALL!
IT ENDS HERE, POYO.
I WON'T LET HIM DO ANY MORE EVIL, POYO.

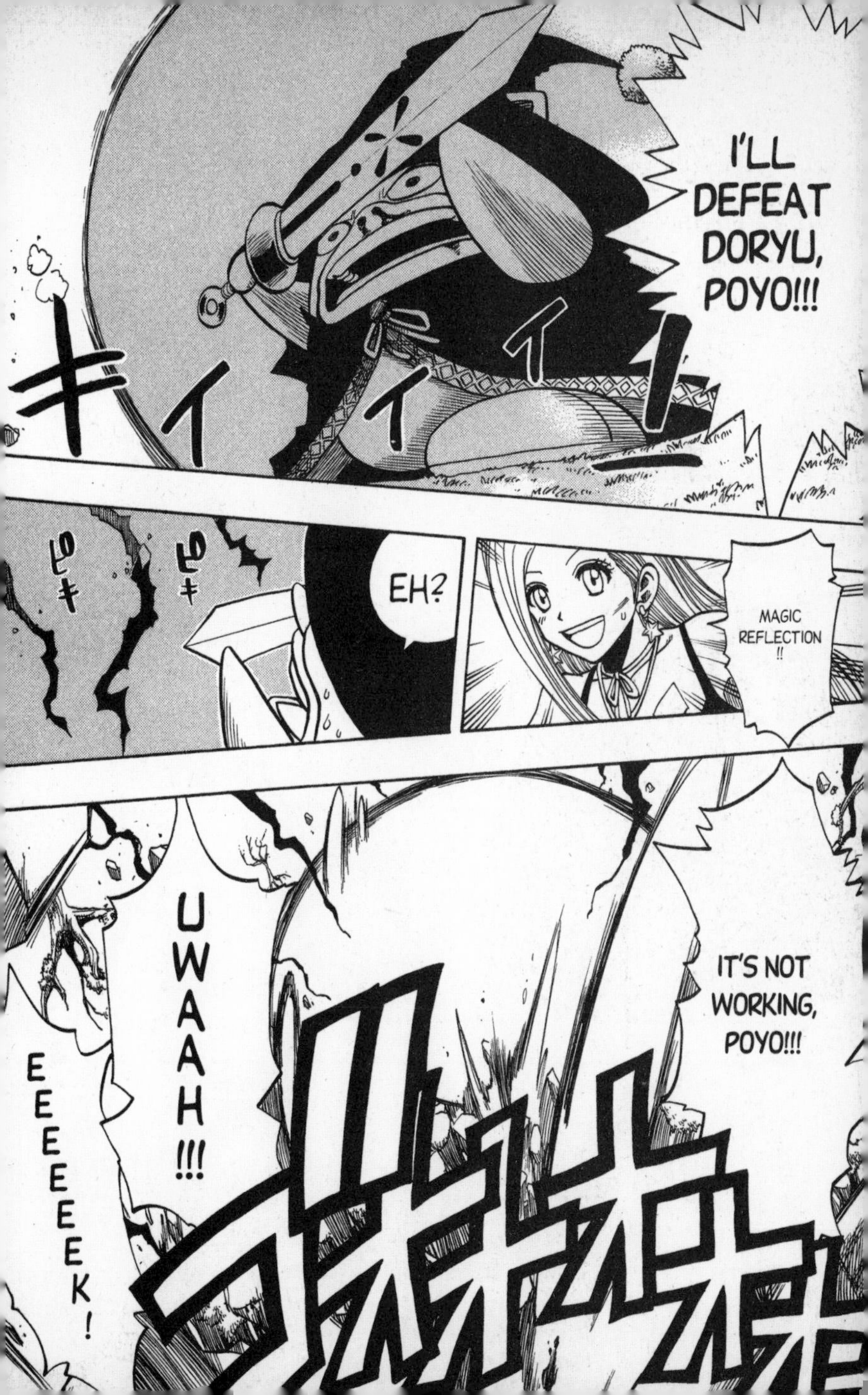
I'LL DEFEAT DORYU, POYO!!!
キイイイー
MAGIC REFLECTION !!
EH?
ピキ
ピキ
IT'S NOT WORKING, POYO!!!
UWAAH!!!
EEEEEEEK!

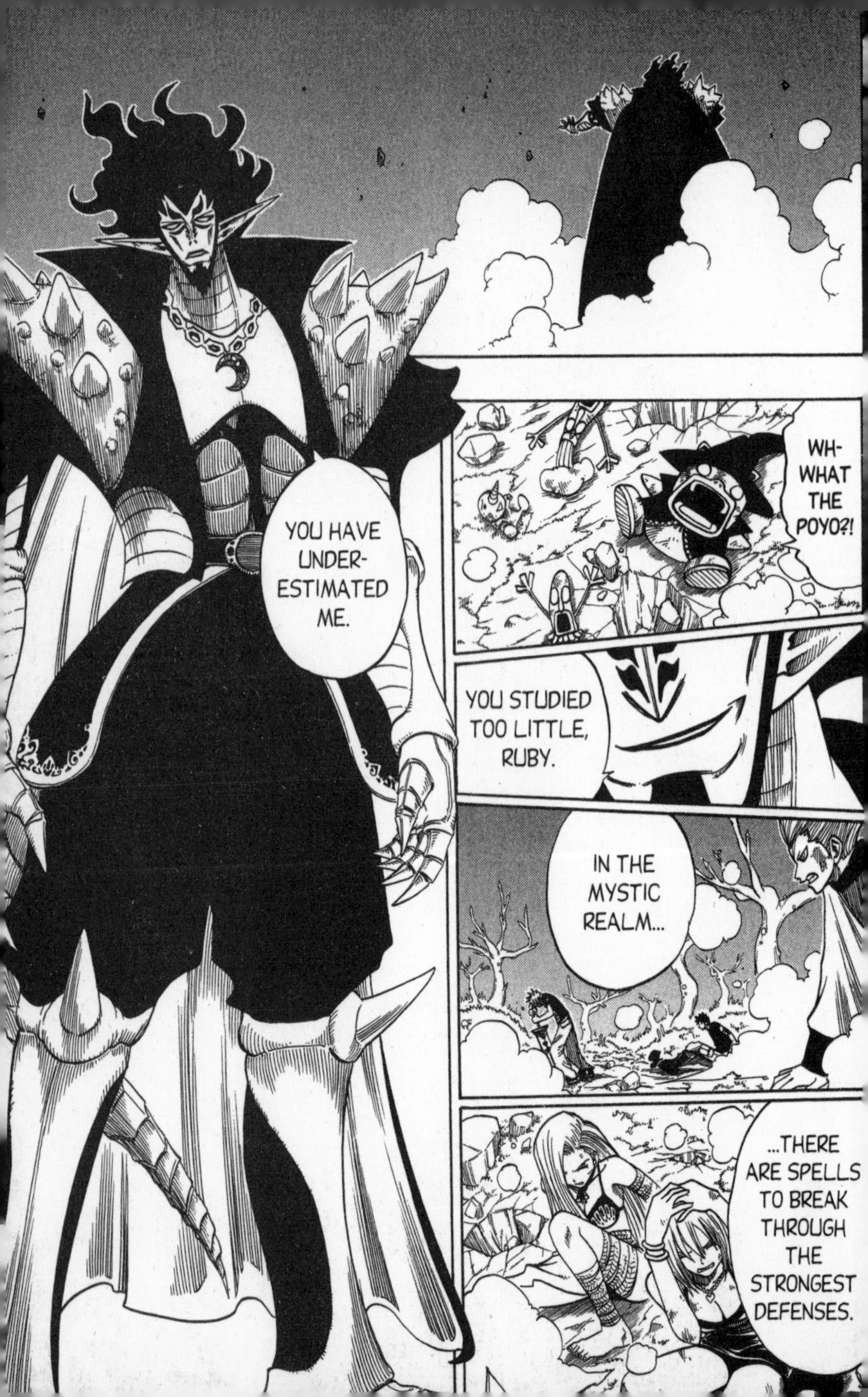
WH-WHAT THE POYO?!
YOU STUDIED TOO LITTLE, RUBY.
IN THE MYSTIC REALM...
...THERE ARE SPELLS TO BREAK THROUGH THE STRONGEST DEFENSES.
YOU HAVE UNDER-ESTIMATED ME.

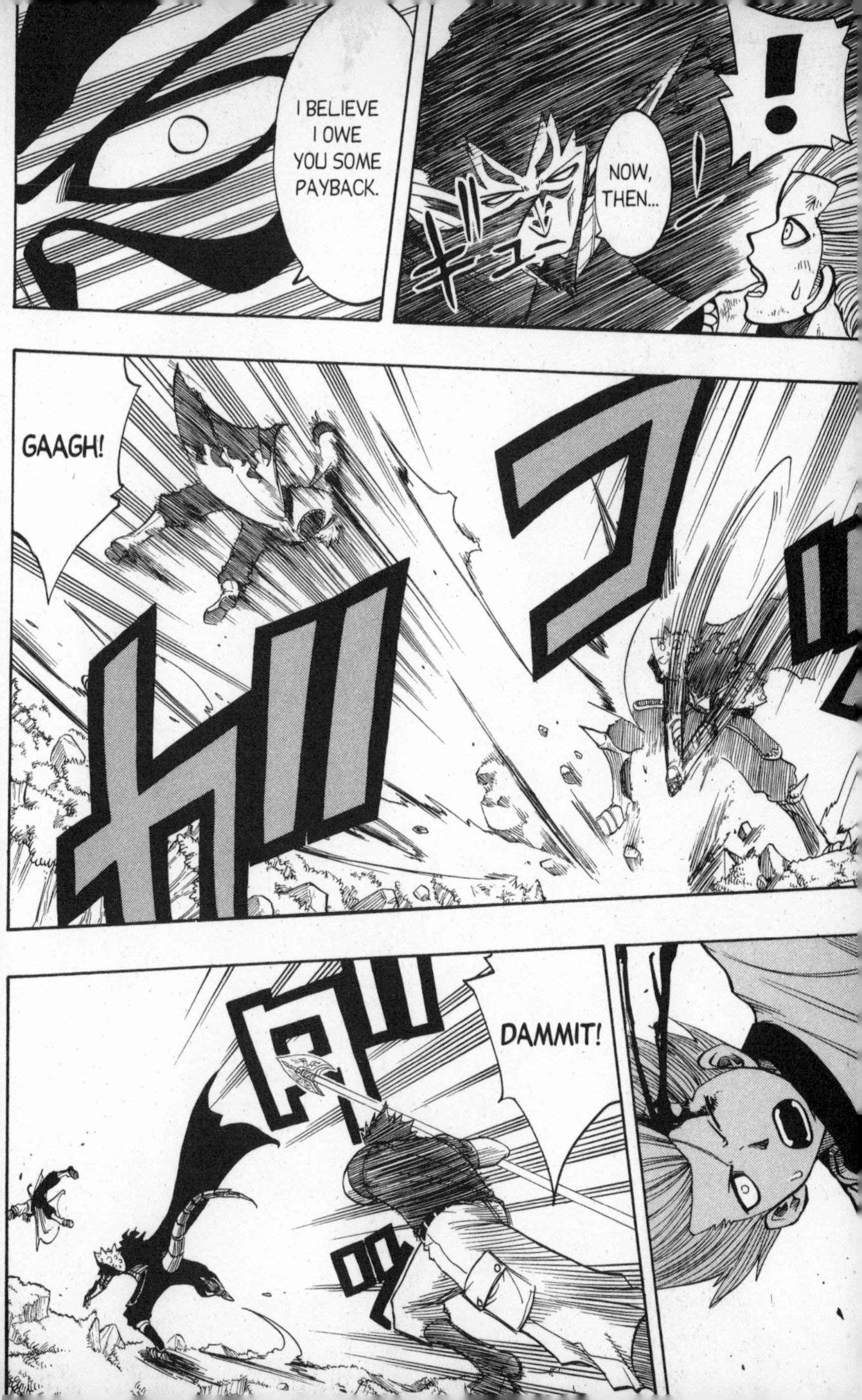
!
NOW, THEN...
I BELIEVE I OWE YOU SOME PAYBACK.
GAAGH!
DAMMIT!

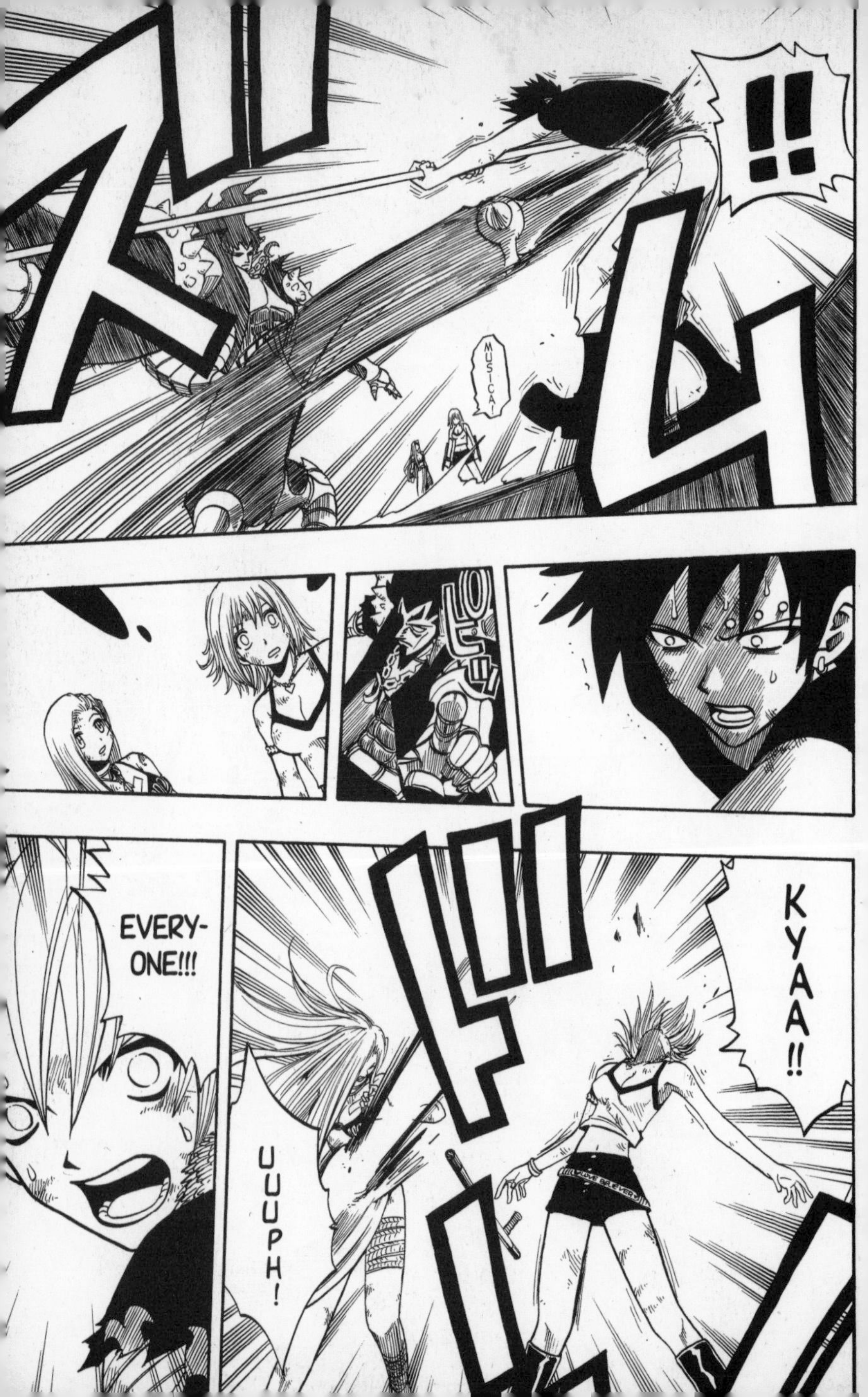
!!
MUSICA!
KYAA!!
UUUPH!
EVERY-ONE!!!

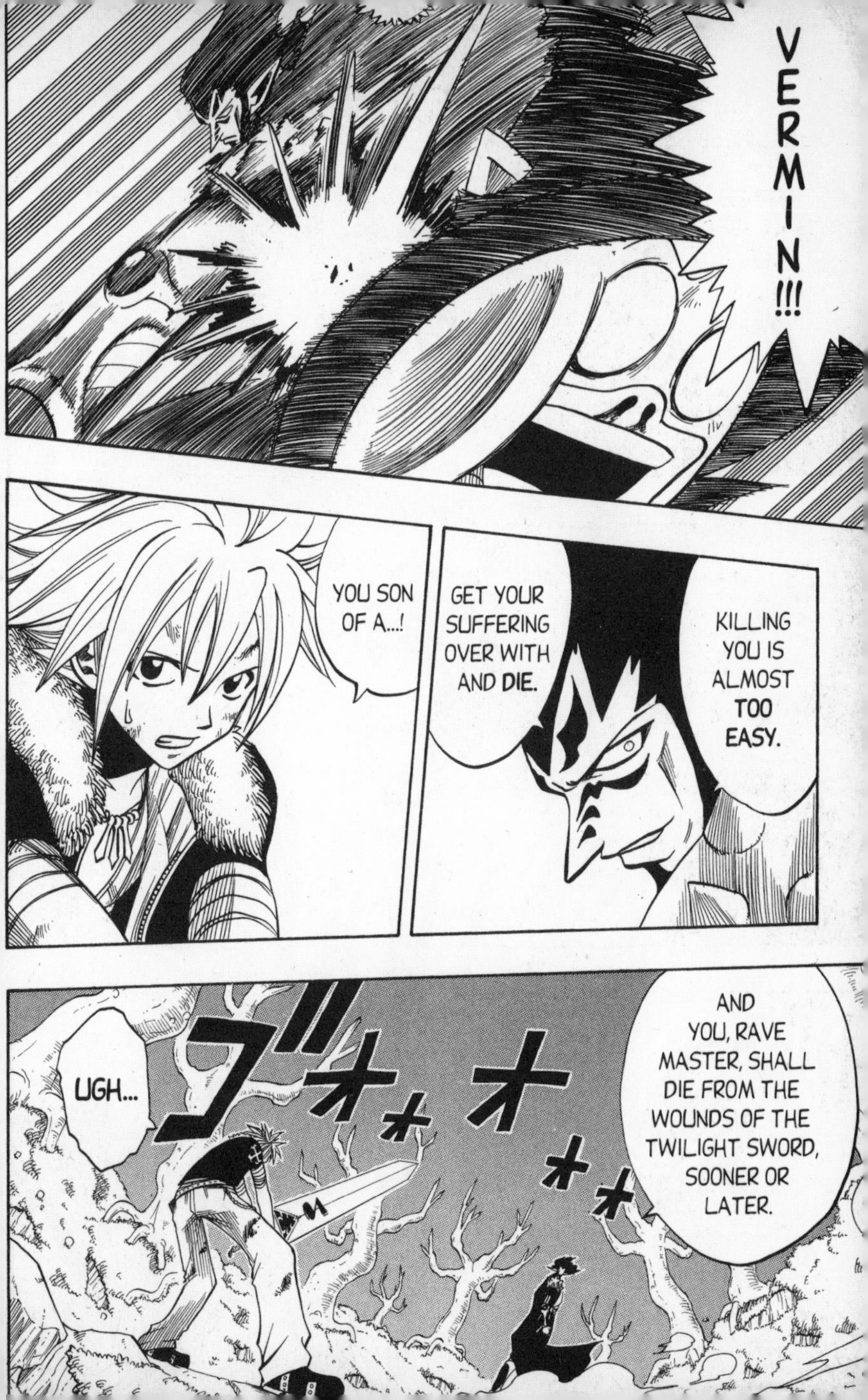
VERMIN!!!
KILLING YOU IS ALMOST TOO EASY.
GET YOUR SUFFERING OVER WITH AND DIE.
YOU SON OF A...!
AND YOU, RAVE MASTER, SHALL DIE FROM THE WOUNDS OF THE TWILIGHT SWORD, SOONER OR LATER.
ブオォオォォ
UGH...

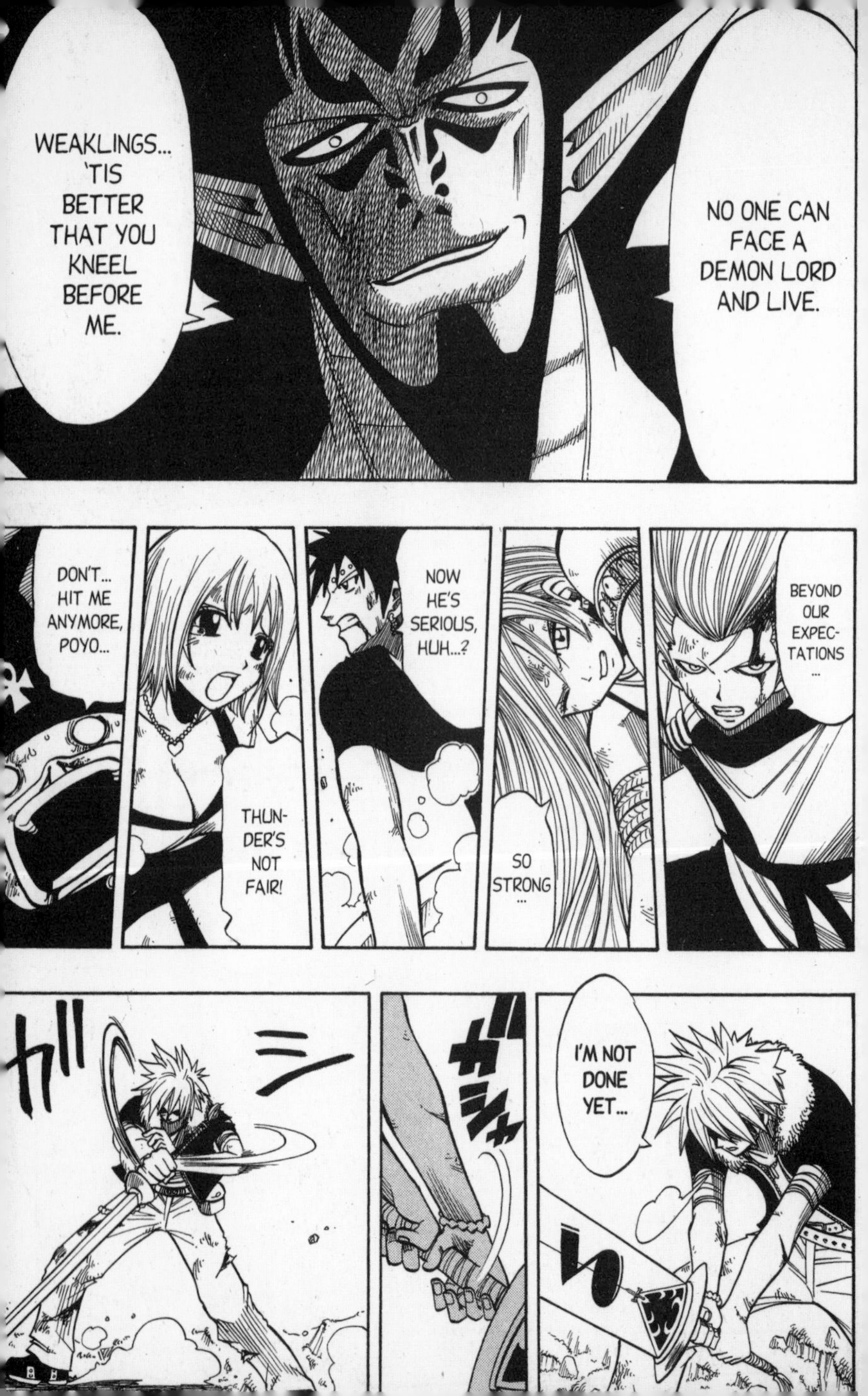
NO ONE CAN FACE A DEMON LORD AND LIVE.
WEAKLINGS... 'TIS BETTER THAT YOU KNEEL BEFORE ME.
BEYOND OUR EXPEC-TATIONS...
SO STRONG...
NOW HE'S SERIOUS, HUH...?
THUN-DER'S NOT FAIR!
DON'T... HIT ME ANYMORE, POYO...
I'M NOT DONE YET...

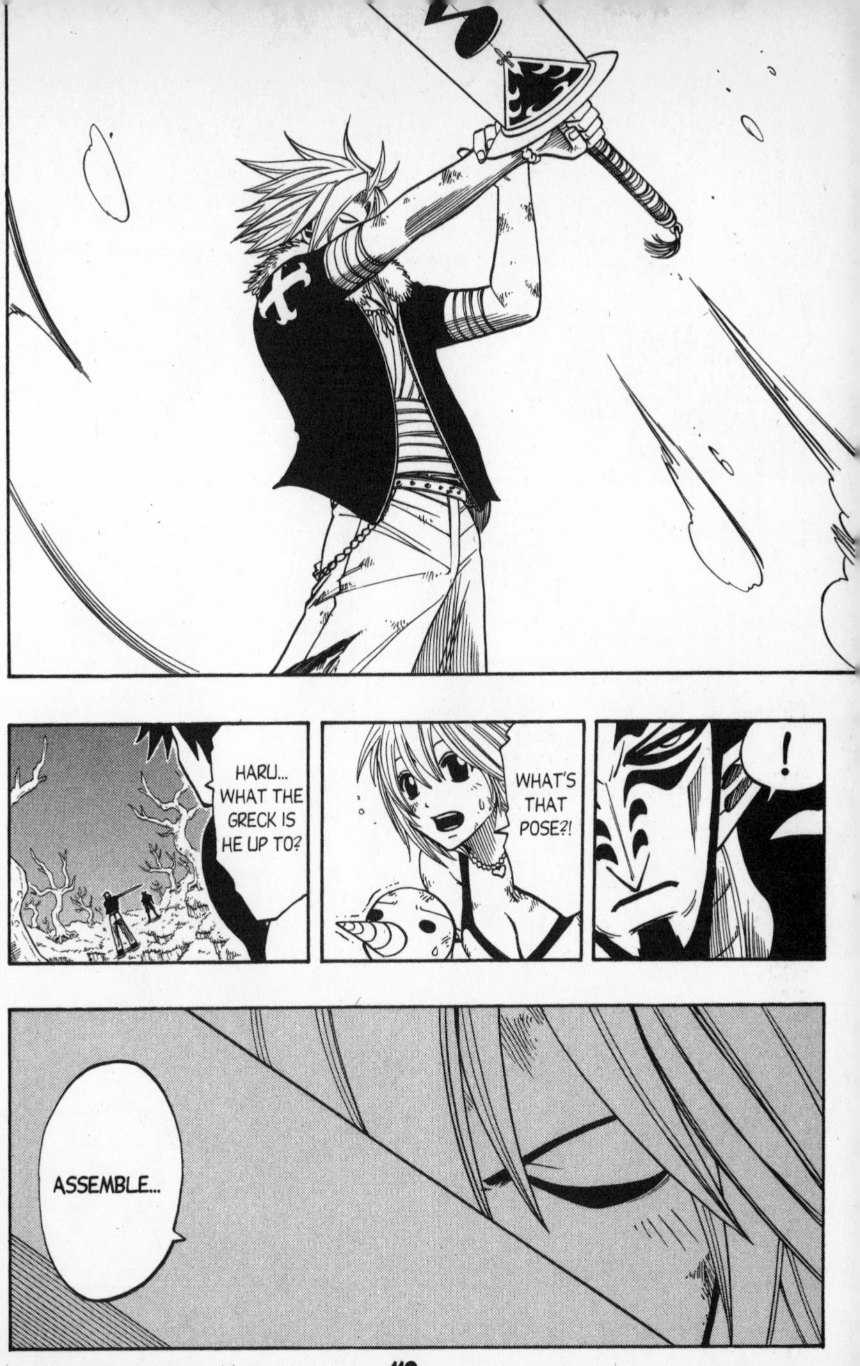
!
WHAT'S THAT POSE?!
HARU... WHAT THE GRECK IS HE UP TO?
ASSEMBLE...

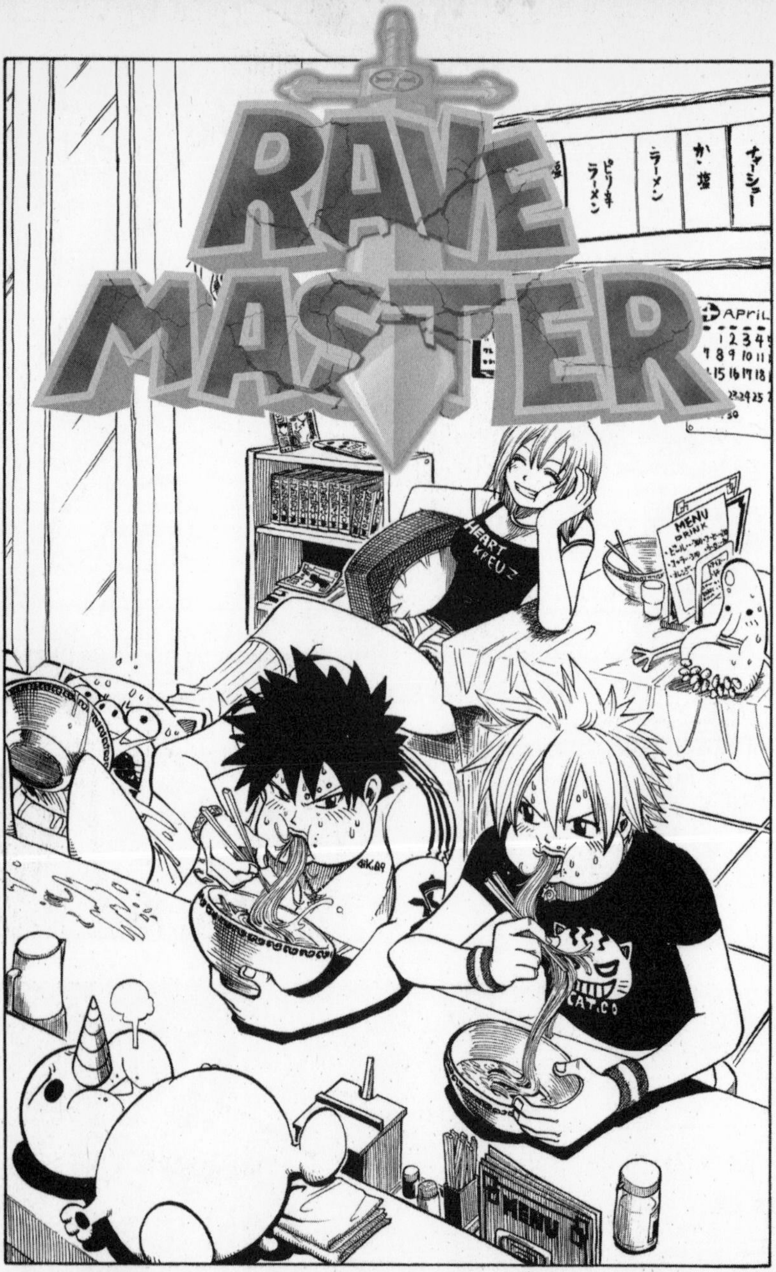
RAVE MASTER
ラーメン
ピリ辛
ラーメン
APRIL
HEART KREUZ
MENU
DRINK
CAT.CO
MENU

RAVE: 135 ✠ "LIGHT'S" TRUMP CARD

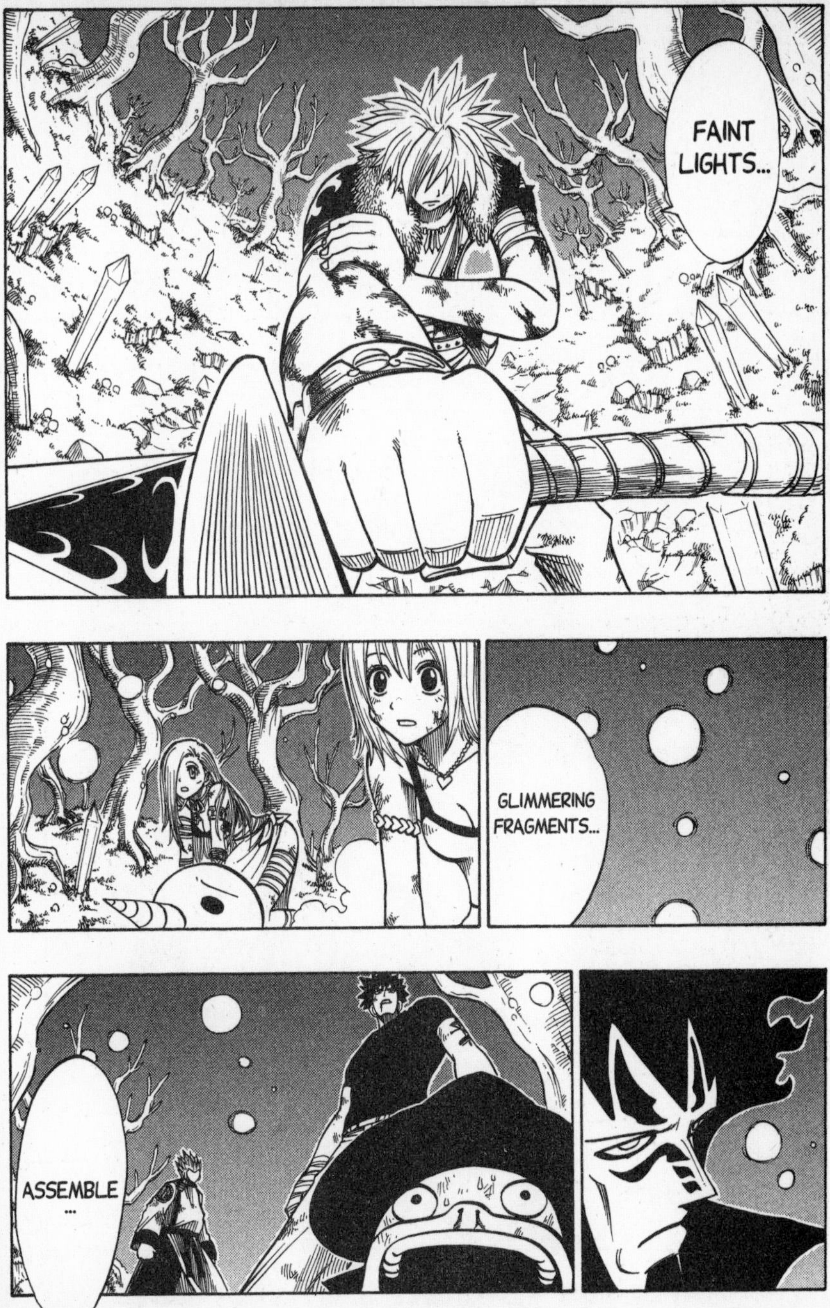
FAINT LIGHTS...
GLIMMERING FRAGMENTS...
ASSEMBLE ...

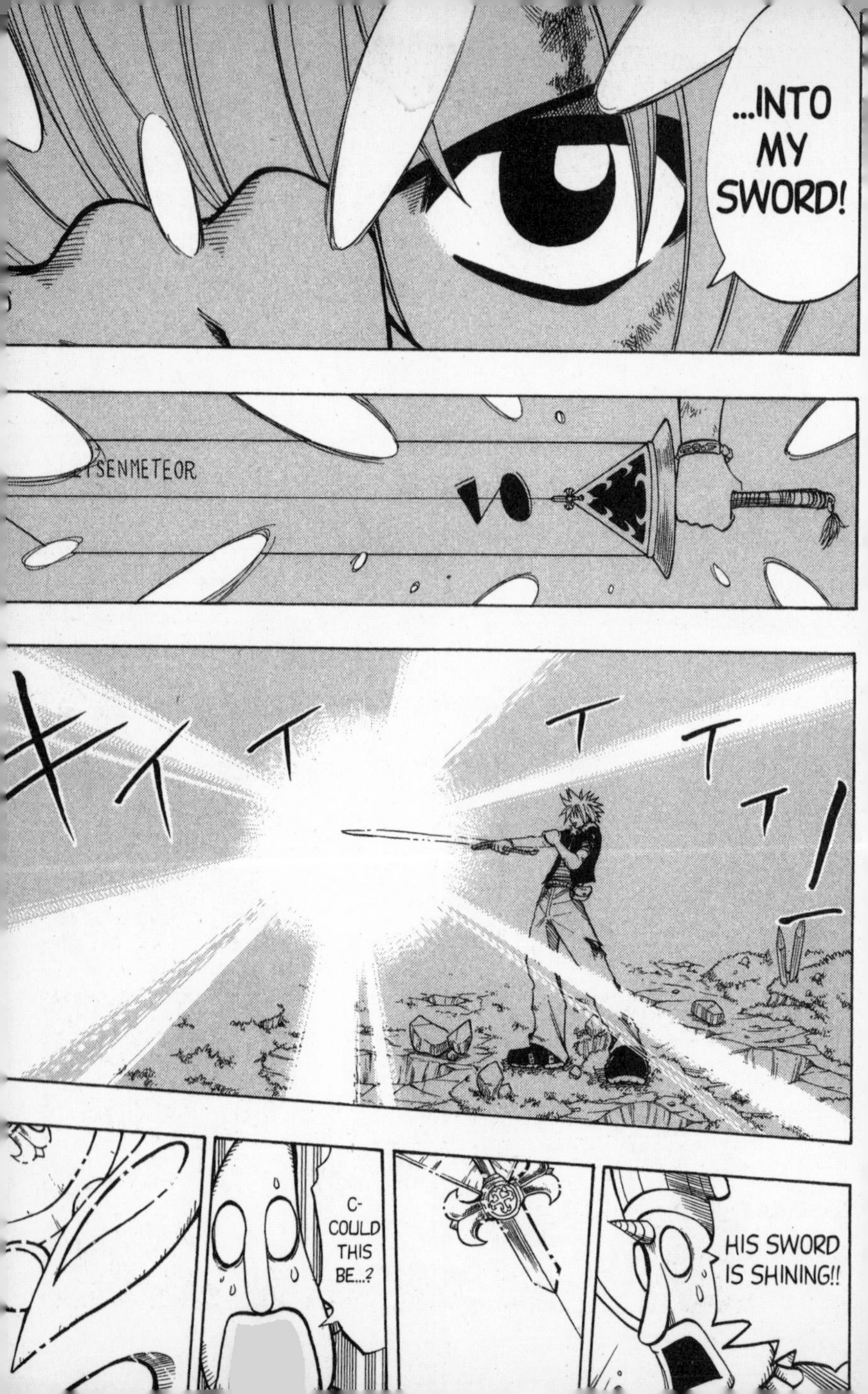
...INTO MY SWORD!
ISENMETEOR
キイイイイー
HIS SWORD IS SHINING!!
C- COULD THIS BE...?

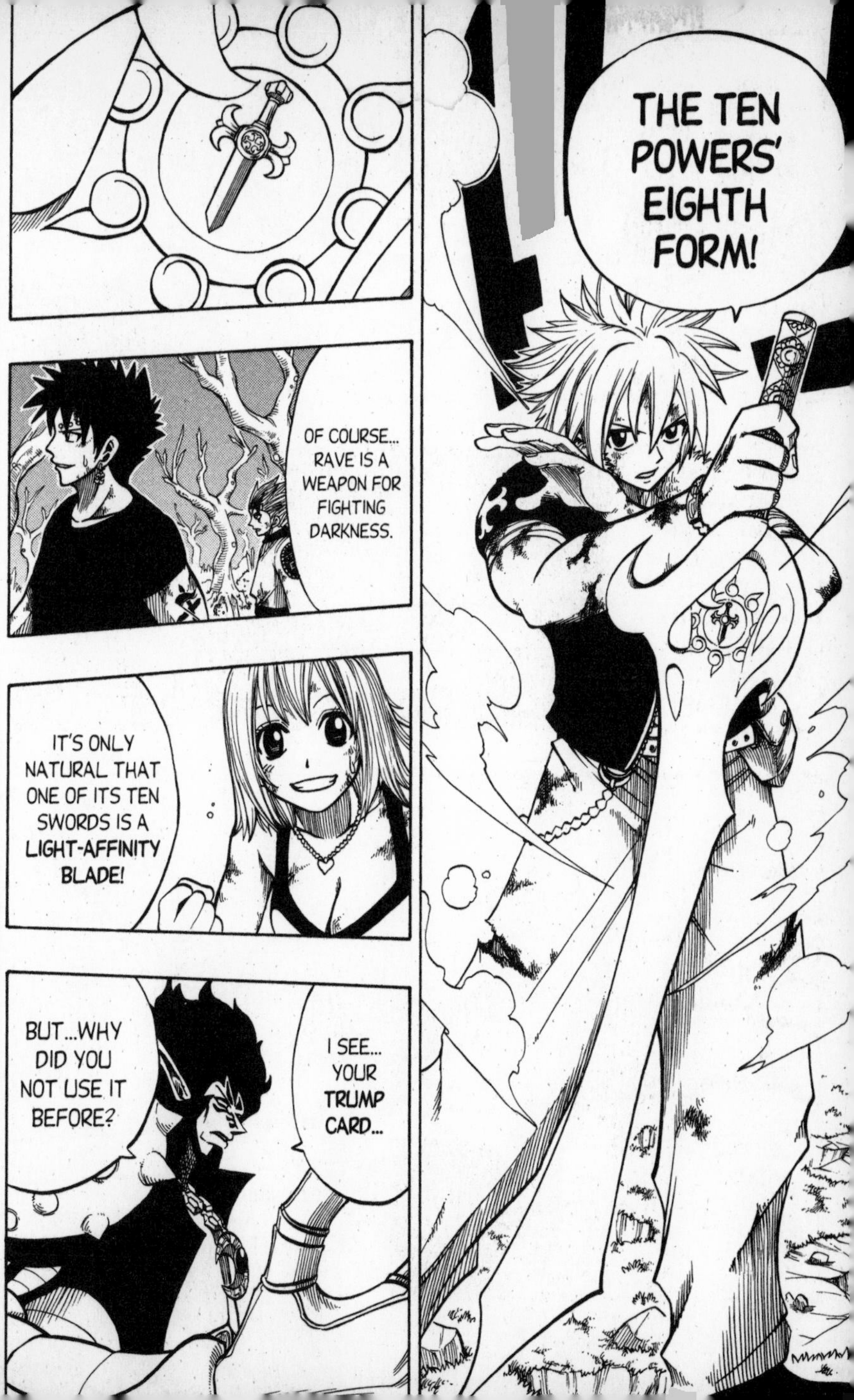
THE TEN POWERS' EIGHTH FORM!
OF COURSE... RAVE IS A WEAPON FOR FIGHTING DARKNESS.
IT'S ONLY NATURAL THAT ONE OF ITS TEN SWORDS IS A LIGHT-AFFINITY BLADE!
I SEE... YOUR TRUMP CARD...
BUT...WHY DID YOU NOT USE IT BEFORE?

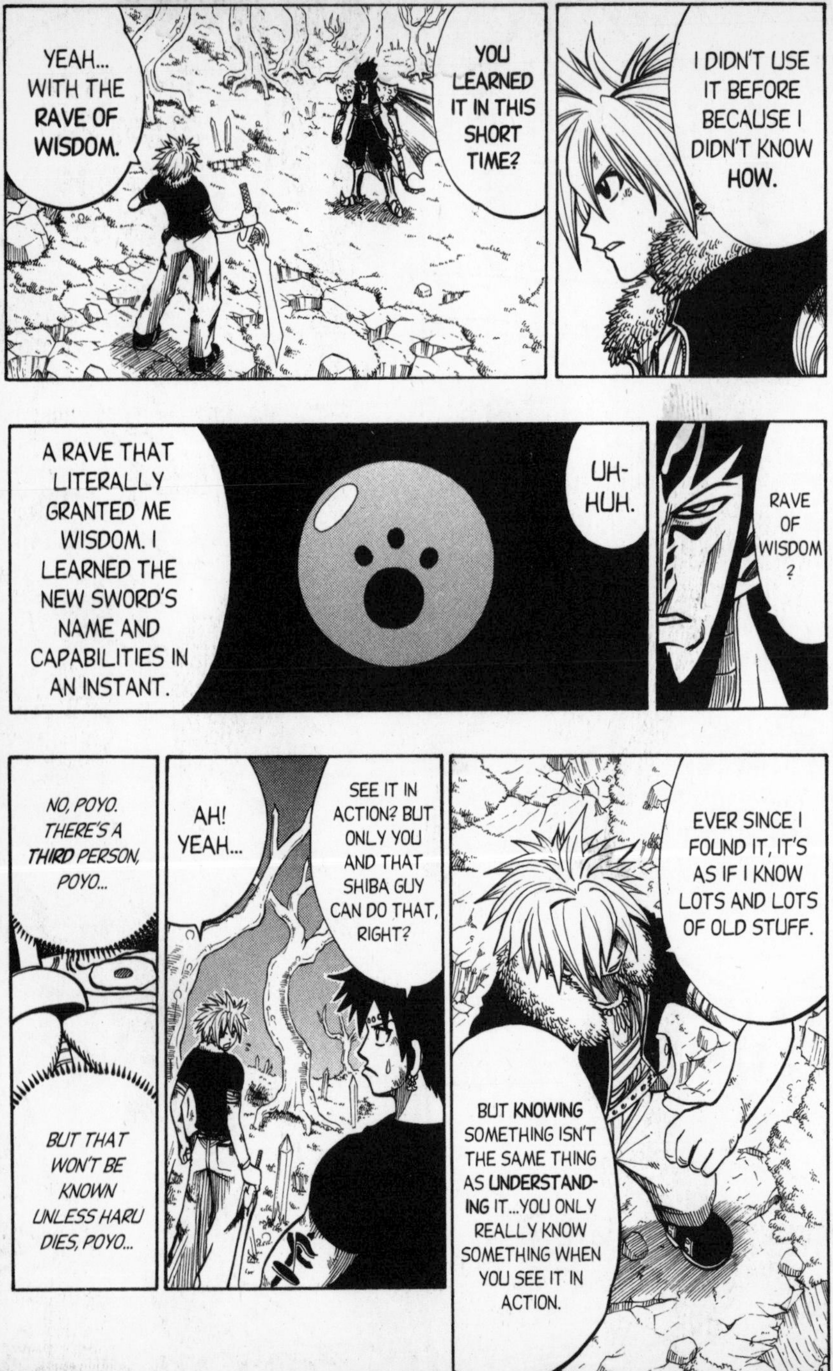
I DIDN'T USE IT BEFORE BECAUSE I DIDN'T KNOW HOW.
YOU LEARNED IT IN THIS SHORT TIME?
YEAH... WITH THE RAVE OF WISDOM.
RAVE OF WISDOM?
UH-HUH.
A RAVE THAT LITERALLY GRANTED ME WISDOM. I LEARNED THE NEW SWORD'S NAME AND CAPABILITIES IN AN INSTANT.
EVER SINCE I FOUND IT, IT'S AS IF I KNOW LOTS AND LOTS OF OLD STUFF.
BUT KNOWING SOMETHING ISN'T THE SAME THING AS UNDERSTANDING IT...YOU ONLY REALLY KNOW SOMETHING WHEN YOU SEE IT IN ACTION.
SEE IT IN ACTION? BUT ONLY YOU AND THAT SHIBA GUY CAN DO THAT, RIGHT?
AH! YEAH...
NO, POYO. THERE'S A THIRD PERSON, POYO...
BUT THAT WON'T BE KNOWN UNLESS HARU DIES, POYO...

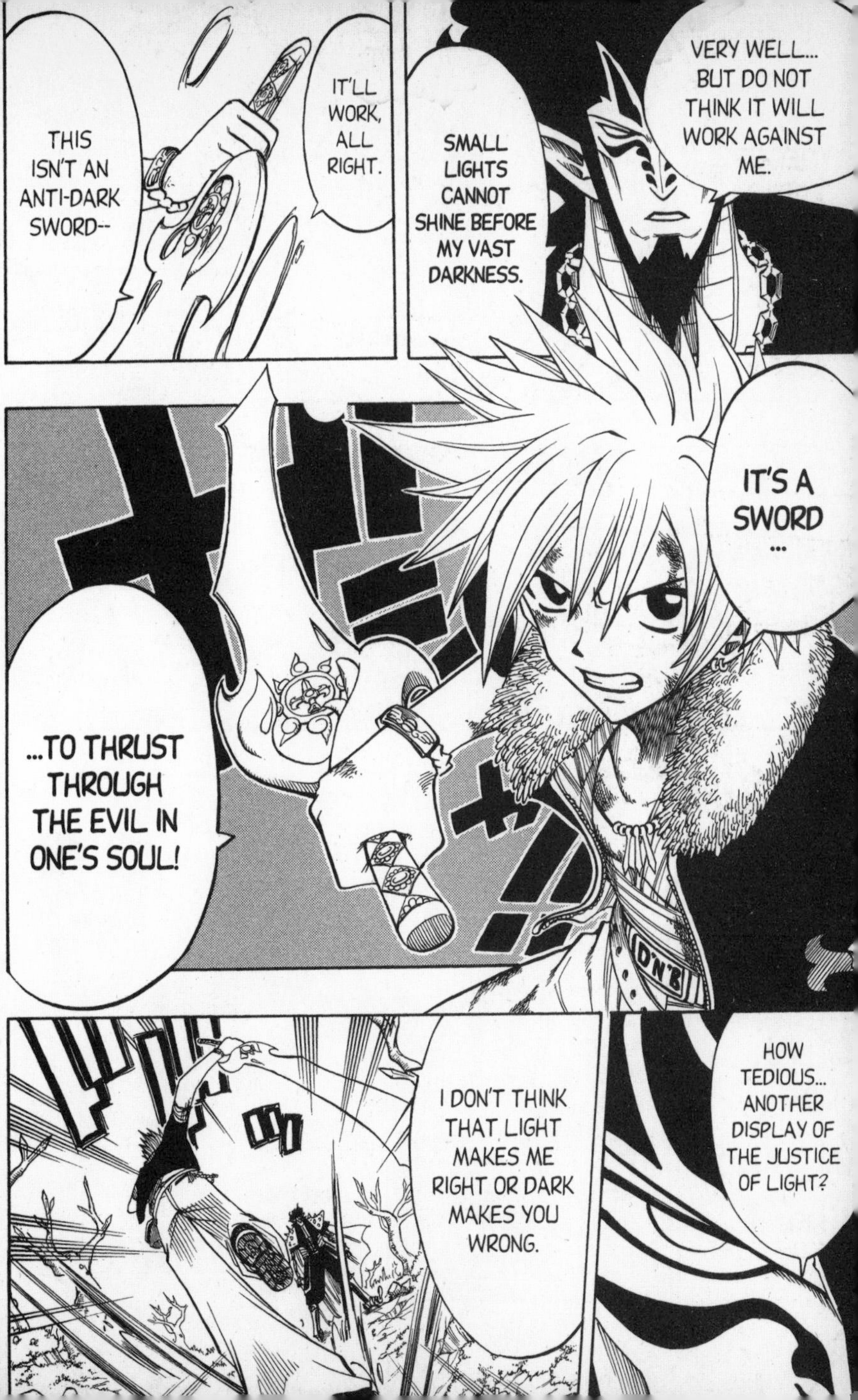
VERY WELL... BUT DO NOT THINK IT WILL WORK AGAINST ME.
SMALL LIGHTS CANNOT SHINE BEFORE MY VAST DARKNESS.
IT'LL WORK, ALL RIGHT.
THIS ISN'T AN ANTI-DARK SWORD--
IT'S A SWORD ...
...TO THRUST THROUGH THE EVIL IN ONE'S SOUL!
HOW TEDIOUS... ANOTHER DISPLAY OF THE JUSTICE OF LIGHT?
I DON'T THINK THAT LIGHT MAKES ME RIGHT OR DARK MAKES YOU WRONG.

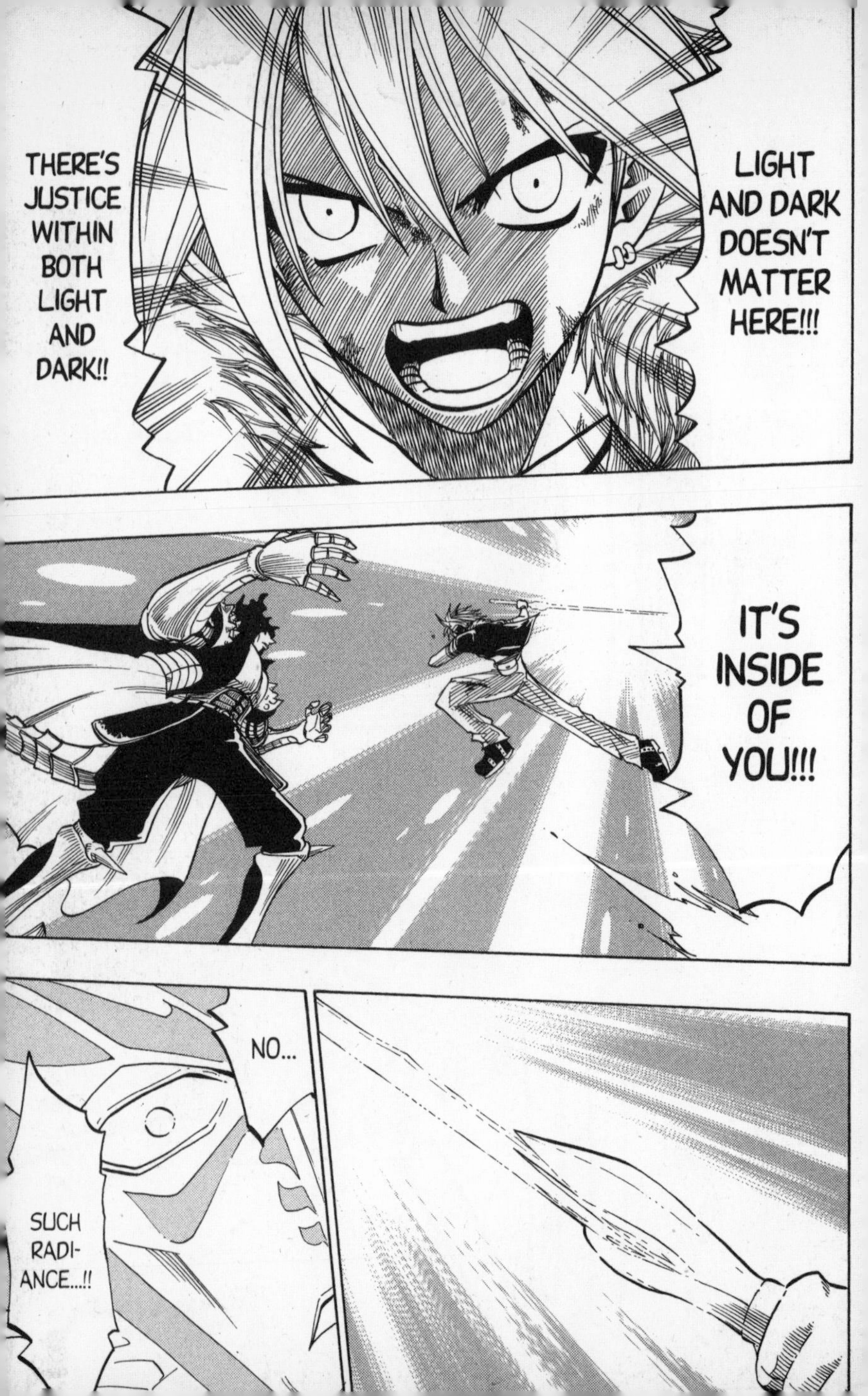
LIGHT AND DARK DOESN'T MATTER HERE!!!
THERE'S JUSTICE WITHIN BOTH LIGHT AND DARK!!
IT'S INSIDE OF YOU!!!
NO...
SUCH RADI-ANCE...!!

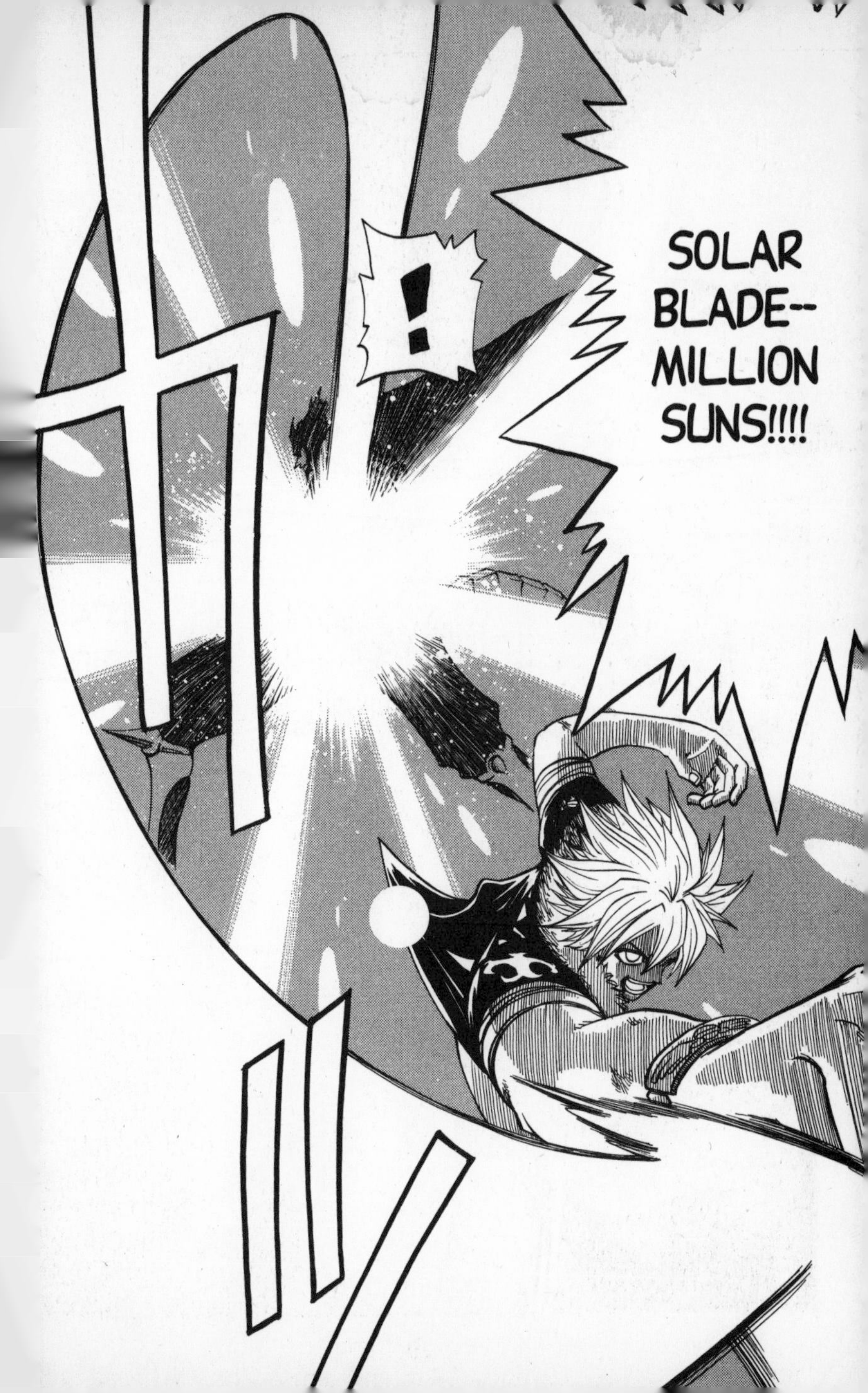
!
SOLAR BLADE-- MILLION SUNS!!!!

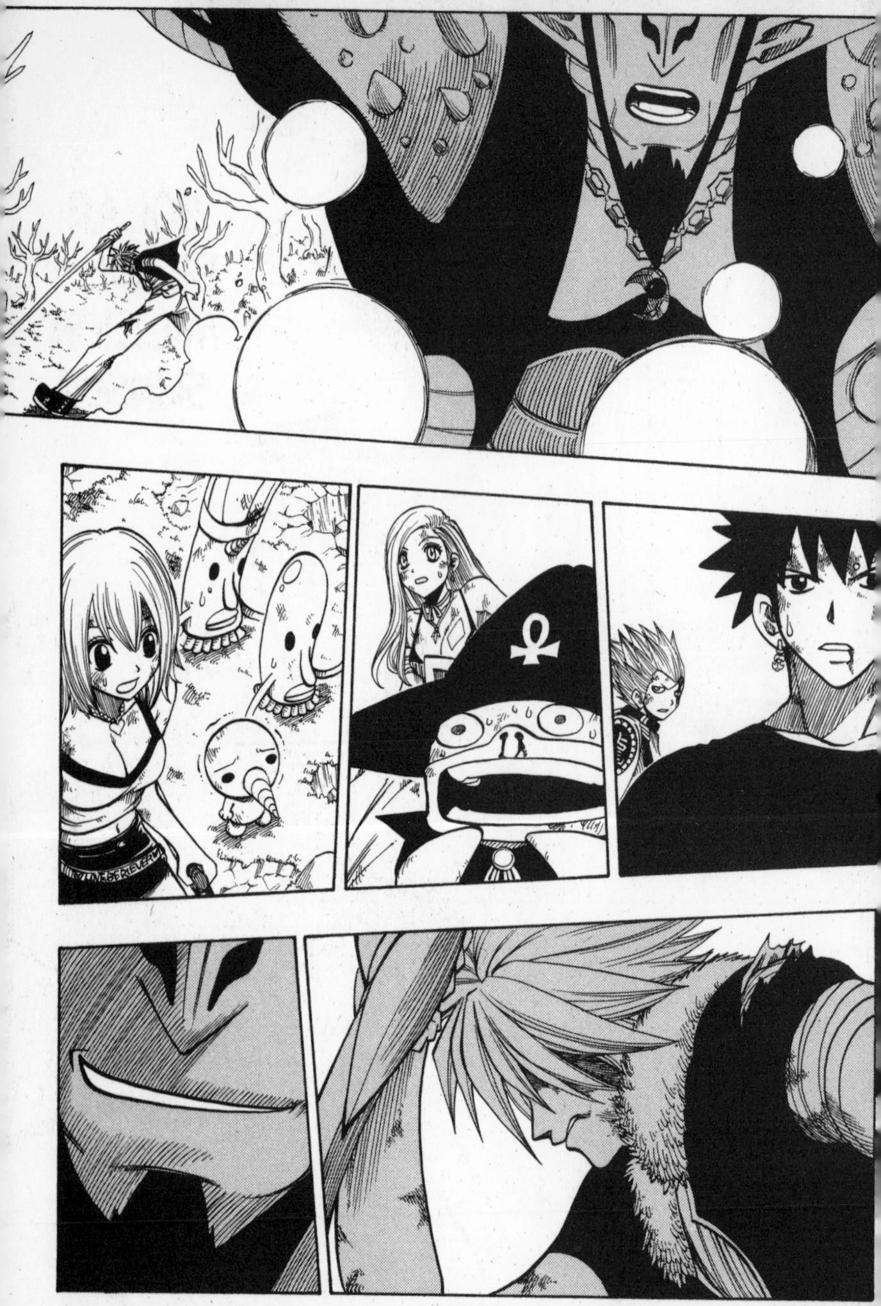

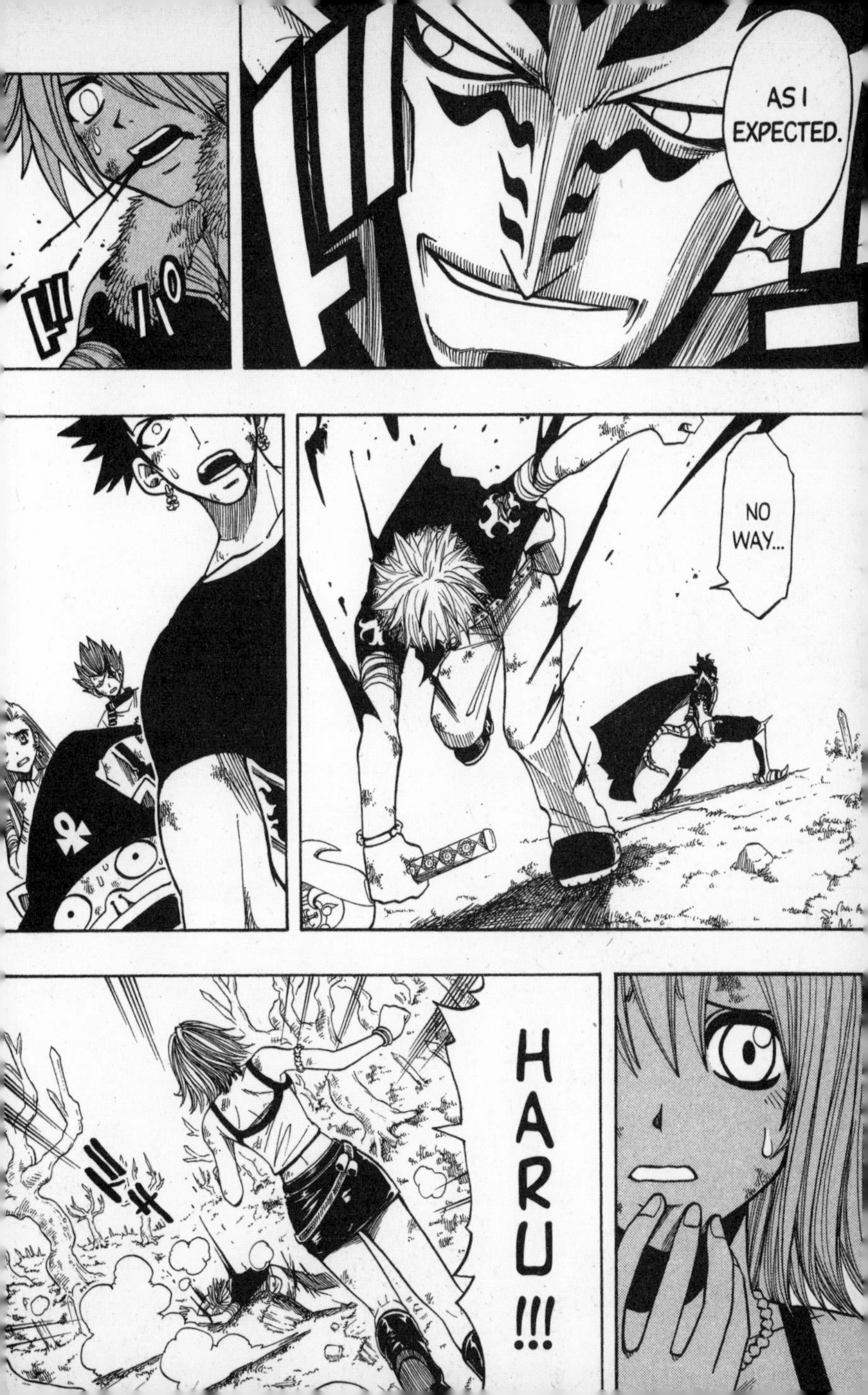
AS I EXPECTED.
NO WAY...
HARU!!!

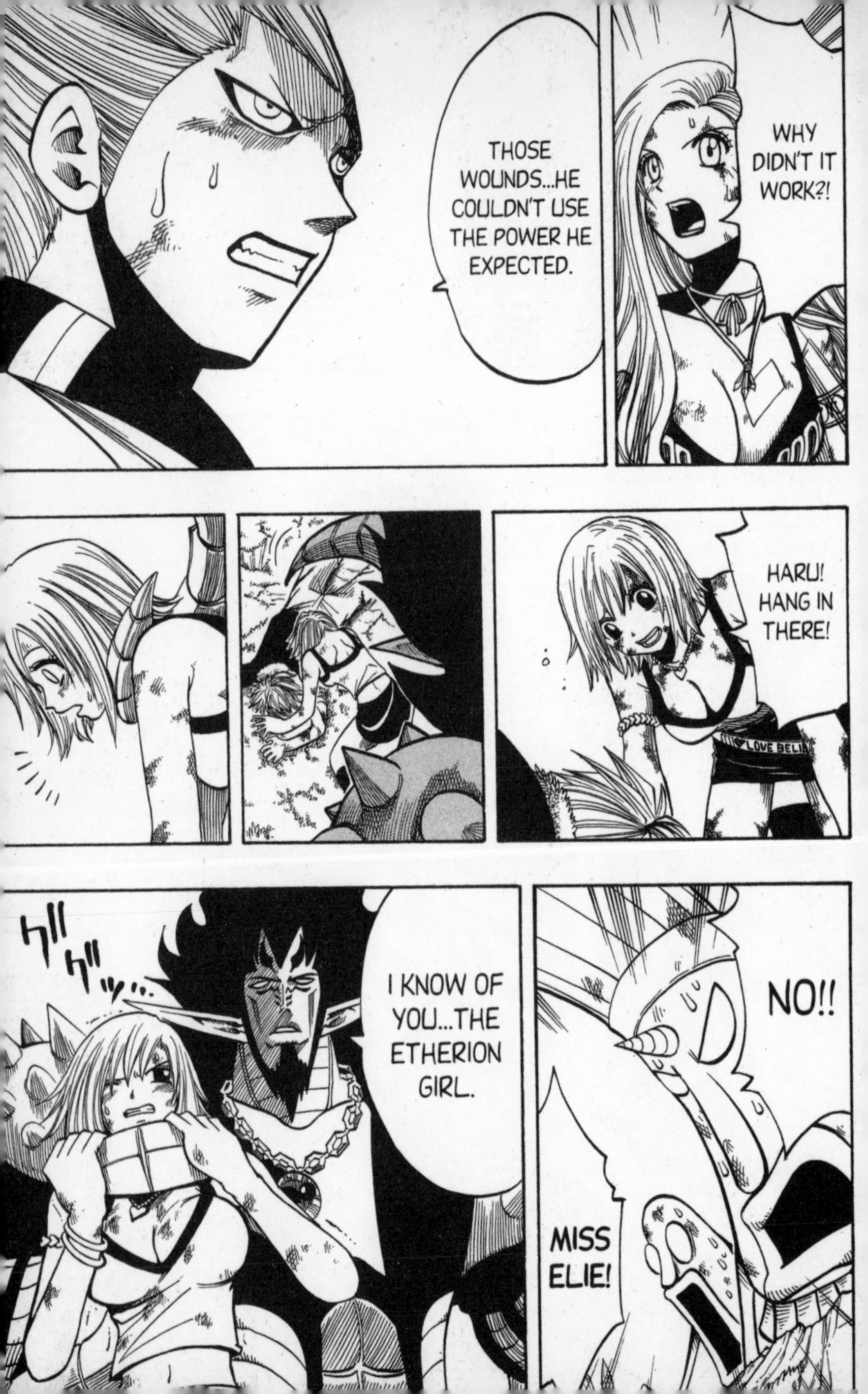
WHY DIDN'T IT WORK?!
THOSE WOUNDS...HE COULDN'T USE THE POWER HE EXPECTED.
HARU! HANG IN THERE!
NO!!
MISS ELIE!
I KNOW OF YOU...THE ETHERION GIRL.

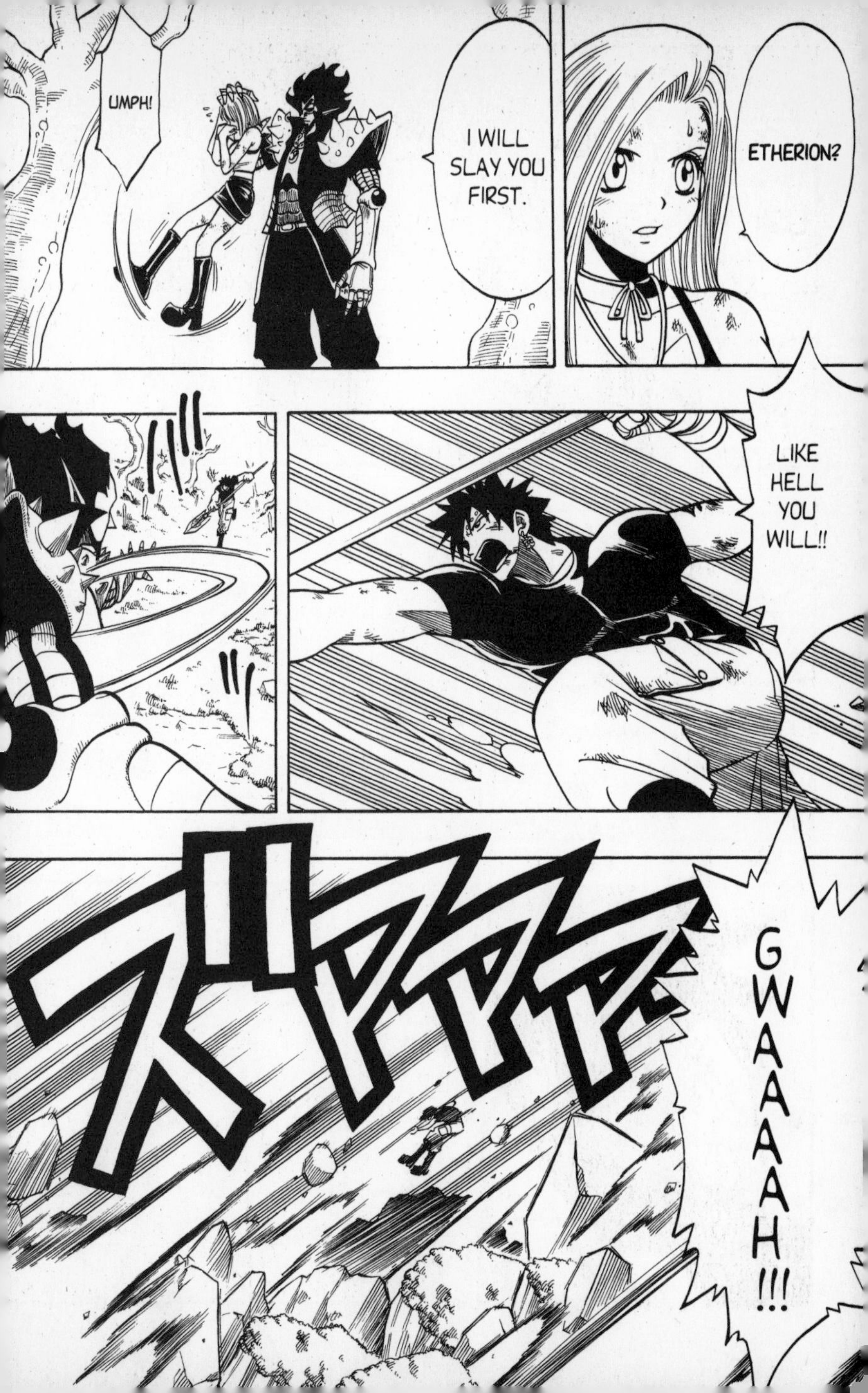
ETHERION?
I WILL SLAY YOU FIRST.
UMPH!
LIKE HELL YOU WILL!!
GWAAAAH!!!

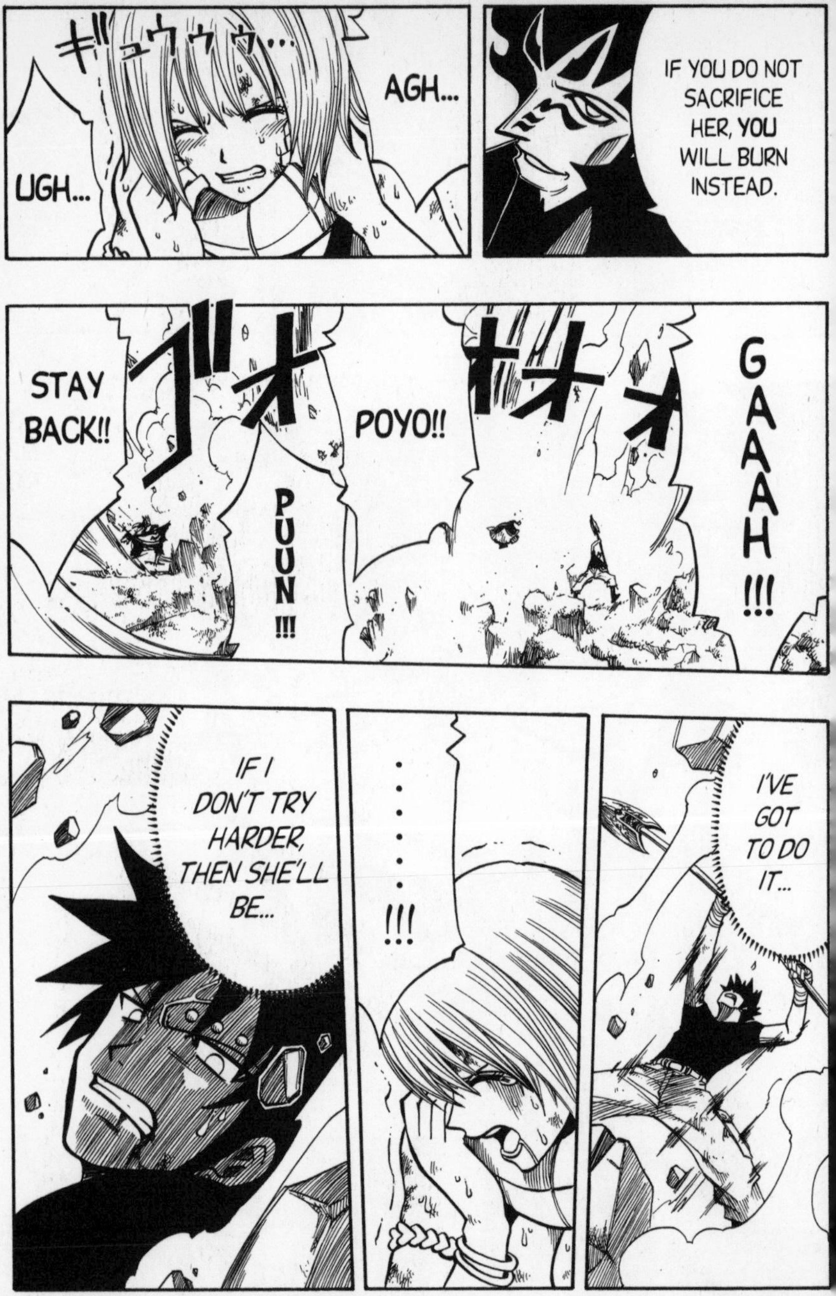
IF YOU DO NOT SACRIFICE HER, YOU WILL BURN INSTEAD.
ギュウウウ...
AGH...
UGH...
GAAAH!!!
ゴオオオ
POYO!!
PUUN!!!
STAY BACK!!
I'VE GOT TO DO IT...
.......!!!
IF I DON'T TRY HARDER, THEN SHE'LL BE...

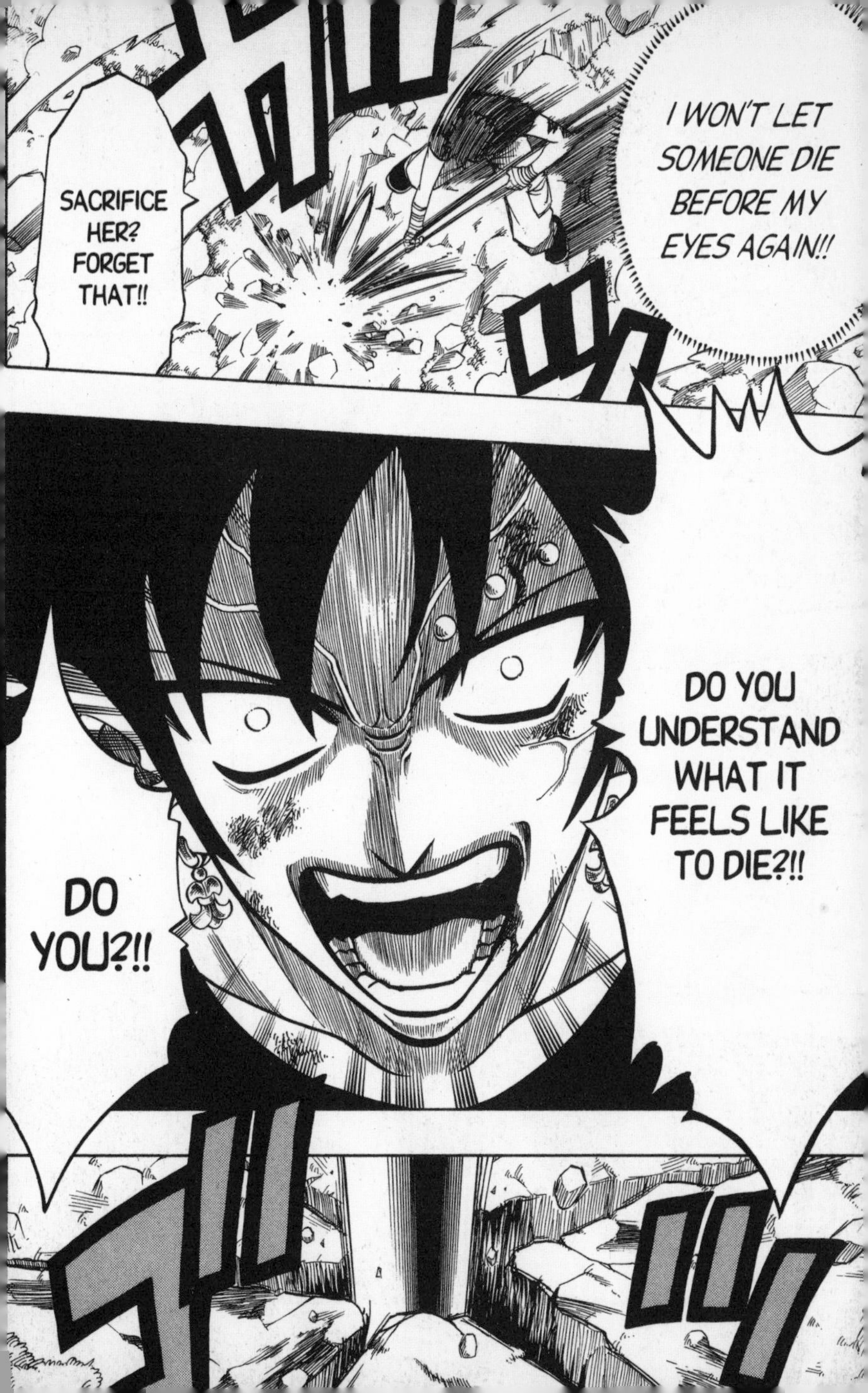
I WON'T LET SOMEONE DIE BEFORE MY EYES AGAIN!!
SACRIFICE HER? FORGET THAT!!
DO YOU UNDERSTAND WHAT IT FEELS LIKE TO DIE?!!
DO YOU?!!

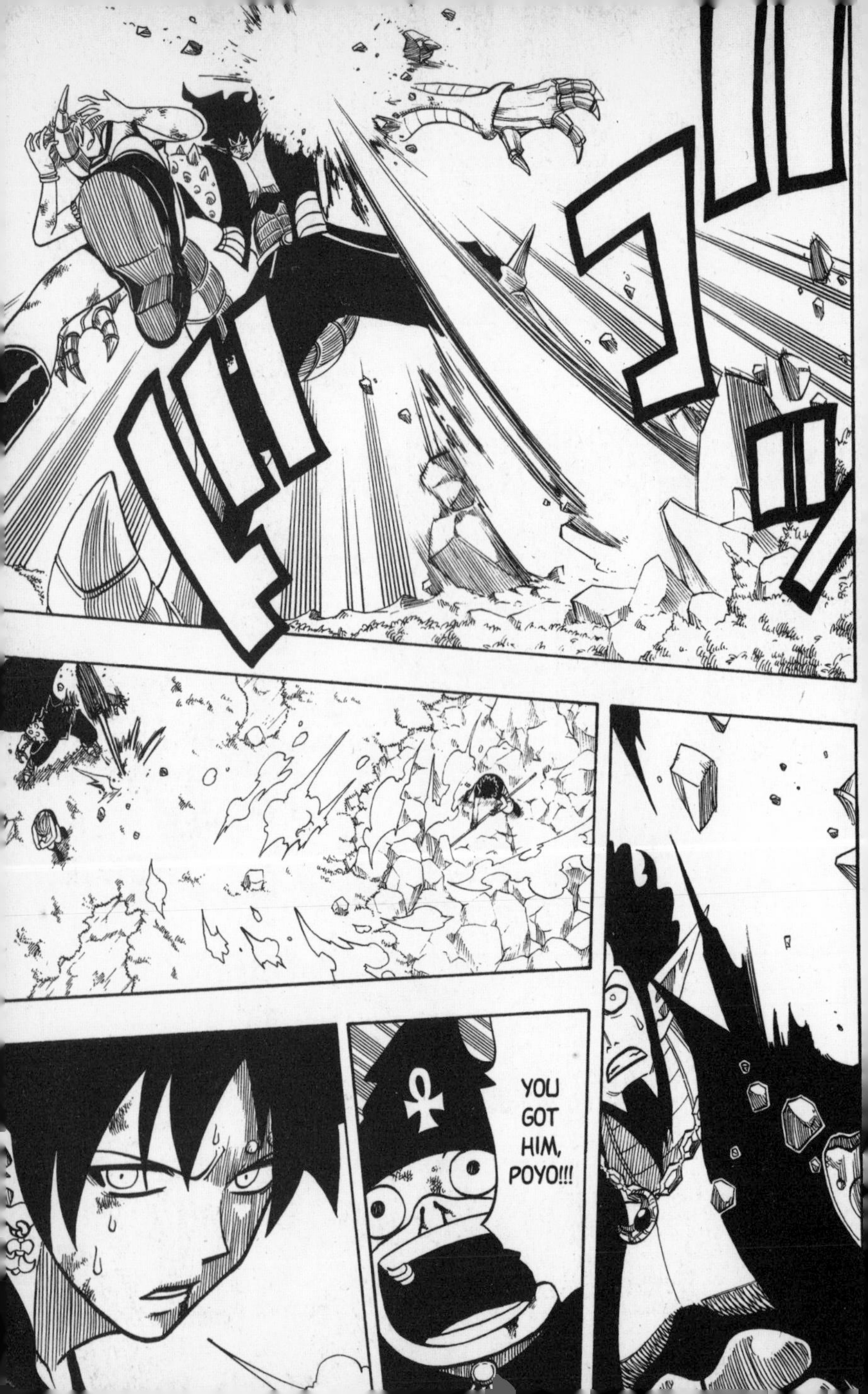
YOU GOT HIM, POYO!!!

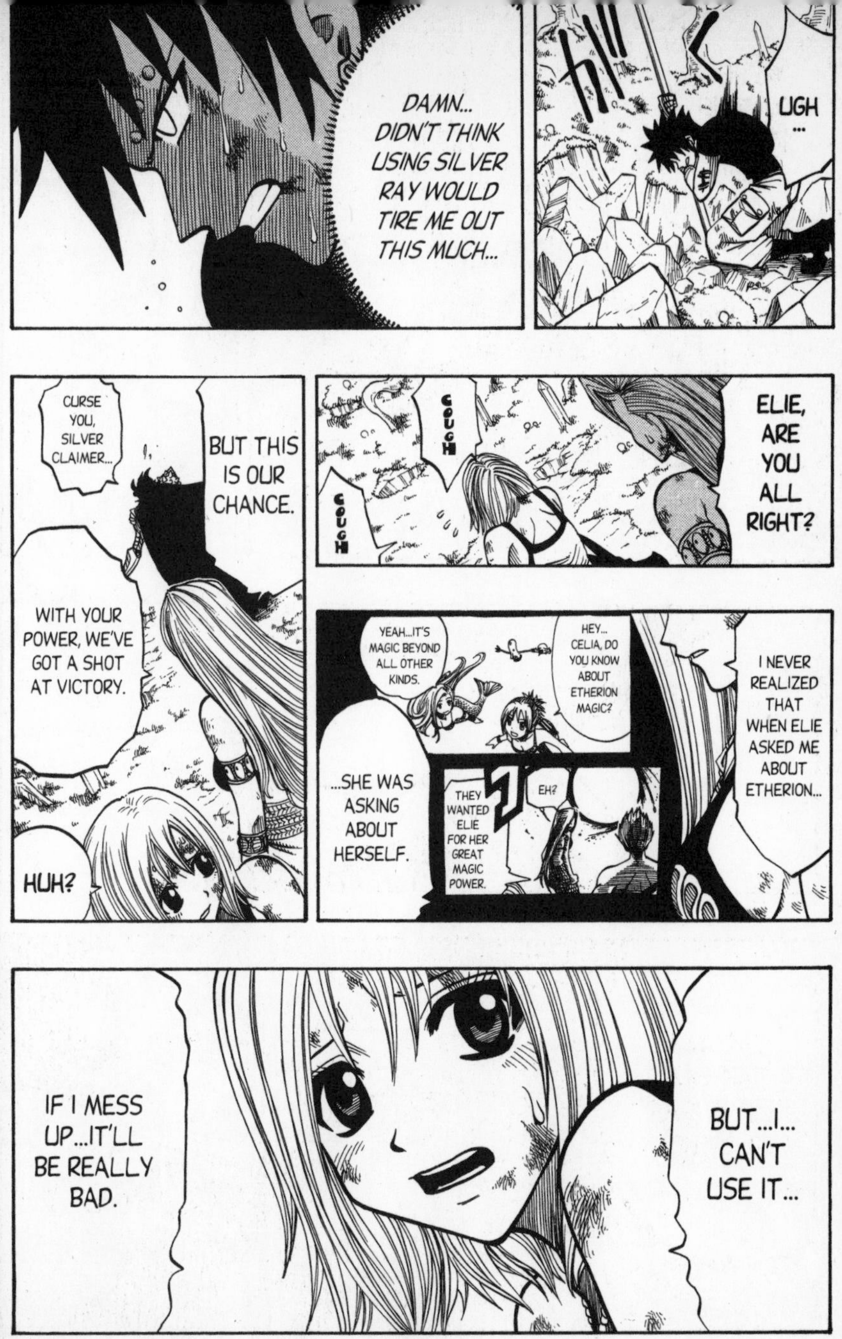
UGH ...
DAMN... DIDN'T THINK USING SILVER RAY WOULD TIRE ME OUT THIS MUCH...
ELIE, ARE YOU ALL RIGHT?
COUGH
COUGH
I NEVER REALIZED THAT WHEN ELIE ASKED ME ABOUT ETHERION...
HEY... CELIA, DO YOU KNOW ABOUT ETHERION MAGIC?
YEAH...IT'S MAGIC BEYOND ALL OTHER KINDS.
EH?
THEY WANTED ELIE FOR HER GREAT MAGIC POWER.
...SHE WAS ASKING ABOUT HERSELF.
BUT THIS IS OUR CHANCE.
CURSE YOU, SILVER CLAIMER...
WITH YOUR POWER, WE'VE GOT A SHOT AT VICTORY.
HUH?
BUT...I... CAN'T USE IT...
IF I MESS UP...IT'LL BE REALLY BAD.

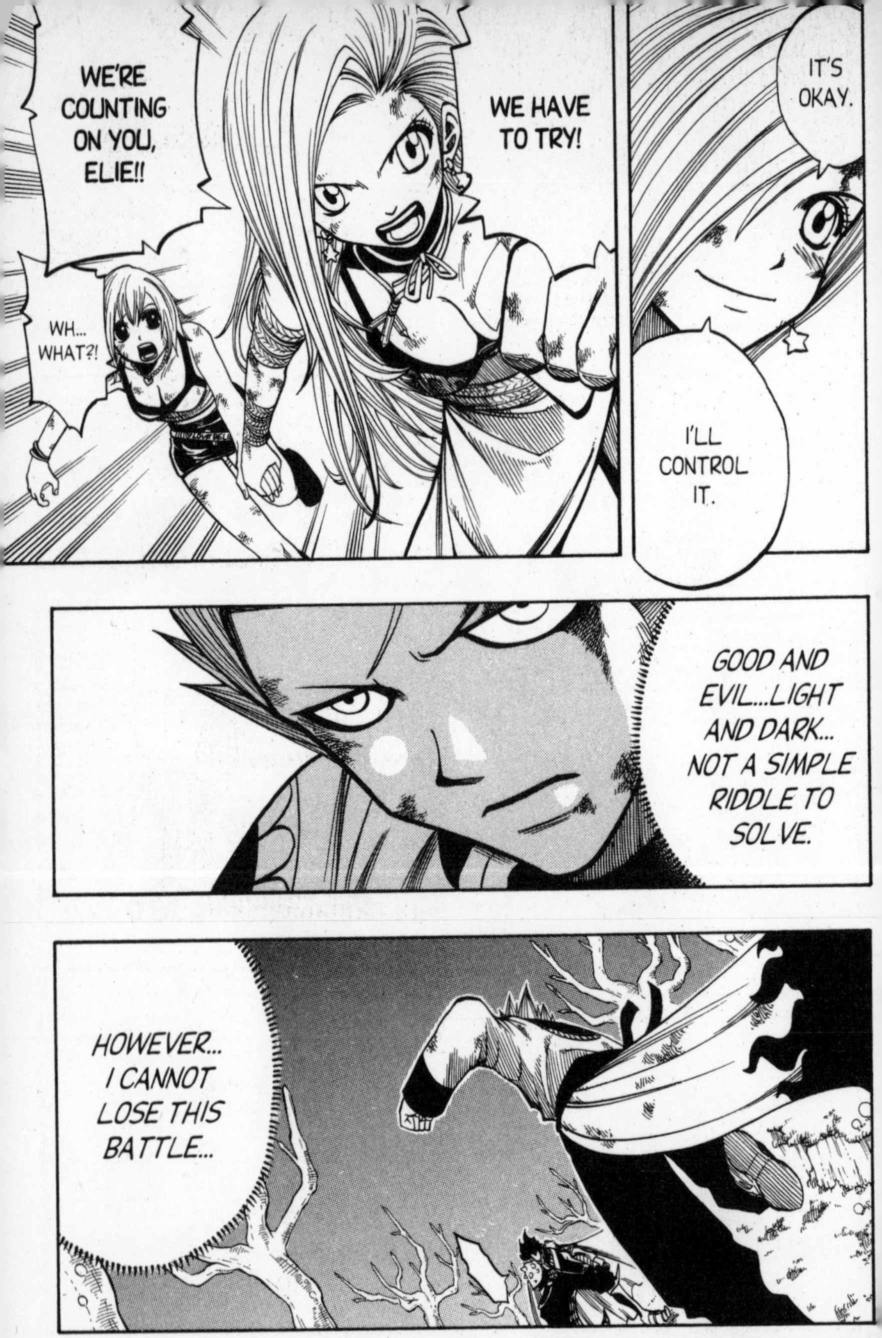
IT'S OKAY.
I'LL CONTROL IT.
WE HAVE TO TRY!
WE'RE COUNTING ON YOU, ELIE!!
WH... WHAT?!
GOOD AND EVIL...LIGHT AND DARK... NOT A SIMPLE RIDDLE TO SOLVE.
HOWEVER... I CANNOT LOSE THIS BATTLE...

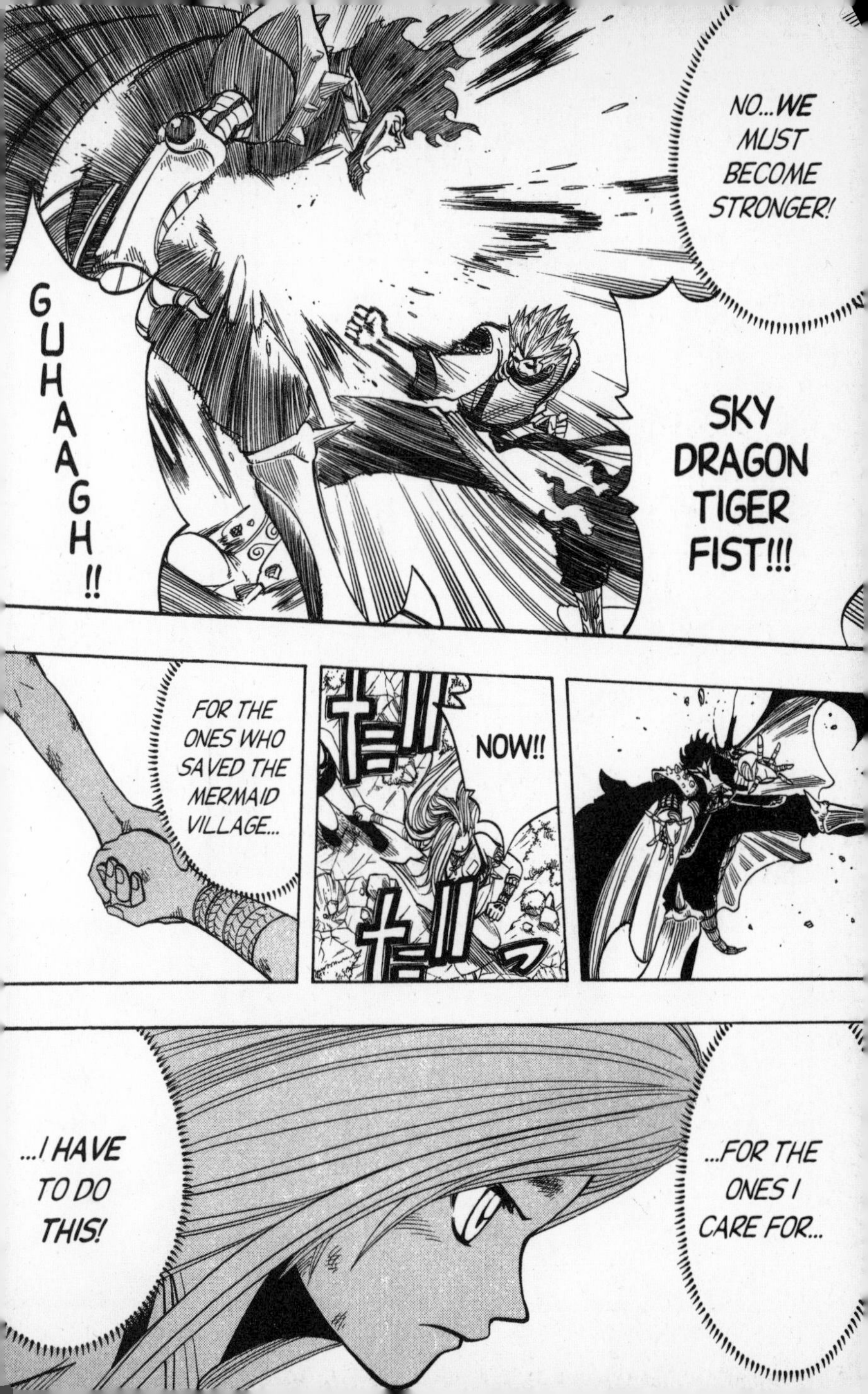
NO...WE MUST BECOME STRONGER!
SKY DRAGON TIGER FIST!!!
GUHAAGH!!
NOW!!
FOR THE ONES WHO SAVED THE MERMAID VILLAGE...
...FOR THE ONES I CARE FOR...
...I HAVE TO DO THIS!

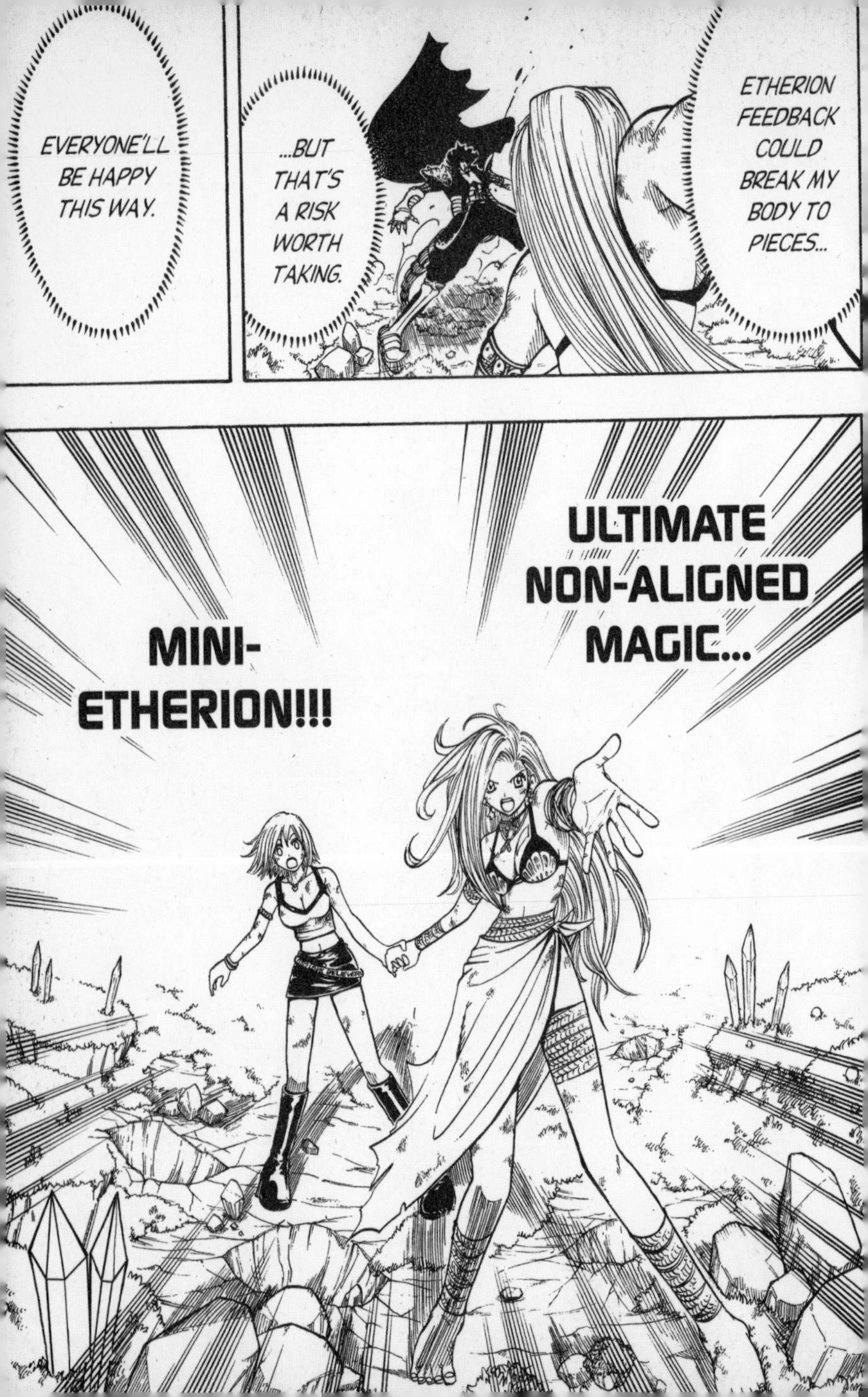
ETHERION FEEDBACK COULD BREAK MY BODY TO PIECES...
...BUT THAT'S A RISK WORTH TAKING.
EVERYONE'LL BE HAPPY THIS WAY.
ULTIMATE NON-ALIGNED MAGIC...
MINI-ETHERION!!!

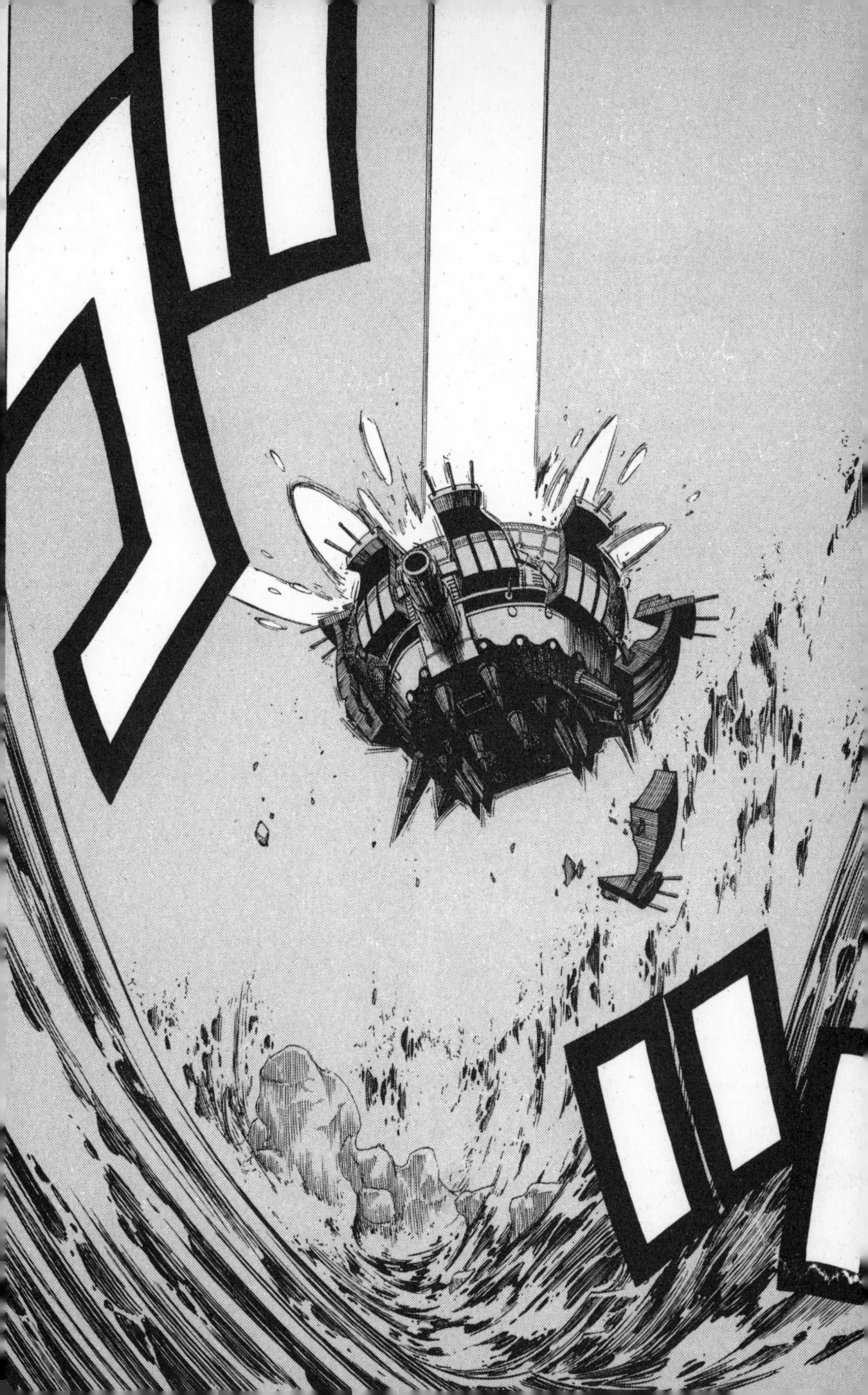

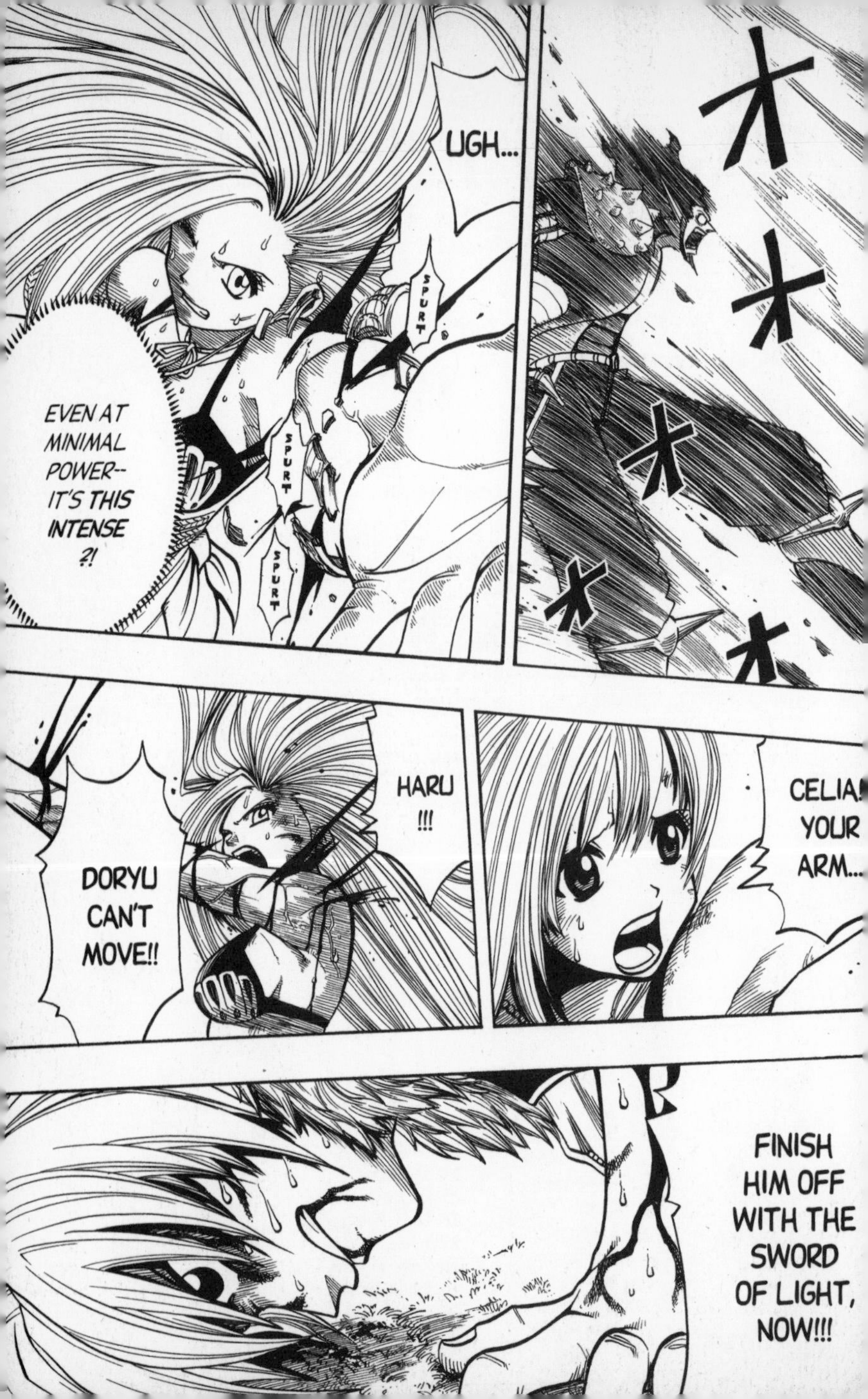
UGH...
SPURT
SPURT
SPURT
EVEN AT MINIMAL POWER-- IT'S THIS INTENSE?!
CELIA! YOUR ARM...
HARU!!!
DORYU CAN'T MOVE!!
FINISH HIM OFF WITH THE SWORD OF LIGHT, NOW!!!

RAVE WORLD MAP

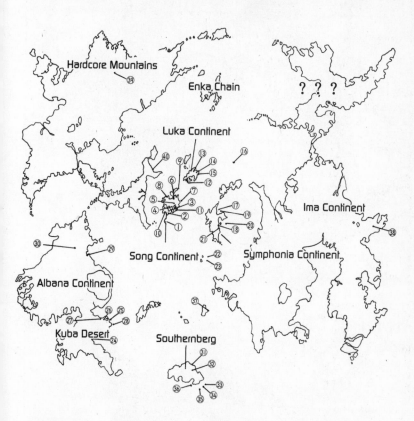

Hardcore Mountains
39
Enka Chain
? ? ?
Luka Continent
40
9
13
14
15
12
6
8
7
5
3
4
11
2
1
10
16
17
19
20
18
21
Ima Continent
38
30
29
Song Continent
22
23
Symphonia Continent
Albana Continent
37
26
25
27
28
Kuba Desert
24
Southernberg
31
32
36
33
34
35

1. Garage Island
2. Hip Hop Town
3. Punk Street
4. Ska Village
5. Tremolo Mt.
6. Experiment
7. Blues City
8. Drum 'N' Bass
9. Sandbar
10. Etherion Research Center
11. Elnadia
12. Elda
13. Rabarrier
14. Tower of Din
15. Bonita
16. Aqua Palace
17. Symphonia Castle
18. Nation of Raregroove
19. Resha's Tomb
20. New Demon Card HQ
21. Raregroove Southern Fort
22. Debacle Village
23. Acappella Island
24. Megaunit
25. Denon Town
26. Elios Village
27. Rudra Capitol
28. Kazan
29. Mary Loose
30. Imperial HQ
31. Site of Silver Knights' Fall
32. Dark Bring Cave
33. Mildesta
34. Syaoran
35. River Saly
36. Deep Sea Shrine
37. Olbesk
38. Location of the Final Rave Stone
39. Former Demon Card HQ
40. Technotica

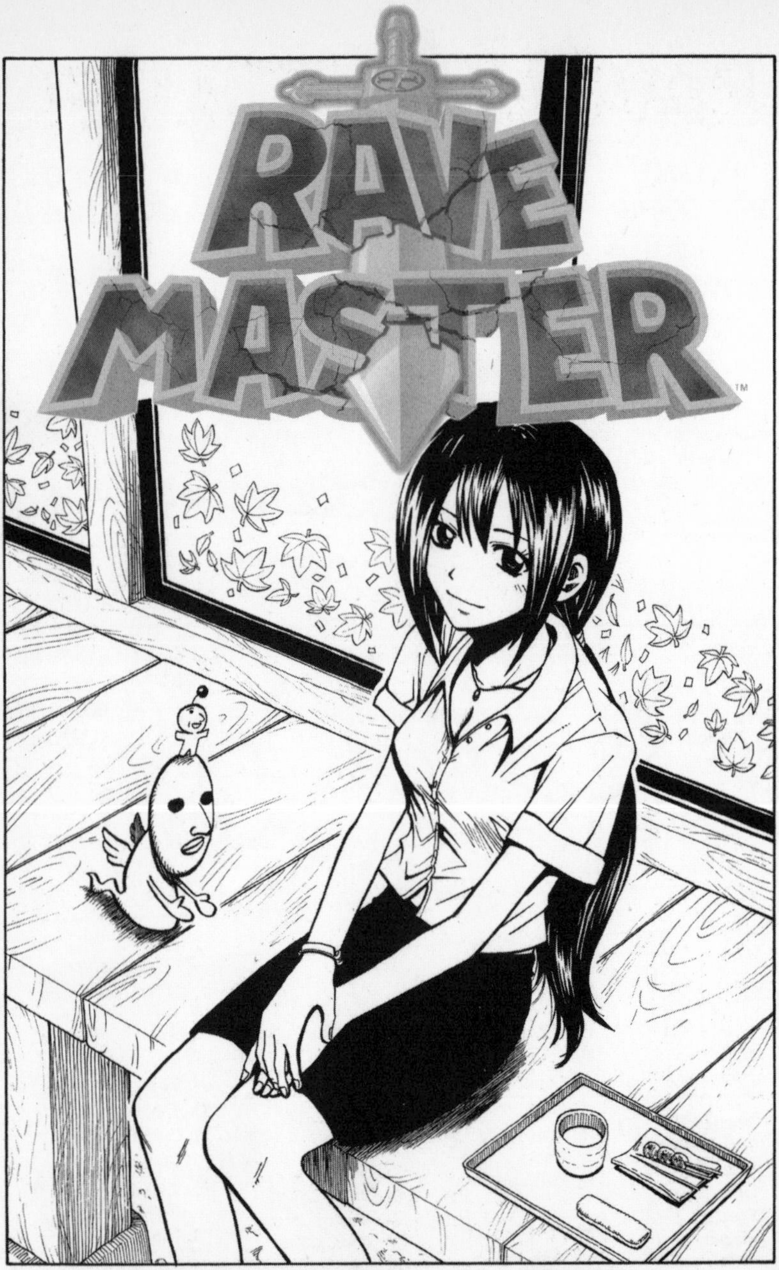
RAVE MASTER

RAVE: 136 LINKED SOULS...

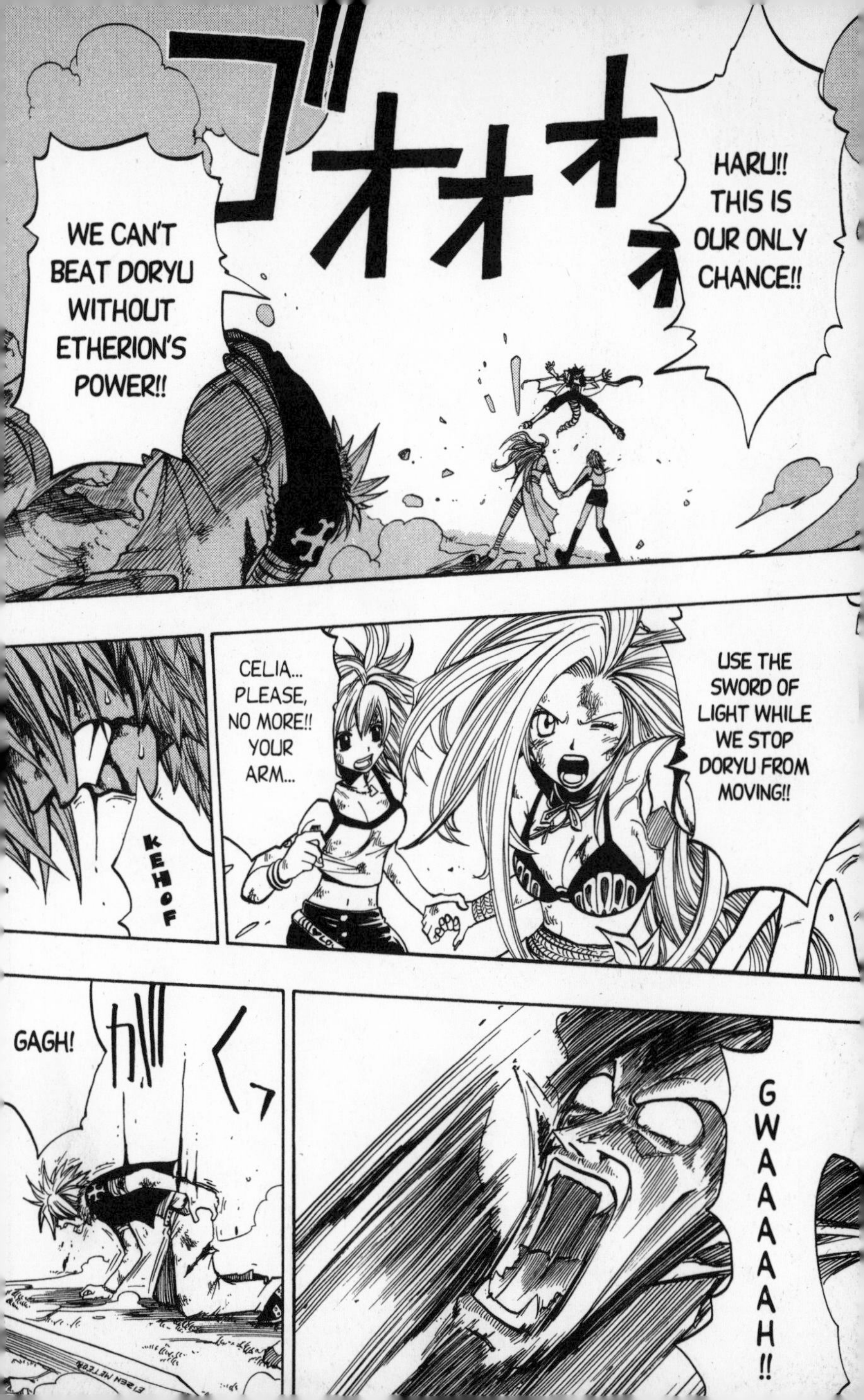
HARU!! THIS IS OUR ONLY CHANCE!!
ゴオオオォ
WE CAN'T BEAT DORYU WITHOUT ETHERION'S POWER!!
USE THE SWORD OF LIGHT WHILE WE STOP DORYU FROM MOVING!!
CELIA... PLEASE, NO MORE!! YOUR ARM...
KEHOF
GWAAAAAAAH!!
カッ
く
GAGH!

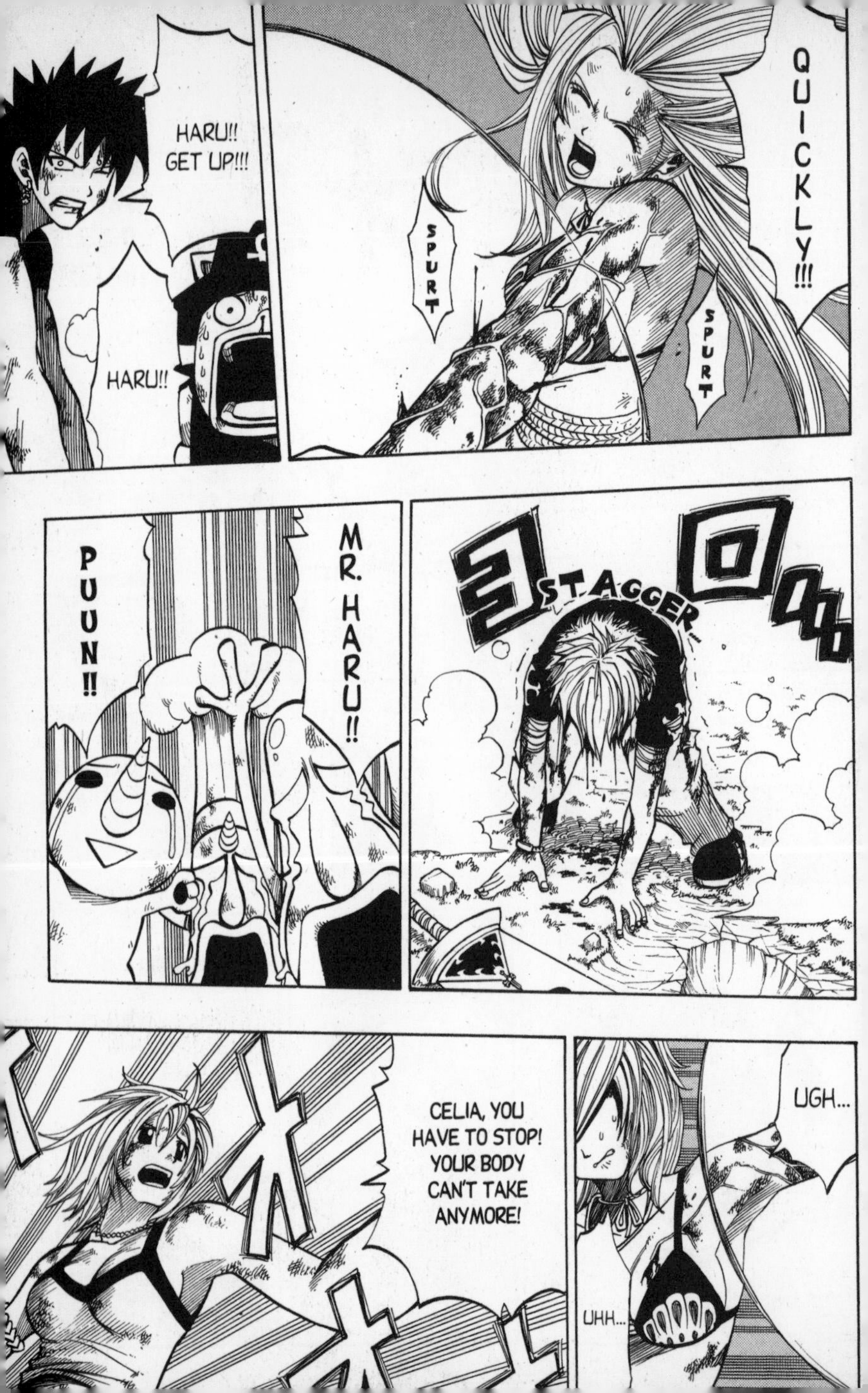
QUICKLY!!!
SPURT
SPURT
HARU!! GET UP!!!
HARU!!
STAGGER...
MR. HARU!!
PUUN!!
UGH...
UHH...
CELIA, YOU HAVE TO STOP! YOUR BODY CAN'T TAKE ANYMORE!

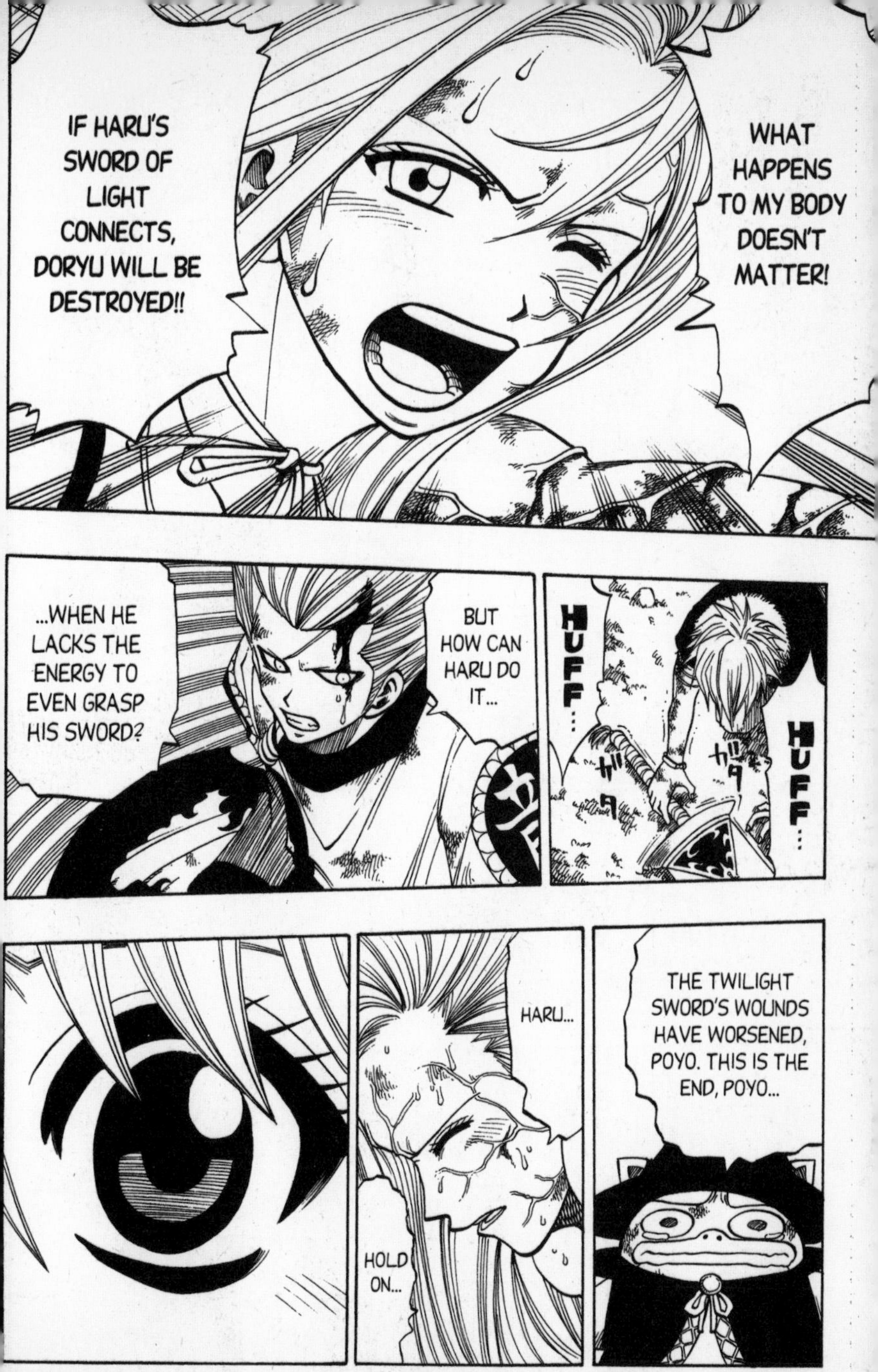
WHAT HAPPENS TO MY BODY DOESN'T MATTER!
IF HARU'S SWORD OF LIGHT CONNECTS, DORYU WILL BE DESTROYED!!
HUFF...
HUFF...
BUT HOW CAN HARU DO IT...
...WHEN HE LACKS THE ENERGY TO EVEN GRASP HIS SWORD?
THE TWILIGHT SWORD'S WOUNDS HAVE WORSENED, POYO. THIS IS THE END, POYO...
HARU...
HOLD ON...

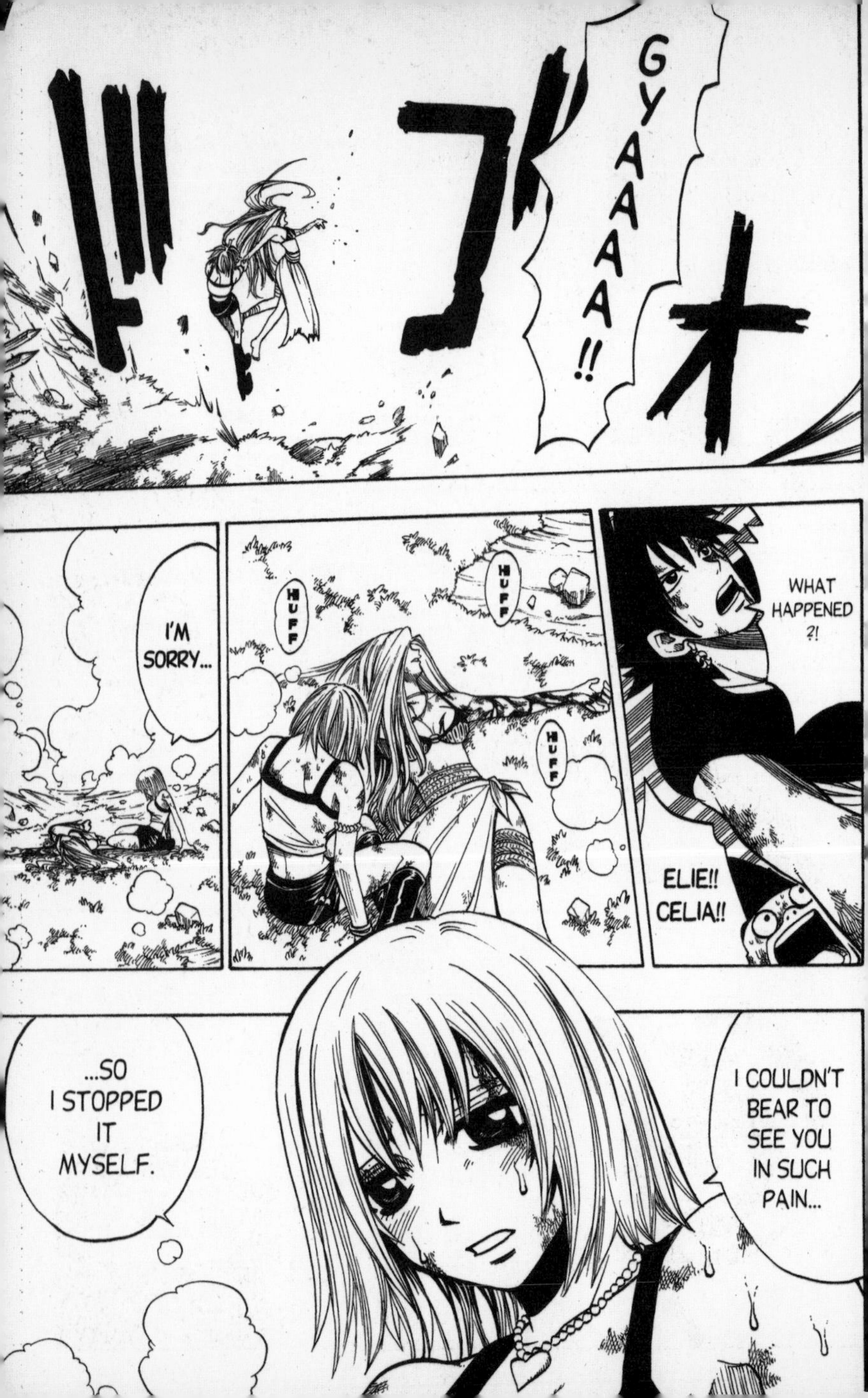
GYAAAAA!!
ドゴオ
WHAT HAPPENED?!
ELIE!! CELIA!!
HUFF
HUFF
HUFF
I'M SORRY...
I COULDN'T BEAR TO SEE YOU IN SUCH PAIN...
...SO I STOPPED IT MYSELF.

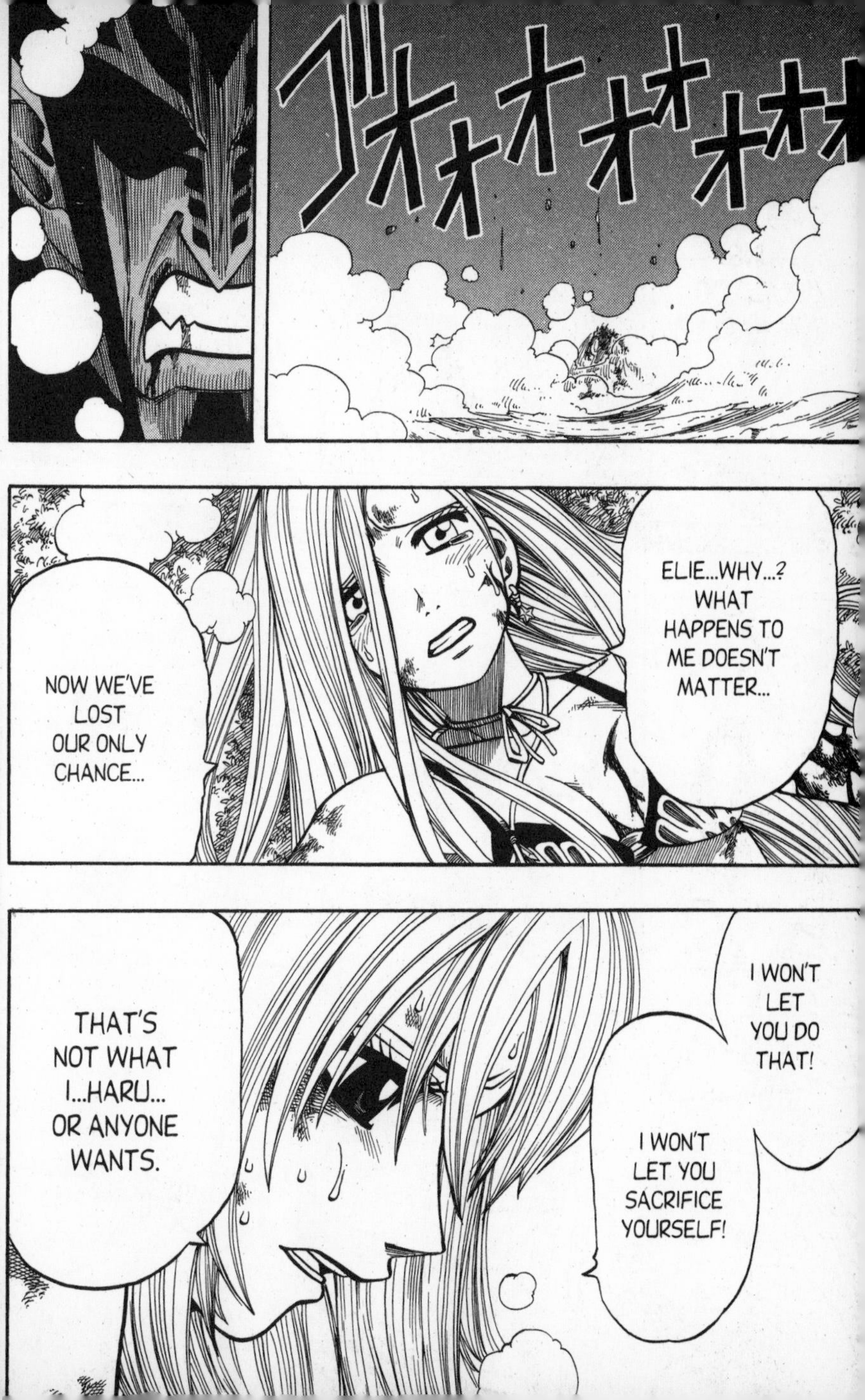
ゴオォオォオォオ
ELIE...WHY...? WHAT HAPPENS TO ME DOESN'T MATTER...
NOW WE'VE LOST OUR ONLY CHANCE...
I WON'T LET YOU DO THAT!
I WON'T LET YOU SACRIFICE YOURSELF!
THAT'S NOT WHAT I...HARU... OR ANYONE WANTS.

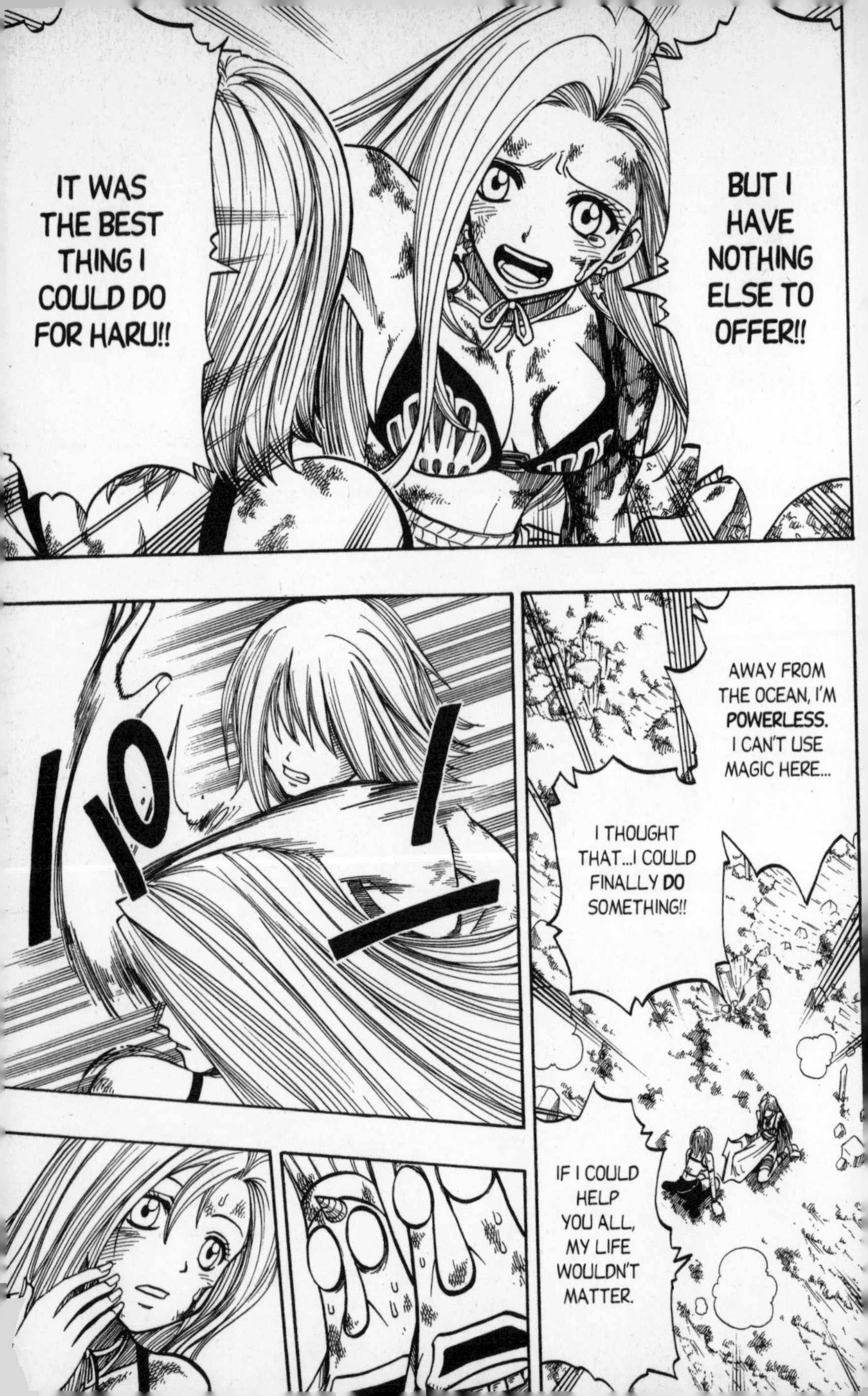
BUT I HAVE NOTHING ELSE TO OFFER!!
IT WAS THE BEST THING I COULD DO FOR HARU!!
AWAY FROM THE OCEAN, I'M **POWERLESS.** I CAN'T USE MAGIC HERE...
I THOUGHT THAT...I COULD FINALLY **DO** SOMETHING!!
IF I COULD HELP YOU ALL, MY LIFE WOULDN'T MATTER.

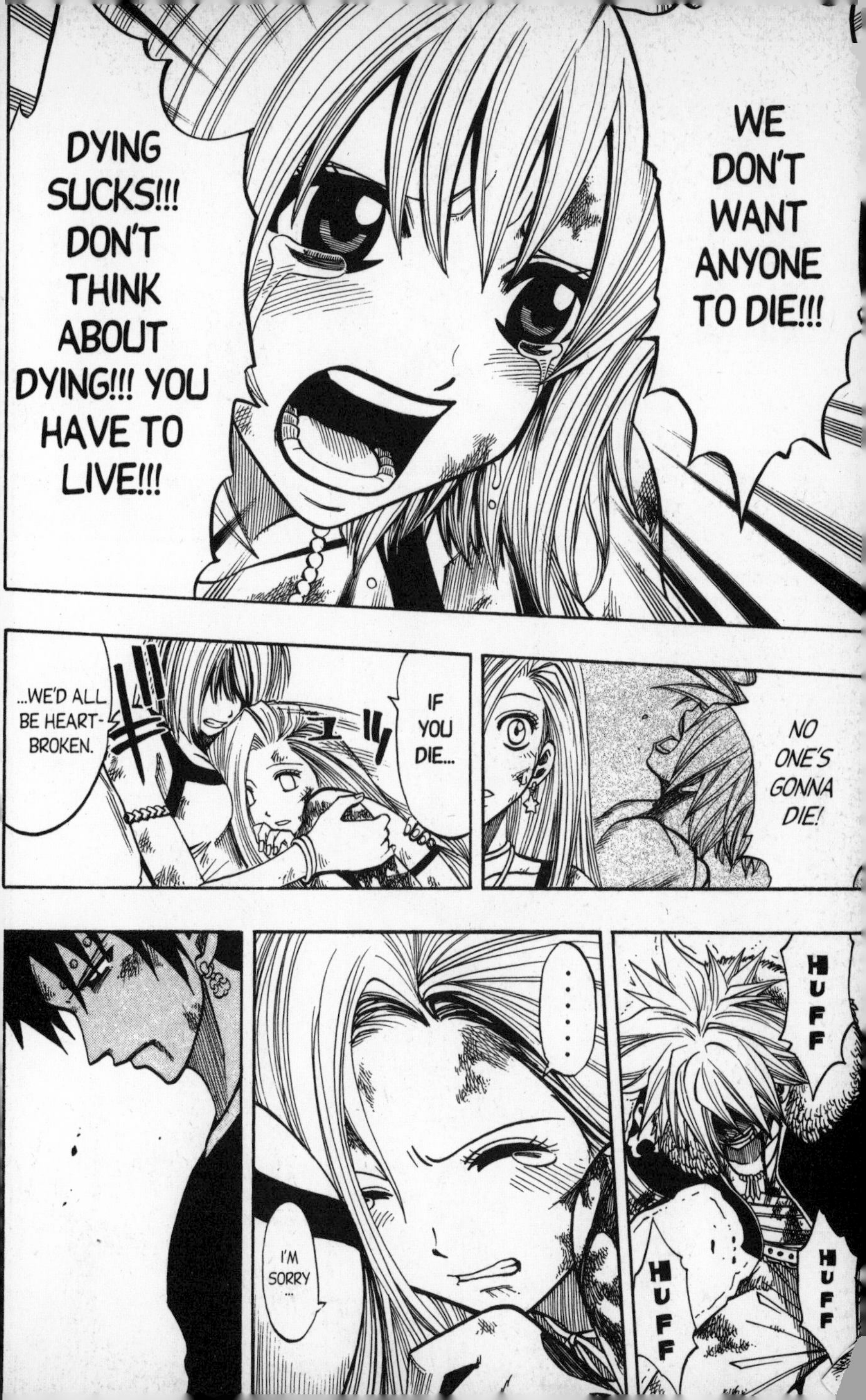
WE DON'T WANT ANYONE TO DIE!!!
DYING SUCKS!!! DON'T THINK ABOUT DYING!!! YOU HAVE TO LIVE!!!
NO ONE'S GONNA DIE!
IF YOU DIE...
...WE'D ALL BE HEART-BROKEN.
HUFF
HUFF
HUFF
......
I'M SORRY...

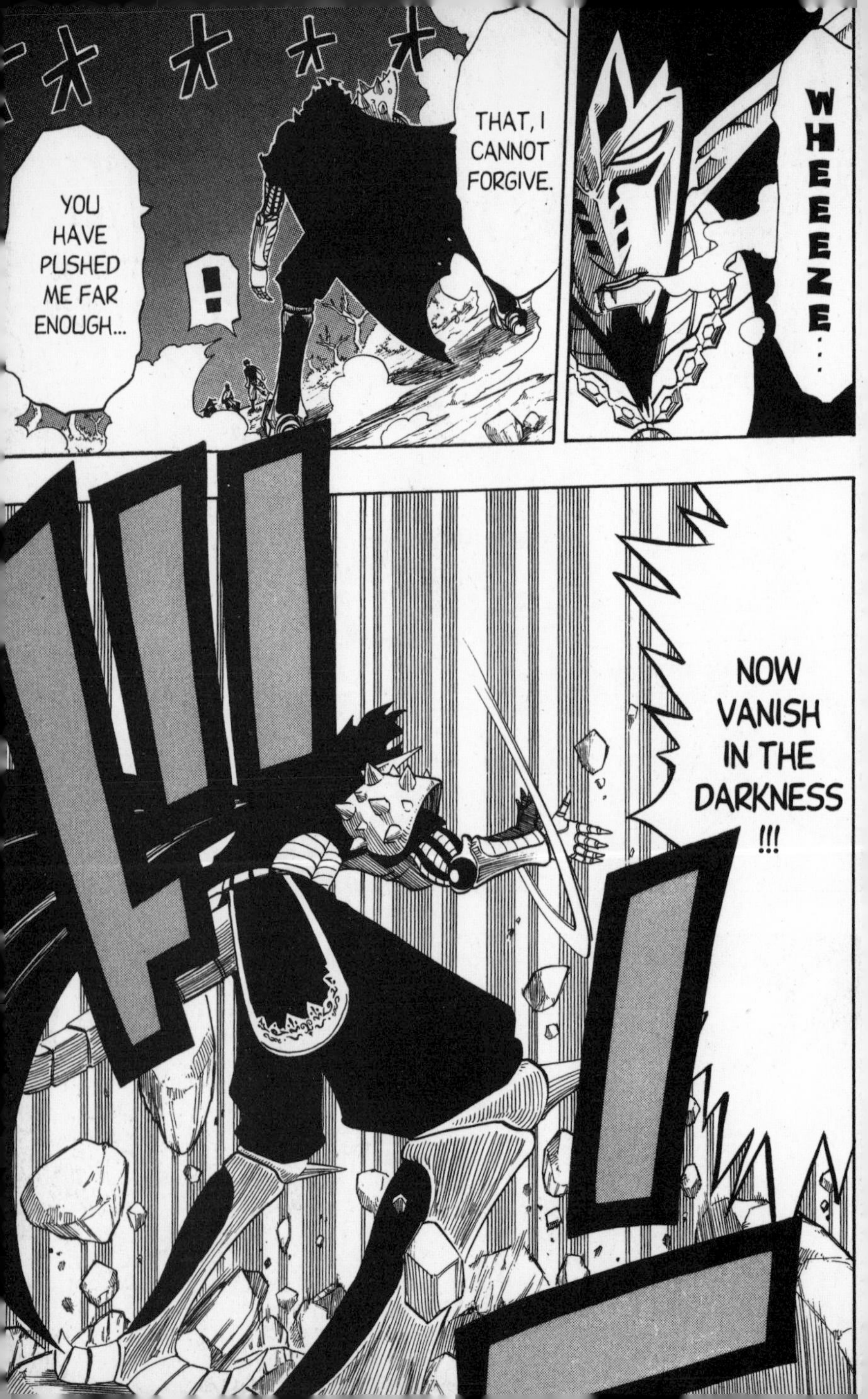
WHEEZE...
THAT, I CANNOT FORGIVE.
YOU HAVE PUSHED ME FAR ENOUGH...
!
オオオオ
NOW VANISH IN THE DARKNESS !!!

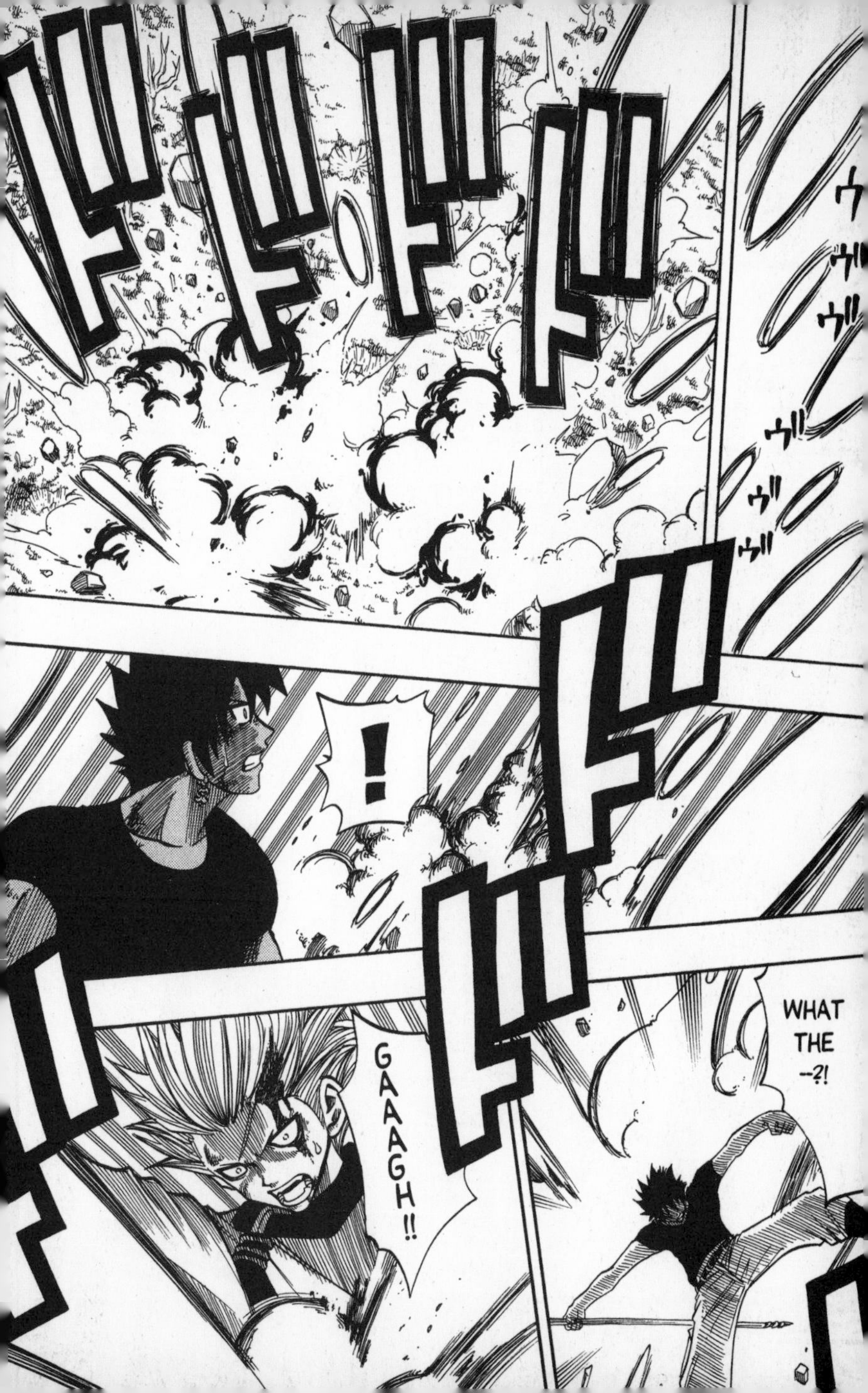
ドドドドド
ウヴヴヴ
ヴヴヴ
!
ドド
WHAT THE --?!
GAAAGH!!

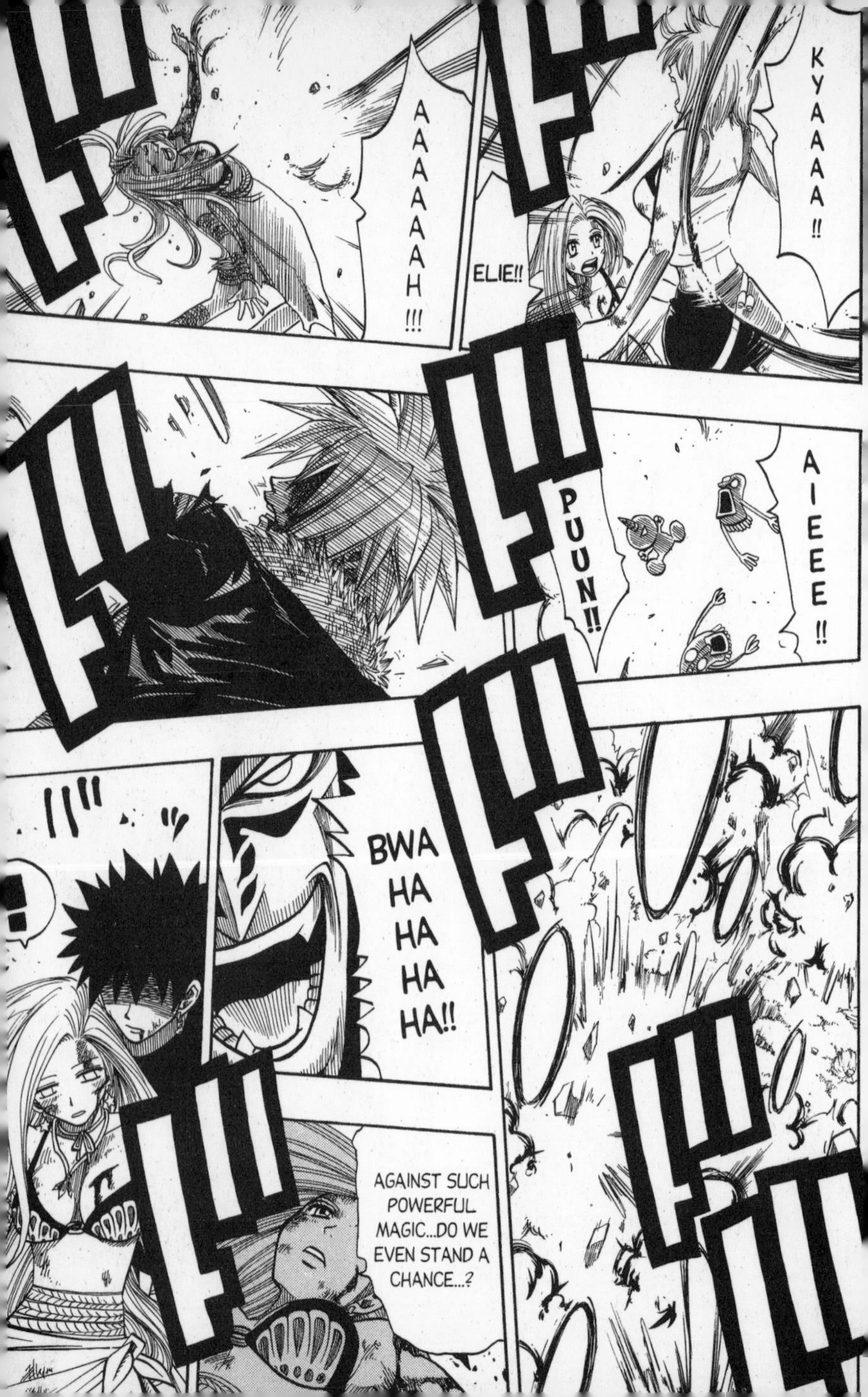
KYAAAAA!!
ELIE!!
AAAAAAAH!!!
AIEEE!!
PUUN!!
BWA HA HA HA HA!!
AGAINST SUCH POWERFUL MAGIC...DO WE EVEN STAND A CHANCE...?

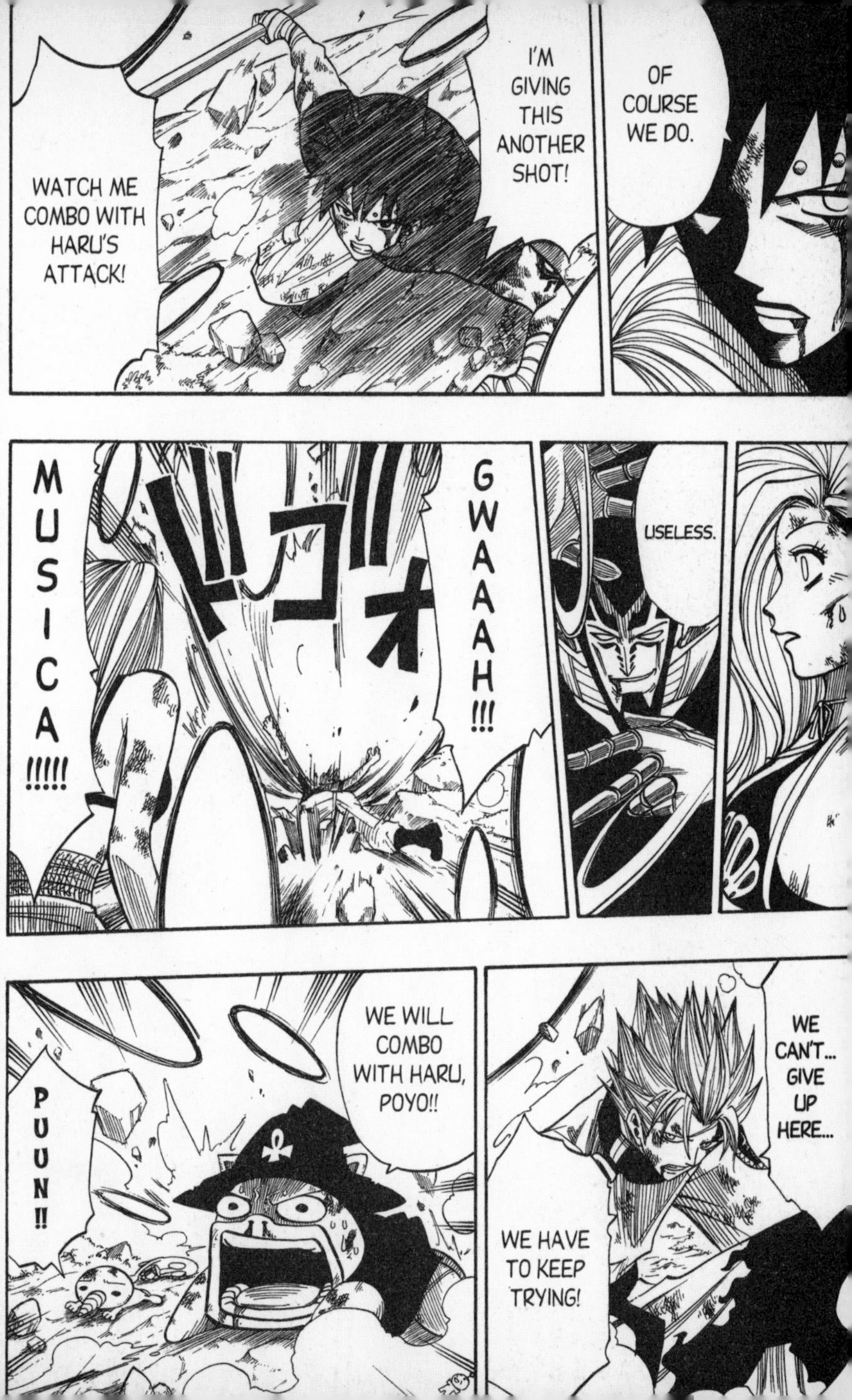
OF COURSE WE DO.
I'M GIVING THIS ANOTHER SHOT!
WATCH ME COMBO WITH HARU'S ATTACK!
USELESS.
GWAAAAH!!!
ドゴオ
MUSICA!!!!!
WE CAN'T... GIVE UP HERE...
WE HAVE TO KEEP TRYING!
WE WILL COMBO WITH HARU, POYO!!
PUUUN!!

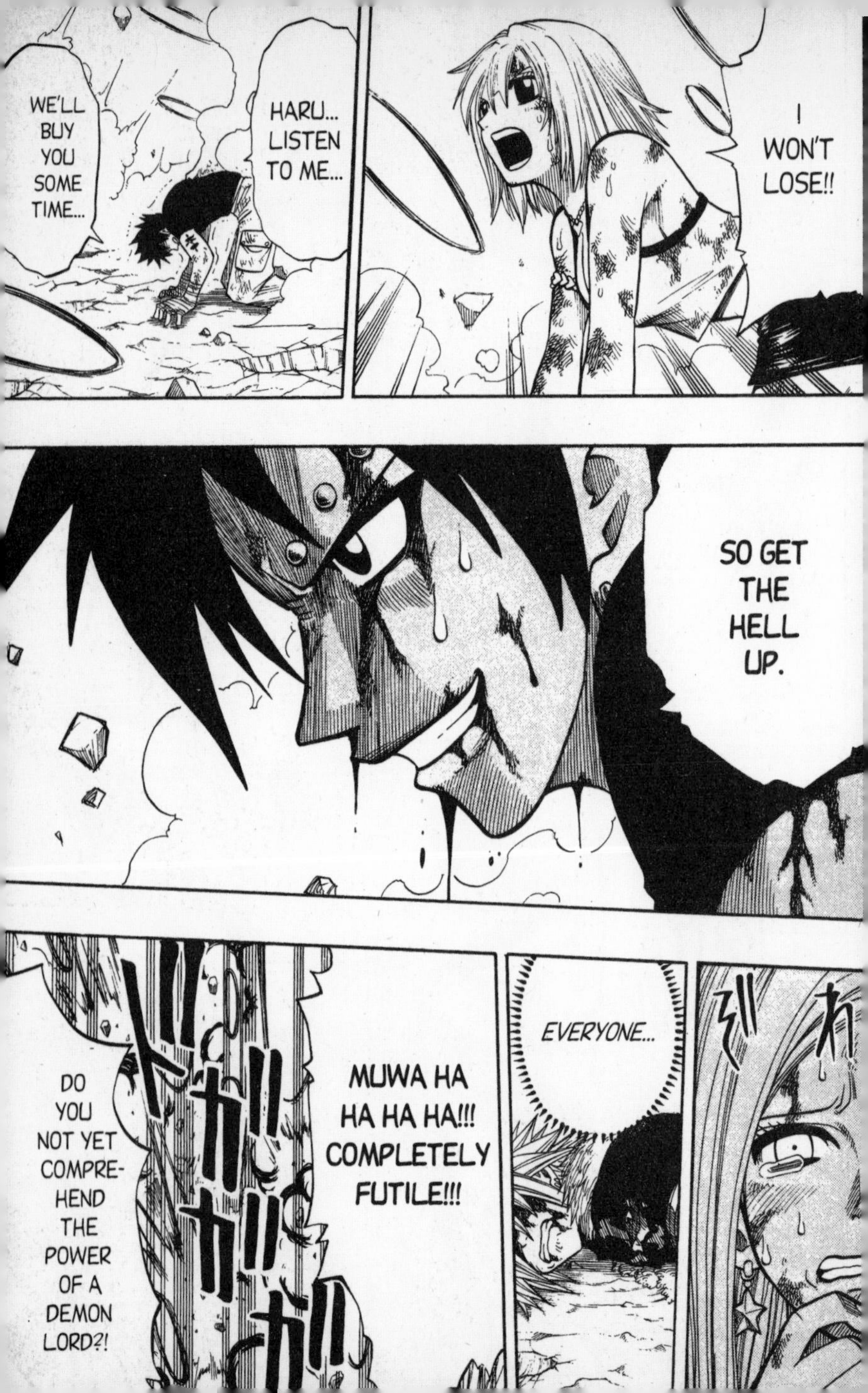
I WON'T LOSE!!
HARU... LISTEN TO ME...
WE'LL BUY YOU SOME TIME...
SO GET THE HELL UP.
EVERYONE...
MUWA HA HA HA HA!!! COMPLETELY FUTILE!!!
DO YOU NOT YET COMPREHEND THE POWER OF A DEMON LORD?!

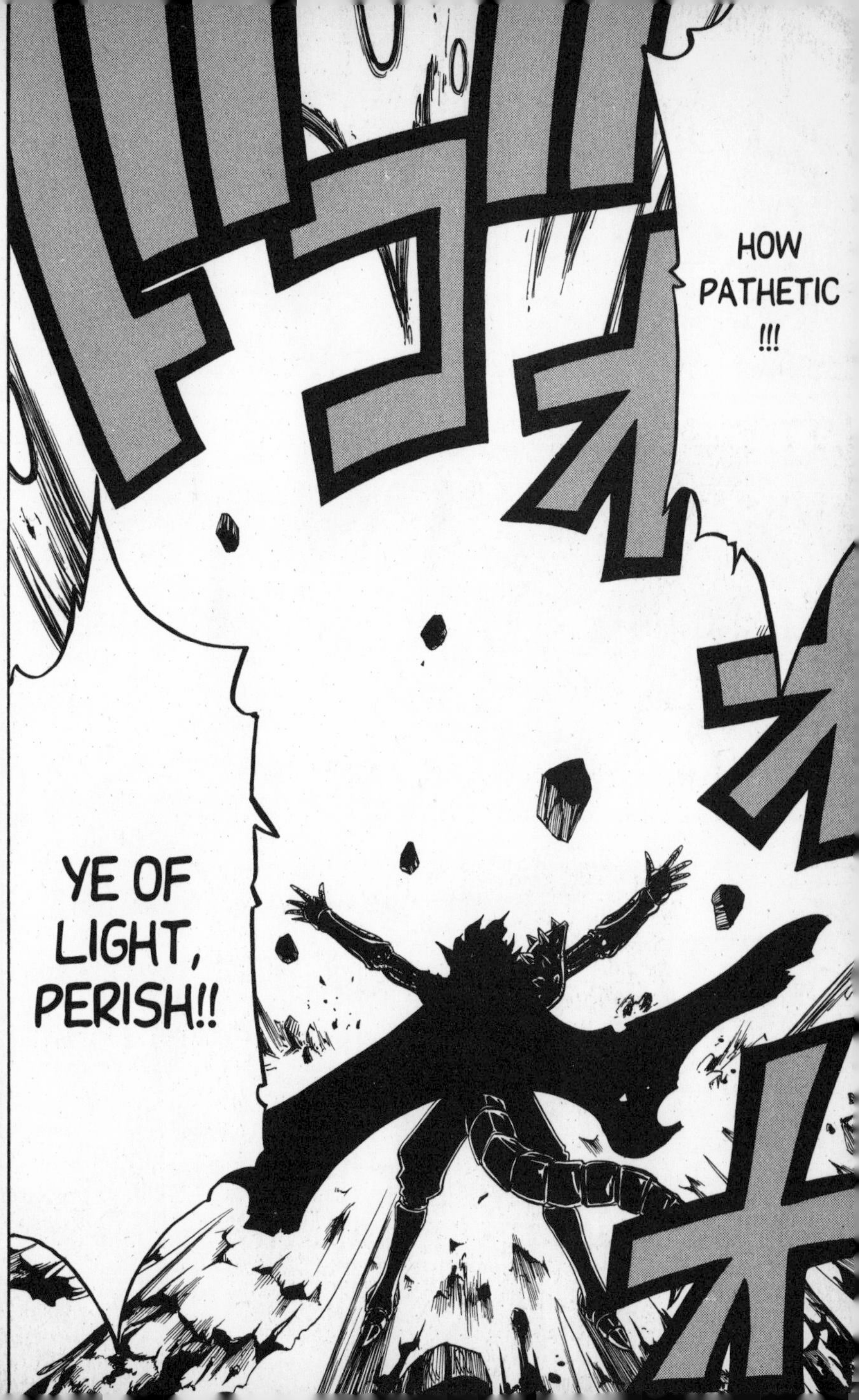
HOW PATHETIC !!!
YE OF LIGHT, PERISH!!

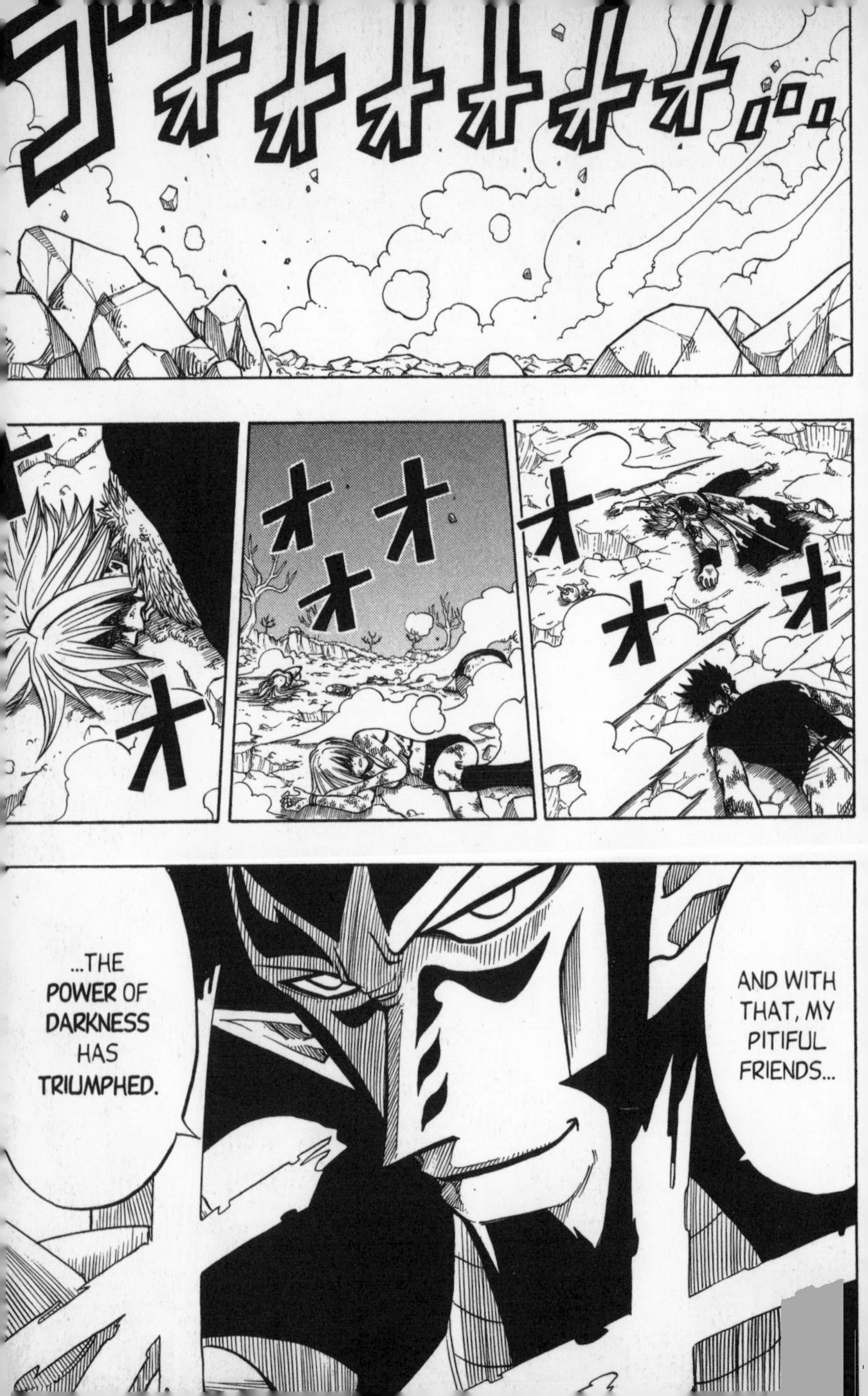
ゴオオオオオオ。。。
オオオ
オオオ
オ
AND WITH THAT, MY PITIFUL FRIENDS...
...THE POWER OF DARKNESS HAS TRIUMPHED.

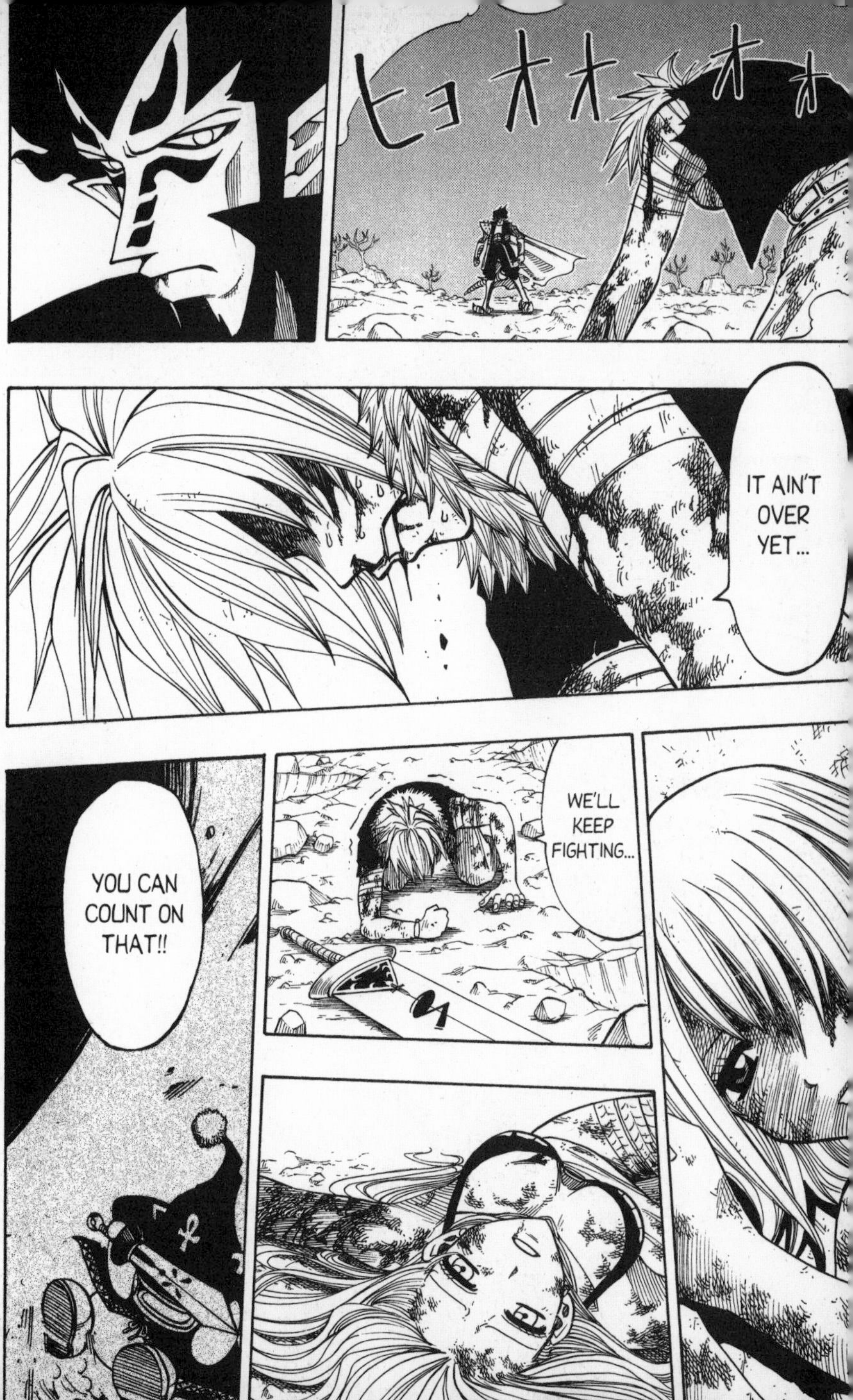
ヒョオオオォ
IT AIN'T OVER YET...
WE'LL KEEP FIGHTING...
YOU CAN COUNT ON THAT!!

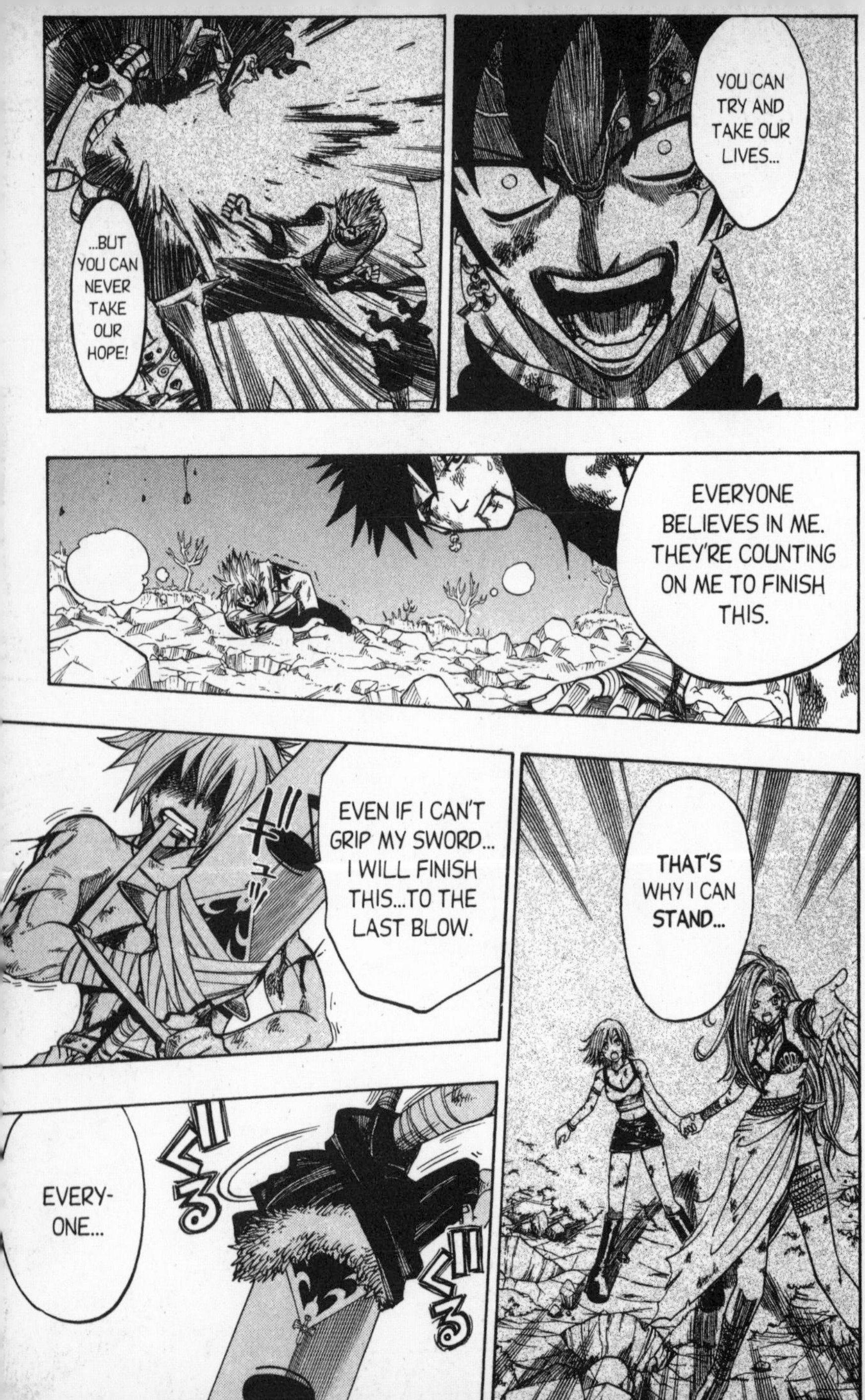
YOU CAN TRY AND TAKE OUR LIVES...
...BUT YOU CAN NEVER TAKE OUR HOPE!
EVERYONE BELIEVES IN ME. THEY'RE COUNTING ON ME TO FINISH THIS.
THAT'S WHY I CAN STAND...
EVEN IF I CAN'T GRIP MY SWORD... I WILL FINISH THIS...TO THE LAST BLOW.
EVERY-ONE...

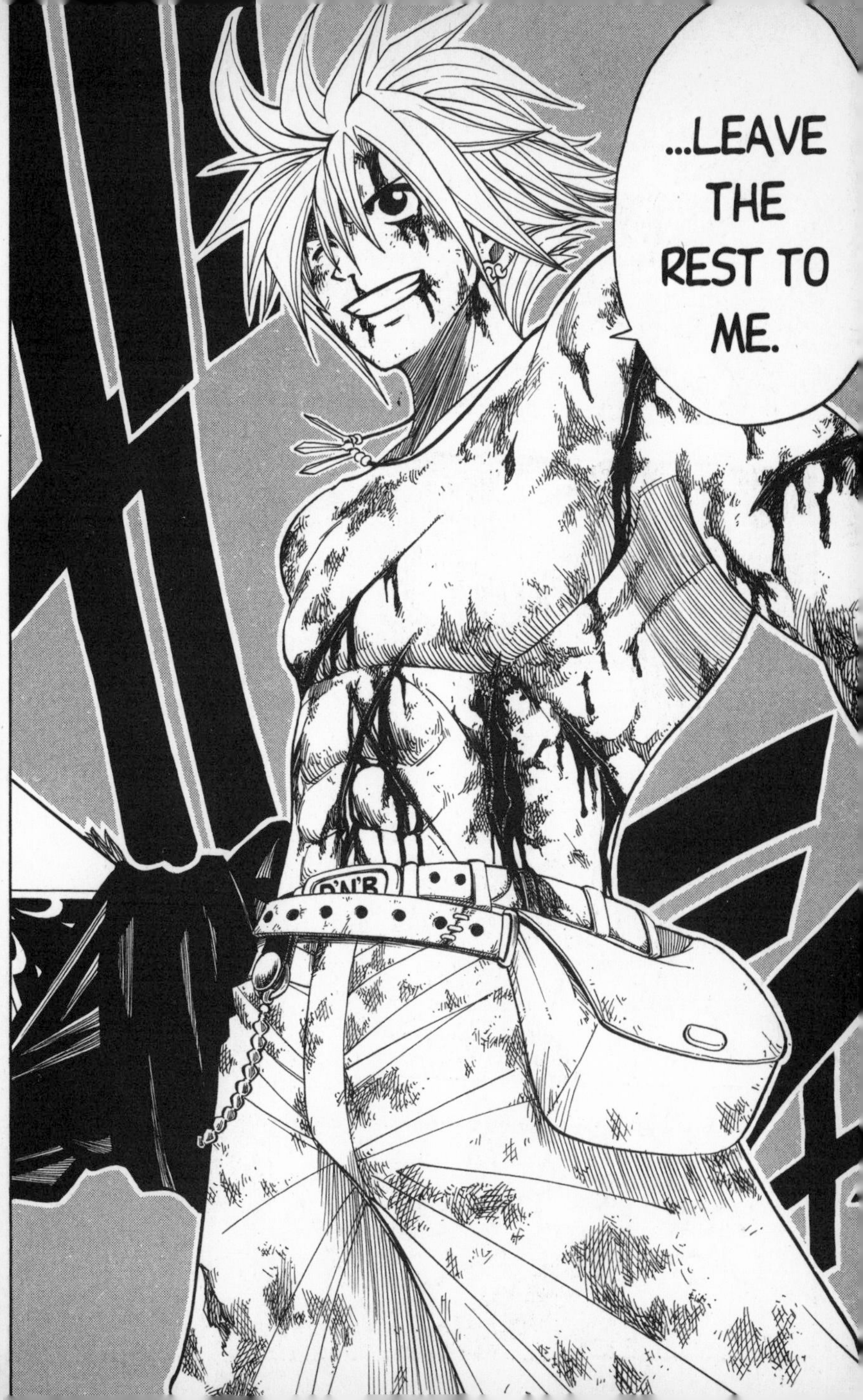
...LEAVE THE REST TO ME.
D'N'B

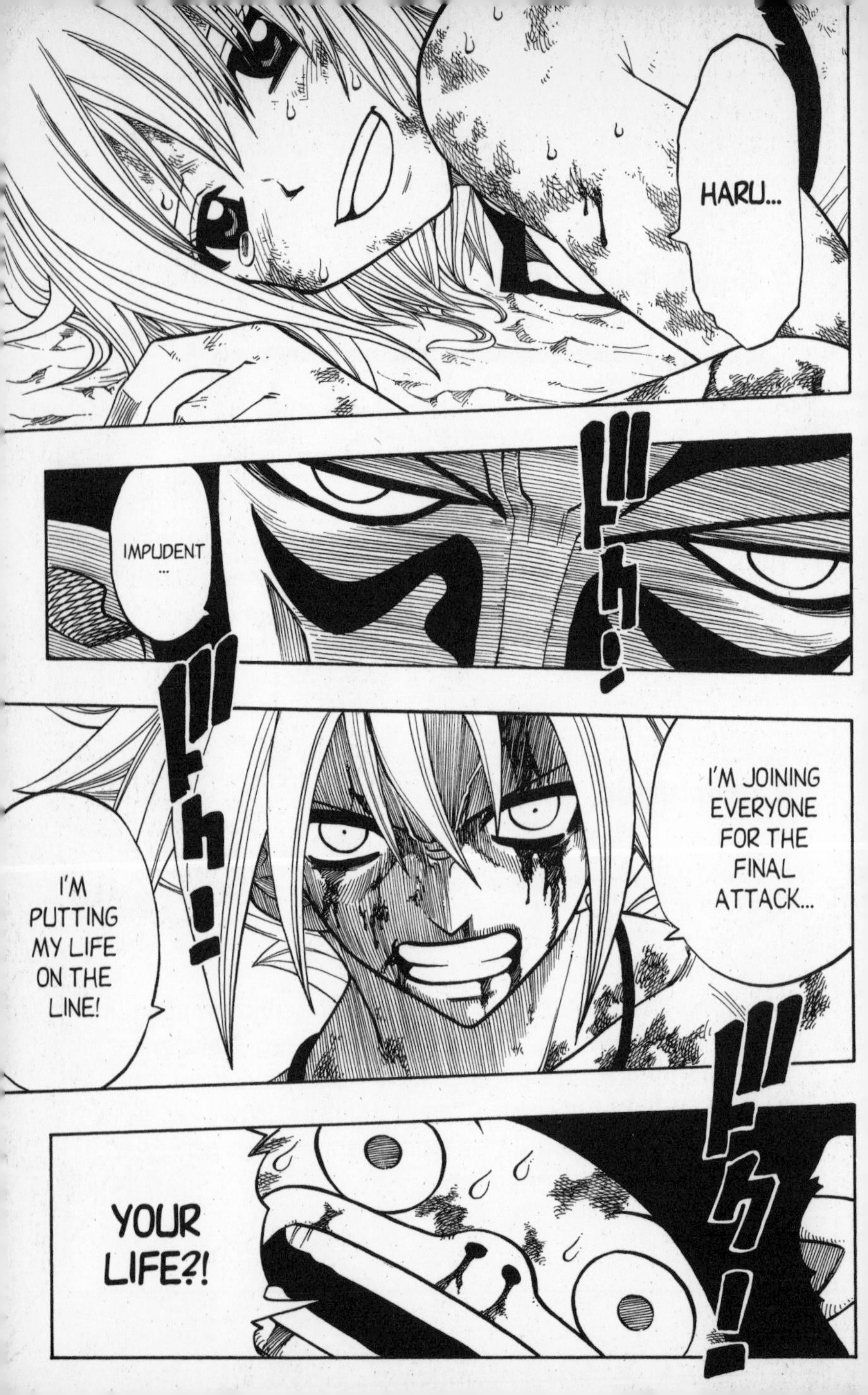
HARU...
IMPUDENT ...
I'M JOINING EVERYONE FOR THE FINAL ATTACK...
I'M PUTTING MY LIFE ON THE LINE!
YOUR LIFE?!

The Ten Powers Sword #4

7. Gravity Blade: GRAVITY CORE

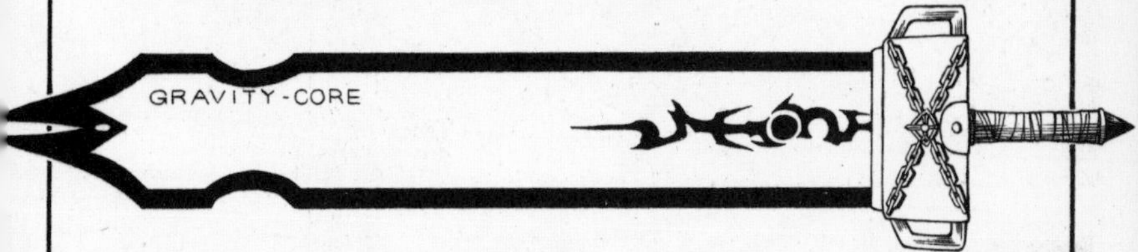
GRAVITY-CORE

Incredibly destructive sword that can cut very hard things. However, the tradeoff is that it's extremely heavy and requires great strength to use. Although more powerful than Explosion, it's a very difficult blade to use.

8. Solar Blade: MILLION SUNS

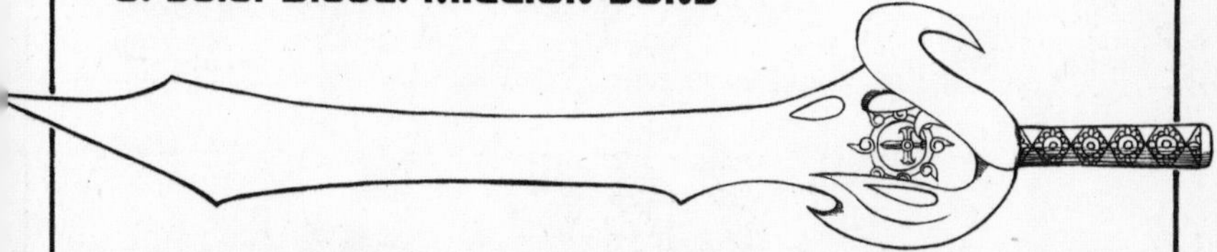

Meaning "the force of a million suns." It would be scary if it were that powerful... Anyway, Haru did say that it wasn't strictly for defeating Dark affinity while telling Doryu that it wasn't a fight between different affinities. However, this Light affinity sword has more than enough power to smash Dark affinity enemies.

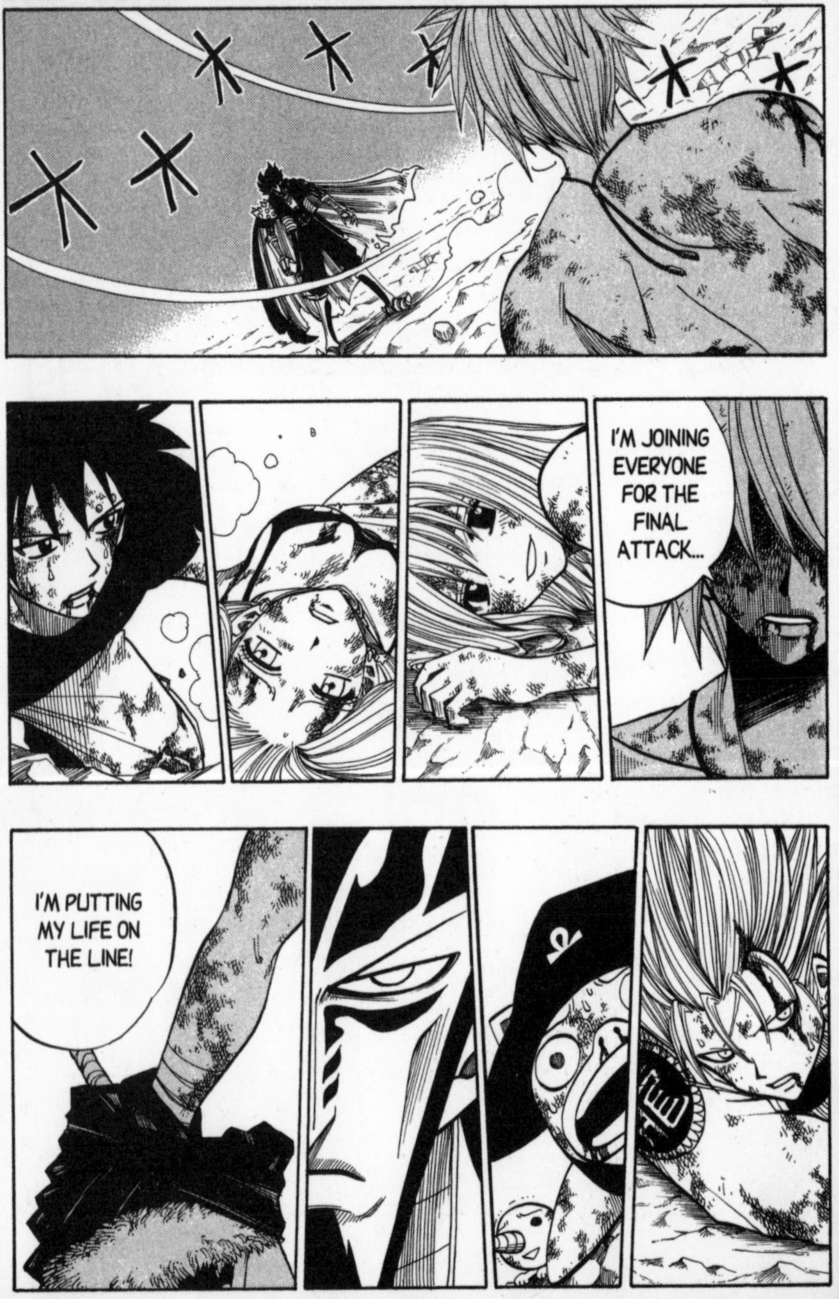
I'M JOINING EVERYONE FOR THE FINAL ATTACK...
I'M PUTTING MY LIFE ON THE LINE!

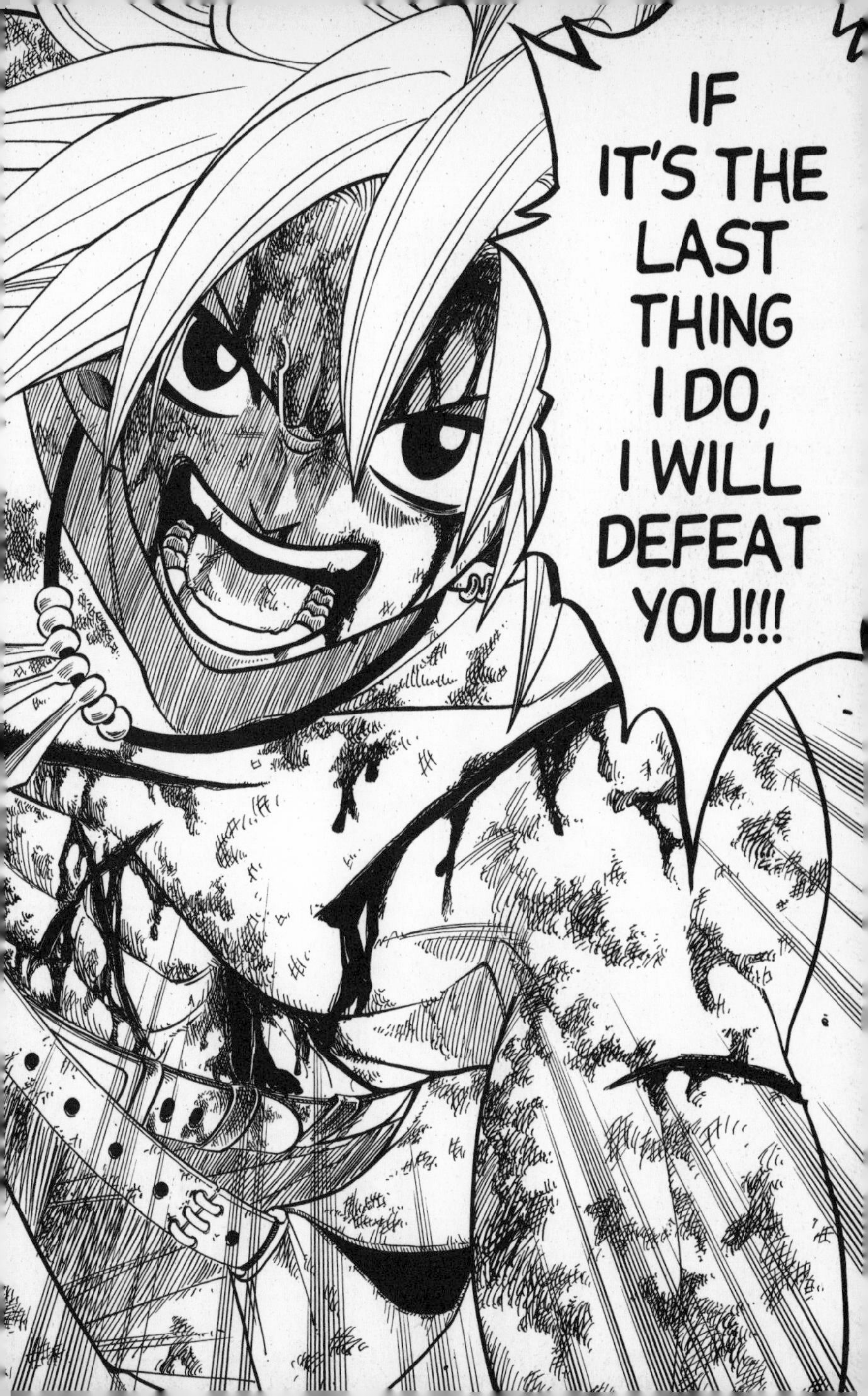
IF IT'S THE LAST THING I DO, I WILL DEFEAT YOU!!!

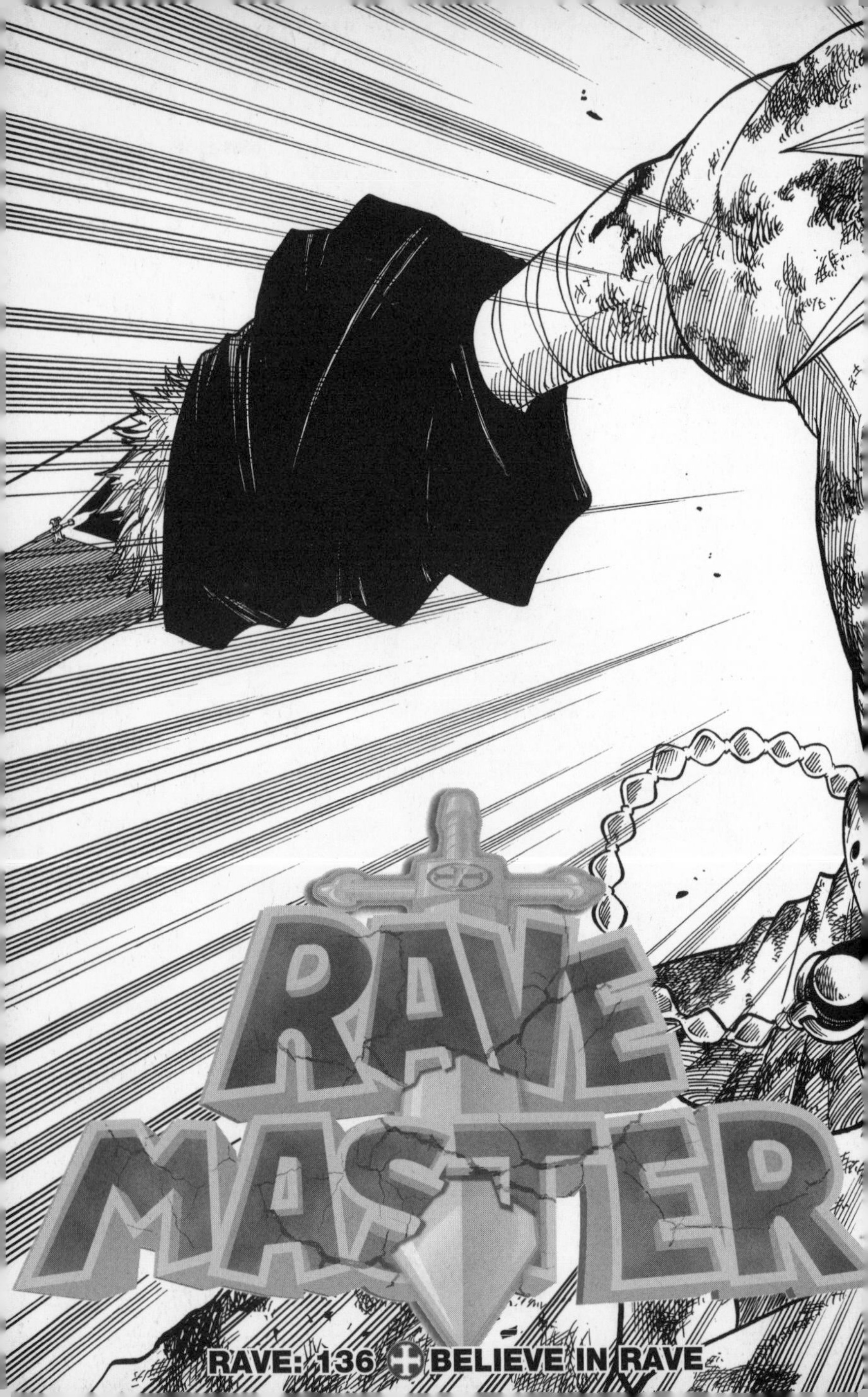
RAVE MASTER
RAVE: 136 BELIEVE IN RAVE

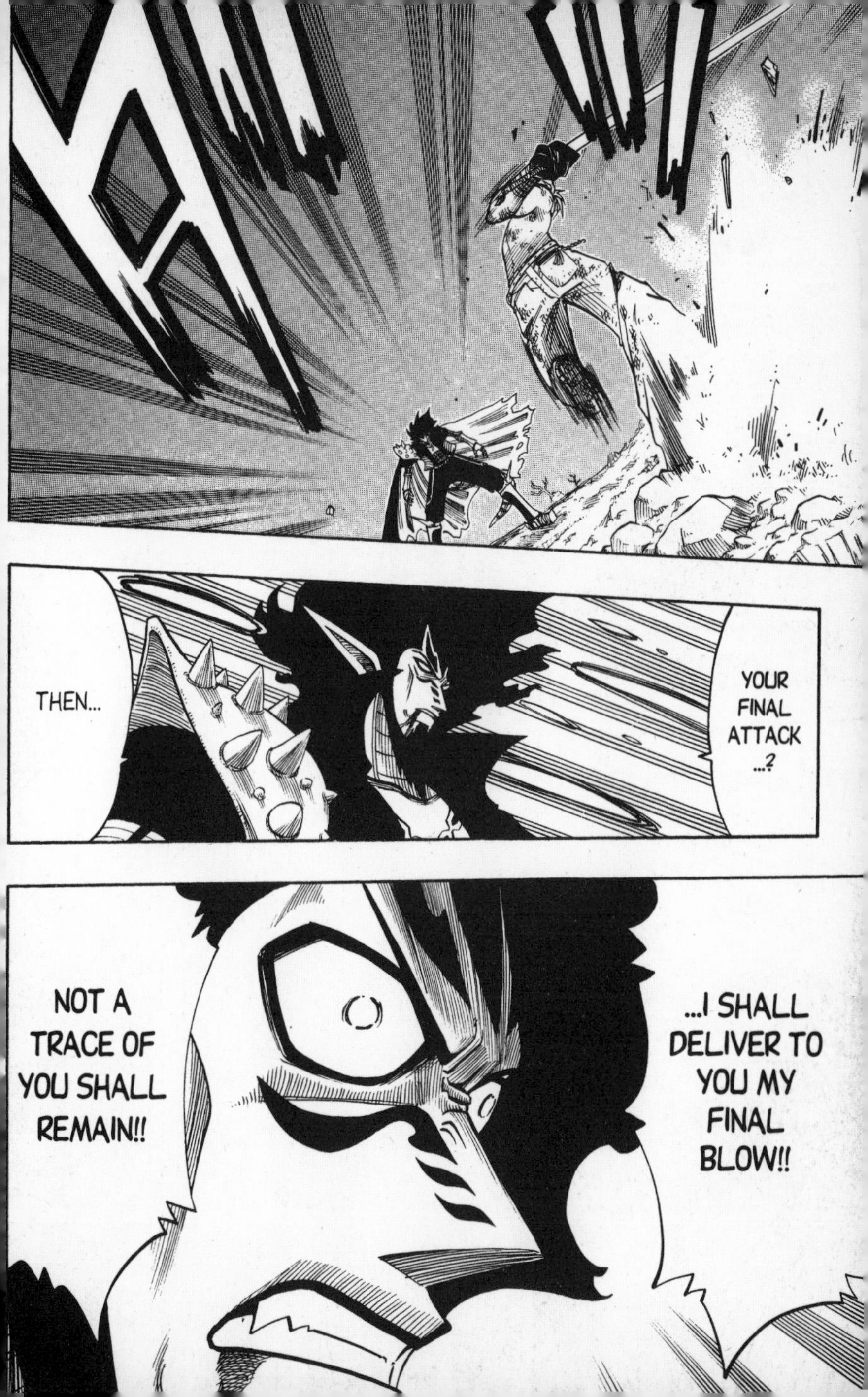
YOUR FINAL ATTACK ...?
THEN...
...I SHALL DELIVER TO YOU MY FINAL BLOW!!
NOT A TRACE OF YOU SHALL REMAIN!!

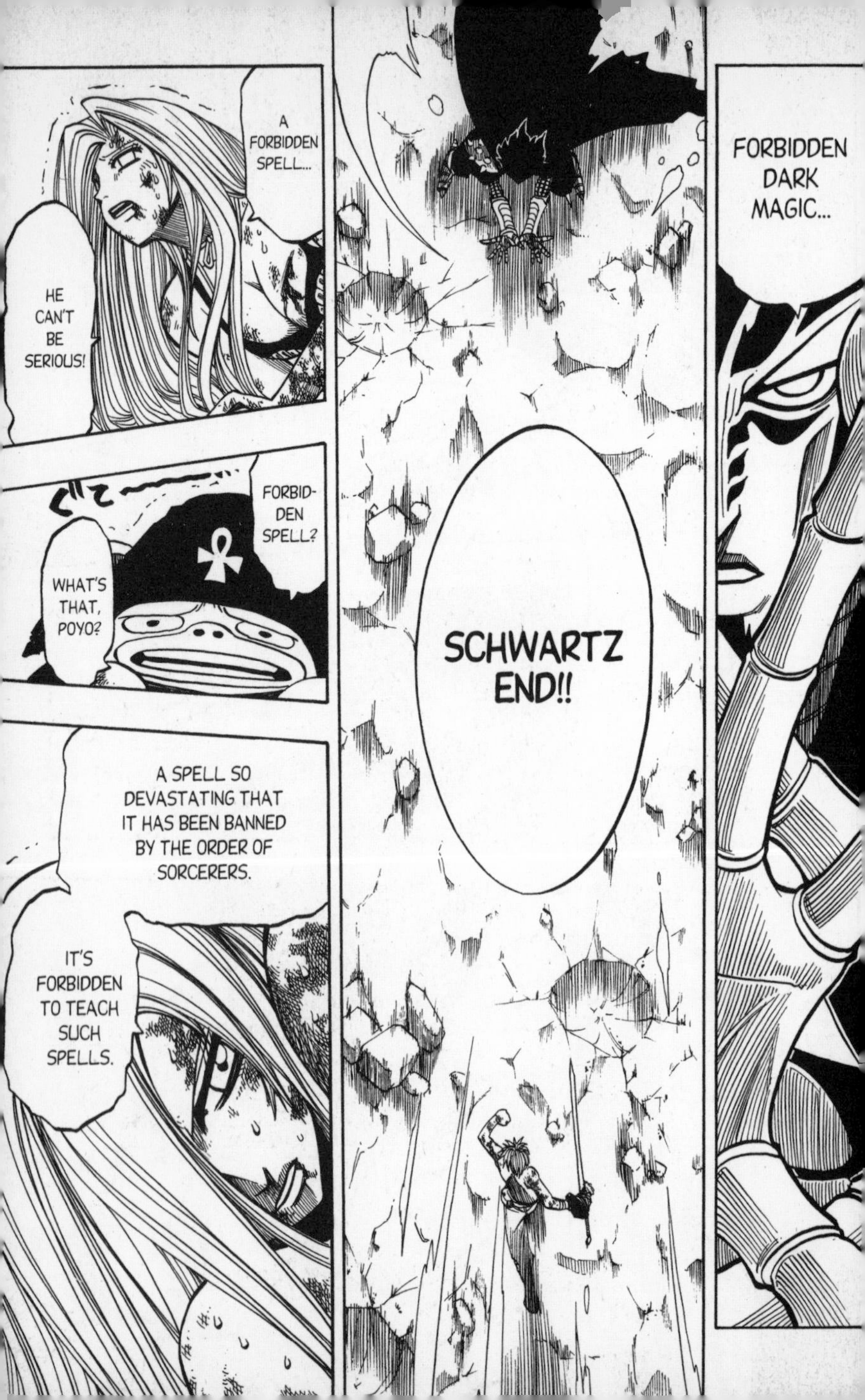
FORBIDDEN DARK MAGIC...
SCHWARTZ END!!
A FORBIDDEN SPELL...
HE CAN'T BE SERIOUS!
FORBID-DEN SPELL?
WHAT'S THAT, POYO?
A SPELL SO DEVASTATING THAT IT HAS BEEN BANNED BY THE ORDER OF SORCERERS.
IT'S FORBIDDEN TO TEACH SUCH SPELLS.

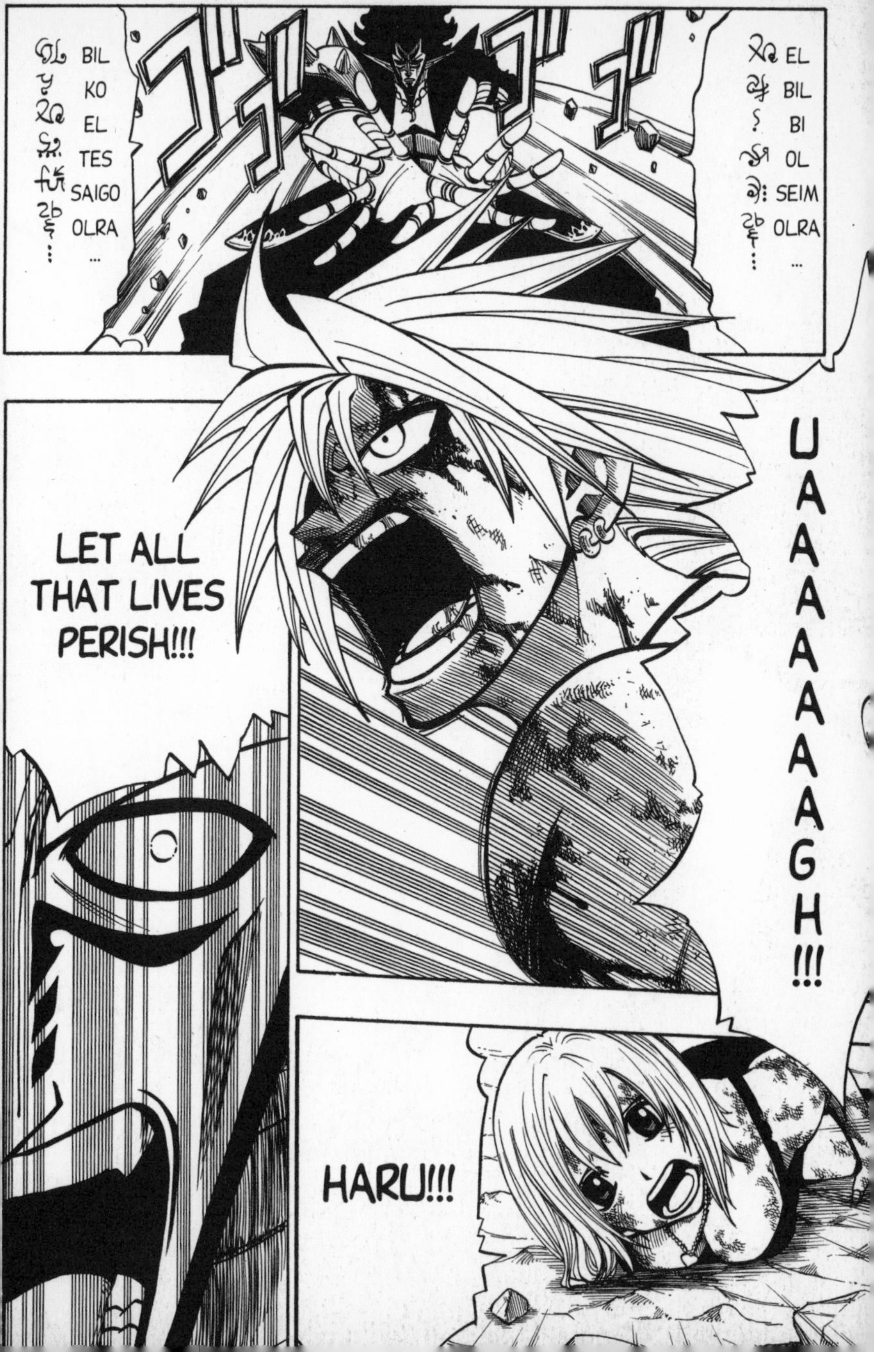
EL BIL BI OL SEIM OLRA ...
BIL KO EL TES SAIGO OLRA ...
UAAAAAAAGH!!!
LET ALL THAT LIVES PERISH!!!
HARU!!!

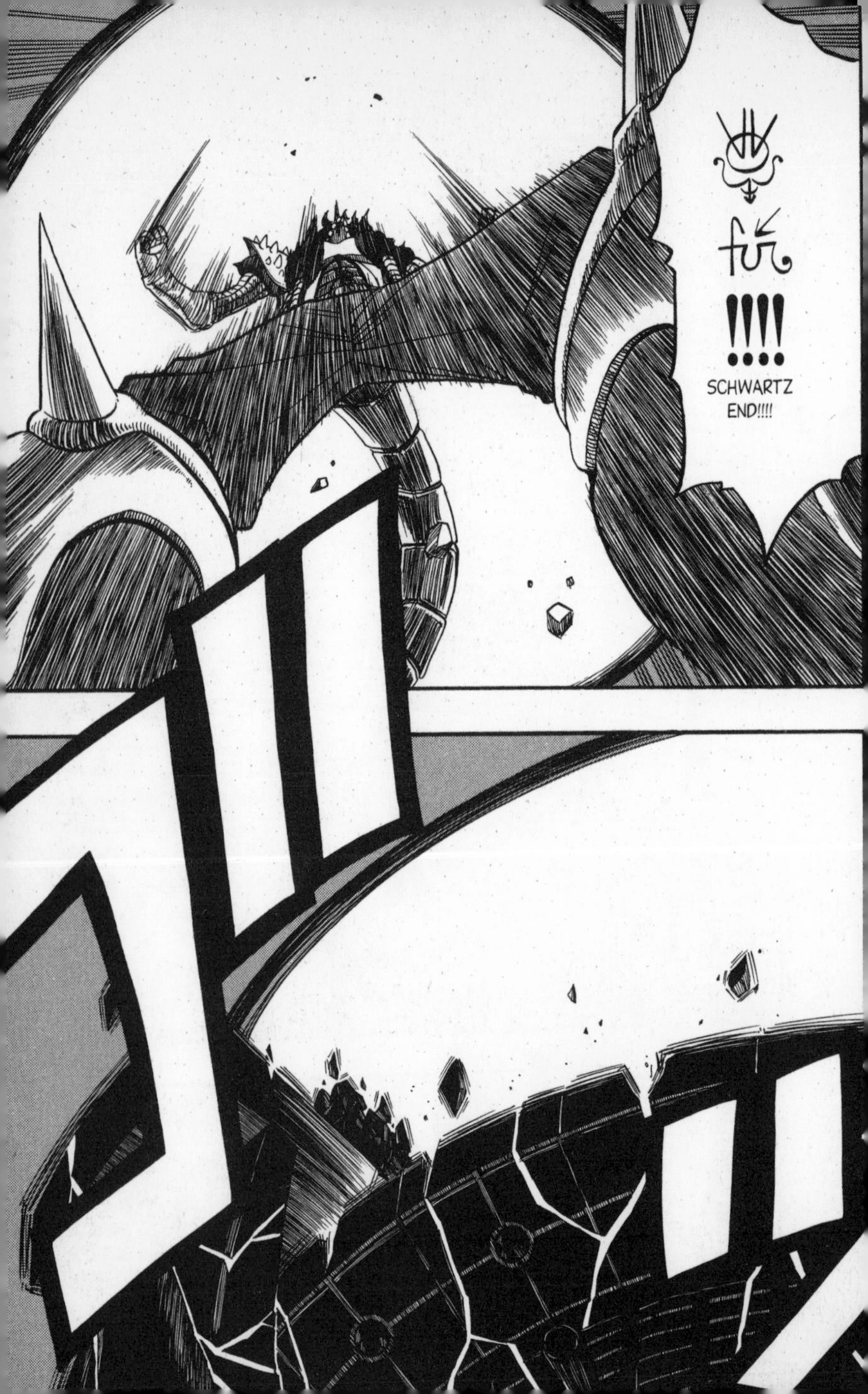
SCHWARTZ
END!!!!

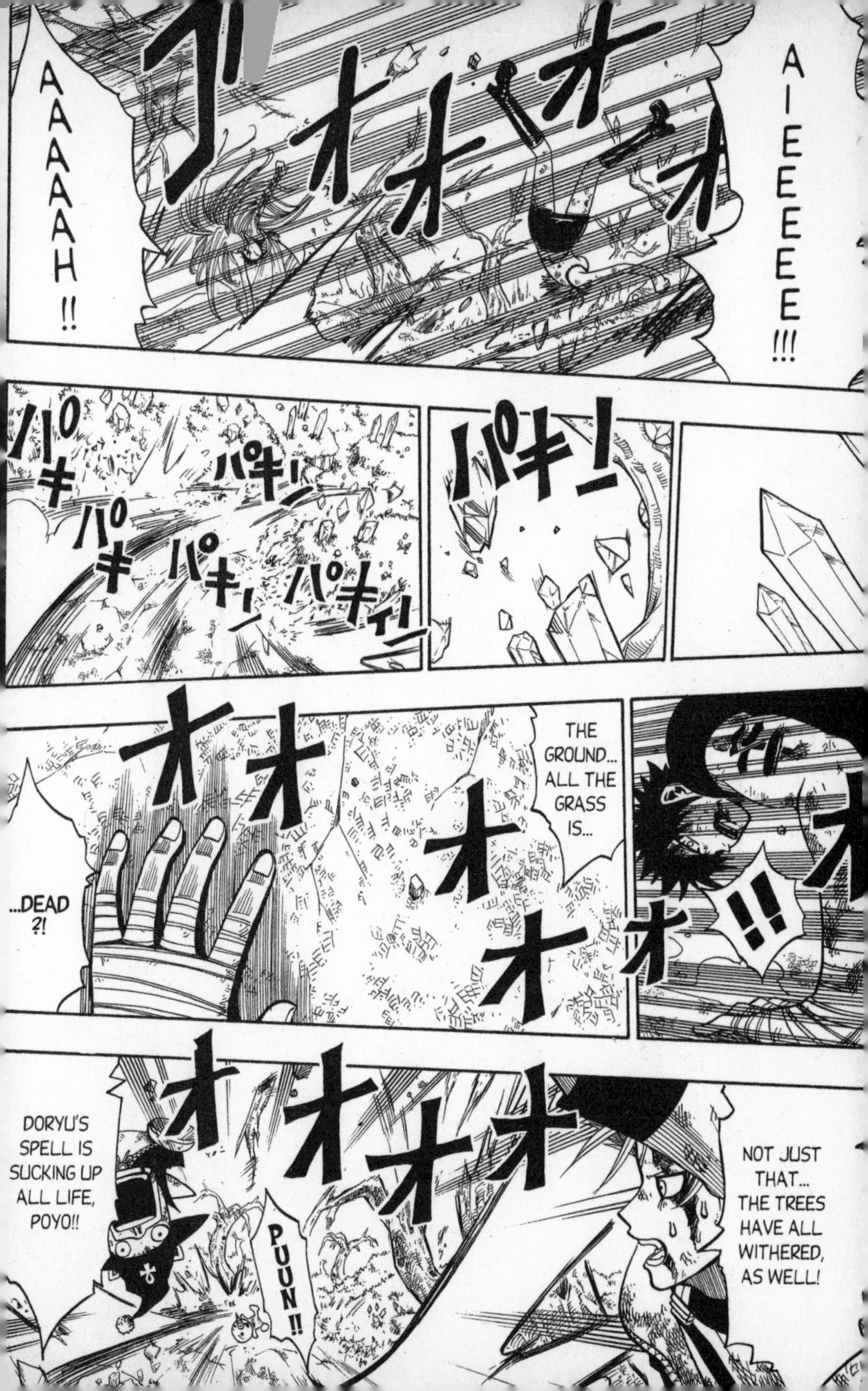

AIEEEEE!!!
ゴオオオオ
AAAAAH!!
パキー
パキ
パキン
パキ
パキン
パキィー
!!
THE GROUND... ALL THE GRASS IS...
オオオオ
...DEAD?!
NOT JUST THAT... THE TREES HAVE ALL WITHERED, AS WELL!
オオオオ
PUUN!!
DORYU'S SPELL IS SUCKING UP ALL LIFE, POYO!!

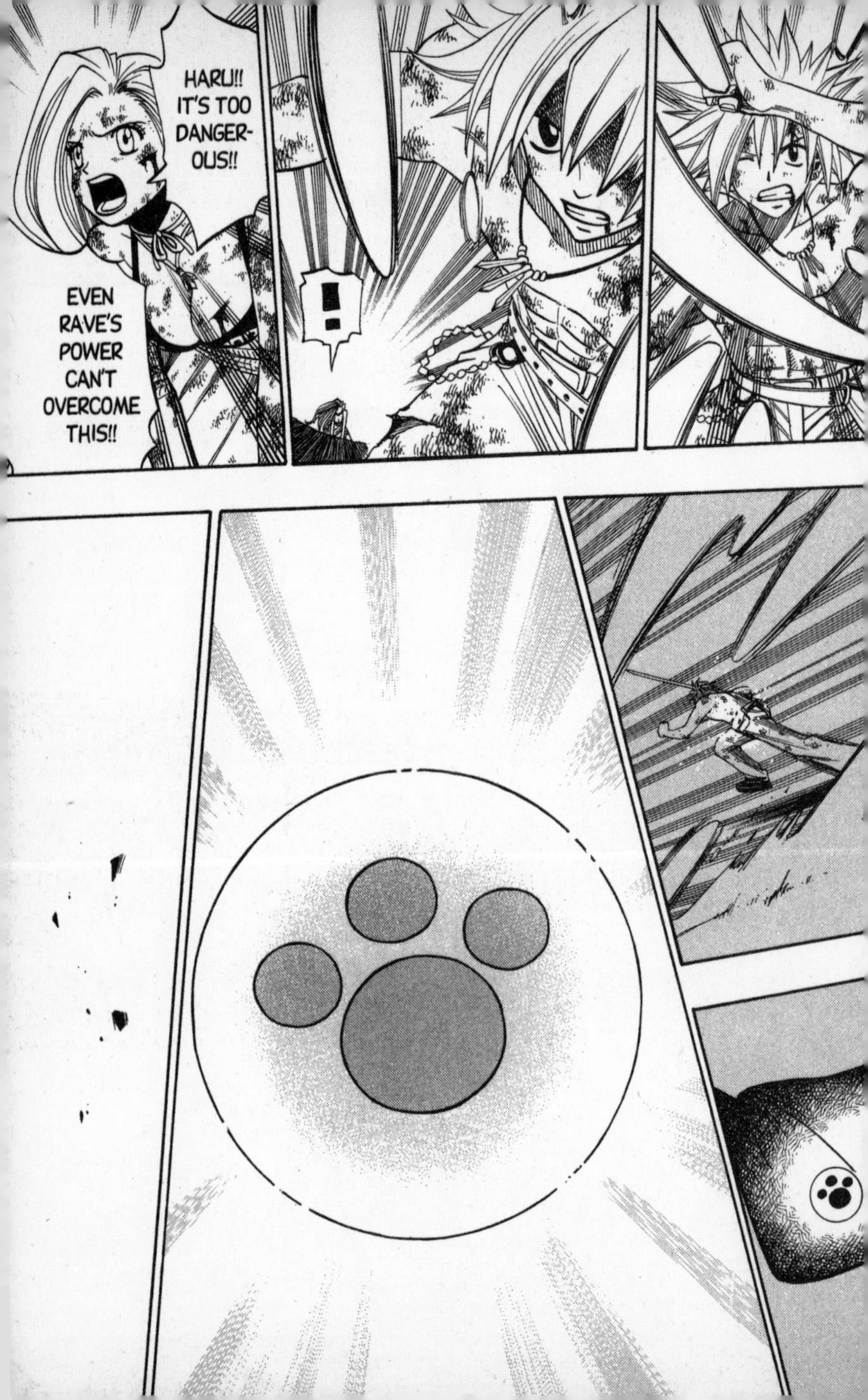
!
HARU!! IT'S TOO DANGER-OUS!!
EVEN RAVE'S POWER CAN'T OVERCOME THIS!!

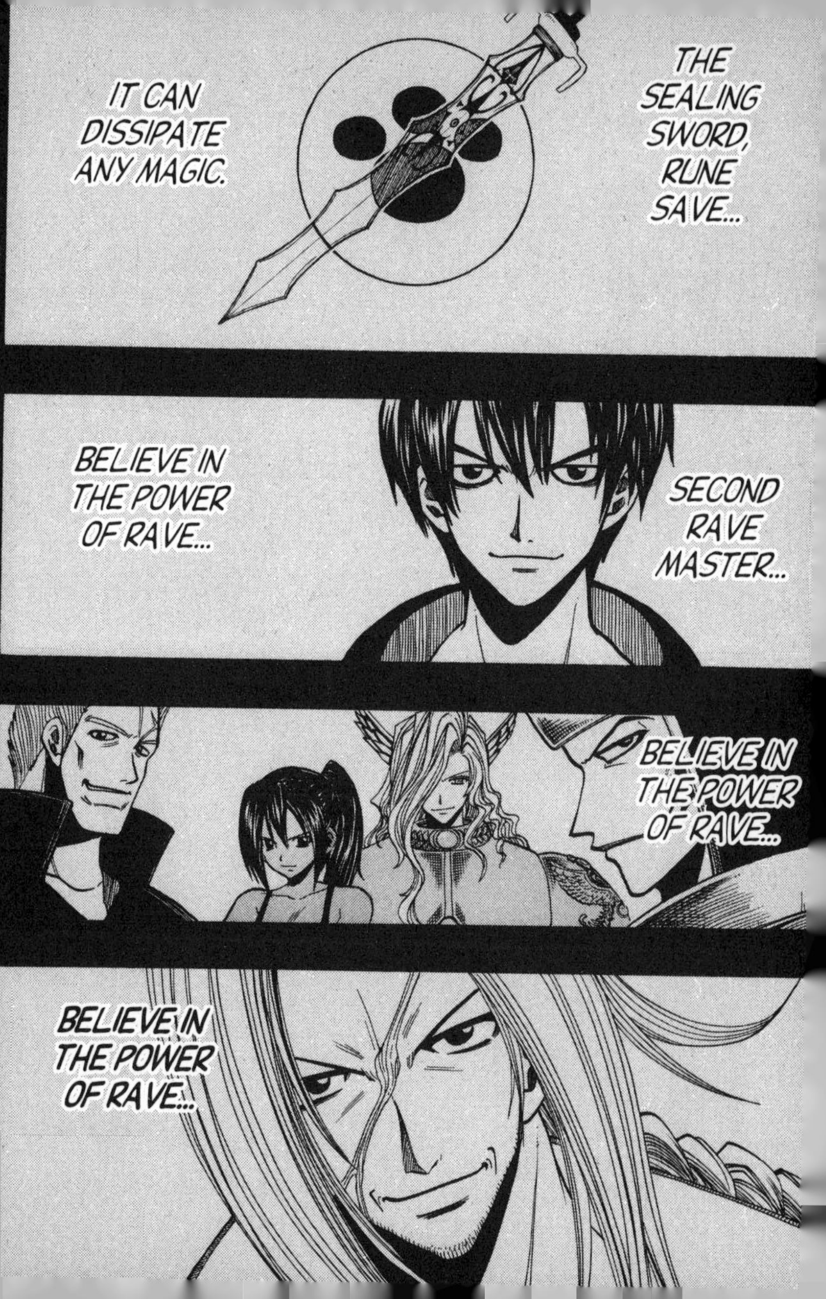
THE SEALING SWORD, RUNE SAVE...
IT CAN DISSIPATE ANY MAGIC.
SECOND RAVE MASTER...
BELIEVE IN THE POWER OF RAVE...
BELIEVE IN THE POWER OF RAVE...
BELIEVE IN THE POWER OF RAVE...

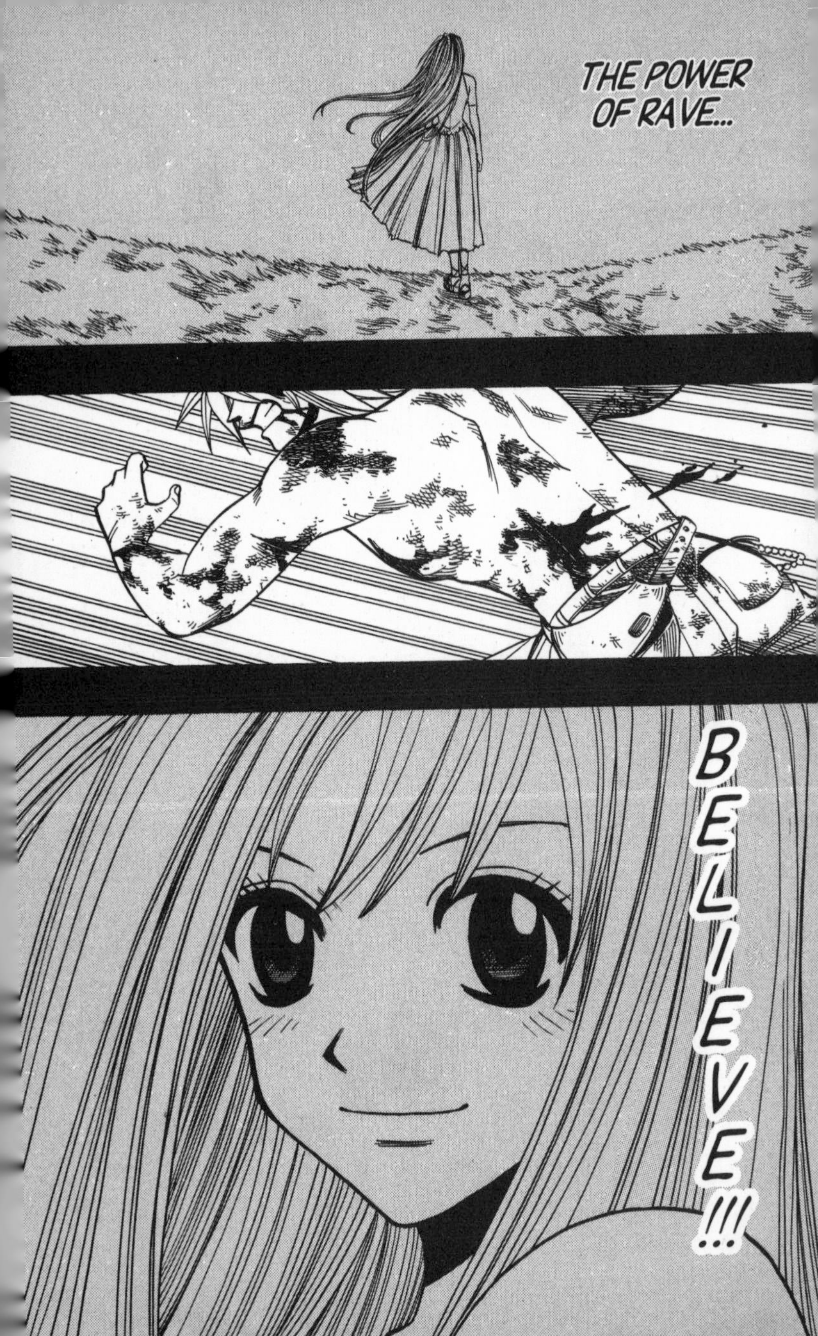
THE POWER OF RAVE...
BELIEVE!!!

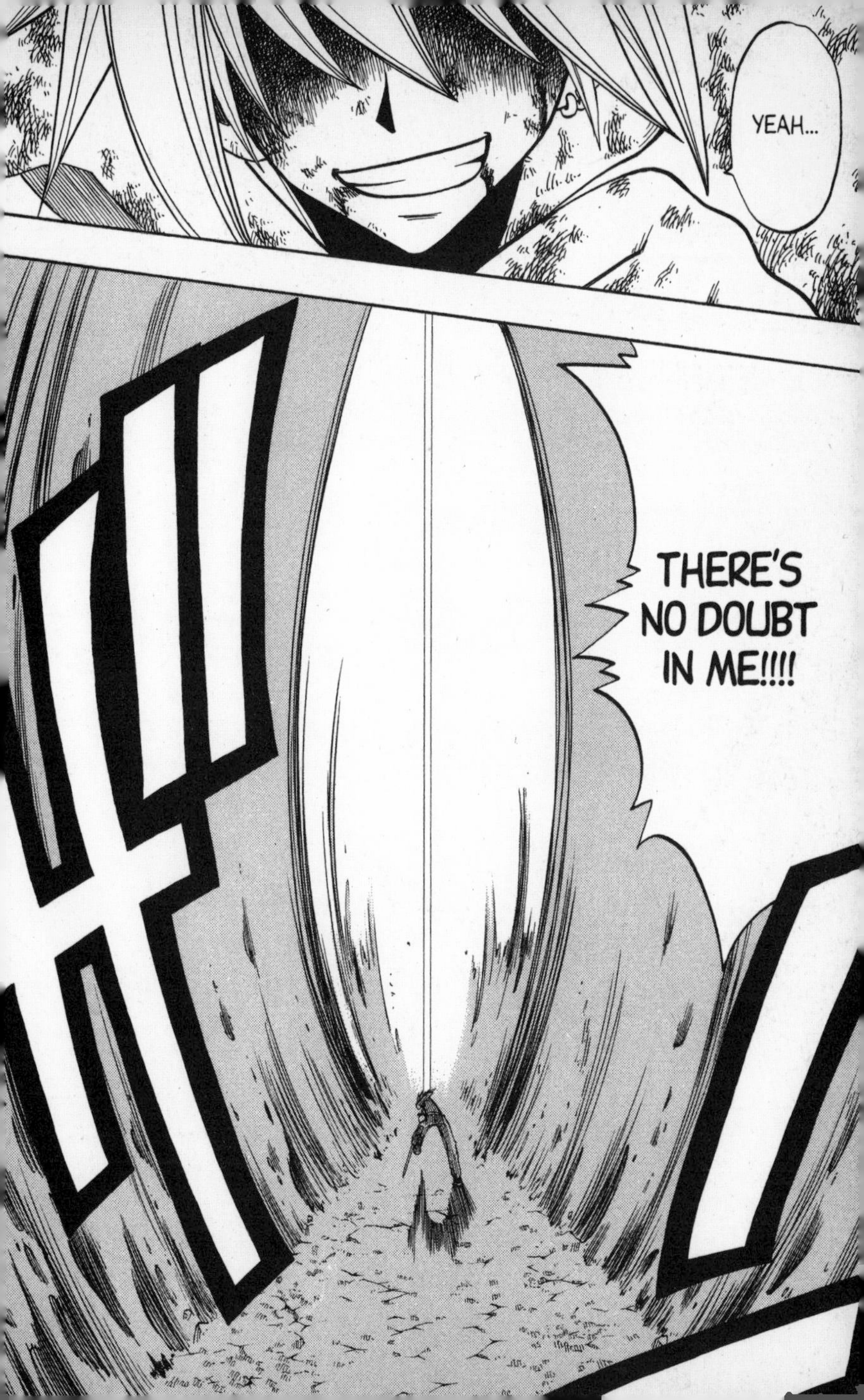
YEAH...
THERE'S NO DOUBT IN ME!!!!

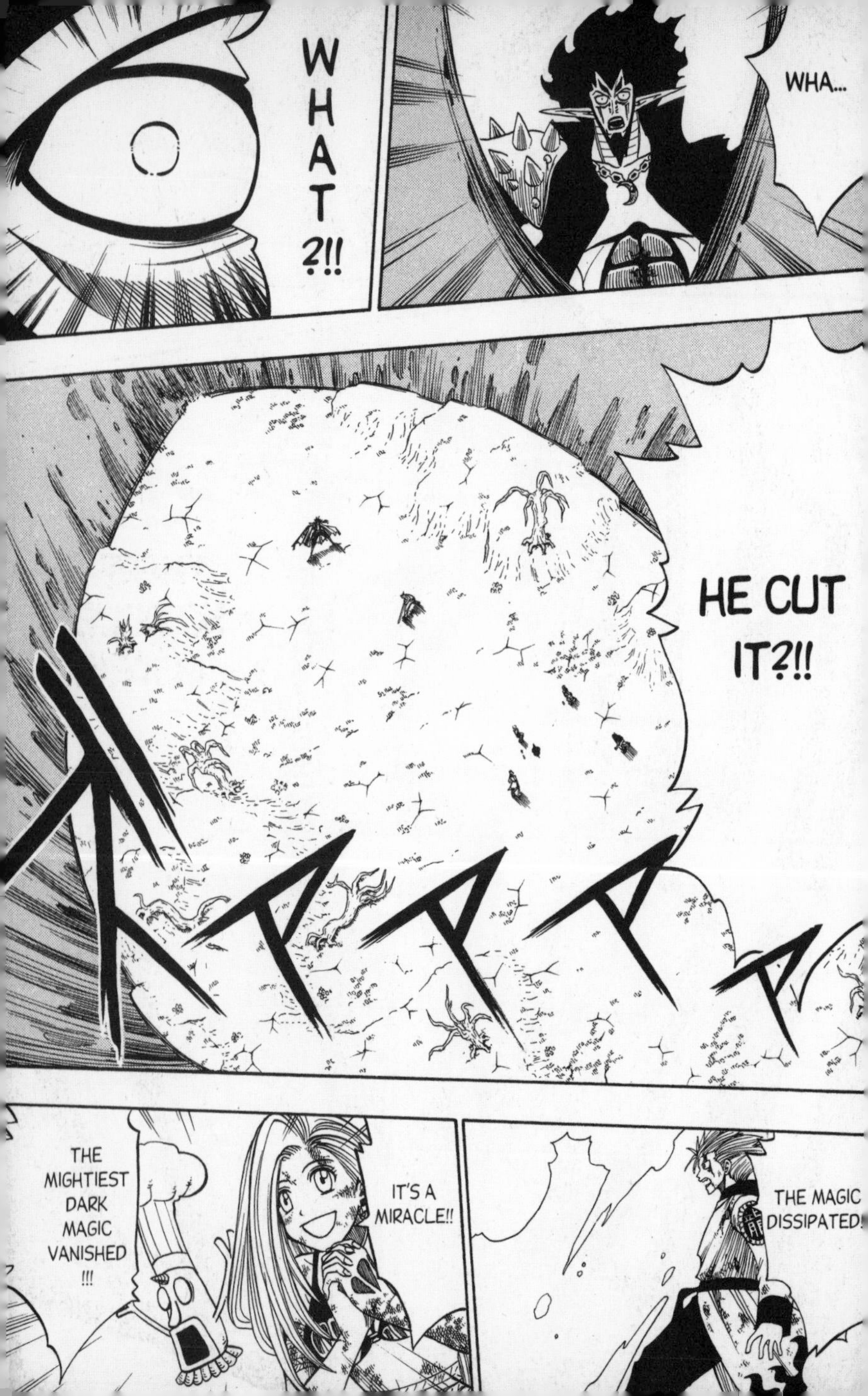
WHA...
WHAT?!!
HE CUT IT?!!
THE MAGIC DISSIPATED!
IT'S A MIRACLE!!
THE MIGHTIEST DARK MAGIC VANISHED!!!

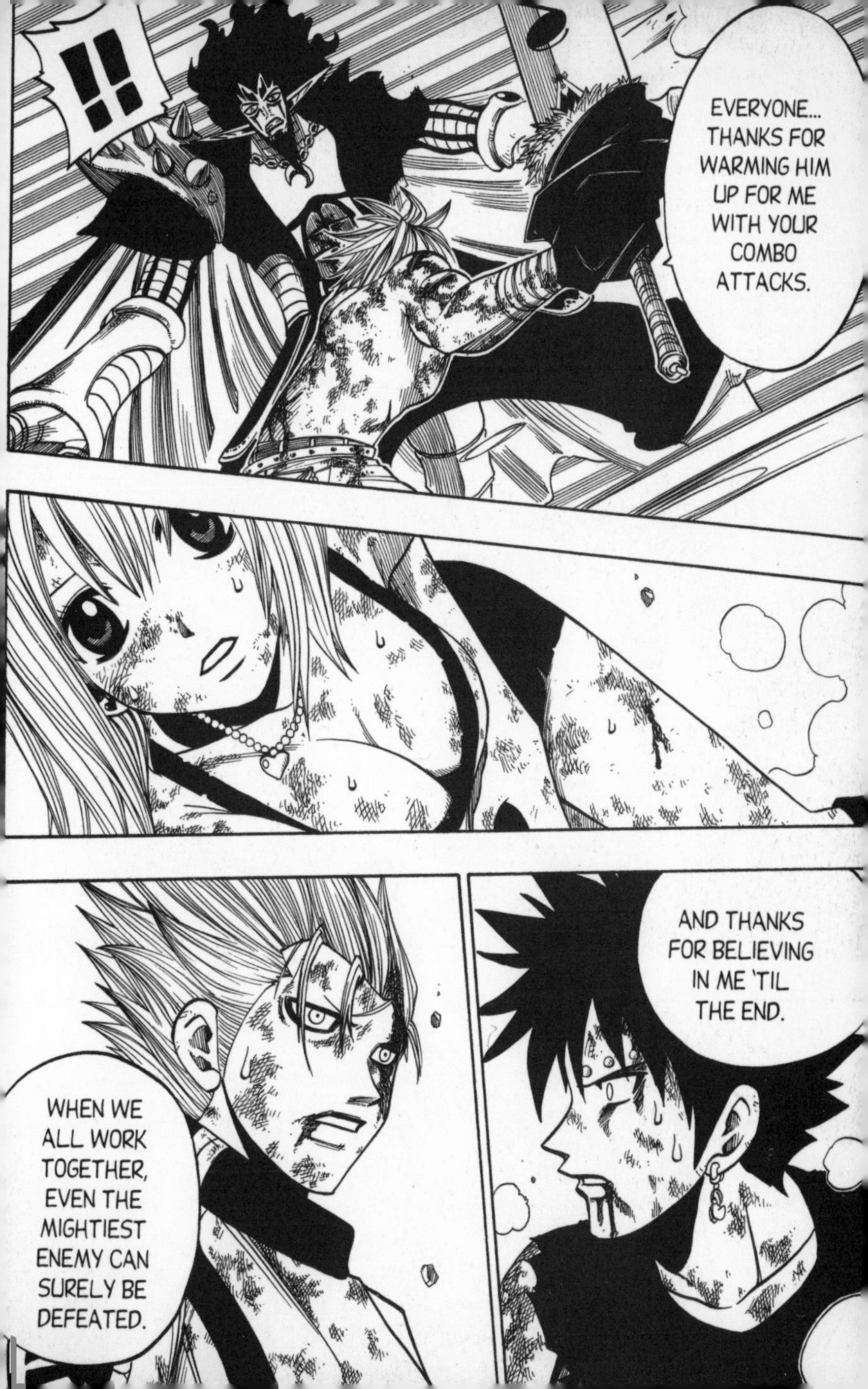
EVERYONE... THANKS FOR WARMING HIM UP FOR ME WITH YOUR COMBO ATTACKS.
!!
AND THANKS FOR BELIEVING IN ME 'TIL THE END.
WHEN WE ALL WORK TOGETHER, EVEN THE MIGHTIEST ENEMY CAN SURELY BE DEFEATED.

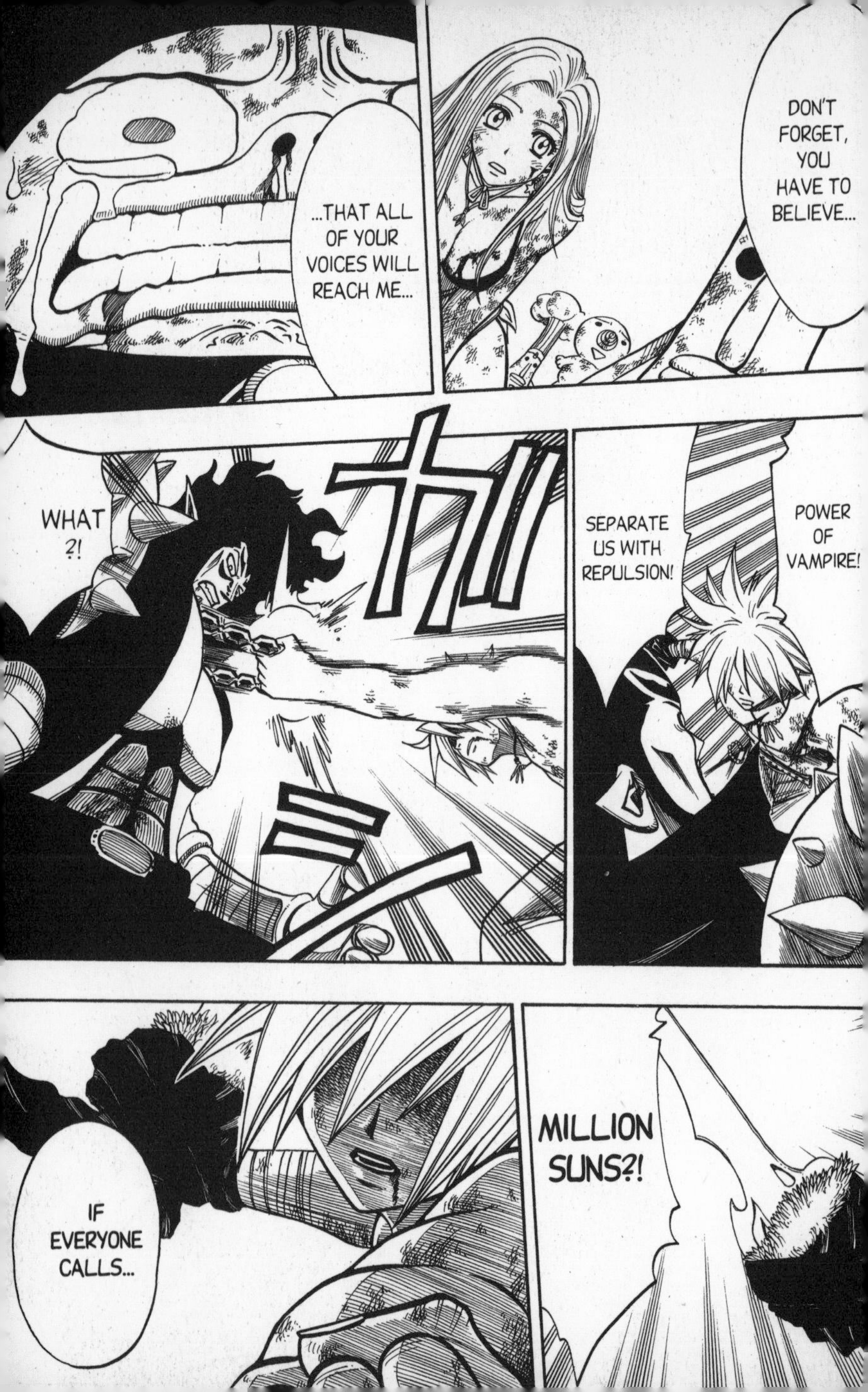
DON'T FORGET, YOU HAVE TO BELIEVE...
...THAT ALL OF YOUR VOICES WILL REACH ME...
POWER OF VAMPIRE!
SEPARATE US WITH REPULSION!
WHAT?!
MILLION SUNS?!
IF EVERYONE CALLS...

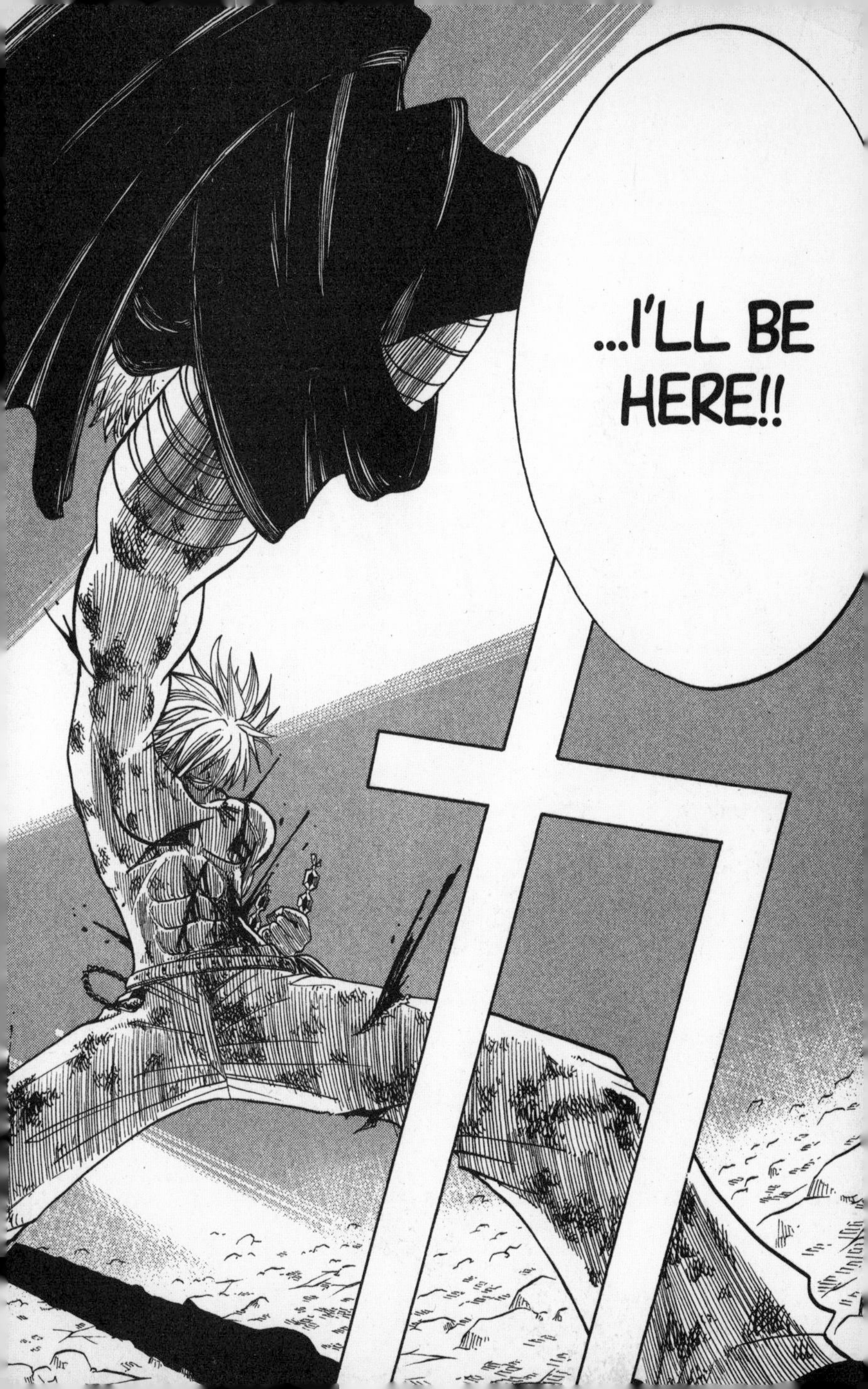
...I'LL BE HERE!!

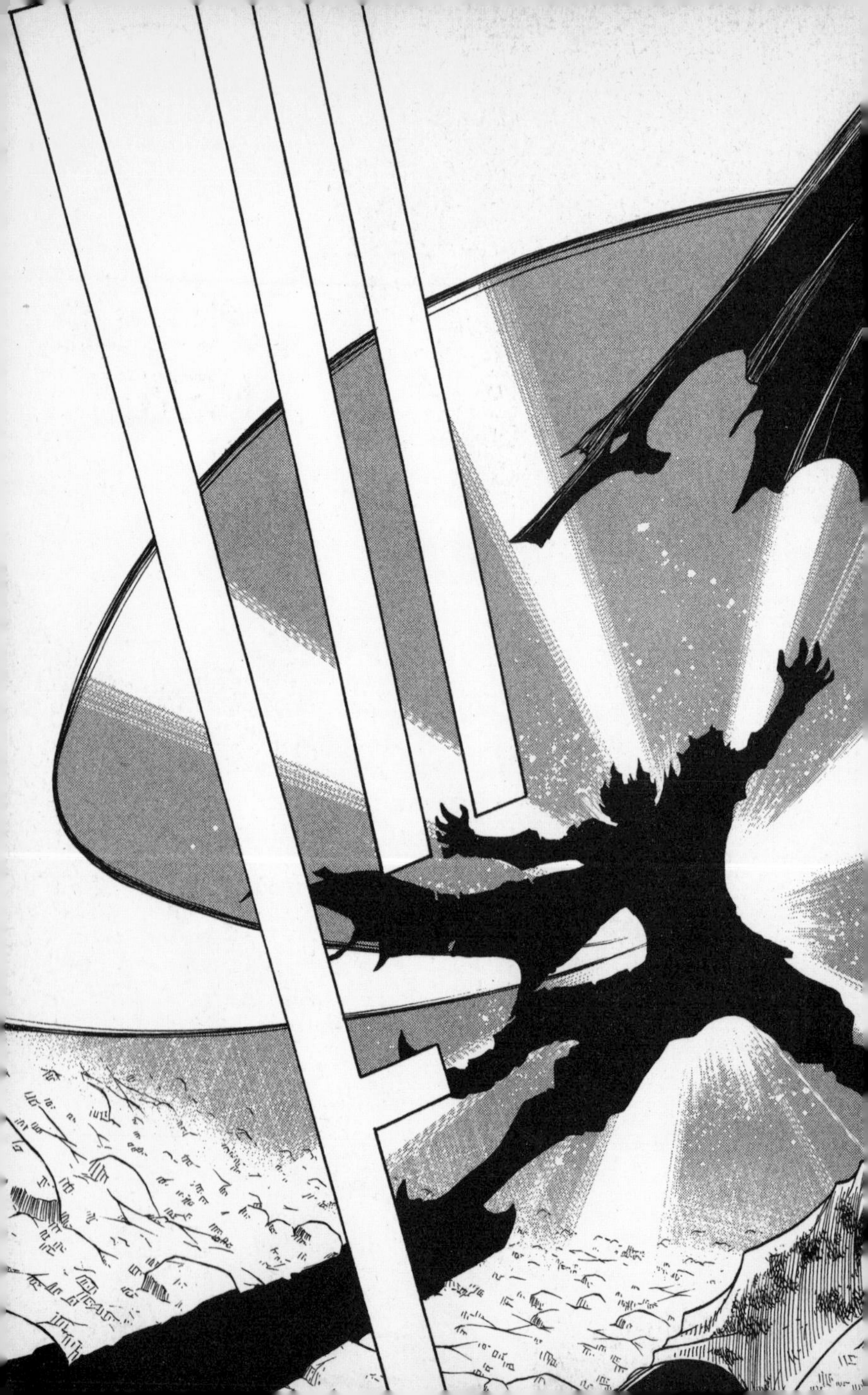

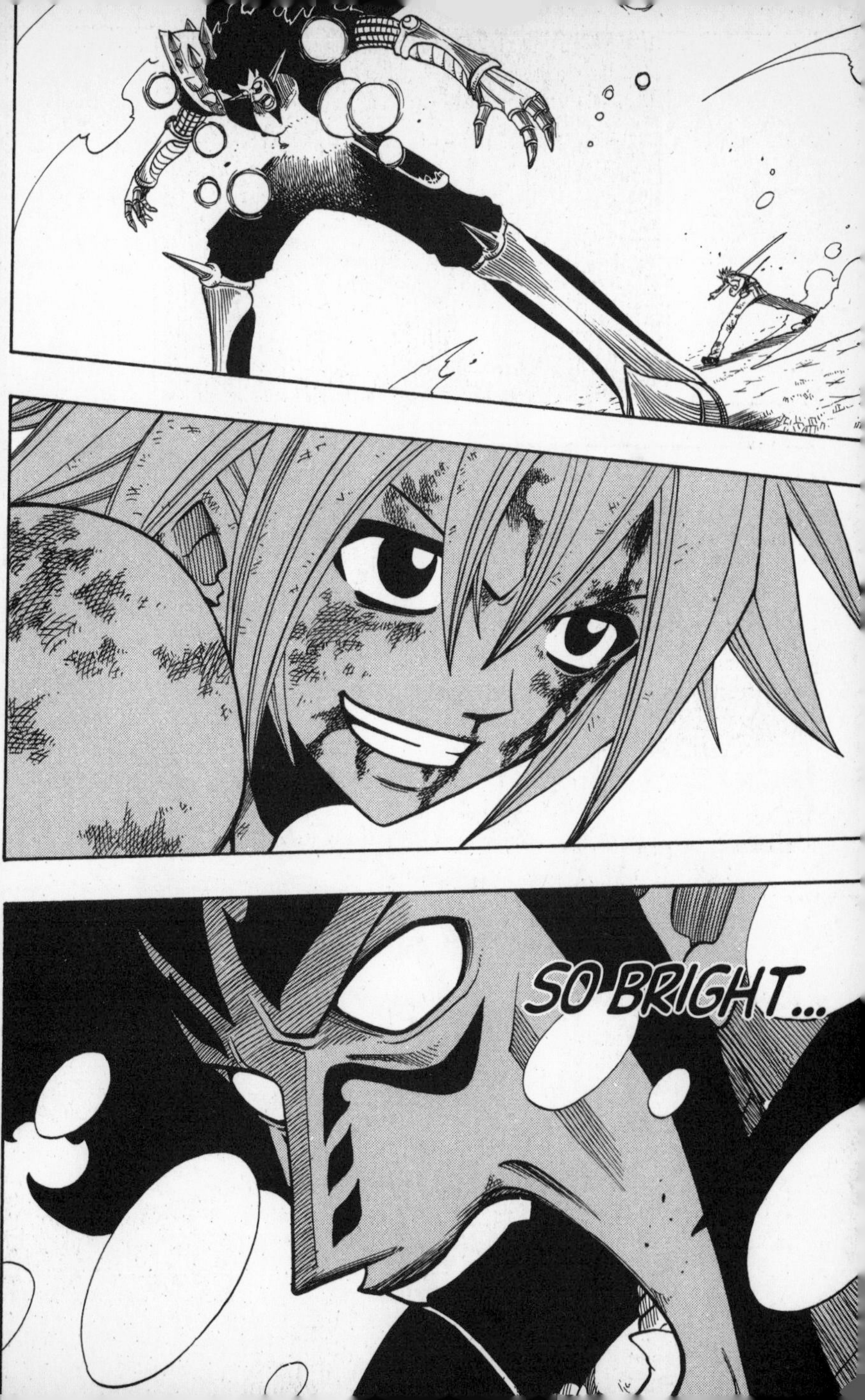
SO BRIGHT...

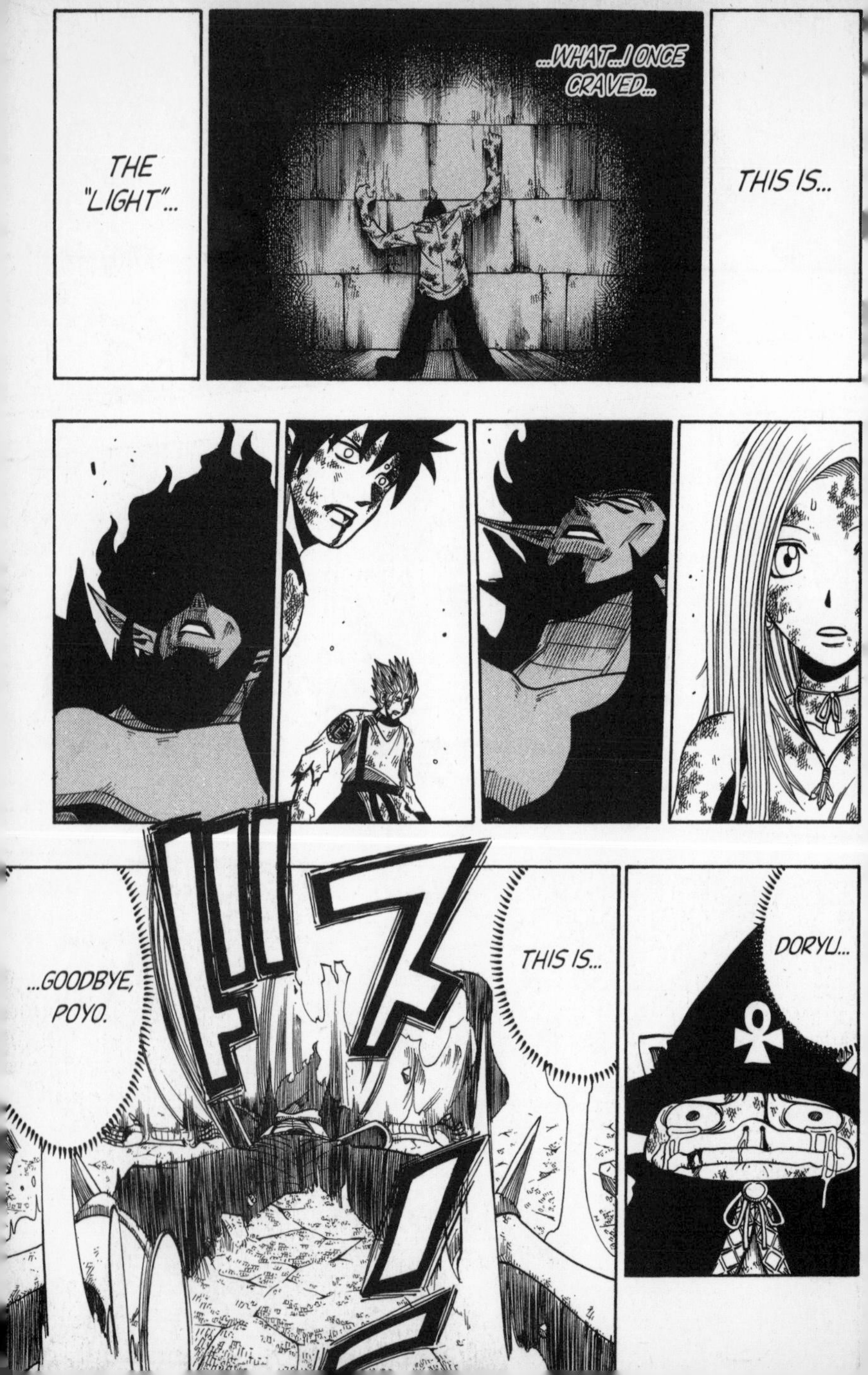
THIS IS...
...WHAT...I ONCE CRAVED...
THE "LIGHT"...
DORYU...
THIS IS...
...GOODBYE, POYO.

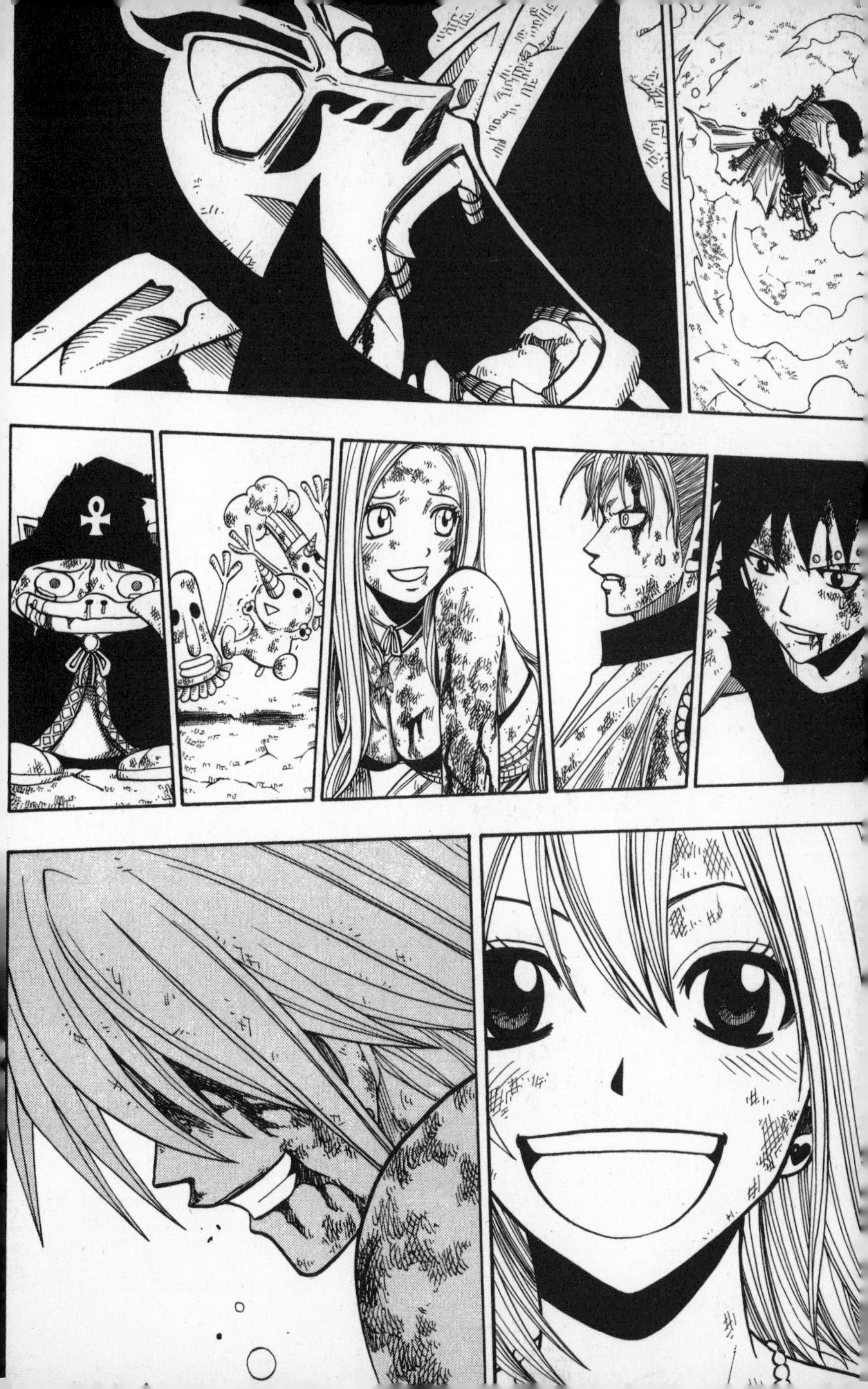

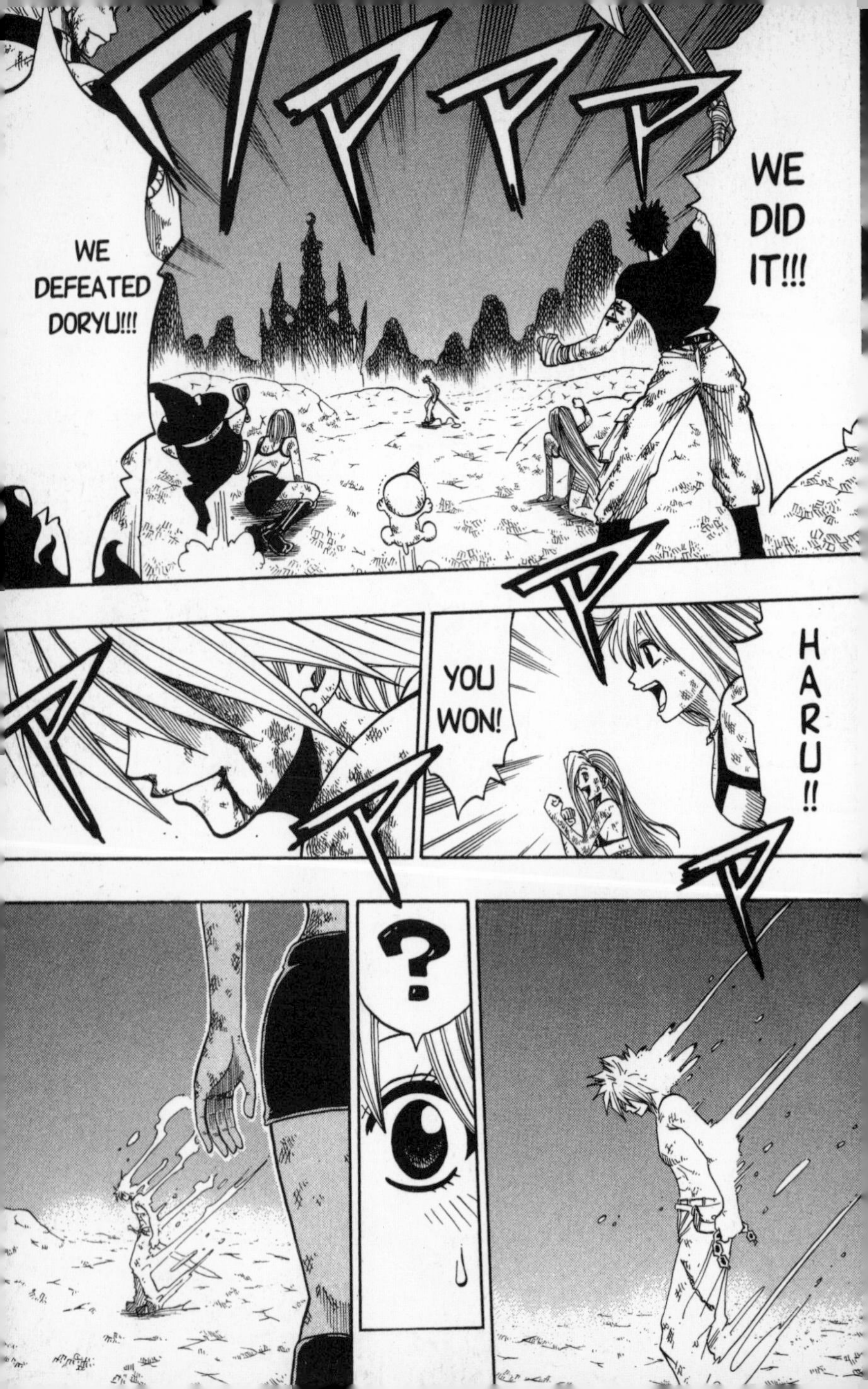
WE DID IT!!!
WE DEFEATED DORYU!!!
HARU!!
YOU WON!
?

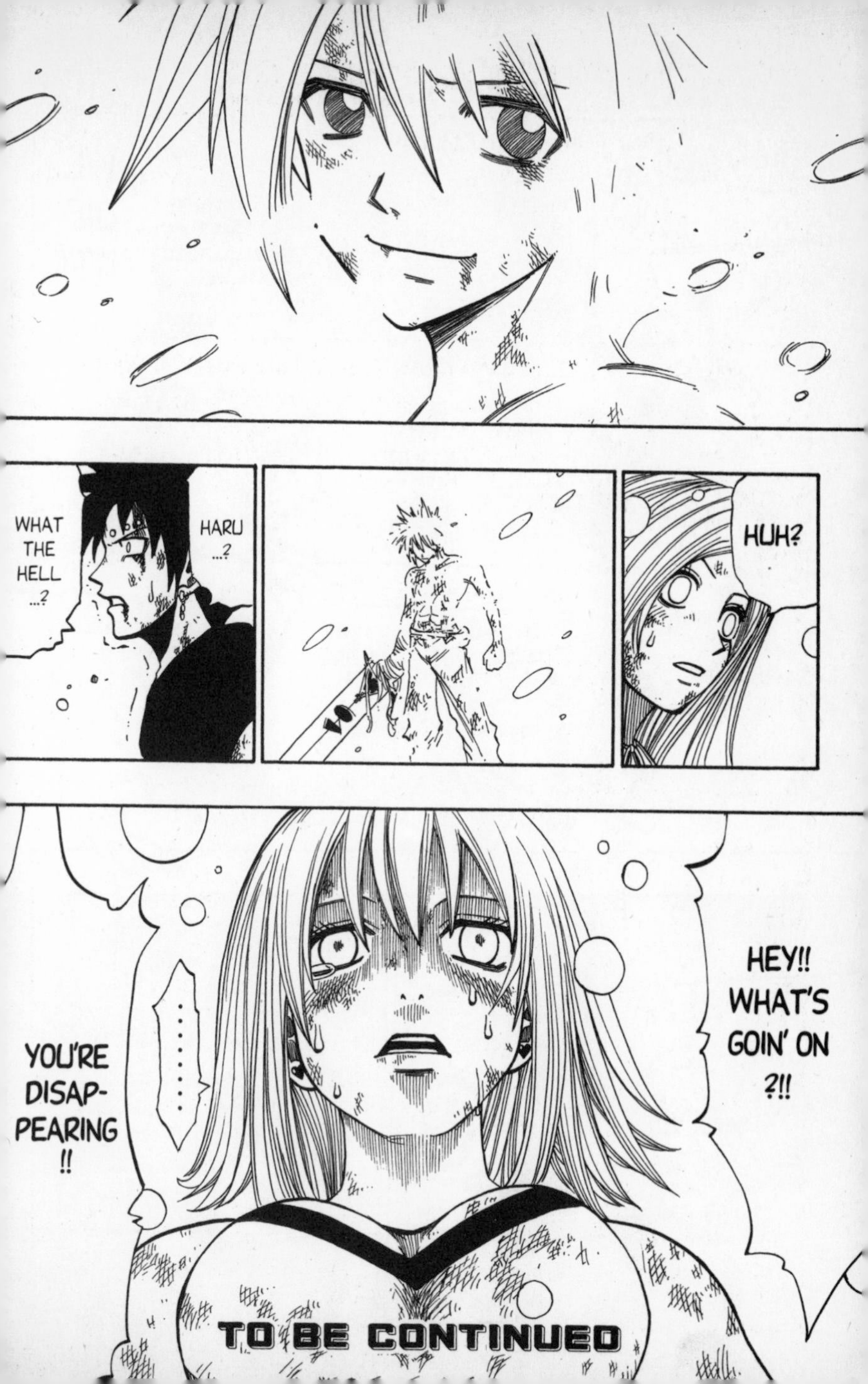
HUH?
HARU ...?
WHAT THE HELL ...?
HEY!! WHAT'S GOIN' ON ?!!
......
YOU'RE DISAP-PEARING !!
TO BE CONTINUED

CHARACTER PROFILES

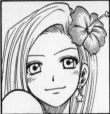

Mermaid: Celia

1) Sea Magic
2) July 23, 0051 / Age: 15
3) 7 ft 1 in / 128 lb / ?
   Human form: 5 ft 3 in /
   108 lb / ?
4) Mildesta
5) What she loves
6) Dancing
7) Star Festival, Haru
8) Oni, what she doesn't
   love

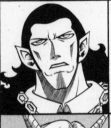

Lord of the Night: Demon Lord Pumpkin Doryu

1) Dark Magic & Blade (Twilight
   Sword) (Jet Black)
   Mother DB (Vampire)
2) Dec 30, 0026 / Age: 40
3) 6 ft 6 in / 205 lb / Type AB
4) Ulburg (Mystic Realm)
5) Collecting Gold
6) All-nighters
7) Night, Halloween
8) Light

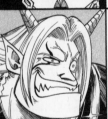

Goldclaimer: Onigami Commander Ogre

1) Gold (Harder than normal)
   Mother DB (Last Physics)
2) Feb 8, 0030 / Age: 36
3) 7 ft 4 in / 331 lb / Type A
4) Capitol of Theatre, Rudra
5) Playing with his sister
6) Near-immortality
7) Women
8) Men

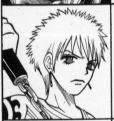

Reina Special Forces: Sopra the Silent

1) Nunchaku & DB (Sound
   Canceller)
2) April 8, 0047 / Age: 19
3) 5 ft 7 in / 132 lb / Type A
4) Blues City
5) Nothing in particular
6) Countering noise
7) Cup of Ramen
8) Pimento

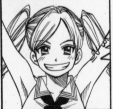

Reina Special Forces: Range the Loud Mouth

1) Voice (DB, Used Sound)
2) Nov 12, 0052 / Age: 14
3) 4 ft 9 in / 86 lb / Type O
4) Hip Hop Town
5) Pet Collecting
6) Mischief
7) Reina, Sopra, friends
8) Ghosts

Reading this Data

1) Weapon
2) Date of Birth / Age
3) Height / Weight / Blood Type
4) Birthplace
5) Hobby
6) Specialty
7) Likes
8) Dislikes

SPEAKING OF CHARACTERS...

Celia was inspired by my love of summer. Every summer I always want to go to the beach, but I'm so busy that I never get a chance to. At first, I received lots of angry "Don't steal Haru!" fan letters from girls, but lately, more and more people have been happy with her.

It's best you never see all my mermaid sketches. Some things are better left a mystery...I think, anyway.

Next is Doryu. I don't know how he happened. I wasn't exactly trying to create a **STUD** with a pumpkin helmet... Ah well...I think he turned out pretty well on paper.

About Ogre...I was laughing to myself thinking--I haven't figured out his Dark Bring yet! How about we make it... THIS! Hmm...Maybe I made him too strong...(^_^) I didn't decide on the Goldclaimer characteristic until just before I started writing the "Bonds of Silver" storyline.

As for Sopra and Range, I planned them as the Up & Down Team from the beginning. Sopra (from soprano) is the "upper" part. Range (as in vocal range) is the "down" part of the team.

Seems like Range is pretty popular. It's not like she ever did much. I guess people just dig girls like that. Next manga I'll make ALL my female characters like that. Well, I'm off to draw!

KNOW YOUR AFFINITY!

* It's simple! Months are on the left; days are on top. Find where the month and day you were born on match and there's your affinity.
If you don't know your birthday...
Boys -> Non-aligned
Girls -> Light affinity
So there.

Affinities are Light (Li)/Dark (Da)/ Fire (Fi)/Water (Wa) /Wind (Wi)/Earth (Ea)/ Thunder (Th) /Sea (Sea) and then Non-Aligned (Non) as the 9th, poyo. Once you know your affinity go to the next page, poyo.

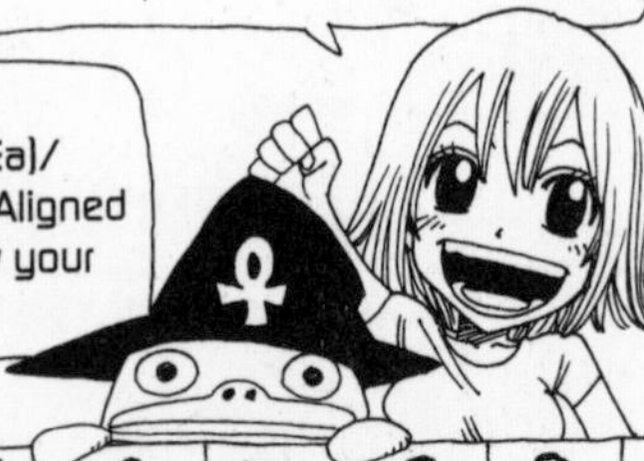

Day / Month	1 11 21 31	2 12 22	3 13 23	4 14 24	5 15 25	6 16 26	7 17 27	8 18 28	9 19 29	10 20 30
1	Li	Th	Da	Sea	Wi	Wa	Da	Fi	Ea	Non
2	Wa	Da	Fi	Sea	Th	Ea	Wa	Ea	Fi	Wi
3	Fi	Wa	Wi	Fi	Ea	Th	Ea	Sea	Wa	Sea
4	Wi	Ea	Th	Sea	Wi	Wa	Li	Fi	Da	Fi
5	Ea	Fi	Wi	Li	Sea	Li	Sea	Wa	Wi	Th
6	Fi	Sea	Wi	Th	Wi	Li	Wa	Da	Th	Sea
7	Th	Wa	Sea	Wa	Wi	Ea	Li	Fi	Da	Sea
8	Wi	Sea	Wi	Ea	Sea	Wa	Th	Wa	Fi	Ea
9	Th	Wi	Ea	Sea	Li	Wa	Wa	Th	Wa	Fi
10	Sea	Li	Da	Th	Fi	Ea	Ea	Wa	Wi	Li
11	Da	Th	Da	Wi	Non	Ea	Fi	Li	Th	Wa
12	Wi	Ea	Th	Fi	Wa	Sea	Li	Sea	Fi	Da

WHAT IF YOU LIVED IN THE WORLD OF RAVE?

Light

HERO TYPE WITH A THIRST FOR JUSTICE!

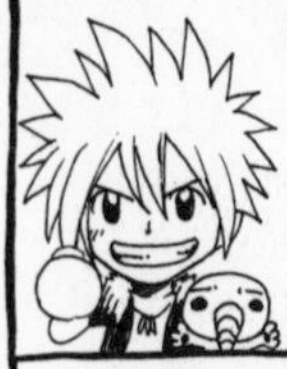

Power	6
Int	3
Movement	7
Luck	9

Other Light people:
Elie, Resha, Shiba

Fire

TYPE TO CHARGE INTO ENEMY WITH BURNING FLAME!

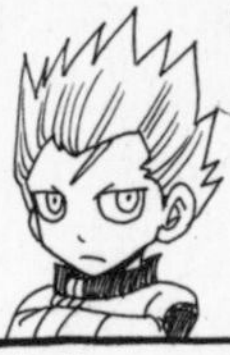

Power	8
Int	7
Movement	6
Luck	4

Other Fire people:
Shuda, Sopra

Thunder

CANNY, FEARSOME FIGHTER TYPE!

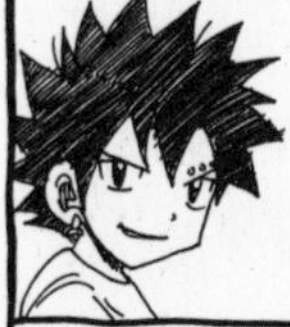

Power	8
Int	4
Movement	8
Luck	5

Other Thunder people:
Go, Range

Earth

TYPE TO HOLD THE FORT WITH STRONG ENDURANCE!

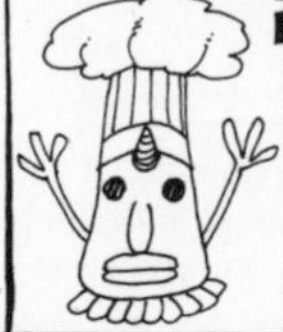

Power	9
Int	7
Movement	2
Luck	7

Other Earth people:
Berial, Ogre, Nakajima

Dark

CHARISMATIC RULER TYPE!

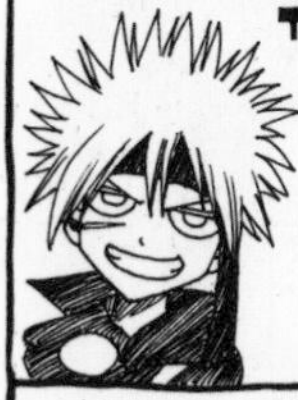

Power	9
Int	8
Movement	7
Luck	6

Other Dark people:
Doryu, Jiggle Butt Gang

Water

COMMANDER TYPE WHO GOES WITH THE FLOW!

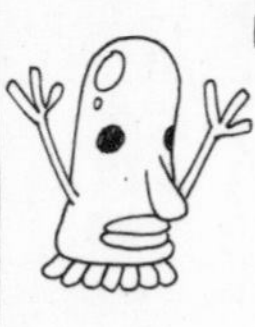

Power	4
Int	8
Movement	8
Luck	5

Other Water people:
Iulius, Deep Snow

Sea

SORCERER TYPE WITH VAST, DEEP KNOWL-EDGE!

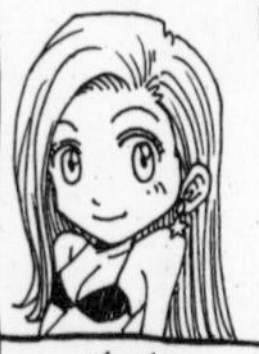

Power	3
Int	10
Movement	6
Luck	7

Other Sea people:
Cattleya, Reina, Remi

Wind

FAST TYPE WHO DOES RECON & SNOOPING!

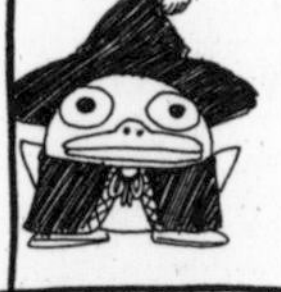

Power	5
Int	5
Movement	10
Luck	5

Other Wind types:
Jegan, Solasido

Non

LONER WRAPPED IN MYSTERY TYPE!

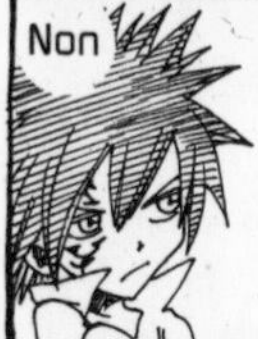

Power	7
Int	7
Movement	7
Luck	7

Normal compatibility with all

Compatibility

You get along well with those of your element, and poorly with those of opposing elements.

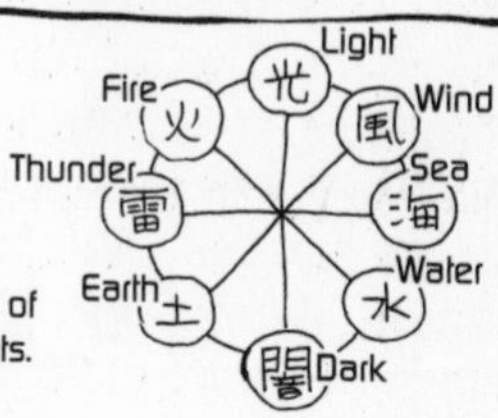

Light
光
Wind
風
Sea
海
Water
水
Dark
闇
Earth
土
Thunder
雷
Fire
火

FYI, Lucia was born Light but changed to Dark. Gale and King were born as Water, but changed to Light and Dark.

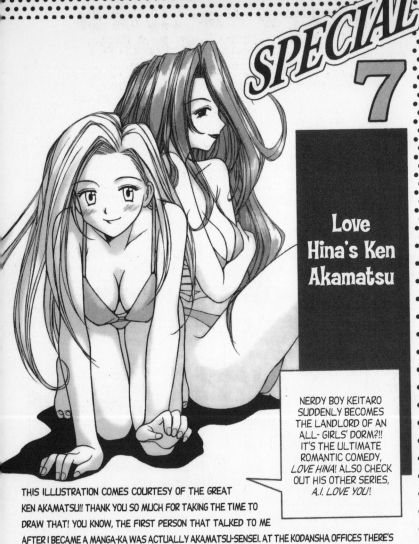

SPECIAL 7

Love Hina's Ken Akamatsu

NERDY BOY KEITARO SUDDENLY BECOMES THE LANDLORD OF AN ALL-GIRLS' DORM?! IT'S THE ULTIMATE ROMANTIC COMEDY, *LOVE HINA*! ALSO CHECK OUT HIS OTHER SERIES, *A.I. LOVE YOU*!

THIS ILLUSTRATION COMES COURTESY OF THE GREAT KEN AKAMATSU!! THANK YOU SO MUCH FOR TAKING THE TIME TO DRAW THAT! YOU KNOW, THE FIRST PERSON THAT TALKED TO ME AFTER I BECAME A MANGA-KA WAS ACTUALLY AKAMATSU-SENSEI. AT THE KODANSHA OFFICES THERE'S A "ROUGH DRAFT ROOM" WHERE SOME OF THE ARTISTS HANG OUT AND DRAW. WELL, ONE DAY I WAS WORKING IN THERE WHEN A MAN COMES UP TO ME AND SAYS "ARE YOU MASHIMA-KUN? I'M AKAMATSU. NICE TO MEET YOU." I COULDN'T BELIEVE THAT HE WOULD ACTUALLY BE THERE...SO I ASSUMED IT WAS AN EDITOR WITH THE SAME NAME. SORRY—THAT WAS A RUDE ASSUMPTION BY ME. WE STILL HANG OUT IN THE "ROUGH DRAFT ROOM" 'TIL THIS DAY. ANYWAY, THANK YOU FOR EVERYTHING— ESPECIALLY THE GREAT ILLUSTRATION!

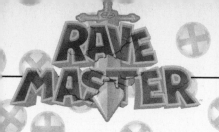

RAVE MASTER Fan Art

MAN, WE'D HATE TO BE ON THE RECEIVING END OF GALE'S THOUSAND-YARD STARE! NICE PENCILING, MICHAELA!

MICHAELA T.
AGE 12
KIHEI, HI

HEY, ASPIRING MANGA ARTISTS! WANT TO SEE YOUR PICTURES IN PRINT? WELL, IF YOU THINK YOU CAN DRAW A COOL-LOOKING HARU, A SEXY ELIE OR A FUNNY PLUE, SEND 'EM THIS WAY! WHAT DO YOU HAVE TO LOSE? NOTHING!

HOW TO SUBMIT:

1) SEND YOUR WORK VIA REGULAR MAIL (NOT E-MAIL) TO:

RAVE MASTER FAN ART
C/O TOKYOPOP
5900 WILSHIRE BLVD.
SUITE 2000
LOS ANGELES, CA 90036

2) ALL WORK SUBMITTED SHOULD BE IN BLACK-AND-WHITE AND NO LARGER THAN 8.5" X 11". (AND TRY NOT TO FOLD IT TOO MANY TIMES!)

3) ANYTHING YOU SEND WILL NOT BE RETURNED. IF YOU WANT TO KEEP YOUR ORIGINAL, IT'S FINE TO SEND US A COPY.

4) PLEASE INCLUDE YOUR FULL NAME, AGE, CITY AND STATE FOR US TO PRINT WITH YOUR WORK. IF YOU'D RATHER WE USE A PEN NAME, PLEASE INCLUDE THAT, TOO.

5) IMPORTANT: IF YOU'RE UNDER THE AGE OF 18, YOU MUST HAVE YOUR PARENT'S PERMISSION IN ORDER FOR US TO PRINT YOUR WORK. ANY SUBMISSIONS WITHOUT A SIGNED NOTE OF PARENTAL CONSENT CANNOT BE USED.

6) FOR FULL DETAILS, PLEASE CHECK OUT HTTP://WWW.TOKYOPOP.COM/ABOUTUS/FANART.PHP

DRAW US! PUUN!

DISCLAIMER: ANYTHING YOU SEND TO US BECOMES THE PROPERTY OF TOKYOPOP INC. AND, AS WE SAID BEFORE, WILL NOT BE RETURNED TO YOU. WE WILL HAVE THE RIGHT TO PRINT, REPRODUCE, DISTRIBUTE OR MODIFY THE ARTWORK FOR USE IN FUTURE VOLUMES OF *RAVE MASTER* OR ON THE WEB WITHOUT PAYMENT TO YOU.

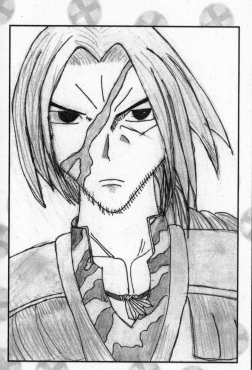

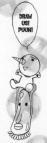

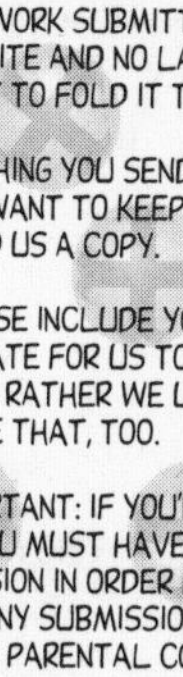

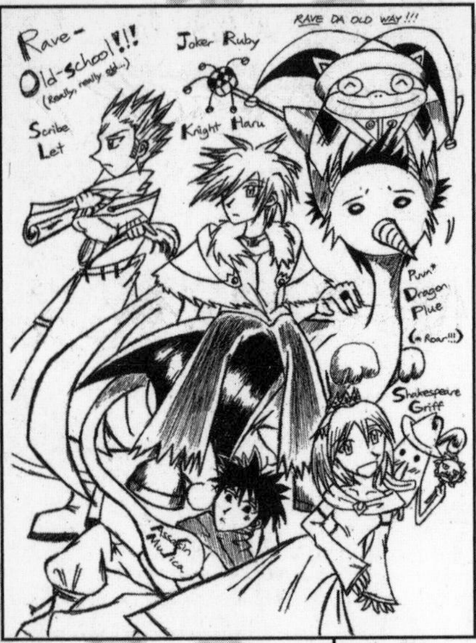
RAVE DA OLD WAY!!!
Rave-Old-school!!!
Joker Ruby
Scribe Let
Knight Haru
Dragon Plue
Shakespeare Griff

FOR THE REST OF THE ARTWORK, WE THOUGHT WE'D FEATURE FANS THAT HAVE SUBMITTED ART MULTIPLE TIMES. KUDOS TO THESE ARTISTS FOR THEIR DEDICATION AND PERSEVERANCE! FIRST UP IS SALLY WITH A ONE-TWO WHAMMY OF FINE ARTWORK. THE DETAIL IN THE GROUP PICTURE IS REALLY IMPRESSIVE...

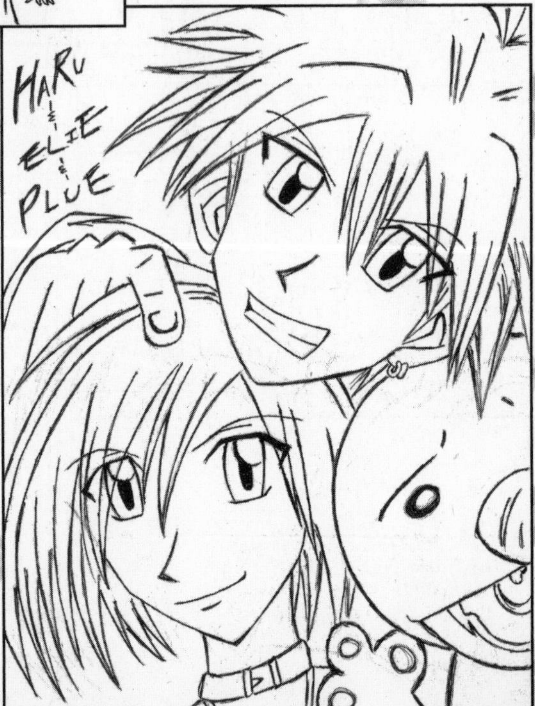
HARU
ELIE
PLUE

...AND THIS CLOSE-UP OF HARU, ELIE AND PLUE LOOKS LIKE A FUN SNAPSHOT TAKEN IN A PHOTO BOOTH. GOOD JOB!

SALLY F.
AGE 14
HACIENDA HEIGHTS, CA

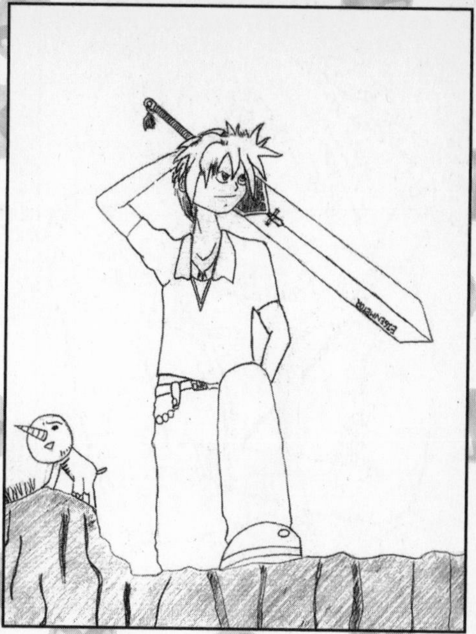

HARU IS STANDING TALL AND SURVEYING THE LANDSCAPE...

...WHILE PLUE IS HOLDING HIS FAVORITE SNACK--BUT YET HE STILL LOOKS WORRIED. MAYBE BECAUSE IT'S HIS LAST ONE? ANYWAY, THANKS FOR THE LETTERS AND ART, RYE. WE'RE GOING TO HOLD YOU TO THAT BEST FRIEND OFFER!

RYE N.
AGE 13
BAKERSFIELD, CA

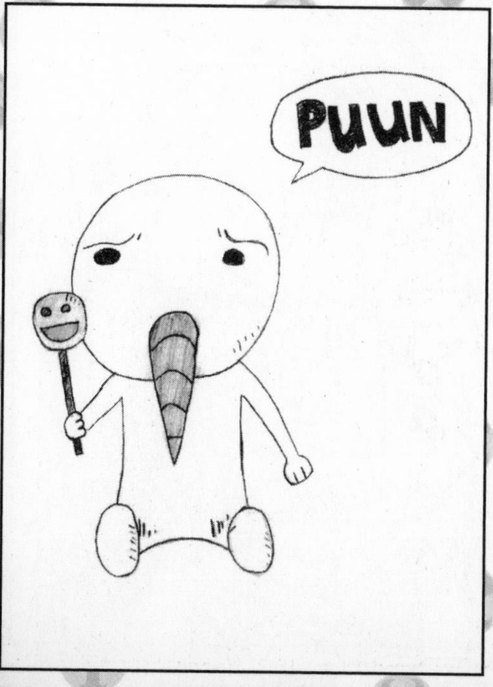
PUUN

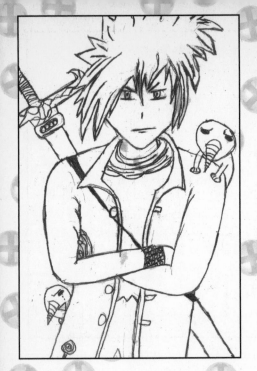

 HERE WE HAVE
HARU LOOKING
VERY CONFIDENT
AND DETERMINED.
I WONDER WHAT'S
ON HIS MIND? HMM...
EVEN PLUE LOOKS
SAD IN THIS ONE.

 THIS IS A NICE CLOSE-UP
OF SIEG. I LIKE PICTURES
THAT MAKE YOU WONDER
WHAT THE CHARACTER'S
THINKING. I CAN ALMOST
SEE THE THOUGHT
BALLOON ABOVE HIS
HEAD NOW...
NICE JOB, MARCO!

MARCO G.
AGE 12
THORTON, CO

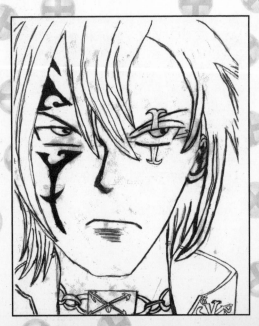

"AFTERWORDS"

YO! THIS TIME I FINALLY GOT A CHAPTER IN COLOR! DRAWING AN EN-
TIRE 20-PAGE CHAPTER IN COLOR WAS REALLY SOMETHING. I DIDN'T
GET ANY EXTRA TIME, EITHER. WELL, I CAN'T COMPLAIN. IT'S WHAT
I WANTED, AFTER ALL (^_^)! I'VE ALWAYS WANTED TO DO MY OWN
FULL-COLOR STUFF LIKE MY IDOL AKIRA TORIYAMA-SENSEI USED
TO DO. SO MY WISH WAS GRANTED THIS ONCE. LOOKING BACK ON IT
NOW, I'VE DECIDED THAT I'M REALLY NOT VERY GOOD AT COLORS
(^_^).

IN THE THREE YEARS SINCE *RAVE MASTER* STARTED, I MUST'VE
DRAWN OVER 100 COLOR PAGES, BUT THEY'RE NOT ALL THAT GOOD.
A LOT WERE DRAWN STRICTLY FOR RESEARCH AND PRACTICE...BOY,
DOES TIME FLY, THOUGH. IT'S NOT THAT THERE IS ANYTHING WRONG
WITH THE COLORS THEMSELVES; IT'S FINDING THE PROPER BAL-
ANCE BETWEEN ALL THE COLORS...IT'S JUST NOT MY EXPERTISE.

WELL, ALL THAT BEING SAID, I'M DEFINITELY NOT GOING TO STOP
TRYING. RIGHT NOW, I'M DRAWING AS WELL AS I POSSIBLY CAN.
PLUS, MY ASSISTANTS ARE PUTTING THEIR ALL INTO IT AS WELL.
WE'VE GOT THAT "LET'S TRY IT AND SEE!" SPIRIT GOING. (THAT'S
ABOUT ALL WE'VE GOT GOING, THOUGH.) SORRY THE RESULTS
AREN'T MORE SATISFYING. IF I EVER GET A CHANCE TO DO ANOTHER
COLOR CHAPTER, I'LL TRY TO MAKE IT MUCH BETTER.

I'M NOT SATISFIED, SO I'LL JUST WORK HARDER!! G'NIGHT!!

- HIRO MASHIMA

That's just...wrong!

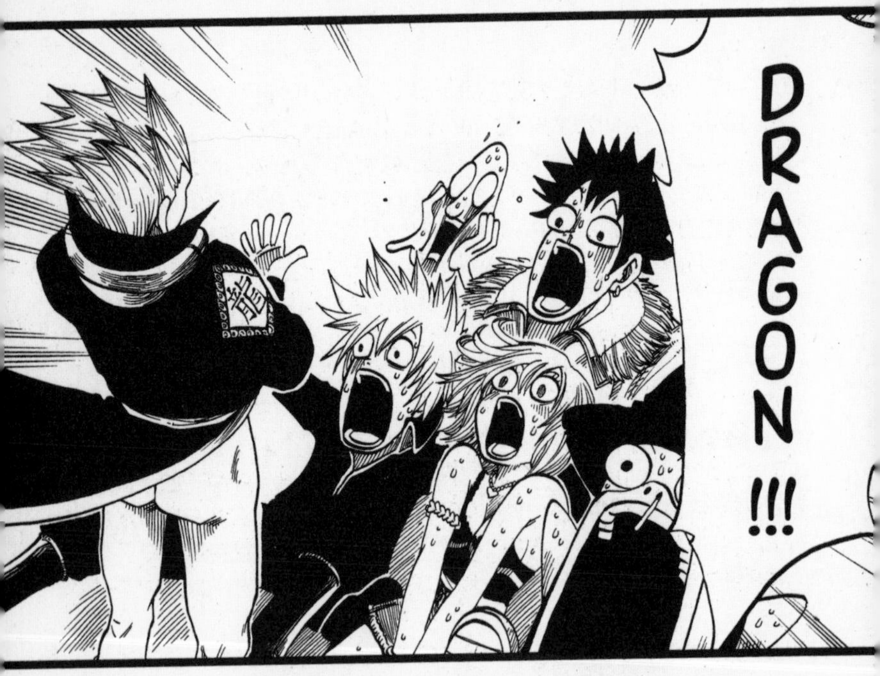
DRAGON!!!

Haru's fading from existence?! Could this be the end of the party for the Rave Master?! And what is Project DR? What threat does it pose to our heroes? It's all in the next volume of Rave Master!

Rave Master Volume 18
Available December 2005

TAKUHAI TOKYOPOP MANGA SUPPLEMENT

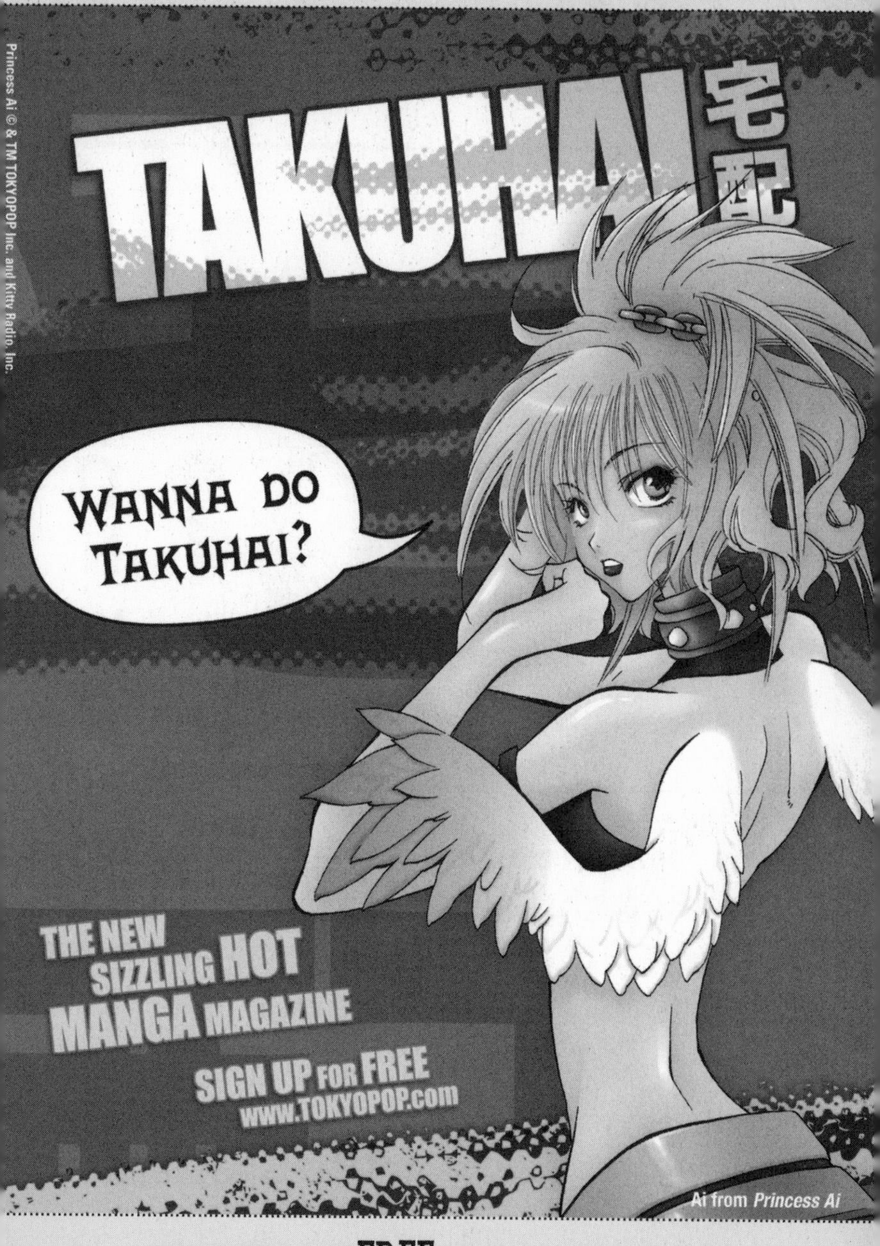

SIGN UP NOW FOR FREE AT: WWW.TOKYOPOP.COM

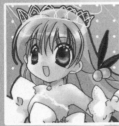
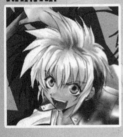

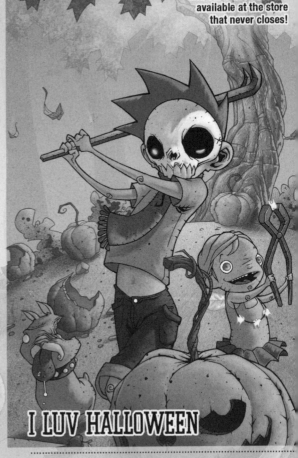

TOKYOPOP MANGA SUPPLEMENT

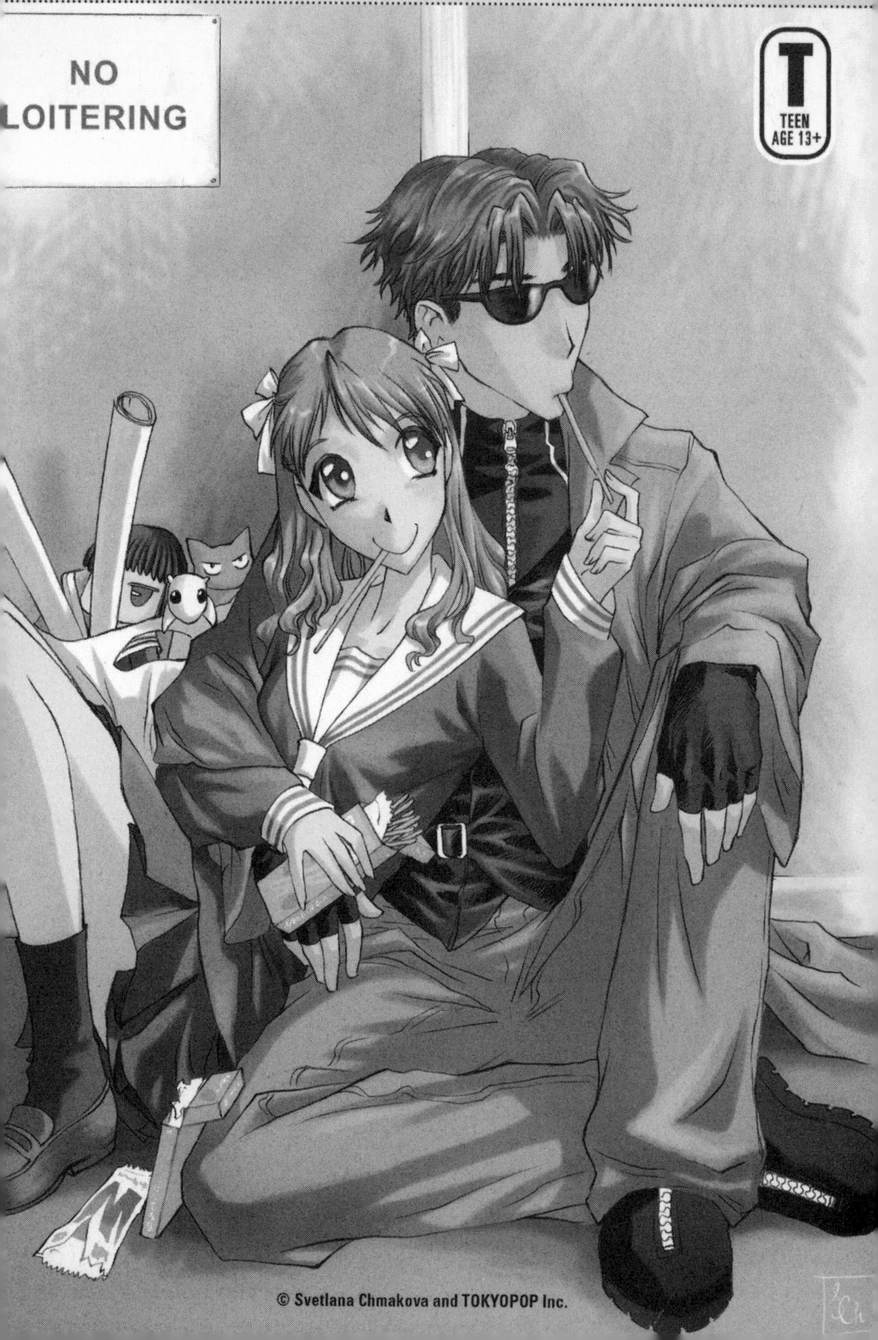
NO LOITERING
T
TEEN AGE 13+

DRAMACON ™

Sometimes even two's a crowd.

When Christie settles in the Artist Alley of her first-ever anime convention, she only sees it as an opportunity to promote the comic she has started with her boyfriend. But conventions are never what you expect, and soon a whirlwind of events sweeps Christie off her feet and changes her life. Who is the mysterious cosplayer that won't even take off his sunglasses indoors? What do you do when you fall in love with a guy who is going to be miles away from you in just a couple of days?

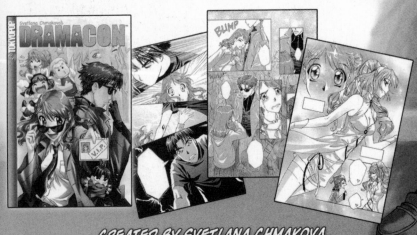

CREATED BY SVETLANA CHMAKOVA, CREATOR OF MANGA-STYLE ONLINE COMICS "CHASING RAINBOWS" AND "NIGHT SILVER"!

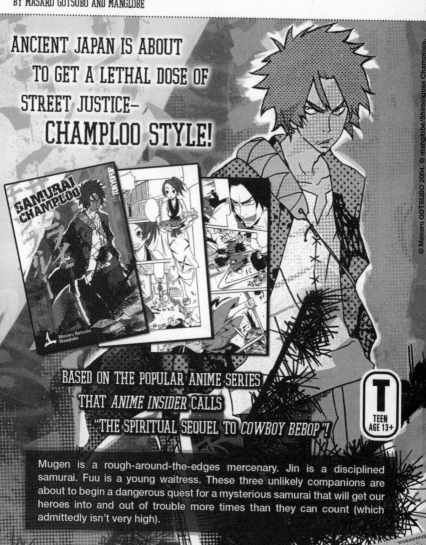

KARE KANO

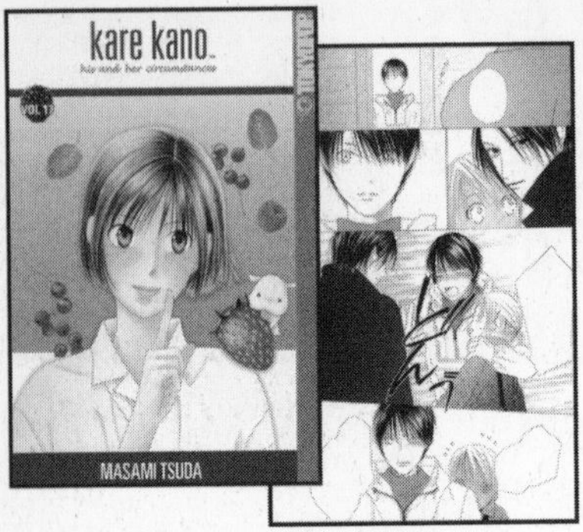
kare kano
MASAMI TSUDA

BY MASAMI TSUDA

Kare Kano has a fan following for a reason: believable, well-developed characters. Of course, the art is phenomenal, ranging from sugary sweet to lightning-bolt powerful. But above all, Masami Tsuda's refreshing concept—a high school king and queen decide once and for all to be honest with each other (and more importantly, themselves)—succeeds because Tsuda-sensei allows us to know her characters as well as she does. Far from being your typical high school shojo, *Kare Kano* delves deep into the psychology of what would normally just be protagonists, antagonists and supporting cast to create a satisfying journey that is far more than the sum of its parts.

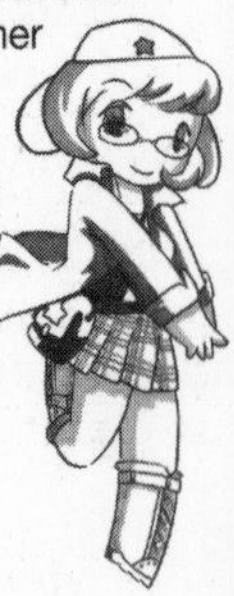

~Carol Fox, Editor

GIRL GOT GAME

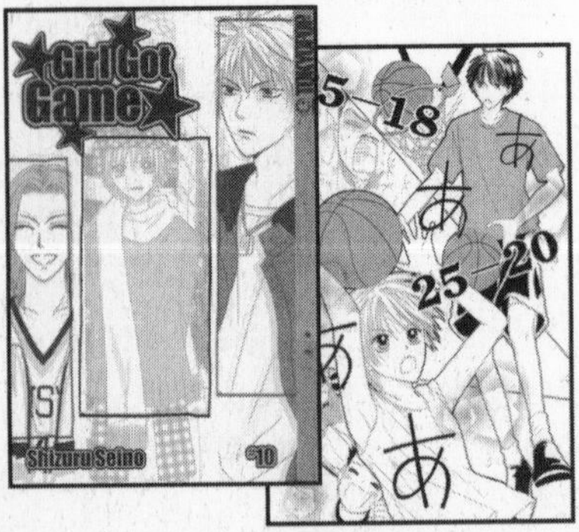
Girl Got Game
Shizuru Seino
10

BY SHIZURU SEINO

There's a fair amount of cross-dressing shojo sports manga out there (no, really), but *Girl Got Game* really sets itself apart by having an unusually charming and very funny story. The art style is light and fun, and Kyo spazzing out always cracks me up. The author throws in a lot of great plot twists, and the great side characters help to make the story just that much more special. Sadly, we're coming up on the final volume, but I give this series credit for not letting the romance drag out unnecessarily or endlessly revisiting the same dilemmas. I'm really looking forward to seeing how the series wraps up!

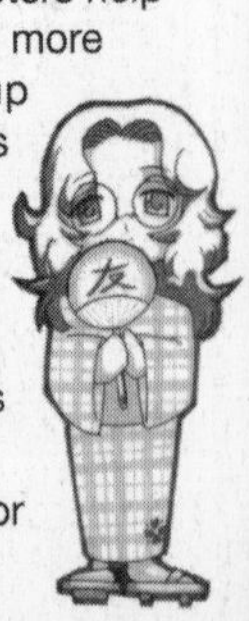

~Lillian M. Diaz-Przybyl, Jr. Editor

STOP!

This is the back of the book.
You wouldn't want to spoil a great ending!

This book is printed "manga-style," in the authentic Japanese right-to-left format. Since none of the artwork has been flipped or altered, readers get to experience the story just as the creator intended. You've been asking for it, so TOKYOPOP® delivered: authentic, hot-off-the-press, and far more fun!

DIRECTIONS

If this is your first time reading manga-style, here's a quick guide to help you understand how it works.

It's easy… just start in the top right panel and follow the numbers. Have fun, and look for more 100% authentic manga from TOKYOPOP®!

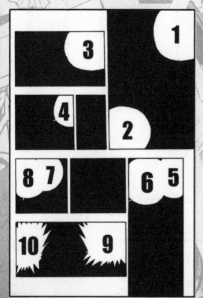

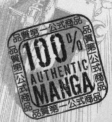